HUMAN BEHAVIOR THEORY
A Diversity Framework

MODERN APPLICATIONS OF SOCIAL WORK

An Aldine de Gruyter Series of Texts and Monographs

SERIES EDITOR

James K. Whittaker

Ralph E. Anderson and Irl Carter, **Human Behavior in the Social Environment: A Social Systems Approach** (fourth edition)

Richard P. Barth and Marianne Berry, **Adoption and Disruption: Rates, Risks, and Responses**

Richard P. Barth, Mark Courtney, Jill Duerr Berrick, and Vicky Albert, **From Child Abuse to Permanency Planning: Child Welfare Services Pathways and Placements**

Kathleen Ell and Helen Northen, **Families and Health Care: Psychosocial Practice**

Marian Fatout, **Models for Change in Social Group Work**

Mark W. Fraser, Peter J. Pecora, and David A. Haapala, **Families in Crisis: The Impact of Intensive Family Preservation Services**

James Garbarino, **Children and Families in the Social Environment** (second edition)

James Garbarino, Patrick E. Brookhouser, Karen J. Authier, and Associates, **Special Children—Special Risks: The Maltreatment of Children with Disabilities**

James Garbarino, Cynthia J. Schellenbach, Janet Sebes, and Associates, **Troubled Youth, Troubled Families: Understanding Families At-Risk for Adolescent Maltreatment**

Roberta R. Greene, **Social Work with the Aged and Their Families**

Roberta R. Greene, **Human Behavior Theory: A Diversity Framework**

Roberta R. Greene and Paul H. Ephross, **Human Behavior Theory and Social Work Practice**

André Ivanoff, Betty J. Blythe, and Tony Tripodi, **Involuntary Clients in Social Work Practice: A Research-Based Approach**

Paul K. H. Kim (ed.), **Serving the Elderly: Skills for Practice**

Jill Kinney, David A. Haapala, and Charlotte Booth, **Keeping Families Together: The Homebuilders Model**

Robert M. Moroney, **Shared Responsibility: Families and Social Policy**

Robert M. Moroney, **Social Policy and Social Work: Critical Essays on the Welfare State**

Peter J. Pecora, Mark W. Fraser, Kristine Nelson, Jacqueline McCroskey, and William Meezan, **Evaluating Family-Based Services**

Peter J. Pecora, James K. Whittaker, Anthony N. Maluccio, Richard P. Barth, and Robert D. Plotnick, **The Child Welfare Challenge: Policy, Practice, and Research**

Norman A. Polansky, **Integrated Ego Psychology** (second edition)

John R. Shuerman, Tina L. Rzepnicki, and Julia H. Littell, **Putting Families First: An Experiment in Family Preservation**

Betsy S. Vourlekis and Roberta R. Greene (eds). **Social Work Case Management**

Heather B. Weiss and Francine H. Jacobs (eds.), **Evaluating Family Programs**

James K. Whittaker, Jill Kinney, Elizabeth M. Tracy, and Charlotte Booth (eds.), **Reaching High-Risk Families: Intensive Family Preservation in Human Services**

James K. Whittaker and Elizabeth M. Tracy, **Social Treatment, 2nd Edition: An Introduction to Interpersonal Helping in Social Work Practice**

HUMAN BEHAVIOR THEORY
A Diversity Framework

Roberta R. Greene

ALDINE DE GRUYTER
New York

About the Author

Roberta R. Greene is Associate Dean, University of Georgia School of Social Work. She is coauthor, with Paul H. Ephross, of *Human Behavior Theory and Social Work Practice;* coauthor, with Betsy S. Vourlekis, of *Social Work Case Management;* and author of *Social Work with the Aged and Their Families* (all: Aldine de Gruyter). Dr. Greene has also authored numerous journal articles dealing with the application of conceptual frameworks to social work practice.

ALDINE DE GRUYTER
A division of Walter de Gruyter, Inc.
200 Saw Mill River Road
Hawthorne, New York 10532

This publication is printed on acid-free paper ⊗

Library of Congress Cataloging-in-Publication Data
Greene, Roberta R. (Roberta Rubin), 1940–
    Human behavior theory : a diversity framework / Roberta R. Greene.
        p.   cm. — (Modern applications of social work)
    Includes bibliographical references and index.
    ISBN 0-202-36089-X (alk. paper). — ISBN 0-202-36090-3 (pbk.)
    1. Social   work   with   minorities—United   States.   2. Pluralism (Social sciences)—United States. I. Title. II. Series.
    HV3176.G77   1994
    36.84'00973—dc20   93-44310
                                                                          CIP

Manufactured in the United States of America
10 9 8 7 6 5 4 3 2

To Nancy, Jeff, Adam, and Kathy, with Love

Contents

Preface

Although the social work literature has attempted to address the knowledge, attitudes, and skills necessary for cross-cultural social services delivery, little has been written about the relationship among diversity frameworks, human behavior theory, and practice methods. This book is the culmination of an extensive literature review of major social work journals and other publications to determine how social work educators and practitioners have used human behavior theory to intervene in the life problems of diverse client populations. The book is not intended as a summary compendium on the topic of cultural diversity. Rather, it is organized by major themes and presents essays on topics related to social work practice in a diverse society.

ACKNOWLEDGMENTS

The author would like to thank the contributors to this volume, particularly Kathryn Thompson, who critiqued many of the chapters. I would also like to thank my family and friends for their encouragement and Joanna Staples for her technical support.

I hope that the text will make a contribution to enhancing practice with social work's diverse constituency.

Introduction

The expanded knowledge base to support cross-cultural social work practice has come to encompass cognitive information, skill-based techniques, methods for developing self-awareness, and an appreciation for cultural differences and principles of cultural dynamics and how they relate to human functioning (Pinderhughes, 1989). In recent years, the profession also has come to recognize human behavior content as central to social work education and as the foundation on which the remainder of the curriculum, particularly practice methods, must be based (Council on Social Work Education [CSWE], 1984; Eure, Griffin, & Atherton, 1987; Griffin & Eure, 1985). A persistent issue related to the human behavior curriculum has been its value to practice within a diversity framework (CSWE, 1984; Federico, 1979; Franklin, 1986; Gibbs, 1986; Granger & Portner, 1985; Lowenstein, 1976; Schlesinger & Devore, 1979; Wetzel, 1986). However, social work educators have suggested that it has been difficult to incorporate sufficient multicultural content into the human behavior curriculum (Granger & Portner, 1985; Proctor & Davis, 1983).

As a result of the civil rights and women's movements, the social work profession has become more aware of its constituency and of the need to reexamine long-held assumptions (Gould, 1984). Faculty at schools of social work are more frequently challenging the "dominant-group definitions of reality and acceptability" (Federico, 1979, p. 188). Moreover, increasing numbers of faculty are beginning to view traditional human behavior theories as being "based on observations of white, middle class, heterosexual individuals and intact families" (Goldstein, 1986b, p. 155). Furthermore, they increasingly are observing that theories of female sexuality and feminine development have been based on a conventional variation in the male model (Gould, 1984). The result has been a reexamination of social work's knowledge base and a lively debate about whether its theoretical foundation applies across gender and cultural boundaries (de Anda, 1984; Longres, 1990).

The social work profession can play an important role in affirming ethnic and cultural pluralism by effectively serving its varied constituency. This book is intended to contribute to this challenge. The purpose of the book is to help students and practitioners better understand how social workers have used human behavior theories to competently address variations in group and community membership within the social worker–client encounter. It specifically examines applications of human behavior theory in multicultural social work practice (including gender and social class as well as racial/ethnic group membership), that is, how human behavior theory applies to differential clinical assessment and intervention with diverse client populations. Throughout the book, the terms *cross-cultural* and *culturally diverse* are used as umbrella terms for diversity of human experiences that is rooted in ethnic, national, or religious identity, race, gender, and social class membership. The extent to which theories of human behavior that support social work practice have been applied universally—or can be applied to the diversities that characterize U.S. society and allow for human differences within cultures—is the major theme of this book.

The goal is to explore how particular assumptions of human behavior theory—psychoanalytic theory, psychodynamic/ego psychology theory, systems theory, behavioral theory, symbolic interaction theory, feminist theory, constructionist theory, small group theory, and ecological perspective—have been used to answer issues related to cultural diversity. The challenges and limitations of each theory's applications and whether each theory has contributed to the understanding of culture-specific and gender-salient aspects of human behavior are discussed.

Chapter 1 discusses the scope of diversity content available for effective transcultural social work practice. It also outlines the various groups that fall under the umbrella of diversity. Chapter 2 outlines how human behavior theory has been used as foundation content for assessment and intervention with diverse populations, discusses the biopsychosocial human behavior paradigm, and explores changing theoretical and ideological perspectives on personality development and culture. Chapters 3–6 emphasize the use of human behavior theory in social work assessment, and Chapters 7–12 in social work interventions.

Chapters 3–12 are organized around a frequently discussed theme in the social work literature related to practice with diverse populations. Chapters 4, 5, and 6 examine three human behavior theories—symbolic interactionism, Eriksonian theory, and role theory-and their influence on social work assessment processes: exploring language, meaning, and social work practice (Chapter 4); examining development-specific practice issues (Chapter 5); assessing changes in professional social work and client roles (Chapter 6).

Chapter 7 begins a discussion of how choice of human behavior theory influences social work intervention processes. Chapter 7 presents social constructionism, a subjectivist theory that focuses on understanding a client's personal story within his or her cultural context. Chapter 8 provides contrast by presenting social learning theory, a positivist theory that emphasizes universal scientific laws and the evaluation of practice with diverse populations. A discussion of client systems with a focus on how to intervene effectively with diverse family forms is undertaken in Chapter 9. Chapter 10 presents a discussion of small group theory and how the practice of social group work with diverse populations relates to social justice and social inequities. Collaborating with natural support systems is outlined in Chapter 11. Finally, Chapter 12 examines how power factors influence client and institutional diversity issues that can be addressed in social work practice.

Questions discussed include the following:

- Does the theory offer concepts that allow for an assessment of a client's developmental transitions from culturally sensitive and gender-specific perspectives?
- What concepts does the theory provide for exploring language usage and meaning in interviewing, assessing, and intervening with diverse client populations?
- Does the theory offer an understanding of cultural factors (including gender and social class) in defining and addressing mental health issues?
- Does the theory offer a means of evaluating diverse social work practice?
- Does the theory suggest ways for the social worker to better understand his or her practice biases?
- Does the theory provide concepts that examine and assess client problems from a multisystems perspective?
- Does the theory offer interventions that stem from a natural helping community context?
- How does the theory help the social worker carry out practice within an empowerment/advocacy sociopolitical context?

Case studies illustrate culturally sensitive interventions for helping individuals, families, and groups.

Social Work Practice Within a Diversity Framework

1

Roberta R. Greene

> *The idea of cultural pluralism, the enrichment which comes from the acceptance and enjoyment of cultural differences, should increasingly affect all disciplines concerned with constructive human relationships.*
>
> (Hamilton, [1940] 1951, pp. 206–207)

During the past 20 years, American society has become increasingly diverse. Although the United States has always been a multigroup society, in recent years the metaphor of America as a melting pot with its goal of homogenization has been challenged as never before. The debate is joined in the social and political arena by those holding an alternative vision: a multicultural society that supports a variety of ethnic group values and life-style choices.

The United States has experienced, and will continue to experience, marked growth in the numbers of people who belong to diverse cultural groups. People have become increasingly aware of or have rediscovered their ethnic identity and cultural group membership. In addition, advocates for civil rights for minorities, women, and gays and lesbians have become more informed consumers of mental health services. The theories and practices for assessment, psychiatric diagnosis, and a range of mental health interventions have come under increasing attack for their gender, race, cultural, and social class bias. Hence, social work practitioners will undoubtedly need to prepare themselves to serve diverse client groups.

These societal forces, combined with accompanying political factors such as increased participation of minorities in the political process, have profoundly affected social work education. As a result, educators have come to better appreciate the importance of teaching social work students within a diversity framework, and researchers are further examining how best to deliver culturally competent social work services.

The consequences of diversity in ethnic background, race, class, gender, sexual orientation, and culture in a pluralistic society also have received increasing exposure in the professional literature. Social work practice with diverse groups in particular requires that practitioners understand the principles of cultural dynamics and how they relate to human functioning (Pinderhughes, 1989). Human behavior theories are used "to deal with vast quantities of data by formulating significant questions, selecting and organizing data, and understanding the data within a larger framework" (Specht & Craig, 1982, p. 8). Social work theorists and practitioners have not had as great an interest in some theories as in others (Ephross-Saltman & Greene, 1993). For example, from the 1950s to the 1970s, Freudian theory and ego psychology dominated the practice world; in 1970, general systems theory also was adopted and gained prominence (H. Goldstein, 1986c; see Greene & Ephross, 1991b, for an extended discussion). In addition, some theory bases have had specific practice applications, such as that of Carl Rogers's theory and its influence on social work interviewing techniques (see Chapter 3).

An ongoing concern related to the human behavior curriculum has been its applicability for practice within a diversity framework (Berger & Federico, 1982; CSWE, 1984; Federico, 1979; Franklin, 1986; Gibbs, 1986; Granger & Portner, 1985; Lowenstein, 1976; Schlesinger & Devore, 1979; Wetzel, 1986). Among the questions raised are:

- How is culture-specific information infused in the social work helping process?
- What theories, or what concepts and assumptions from certain theories, are best suited for transcultural social work practice?
- How has human behavior theory most effectively been used transculturally to explain behaviors and structure the helping process?

As a result of these concerns, the social work profession has reexamined its use of human behavior theory, and social workers have engaged in a lively debate about whether the theoretical foundation of human behavior theory applies across cultural boundaries or equally to females and males within diverse cultures (Collins, 1986; de Anda, 1984; Longres, 1990).

The social work profession can play an important role in affirming ethnic and cultural pluralism by effectively serving its varied constituency (Sanders, 1975). This chapter outlines the various groups that fall under the umbrella of diversity. It also discusses the scope of diversity content available for effective transcultural social work practice.

HISTORICAL ADVOCACY

The skilled [social work] bureaucrat is able to negotiate the constraints of the organizational environment in order to maintain maximum range for discretionary behavior to be enacted in the client's behalf. (Solomon, 1976, p. 15)

Over the past three decades, historical and social events in the United States have brought about an increase in the number of groups that either define themselves as minorities or seek redress from the general society. Starting in the 1960s, the tumultuous changes in the body politic, including urban upheavals and the demand for community control, presented social work with "formidable challenges" (Tidwell, 1971, p. 59). The civil rights and women's liberation movements, with the accompanied acceleration in social change, required that the social work profession reassess its priorities and direction.

These social and political forces particularly gave impetus to an advocacy approach to the social work curriculum (see Chapter 12 and Epilogue for a discussion of gay and lesbian content in the social work curriculum). Students and faculty activists asserted that variations in cultural group patterns that historically were less visible in the curriculum should be given more attention (Arnold, 1970; Glasgow, 1971). The strain and struggle to incorporate the study of ethnic and minority group life into the social work curriculum was reflected in professional journals, in professional conferences, and in the task forces appointed by the Council on Social Work Education (CSWE) (Francis, 1973; Mackey, 1973; Miranda, 1973; Murase, 1973; Ruiz, 1973). Moreover, faculty groups within CSWE urged that information about the life-styles of diverse client groups become an integral part of social work education.

Reassessment of curricula eventually led to a heightened commitment to understanding diverse groups and "activities related to ethnic minority concerns" (Pins, 1970, p. 32A). As a result, CSWE established accreditation standards that required schools to make a special effort to assure cultural diversity in their student body, faculty, and staff and to provide a curriculum that would include a body of knowledge on women and various diverse groups (CSWE, 1970; 1971; Dumpson, 1979).

Currently, three CSWE curriculum standards reflect the profession's interest in a curriculum that respects diversity (Table 1.1). According to CSWE (1991–1992), such populations include, but are not limited to those distinguished by age, religion, disablement, sexual orientation, and culture. CSWE also mandates that content on social justice and the dynamics and consequences of oppression as well as on populations-at-risk be included in curricula.

DEFINING DIVERSITY

There are many perspectives on how ethnic group membership, social class, minority group status, and culture affect individual and group life. . . . Those who have been assigned official responsibility "to help" have a particular obligation to be aware of inequality. (Devore & Schlesinger, 1987a, p. 3)

Table 1.1.   Curriculum Policy Statement

Diversity:

M6.6 Professional social work education is committed to preparing students to understand and appreciate human diversity. Programs must provide curriculum content about differences and similarities in the experiences, needs, and beliefs or people. The curriculum must include content about differential assessment and intervention skills that will enable practitioners to serve diverse populations.

Each program is required to include content about population groups that are particularly relevant to the program's mission. These include, but are not limited to, groups distinguished by race, ethnicity, culture, class, gender, sexual orientation, religion, physical or mental ability, age, and national origin.

Promotion of Social and Economic Justice:

M6.7 Programs of social work education must provide an understanding of the dynamics and consequences of social and economic injustice, including all forms of human oppression and discrimination. They must provide students with the skills to promote social change and to implement a wide range of interventions that further the achievement of individual and collective social and economic justice. Theoretical and practice content must be provided about strategies of intervention for achieving social and economic justice and for combatting the causes and effects of institutionalized forms or oppression.

Populations-at Risk:

M6.8 Programs of social work education must present theoretical and practice content about patterns, dynamics, and consequences of discrimination, economic deprivation, and oppression. The curriculum must provide content about people of color, women, and gay and lesbian persons. Such content must emphasize the impact of discrimination, economic deprivation, and oppression upon these groups.

Each program must include content about populations-at-risk that are particularly relevant to its mission. In addition to those mandated above, such groups include, but are not limited to, those distinguished by age, ethnicity, culture, class, religion, and physical and mental ability.

Source: Council on Social Work Education. Curriculum Policy Statement for Master's Degree Programs in Social Work Education. Approved by the Board of Directors July 19, 1992.

   Clearly, the history of social work education suggests that there has been growing attention to curriculum content relevant to a diverse client constituency. Select human behavior theory and practice issues as they relate to members of these various constituents are discussed throughout the text. However, it is important to understand that there is often as much diversity within a particular group as between groups. Therefore, each client must be seen as an individual who may or may not subscribe to general group norms and beliefs. Therefore, a client should be asked to differentiate his or her own experiences as a member of particular diversity or reference group.

   In this section, there is a general introduction to nine diverse groupings that are often affected by social, economic, and legal bias or oppression. The list should not be considered exhaustive. In addition, terminology preferred by various racial and ethnic groups has changed over time, and currently may not reflect unanimous agreement. Therefore, terms used here and in various chapters generally reflect the terminology used at the time a particular piece of literature was written. For example, although the term *Native American* was used in journal articles of the 1970s, the term *American Indian* is currently more prevalent. Furthermore, social workers should be alert to how individuals or a group of individuals describe or define themselves. For example, people who are deaf are increasingly arguing that they are a subculture characterized by language, the American Sign Language. That is, instead of perceiving deafness as a disability or as merely a medical condition, growing numbers of people who are deaf consider themselves members of a shared cultural group (Dolnick, 1993).

The groups discussed here are:

1. minority groups, as they are defined by limited political power;
2. ethnic groups, which are characterized by a shared peoplehood;
3. women, in terms of gender roles and power issues;
4. the aged, who are affected by devalued status;
5. members of certain social classes, in terms of their economic and educational (dis)advantage;
6. developmentally disabled people, who are perceived as limited by handicap;
7. people of varying sexual orientations, affected by misconceptions of life-style and affectional ties;
8. religious groups, as defined by their spiritual needs, religious beliefs, and practices; and
9. oppressed populations, who face discrimination and limited political power.

Case studies that illustrate social work practice with these diverse groups appear in subsequent chapters.

people of color Minority Groups

Social work practice with minority clients addresses individuals, families, and members of communities who historically have been oppressed or have had limited power in U.S. society (Green, 1982; Lum, 1986). Devore and Schlesinger (1987a) have suggested that the term *minority group* be used to mean "the underprivileged in a system of ethnic stratification" (p. 13). However, Hopps (1987) proposed the term *people of color* as the best term to define those individuals "most affected by racism and poverty" (p. 161).

Because minority group members are in a relatively less powerful position in society, they may be denied access and opportunities available to others, such as adequate housing, employment, and health care.

The term *minority* has been extended over the years to include more groups, including people affected by racism, poverty, or discrimination. Among the groups that have been included by law in the term minority are American Indians, Alaska Natives, African-Americans, Asian-Americans and Americans from the Pacific Islands, and Hispanics of various national ancestry. Developmentally disabled persons also are protected by law (P.L. No. 95-602). Women, gays, lesbians, the elderly, and people with Spanish surnames sometimes are referred to as minorities. However, the term has no scientific criteria; moreover, it often is defined differently by government policy and regulations as well as by group members themselves (Hopps, 1987). Also, there is considerable variation in culture and life situations among subgroups of people identified as members of a particular minority or ethnic group.

In addition, there is no scientific agreement about the term *race* (Green, 1982; Johnson, 1987). Race is currently considered by most social scientists to be a social concept with "no standing as a scientific or analytic category" (Green, 1982, p. 6). The disuse of the term *race* as a scientific category relates to the understanding that there are only superficial physical differences between people, such as skin color, and that people differ more within a race than between races.

However, because people of color have experienced oppression, stereotyping, and denial of opportunity, the term *race* is often associated with stratification of power (Green, 1982). Therefore, there is concern among members of the social work profession about how color differences are portrayed and "the uses to which [group classification] might be put. . . . [At the same time,] social workers must be alert to the possible misuse of 'color blindness' as a way to avoid remediation of the effects of past discrimination" (Hopps, 1987, p. 162).

Ethnic Groups

Members of an ethnic group think of themselves as a "people" or as having a common culture, history, and origin. An ethnic group maintains a distinction between itself and perceived outsiders; however, it is "a dynamic system constantly changing, adjusting, and adapting to the wider environment of which it is a part" (Holzberg, 1982, p. 254). Ethnic groups consist of subgroups with diverse life-styles, languages, histories, and cultural strengths and supports.

Women

Every known society has a gender-based definition of economic and social roles. Although every society makes a distinction between gender roles, the way in which gender is symbolized varies across cultures. Stockard and Johnson (1992) have pointed out that although women's status in a culture is multidimensional, "there is no evidence, historical or contemporary, of any society in which women as a group have controlled the political and economic lives of men" (p. 91).

In addition to possible structural inequities, the concern in social work practice is whether practitioners have differential perceptions of clients by gender that adversely affect the help rendered (Jayaratne & Ivey, 1981). Gender-sensitive social work practice, although variously defined, usually incorporates a therapeutic model that rejects traditional power arrangements for both males and females. Many feminists have suggested that gender-sensitive practice follows a therapeutic model that would produce a nonsexist role model, espouse self-actualization regardless of role stereotyping and social demand, and provide for women a unified feminist ego ideal (Orlin, 1979–1980).

The Aged

Every society ascribes certain qualities to its aged members. Reviews of the contemporary literature indicate that attitudes toward older adults are mixed at best (Hooyman & Kiyak, 1988). In the youth-oriented society of the United States, the image of the older person as unproductive is commonplace (Butler, Lewis, & Sunderland, 1991). The view has been so pervasive that the term *ageism* was coined to describe the prejudice and stereotypes applied to older people solely on the basis of their age (Butler, 1969). Ageism is an attitude that can result in actions that subordinate a person or group because of age, and thereby brings about unequal treatment. That ageism exists in the mental health field has been well documented in numerous studies indicating that allied health professionals are reluctant to enter the field (Greene, 1984). Throughout the 1960s, gerontologists (Posner, 1961; Soyer, 1960; Wasser, 1964) urged social workers to counteract negative societal attitudes and work with older adults and their families. In the 1970s, as the field of geriatrics became recognized and better funded, more professionals entered this area of practice. Despite professionalization and efforts to eliminate stereotypes, many misconceptions and barriers to effective service remain, and shortages in social work personnel have been projected (Greene, 1989).

Members of Varying Classes or Socioeconomic Circumstances

There is no consensus among theorists about whether or how to identify, measure, and classify different social strata. Although conceptions about social and economic inequality and stratification are complex, they generally deal with "maldistribution of wealth, variation in educational attainment, occupations, and patterns of deference accorded certain groups" (Devore & Schlesinger, 1987, p. 23). One often used means of classifying social strata, however, is a six-part classification by Hollingshead and Redlich (1958a,b). It comprises members of the

1. upper-upper class: the most wealthy—often "old wealth";
2. lower-upper class: the newly wealthy;
3. upper-middle class: successful professional and business people;
4. lower-middle class: white-collar workers;
5. upper-lower class: blue-collar workers; and
6. lower-lower class: unemployed and recipients of public assistance.

In a study of the "average" person's conception of social class, Coleman and Rainwater (1978) found that people tend to associate social class with social standing, namely social rank, no matter how achieved. Although respondents used the social class concept to refer to high or low status and acceptance, they wished it was used to refer to "a person's true quality [and] moral goodness" (p. 17).

The social work profession has a strong interest in social welfare and how to redress incongruities between client needs and resources. Social workers also serve a large proportion of lower income clients. However, the research literature suggests that clinical assessments and psychotherapeutic interventions may be biased by middle-class ideology (Franklin, 1986). Equally important to how social workers perceive clients is the way in which such clients perceive their economic and political opportunities. Many social workers are concerned about people who are viewed as members of the "underclass," the structural inequities and personal hopelessness that appears to accompany that status, and the profession's role in solving these difficulties.

Developmentally Disabled People

People who have had less than successful or variations in developmental processes that impair cognitive and social functioning are *developmentally disabled*. Identification of people who are developmentally disabled has been greatly influenced by legislative and regulatory policy. According to the

Developmental Disabilities Act of 1984 (P.L. No. 95-602), individuals are termed developmentally disabled if they experience substantial physical or mental limitations before age 22 in each of seven major life activity areas in which they require long-term assistance:

1. self-care, for which they need assistance in feeding, hygiene, and appearance;
2. receptive and expressive language, to communicate effectively;
3. learning, if their learning interferes with cognition or visual or oral communication;
4. mobility, if they are unable to use fine and gross motor skills;
5. self-direction, to enable them to make decisions concerning social and individual activities;
6. capacity for independent living, if they are unable to perform "normal" societal roles in a safe manner; and
7. economic self-sufficiency, if individuals are in situations that prevent working or self-support (McDonald-Wikler, 1987).

Developmentally disabled individuals seeking social services are most likely to be diagnosed as having mental retardation, cerebral palsy, autism, orthopedic problems, hearing problems, epilepsy, or specific learning disabilities. Clients facing these difficulties are more likely to be poor, strained by care demands, and need counseling, multiple supportive services, and advocacy; consequently, the social work role with developmentally disabled clients is rapidly expanding to meet these needs (National Association of Social Workers [NASW], 1982).

People of Varying Sexual Orientation

Sexual identity has three components: (1) gender identity, or the individual's perception of himself or herself as male or female; (2) gender role, or the set of role behaviors expected of males and females; and (3) sexual orientation, or the individual's gender and affectional partner, i.e., whether that person is of the same or opposite gender (Berger, 1987). For many years prior to 1973, homosexuality was included in the American Psychiatric Association's (APA) *Diagnostic and Statistical Manual* (DSM) as a mental illness requiring treatment. Because homosexuality was never shown to meet the definition of mental disorder, this portrayal of gays and lesbians was challenged. On December 15, 1973, the APA board of directors voted to remove homosexuality as a psychiatric disorder behavior, and currently views homosexuality as a particular life-style (APA, 1980; Harrison, Wodarski, & Thyer, 1992).

However, many misconceptions of the sexual orientation of gays and lesbians still exist. Conflicting and inaccurate definitions of homosexuality and the perpetuation of myths often impede social work services (Berger, 1983, 1987). Research has underscored that homosexual men and women are diverse in developmental experiences, family constellation, roles, and personality (Crawford, 1988; Woodman, 1987). Yet, far too often, gays and lesbians are portrayed as deviant or pathological (Kravetz, 1982; Lowenstein, 1980).

This far too common misconception is known as *homophobia*, which is a belief system that supports negative myths and stereotypes about gays and lesbians. This belief system may lead to the use of offensive language and a devaluation of homosexual life-styles, and also may erroneously suggest that discrimination on the basis of life-styles is justifiable (Morin & Garfinkle, 1978). Because practitioners who subscribe to a homophobic belief system are less likely to understand homosexual clients and can seriously undermine their therapeutic work, it is important for practitioners to clarify their belief systems and to obtain accurate information about this client constituency (Cummerton, 1981).

Religious Groups

Although the definition of religion is complex, it usually includes reference to a supernatural power or being, a sense of faith, and how a person perceives his or her ultimate concerns (Favor, 1986). In addition to a person's spirituality, religion also tends to refer to an institutionally patterned system of beliefs, values, and rituals. Because social workers sometimes perceive religion as a private concern of clients, they may ignore spiritual issues in professional practice (Sanzenbach, 1989). Researchers in recent literature have increasingly questioned this assumption, and suggest that understanding a client's religious beliefs and practices is important in assessing individual and collective behavior (Canda, 1989). It is critical for social workers to know a person's sense of spirituality in order to understand that person's maturational development. In addition, knowledge of religious beliefs, values, and rituals enable practitioners to better comprehend the culture in which the client lives (Kolberg, 1976; Holland, 1989).

Oppressed Populations

Diversity content in social work education encompasses groups of people who experience the effects of social and economic injustice, including all forms of discrimination. Effective cross-cultural social work practice also addresses strategies of intervention to achieve social and economic justice and to combat the causes and effects of institutionalized forms of oppression (CSWE, 1992). Social workers who understand and use advocacy and empowerment techniques can be instrumental in assisting clients to exert their personal, political, and economic power.

Clearly, the groups to be addressed under the rubric of diversity in social work practice have been variously defined. Currently, many social workers who espouse a postmodernist approach, as expressed in feminist theory (Chapter 12) and social constructionism (Chapter 7), have challenged the accepted or traditional ideas about race, gender, and class. These scholars have suggested that it is ineffective to think about clients in categories, such as "women" or "African-American" (Scott, 1989; Tice, 1990; see Chapter 2 for a discussion of whether human behavior theory can be universal). Rather, they have suggested that social workers be open to multiple meanings, respect clients' multiple perspectives, and "celebrate [client] differences" (Sands & Nuccio, 1992, p. 489).

CURRICULUM FOR DIVERSE SOCIAL WORK PRACTICE

The cross-cultural and pluralistic perspective in social work implies a conscious effort to break loose from the tendency to see social work practice exclusively in terms of one culture, class, or nation. (Sanders, 1974, p. 86)

The social work commitment to a diversity framework reflects an appreciation and understanding of the consequences of diversity in ethnic background, gender, race, class, sexual orientation, and culture in a multicultural society. The ability to work with and to understand individual life-styles and the distinct needs and aspirations of diverse ethnic groups and special populations, to view these differences nonjudgmentally and with respect, and to incorporate this understanding into practice is fundamental for culturally sensitive social work practice (Greene & Ephross, 1991b). The goal is to be able to practice effectively with people of both genders in varying cultures and socioeconomic and life situations.

Various groups fall under the umbrella of diversity, and definitions of what constitutes multicultural or gender-sensitive social work practice may vary. A social worker who can work effectively with people and communities other than his or her own may be considered culturally competent (Crompton, 1974). In addition, cross-cultural social work services to individuals, families, and groups uses ethnographic information in the planning, delivery, and evaluation of such services (Green, 1982). Social work practice within a diversity framework also recognizes the culture of the client in understanding help-seeking patterns; in defining problems; in selecting solutions and interventions; and in planning service, policy design, and implementation.

Despite the profession's value commitment and increased attention to a diversity framework, content related to diversity in the curricula of schools of social work remains fragmented (Granger & Portner, 1985; Lister, 1987). Currently, the literature on cultural content in social work practice remains diffuse, and there is no consensus on a theoretical framework with which to address our multicultural constituency (Lister, 1987; Lum, 1986; Montiel & Wong, 1983; Tully & Greene, 1994). To compound the problem, relevant terms are ill defined, and there is no agreement about how best to build diversity content into the curriculum. Nonetheless, the growth of diversity as a social force has become so powerful that it clearly is essential that the profession prepare social work professionals for effective practice with diverse groups.

Content on human diversity is not a single component; rather, diversity content is multidimensional, addressing numerous communities and groups and encompassing multiple sources for effective practice. Diversity content and applications are presented in all five domains of social work education: (1) research, (2) practice methods, (3) social policy, (4) human behavior, and (5) field education. The expanded knowledge base to support social work practice within a diversity framework encompasses cognitive information, skill-based techniques, and methods for developing self-awareness and an affirming appreciation for cultural variations or differences.

The differential use of theory-informed practice with diverse populations is central to transcultural client–social worker encounters. The ability to organize the helping process and to work sensitively with diverse populations requires the selective and differential use of knowledge, attitudes, and skills pertaining to social welfare policy, research methods, practice methods, human behavior theory, and an evaluation of the effectiveness of interventions in the field. Although this book emphasizes the application of human behavior theory to social work practice with diverse constituency groups, it initially explores the multiple sources of learning to achieve practice competency.

KNOWLEDGE, SKILLS, AND ATTITUDES

A vast body of knowledge identifies how ethnicity and membership in various social class groups shape approaches to the problems of living. (Devore & Schlesinger, 1987a, p. 3)

Three of the traditional elements of social work learning are involved in developing culturally sensitive practice: knowledge, skills, and attitudes. The knowledge component, or culture-specific information, overlaps with the attitude or value dimension and is broad, cutting across all curriculum areas including social welfare policies and services, social work practice, social work research, human behavior in the social environment, and field practicum. The knowledge component, in large measure, stems from the idea that false assumptions and prejudice can most readily develop when people lack information or have misinformation about a member of a particular group. Moreover, it is imperative to understand the impacts of oppression, as well as a cultural group's history, normative life experiences, and family and community patterns. The practitioner then must be able to individualize or understand how these factors affect a particular client's life experiences (Schlesinger & Devore, 1979).

According to Robertson (1970), detailed information on and facts about diverse populations are necessary to combat myths and stereotypes. Kim (1973) has pointed out that "the myth that Asian-Americans comprise a homogeneous model minority ignores the many difficulties these heterogeneous populations face" (p. 44). He suggested that practitioners need to know that communities referred to as Asian-American contain groups with great variations in their immigration patterns, size, group cohesion, stability, and educational, professional, political, and economic life. In addition, a particular client must be assessed to ascertain his or her interpretation of cultural and other life experiences.

Factual information alone may not improve specific practice behaviors (Caster, 1993; Gallegos & Harris, 1979; Ifill, 1989; Proctor & Davis, 1983). Teaching approaches that help students move beyond cognitive learning, including a focus on affective processes and skills development, are increasingly popular. Skills necessary to provide culturally competent social work services include those for interpersonal interacting, gathering information, developing relationships, and constructing helpful interventions. Skill development has routinely included methods for interviewing as well as for giving practice feedback of basic facilitative skills such as attending, responding, reflecting, questioning, and summarizing feelings (Blue, 1986).

To provide transcultural social work, practitioners must become competent in the skills necessary for services not only to individuals, but to families and groups (see Chapters 9 and 10). Delivering family-centered interventions from a cross-ethnic or cross-cultural perspective involves being open to cultural differences, understanding the relativity of practitioners' own biases, and providing a culturally relevant assessment for families of different cultural backgrounds (Burke, 1982; McGoldrick, Preto, Hines, & Lee, 1991; Stack, 1974). Culturally sensitive social work practice with groups encompasses understanding how a group experience can universalize the needs of minority ethnic group members and affirm their cultural traditions and experiences (L. E. Davis, 1984; Lee, 1988).

For at least four decades, researchers have argued that a social worker's feelings and attitudes toward minority clients, particularly when hidden and negative, potentially interfere with effective interracial practice (Brown,

1950). Briar (1961) and Fischer (1978) assessed the impact of client group membership, such as race and social class, on the clinical judgment process. They found that clinicians tended to assess working-class clients more negatively than middle-class clients. Similarly, practitioners of older clients were found to be influenced by their emotional response to that population (Genevay & Katz, 1990). The classic study by Hollingshead and Redlich (1958a) established the effects of social class on mental health and diagnosis; and the equally well-known study by Broverman, Broverman, Clarkson, Rosekrantz, and Vogee (1970) pointed out the effects of therapists' bias on judgments about mental health of clients related to client gender.

These interests, sentiments, feelings, attitudes, values, awareness, judgment, and so forth compose the affective or value-oriented content of cross-cultural social work (Montalvo, 1983). Affective learning, usually thought of as experiential, requires an exploration and clarification of the practitioner's worldview. Through affective learning, practitioners often focus on an awareness of their own cultural upbringing so that they will develop the ability to distinguish their own worldview from the worldview of others (Chau, 1989, 1990). Practitioners may approach affective learning through modeling behavior in role plays, an examination of popular-culture movies, through novels, through autobiographies, by writing a "coming out" letter, or by discussing a person's first encounter with racism, sexism, or classism (Freedman, 1990a).

Norton (1978) has proposed that, to understand the client's dual perspective in which the client and social worker simultaneously compare the values, attitudes, and behavior of the larger societal system with those of his or her immediate family and community system, it is necessary to have experiential learning in class and in the field practicum. This could take the form of candid discussion and labs. Experiential learning opportunities can narrow the gap between a practitioner's personal life and his or her work expectations.

The nature of the causal relationship among knowledge, attitudes, and behaviors remains a central issue in cross-cultural social work. The evolution of practice appears to be moving from a framework that encompasses minority *content* to an approach that includes *minority practice.* The shift from minority content to minority practice places more emphasis on skills and affective components (Ifill, 1989). Similarly, there is a growing recognition that ethnic and gender-sensitive practice must pay attention to perceptions that bias practice (Granger & Portner, 1985). For example, Boneparth and Stoper (1988) proposed that social work practice involves understanding the policy implications of role equity and equalizing opportunities for men and women, whereas Dubray (1985), in a study of value differences, found that cultural conflict often arises when Anglo-American counselors practice with American Indians. He suggested that further information about American Indian clients' values is a necessary starting point in implementing the objectives of effective social work programs. Understanding such differences must begin with an appreciation of diversity both within the American Indian heritage as well as in contrast with other North American peoples (Carpenter, 1980).

Experiential learning increasingly is conceptualized in behavioral terms and includes opportunities, such as participant observation or social simulations, for practitioners to explore how they should act during an interview of the client. Experiential learning in the classroom and the field practicum begins the process that allows social workers to understand and interact with people who are culturally different from themselves.

Ideally, experiential experiences can enable students who wish to achieve effectiveness in transcultural social work to confront and possibly overcome their biases and to better understand how members of a community articulate their own problems and concerns (Fox, 1983). Self-awareness, which encompasses the ability to challenge preconceived ideas and attitudes about particular client populations, is the goal of much affective learning content. This is a gradual and ongoing process of becoming more receptive to cultural differences. The process begins with awareness, that is, increasing one's consciousness of people and events outside one's own experience; moves to openness, a further ability to accept information and experiences with those who are culturally different; and results in an immediate alertness to others (Montalvo, 1983). Because this self-knowledge enables practitioners to be more culturally responsive and "give unbiased attention to concerns of the larger society and those unique to racial and ethnic groups" (Chau, 1990, p. 131), self-awareness can heighten the skills component.

MODELS OF CROSS-CULTURAL SOCIAL WORK PRACTICE

Readers [of Group Work with the Poor and Oppressed] will yield increased knowledge of empowerment theory and practice (knowing) that can be generalized to work with all groups (doing), and increased understanding of the . . . contemporary social work commitment (feeling). (Germain, 1989, p. 1)

Social workers may turn to a number of practice models as a means of becoming more effective multicultural practitioners (Chau, 1990; Devore & Schlesinger, 1987a; Green, 1982; Lum, 1982, 1986). A major argument for an overarching model is that it is impossible to gain intimate, comprehensive, detailed knowledge on all groups. Models can offer a unified methodology for knowledge, theories, values, and related skills. A process approach may help establish critical thinking and the ability to make theoretical connections (Crompton, 1974; Lum, 1982). Among those theorists who argued from an integrative perspective for examination of the overall approach to diversity is Latting. Latting (1990) suggested that prejudice be thought of as an inability to think critically, and that students work to achieve the skill of critical thinking to prepare for social work practice with diversity. From another perspective, Hopkins (1980) suggested that the basis for racism, ageism, and sexism is institutional inequality. He proposed that, to overcome institutionalized barriers, classroom instructors must address issues of social stratification. In addition, Lum (1986) has offered a process model for practice with people of color or ethnic minorities. He suggested that the common experiences of racism, discrimination, and segregation "bind minority people of color together and contrast with the experience of white Americans" (p. 1). Therefore, generic concepts—those that apply to all people—do not address cultural dimensions of meaning. He argued that social workers need to understand ethnic customs and beliefs, interdependent family networks, and behavioral survival skills, and need to tie them to a practice model.

Green's (1982) model for ethnic competence in social work practice draws on anthropological views of ethnicity and stipulates that practitioners are responsible for conducting themselves in a manner that is congruent with the behavior and expectations that members of the group being served view as appropriate behavior. He has contrasted two views of ethnicity: (1) the categorical perspective, which attempts to explain differences between and among groups by the degree to which members follow distinctive cultural traits, such as ways of eating, dressing, or behaving, and (2) the transactional approach, which focuses on the way in which people of different groups interact and communicate to maintain their sense of cultural distinctiveness. The transactional view emphasized in Green's model is based on how the boundaries between groups are managed. He has delineated five major features of ethnic-competent practice: (1) an awareness of one's own cultural limitations; (2) an openness to cultural differences; (3) a client-oriented, systematic learning style; (4) use of cultural awareness; and (5) an acknowledgment of cultural integrity.

Devore and Schlesinger's (1981) model suggested that practitioners need to consider the effects of their own ethnicity before they can offer ethnic-sensitive social work services. This thought process involves discovering "ME— not always nice, sometimes judgmental, prejudiced and noncaring" (p. 83). According to Devore and Schlesinger (1987b), ethnic-sensitive practice is based on three major principles:

1. Simultaneous attention must be given to individual and systemic concerns as they emerge out of client needs and professional assessment.
2. Practice skills must be adapted to the particular needs and dispositions of ethnic and class groups.
3. Practice must recognize that the "route of the social worker" (p. 515) affects problem definition and resolution.

Overall, effective multicultural practice requires the simultaneously simple and complex activity of putting the client—with all that implies about the particular aspects of the client's life experience and meaning system—at the center of the helping process. It involves, at the very least, an attitude of respect for the client's experiences and life-style, an appreciation of the right to client self-determination, sufficient interpersonal skills and professional interventions to meet client needs, knowledge about the clients' group's life, and an understanding of the basic dynamics of human behavior. The argument for understanding the dynamics of human behavior involves a *differential* use of theory-based practice, that is, a practice in which social work practitioners obtain sufficient information about various patterns of human behavior and development—contexualized by specifics of gender, race, socioeconomic class, and particular client time and locale—to be able to take an inquiring stance about the client's or client system's life experiences.

A Diversity Framework for Human Behavior: Conceptual and Historical Reformulations

2

Roberta R. Greene

> *Groups urging ethnic identity do a service to all Americans. The capacity to value difference is a positive phenomenon, it mitigates against human suspicion of others unlike ourselves and against the need to measure everyone by a single standard of behavior.*

(Cooper, 1973, p. 78)

Throughout the profession's history, social work has had a value commitment to understand and address client differences. However, the approach to client diversity has varied. A review of the literature suggests that the social work profession's thinking about how to prepare practitioners to capably meet the needs of diverse client groups has evolved over time and reflects the changing body politic of the United States (Lukes & Land, 1990; Mirelowitz & Grossman, 1975). The following section addresses the profession's search for a human behavior curriculum for diverse social work practice.

HUMAN BEHAVIOR THEORY AND DIVERSITY CONTENT

> *As we enter into the 1990s, the demand for culturally competent practice—a legacy of the '80s fueled by demographic forces and a critical interest in ethnicity—will continue to shape practice.* (Chau, 1991, p. 1)

A *theory*, a logical system of concepts that provides a framework for organizing and understanding observations, enables social workers to carry out their professional responsibilities through a planned process (Greene & Ephross, 1991b). However, not all theories of human behavior in the social work environment are thought to have equal utility in addressing diversity and cross-cultural and ethnic concerns. To effectively deliver cross-cultural social work services, many theorists suggest that practitioners must be armed

19

with theories that are as universal as possible in their practice application (Chess & Norlin, 1988; Newman & Newman, 1987). The extent to which theories of human behavior that support social work practice have been applied universally—or can be applied to the diversities that characterize U.S. society and can allow for human differences within cultures—is explored throughout this book.

Social workers turn to human behavior theories to provide a knowledge base for understanding and action (Bloom, 1984). Human behavior content encompasses theories and knowledge about biopsychosocial development across the life span, and addresses the range of social systems in which individuals live—families, groups, organizations, institutions, and communities (CSWE, 1992). Human behavior content also deals with the impact of social and economic forces on individual and social systems.

The social work profession has long accepted human behavior theory as the crucial knowledge base to be used by social workers to formulate a psychosocial assessment and a treatment or intervention plan (Boehm, 1959a,b; Butler, 1959; Eure, Griffin, & Atherton, 1987; Griffin & Eure, 1985; Towle, 1960). The theoretical model of human behavior is "a point of departure in problem solving . . . and provides guidelines about how to carry out the social work role" (Greene & Ephross, 1991b, p. 6).

The idea that a theory, by defining parameters or conceptual boundaries, can affect social workers' practice perspectives has been expressed in a number of ways (Bartlett, 1970; E. G. Goldstein, 1986c). For example, Greene (1986) suggested that having an assessment and treatment orientation is one of the most critical aspects of the professional use of self. Meyer (1982) best summed up the need for a set of human behavior assumptions, a system for data collection, and a basis for making decisions: "What one is trained to see one addresses in assessment and intervention" (pp. 19–20).

To achieve this practice goal, a viable person-environment model to understand human behavior within a diversity framework is essential. Theories best suited to social work practice with diverse populations should apply to different gender, ethnic, racial, and social class groups. Theories for diverse practice also should enable social workers to better understand client similarities and differences (Newman & Newman, 1987; Specht & Craig, 1982).

Social work educators throughout the profession's history have turned to a variety of theoretical models in their search for a common theoretical orientation that will enable them to effectively organize and teach human behavior content. Their expectations for the human behavior curriculum have reflected prevailing social and political contexts, have been accompanied by changes in instructional emphases, and have predicted changes in the theories used in practice (Brooks, 1986; Ephross-Saltman & Greene, 1993). At times, debate about which theory best meets the purposes of the profession has been so intense that it has generated ideological feuds and rivalries

(Gould, 1987; Guidry, 1979; Mohan, 1980). The early stages of social work, which arose in response to dislocations brought about by the Industrial Revolution, were characterized "more by direct action than any concern for the elegance or utility of theory" (Findlay, 1978, p. 53). During the late 1920s to the mid-1950s when social work became increasingly professionalized and emphasized individual therapeutic practice, psychoanalytic theory dominated practice. Social workers in such counseling roles were said to have a narrow psychological approach to human behavior (Solomon, 1987).

Throughout the 1960s, social workers were ambivalent about the utility of the Freudian medical model, an approach that emphasized diagnosis, treatment, and cure as a practice approach. The emphasis in human behavior theory began to shift from a psychoanalytic formulation of intrapsychic processes, mainly concerned with the relative functioning of id, ego, and superego, to a greater consideration of the person-in-situation and the consequences of cultural group membership on behavior (Janchill, 1969). By the 1970s, different modes of helping proliferated, such as the short-term therapies, and family and couples approaches (Schwartz, 1984). Humanistic and behavioral therapies as well as general systems theory received greater attention. By the 1980s, there no longer appeared to be a monolithic orientation to treatment. Rather, a number of helping orientations prevailed (Ephross-Saltman & Greene, 1993; Schwartz, 1984).

Both historical and conceptual reasons can explain the shifts in theoretical emphases of social work's guiding theory base. A major reason was social work's historical shifts between individual therapy on the one hand, and social reform on the other (Morell, 1987; Siporin, 1980). Different theories were seen as more likely to achieve one or the other goal.

Another reason for the change in emphases was social workers' dissatisfaction with the perceived biases inherent in particular human behavior theories. For example, some social work educators contended that much of the psychological literature, particularly that of Erikson and Freud, reinforced cultural stereotypes of women (Brown, 1976; Gould, 1987; Lowenstein, 1976; Meisel & Perkins, 1974; Schwartz, 1973). These educators raised concerns about the social work biases in the knowledge base, the selection of slanted textbooks, and limited opportunity in field activities (Berkun, 1984; Kravetz, 1982; Schwartz, 1973; Wetzel, 1976). The goal of these educators in challenging traditional paradigms has been to achieve a more inclusive curriculum. For example, they defined a gender-inclusive curriculum as one that would not polarize between men and women, but rather would examine "gender as a process accomplished through social interaction" (Hurtado, 1989, p. 835).

Racial minorities also raised concerns about the human behavior curriculum and whether the complex interactions among biological, psychological, and sociocultural variables were being addressed. For example, African-

American educators pointed out that there was an absence of accurate information about black family life in the human behavior curriculum to combat myths and stereotypes (Billingsley, 1969; Delaney, 1979; Dumpson, 1979; McAdoo, 1981). Scholars called for universal principles of psychological and social functioning, as well as attention to the unique experiences of African-Americans and other minorities (Petro & French, 1972).

Gradually, advocacy efforts of social work educators promoted an awareness that theoretical orientation plays a critical role in choosing among various strategies for enhancing the social functioning of clients. Many educators urged that the theory underlying social work practice should consider the cultural group to which a client belongs. For example, Goldstein (1980) challenged traditional human behavior theories as "based on observation of white, middle class, heterosexual individuals and intact families" (p. 175), whereas Trader (1977) cautioned that "most, if not all theories are culture-bound" (p. 10), requiring practitioners to question whether a particular theory fits the needs of a minority group client.

The effects of the civil rights and women's liberation movements were instrumental in helping the social work profession become more aware of its constituency and the need to reexamine long-held assumptions about human behavior theory (Gould, 1984). Social work educators began to question whether one set of principles and values, namely Anglo-Euro-American, could apply to all humans at all times (Edwards, 1982). Faculty increasingly challenged the "dominant-group definitions of reality and acceptability" (Federico, 1979, p. 188). For example, Gould (1984) observed that the theory of female sexuality and feminine development was based on a conventional variation in the male model. She and others argued that it is impossible to have a gender-sensitive curriculum that uses one set of norms or places everyone into a monolithic category (Tice, 1990).

Edwards (1982) stated a similar concern about the application of generic concepts to all people in all situations:

> The most profound expression of this practice is the clinical approach to blacks and other ethnic minorities. There is a basic assumption that the study of *general* human behavior within the social environment may lead to feelings, intuition and knowledge that will be beneficial to all in the treatment context. Social scientists and people with a social concern have for several generations articulated and overemphasized the commonality and universality of traits within the species. (p. 430)

In this vein, theories were reevaluated that often appeared to omit consideration of racial, cultural, and ethnic factors and that sometimes stressed sexist interpretations (Granger & Portner, 1985). Of particular importance was the theoretical perspective on problem resolution (Proctor & Davis, 1983).

Fit between client and theory could occur better, according to Trader (1977), if the theory base considered the cultural group to which a client belongs. She suggested that, particularly in practice with oppressed minorities, social workers must use a theory that would strike a balance between pathology and health, practitioner and client control, the personal and societal impact on behavior, internal and external views on change, and rigidity and flexibility in its adherence to its postulates.

Over the past two decades, the human behavior knowledge base has expanded and the content has moved away from any single-theory approach that emphasizes individual behavior and staged development. Instead, the focus has been on multiple theories that better address the person-in-environment (Parsons, Hernandez, & Jorgensen, 1988). For example, postmodern philosophy, which rejects fixed categories and universal laws, also is triggering a reconceptualization of social work knowledge (Sands & Nuccio, 1992; see Chapter 7). This theoretical thrust suggests that each client's life story has its own special meaning that can be interpreted within political and social contexts. Clearly, beginning in the late 1960s, when CSWE intensified its examination of how minority content fits into curriculum, human behavior and the social environment has increasingly been taught within a human diversity framework (Brooks, 1986; Ifill, 1989).

EVOLVING PERSPECTIVES: BIOLOGICAL, PSYCHOLOGICAL, AND CULTURAL ASPECTS OF HUMAN DEVELOPMENT

Seeing only one "normal" pattern [of human development] ignores the cultural, social, and genetic factors that lead to multiple views of appropriate life goals and multiple resources and behavioral networks to achieve them. Therefore, human behavior must be understood as resulting from the interplay of equally important psychological, social, cultural, and biological factors. (Federico, 1979, p. 181)

Human behavior is a result of the complex interactions of biological, psychological, and sociocultural factors. Understanding the interplay of biological, psychological, social, and cultural elements of development in the life space of individuals, families, and small groups is central to clinical social work practice (Caroff, 1982). The social, psychological, and physical aspects of a person's development, at any stage of the life cycle, are intimately related. When people experience a dysfunction in any one, it may lead to a request for social work services. All three aspects and the interaction among them demand attention so that the clinical social worker can understand the presenting problem and devise an appropriate plan of intervention (Greene & Ephross, 1991b).

A basic ingredient of social work practice is an evaluation of a client's ability to move through a series of lifelong biopsychosocial transitions (Greene, 1986). The idea that clinical social work assessments and interventions should be based on an understanding of human behavior related to the whole person is a strong theme in the social work literature:

> The client of a social agency is like all the other persons we have ever known, but he [she] is different too. . . . Nevertheless, the person is a whole in any moment of living . . . he [or she] is product-in-process, so to speak, of his [or her] constitutional makeup, his [or her] physical and social environment, his [or her] past experiences, his [or her] present perceptions and reactions, and even his [or her] future aspirations. It is this physical-psychological-social-past-present-future configuration that he [or she] brings to every life-situation he [or she] encounters. (Perlman, 1957, pp. 6–7)

Biological Aspects

The assessment of biological factors includes genetic endowment; the physiological, induced changes and functional capacities of vital organ systems that contribute to health, well-being, and life expectancy; social factors involving the capacity for carrying out social roles with respect to other members of society; and psychological components, which are the coping strategies and adaptive capacities of the individual vis-à-vis environmental demands (Birren, 1969; Greene, 1986).

Biological aspects of human functioning, closely associated with an individual's capacity for survival or position along his or her life span, include changes in the structure and functions of body organs and systems that occur over time (Zarit, 1980). Physiological changes encompass all time-dependent changes in structure and function of the organism, the efficiency of these changes to meet life demands, and increased vulnerability to disease and death, such as lung capacity, margin of stress, and speed of reaction time.

Although social workers, particularly those in health settings, are interested in physiological functioning and health status, they are also concerned with the whole person. This means effective practitioners also may need to assess a client's nutritional habits, ease of mobility, energy level, availability and use of medication, and understanding of medical or health regimes (Greene, 1986).

Based on a biopsychosocial paradigm, social work practice with diverse populations requires an understanding of the psychological and social issues of wellness and illness. There is considerable evidence that an individual's approach to issues of health and illness is closely interrelated with psychological and sociocultural aspects of human behavior. For example, in some groups, people are expected to experience pain stoically, whereas in others, individuals may vigorously express their pain. Therefore, how a person reacts to symptoms related to a particular illness is personal, but also related to cultural differences in approach to wellness and illness, such as beliefs about what causes an illness and how an illness is expected to be cured (Devore & Schlesinger, 1987a).

A useful concept in thinking about the relationship of health and culture is the *illness trajectory*, that is, the path or progression of the illness as it relates to all persons involved (Kumabe, Nishida, & Hepworth, 1985; Table 2.1). The concept of the illness trajectory suggests that the social worker examine the patient, family, ethnic group, community, and care provider fit or participation in the treatment process. The dimensions of the illness trajectory include the *knowledge component*, which deals with how the patient perceives and understands his or her illness; the *emotional components*, which involve the patient's feelings and coping styles related to his or her illness; and the *role behaviors* of persons involved, which include the expected responsibilities of patients and caregivers.

Social workers engage in practice with several diverse populations about whom knowledge of biopsychosocial functioning within the U.S. societal context is critically important. For example, advocacy techniques are central to social work with people with acquired immune deficiency syndrome (AIDS), and is an area of practice in which the profession's concern with social policy and societal justice overlaps with a need to have current information about human biology.

Social work practitioners also are increasingly working with people with developmental disabilities. From the biopsychosocial perspective, the focus of attention moves to what Black and Weiss (1991) have discussed as the *social construction of disability*, that is, the idea that people with chronic illness and disability often face discrimination in U.S. society and are viewed by many activists and scholars as an oppressed minority group (Fine & Asch, 1988; Fox, 1986). Indeed, more than 20 years ago, some human services professionals who sought to implement normalization principles noted that "handicappism" should be added to racism, sexism, and ageism as examples of institutionalized oppression. An idea that is receiving increased attention is that such social discrimination requires social work interventions that increase societal participation and access to services.

Psychological Aspects

The psychological aspects of human behavior theory examine the behavioral, developmental, affective, and cognitive aspects of human functioning (Maier, 1987). Psychological functioning generally includes factors related to

Table 2.1. The Illness Trajectory

Perspectives	Patient ↔ Family ↔ Ethnic Group → Community → Care Providers ↔ Others		
		Dimensions of Trajectory	
↑ Phases of Trajectory	Knowledge, art, and beliefs about	Emotional components	Role behaviors of persons involved
OUTCOME Wellness Chronic Illness or disability Death	Good health, well-being Chronic illness, chronic disability Death and dying	Perceptions of wellness, Disabling conditions and death Emotional reactions Coding responses	Dying person Chronically ill or handicapped Family Community Care providers, etc.
TREATMENT	Who should treat Modes of treatment Side effects Setting for treatment Goals of treatment	Perception of treatment Perceptions of care providers and of care system Emotional reactions Coping responses	Patient Family Community Care providers, etc.
ILLNESS	Causes and symptoms Characteristic patterns Long-term illness Diagnosis Prognosis	Perceptions of illness Emotional reactions Coping responses	Patient Family Community Care providers, etc.

Source: Kumabe, K. T., Nishida, C., & Hepworth, D. H. (1985). *Bridging Ethnocultural Diversities in Social Work and Health*. Honolulu: University of Hawaii, School of Social Work, p. 43. Reprinted with permission of the authors.

personality, sense of self-esteem and competence, judgment, problem-solving ability, appropriateness of affect, and interpersonal skills.

The psychological aspects of human behavior theory are often best known to social work practitioners. In addition, an interest in the client's "characteristic ways of functioning" and the manner in which the client deals with himself or herself as well as others has long been an interest in social work assessment (Perlman, 1957, p. 9). However, the conceptual approach to psychological development has changed over the decades. Before World War II, the social work profession emphasized a psychological orientation to human development. In the 1950s and 1960s, the teachings of Sigmund Freud, Otto Rank, and Erik H. Erikson, with their focus on an individual psychoanalytic orientation, held sway (Ephross-Saltman & Greene, 1993; Maier, 1987).

Starting in the 1960s, women, minorities, and gay and lesbian rights advocates called for a reexamination of the human behavior curriculum. Feminist scholars challenged orthodox and neo-Freudian concepts of the psychology of human development such as *anatomy is destiny*—women's nature, for example, as nurturer, is solely determined by anatomy—and *penis envy*—the female child considers herself defective because she does not have a penis (Gould, 1984; Wesley, 1975; Wetzel, 1986). Feminist scholars have continued to argue for a change in traditional paradigms and a systematic way of integrating current research on women's development (Russo, 1991; Tice, 1990).

A major dissatisfaction with the curriculum among feminist scholars was that principles of human behavior were applied without examination as if they were universal. For example, Tice (1990) proposed that a gender-inclusive curriculum would not collapse the "multiplicity of women's expressions, preoccupations, and experiences into the universal woman" (p. 136). Gilligan's *In a Different Voice* (1982), on the other hand, suggested that human development texts need to consider differences among women of color and among women in general in divergent historical circumstances (see Chapter 12).

Minority group educators also advocated for human behavior content that more effectively addressed diversity. For example, Farris, Neuhring, Terry, Bilecky, and Vickers (1980) called for curriculum content on the self-concept formation among Native American children; Balgopal, Munson, and Vassil (1979) urged schools of social work to include content related to the societal-institutional facet, the group-interactional facet, and the individual-psychological facet of developmental theory among ethnic minority children.

During the 1970s and 1980s, social work educators urged that more attention be given to the psychological development and needs of men and women who are homosexual (Berger, 1984; Cornett & Hudson, 1987; Needham, 1977). For example, Berger (1983, 1984) stated that social workers have little accurate information about older gay and lesbian clients. Needham (1977) urged social workers to remember the social work ethic of "accepting the client where he or she is" (p. 389). Cornett and Hudson (1987) suggested that the psychoanalytically oriented theories of Erikson, Gould, and Vaillant could be applied successfully with gays.

Advocacy for such changes in the social work curriculum ultimately has resulted in the profession broadening its person-environment knowledge base and has increasingly promoted the idea that positive personal identity and self-respect are intimately tied to cultural group membership.

Cultural Aspects

Culture is the way of life of a society and comprises institutions, language, artistic expression, and patterns of social and interpersonal relationships. Culture encompasses the values, knowledge, and material technology that people learn to see as appropriate and desirable. It prescribes ways of behaving, or norms of conduct, beliefs, values, and skills. As such, culture establishes the parameters that guide, structure, and may limit thinking and behavior (Berger & Federico, 1982). A culture is distinguishable by the manner in which groups guide and structure behavior and in the meaning they ascribed to it. "Cultures differ in their world view, in their perspectives on the rhythms and patterns of life, and in the concept of the essential nature of the human condition" (Devore & Schlesinger, 1981, p. 9).

Culture can be thought of as those elements of a people's history, tradition, values, and social organization that become implicitly or explicitly meaningful to the participants (Green, 1982). As such, it shapes the cycle of development or growth of its members through socialization in the family as well as through community groups and societal institutions. Culture comprises those things that are relevant to communication across a social boundary and that become most important when moving from one cultural group to another (Green, 1982).

The early or beginning conceptual frameworks for social work practice addressed the need to appreciate a client's cultural background and heritage: Richmond (1917) cautioned that it would be an error for caseworkers to ignore the special characteristics of immigrant populations. Hamilton ([1940] 1951) stated that the distinguishing feature of social work was its attention to, and integration of, information about a client's cultural patterns into practice. Perlman (1957) echoed this principle a decade later: The ability to take a "cultural life history" (p. 207) and to incorporate such cultural information in social work practice is a key component of social work practice.

Although the literature provides evidence of social work's historical commitment to understanding a client's cultural background, how best to serve a client within a cultural context has been debated over the decades. Devore and Schlesinger (1987b) have suggested that social workers have tended to encourage integration of minority groups into U.S. society. That is, along with the rest of society, social workers long subscribed to the melting pot theory, in which the United States was expected to become a society in which cultural diversity would eventually all but disappear. Although the melting pot perspective factored in the cultural component in the client assessment, it de-emphasized cultural differences. This de-emphasis dominated the profession's practice perspective from the late 1940s and until the civil rights and women's liberation movements of the 1960s.

By the 1970s, social worker educators frequently advocated for greater attention to cultural diversity in the curriculum and in service delivery. Petro and French (1972) argued that, although life experiences of blacks differ from those of other minorities and whites, largely because of racism, before the 1970s there was relatively little in the social work literature on racial or ethnic differences in developmental issues such as self-esteem. Billingsley (1971) further suggested that the myth prevalent in social work that "people are people" and "race does not matter" was a barrier to understanding and liberating black people (p. 33). He called for major societal institutions to abandon "the single standard of excellence based on white European cultural norms" (1968, p. 77). These observations appear to be a further recognition of an inherent contradiction in the American ethos, which simultaneously called for tolerance and conformity.

To understand this paradox, it is necessary to proceed with the history of social work's perspective on the concept of culture. During the 1970s, social work educators increasingly came to realize that they should offer educational approaches that trained practitioners to work in a pluralistic society, a society in which there are distinct, identifiable subcultures that affect how people think, feel, and act (Devore & Schlesinger, 1987b; Sanders, 1975). For example, Sanders (1974), then dean of the School of Social Work of the University of Hawaii, urged the profession to make a "conscious effort to break loose from the tendency to see social work practice exclusively in terms of one culture, class, or nation" (p. 86).

As a result of consciousness-raising and the curriculum review process, concepts related to diversity were revised: For example, the melting pot theory all but lost its credibility (Green, 1982; Lum, 1986). In addition, most social workers took exception with the *culture of poverty* argument. This argument attributed the conditions of the ghetto to the personal pathologies of its members (for example, people in poverty are "not motivated" or are "lazy") and characterized minority families in negative terms (Lewis, 1966).

Ryan (1971) coined the term *blaming the victim* to describe how the ills of society, such as unemployment, low wages, and crowded living quarters, are attributed to the people suffering from them. Ryan suggested that conditions in the ghetto would change only when white society decided to accept structural and governmental reform or a change in the balance of power.

The effect of rethinking these social concepts led to a shift of focus in curriculum from the pathology of clients to a strengths model. That is, rather than examine so-called client personality flaws, social workers were encouraged to help practitioners better understand the respective histories of clients as individualized members of various ethnic and minority groups (Saleebey, 1992). In addition, social workers were taught the importance of reinforcing a minority person's values, norms, language, and traditions as well as general daily living patterns (Lum, 1986).

Several perspectives have been offered to better understand a particular client's cultural life, and to free them from culture-bound practice (de Anda, 1984). For example, the *dual perspective* is the art, theory, and practice of consciously and systematically perceiving, understanding, and comparing simultaneously the values, attitudes, and behaviors of the minority client's immediate family, community, or cultural system with those of the larger system (Norton, 1978). The dual perspective suggests the social worker recognize that all clients are part of two systems: (1) the dominant or sustaining system—the source of power and economic resources—and (2) the nurturing system—the immediate social environment of the family and community (Chestang, 1972).

Miller (1980) proposed that the use of the dual perspective allows for an assessment of the institutional and dominant environment factors as well as those more directly associated with the client that may bring about stress. He concluded that, through the dual perspective, social workers can decide "whether the target of change should become the client, the larger system, or both, or whether it is appropriate to intervene at all" (p. 60).

Social work practice often focuses on the conflicts that arise for the individual who must transverse two cultural systems. Lukes and Land (1990) have suggested this perspective would be useful in social work practice with homosexual clients, whereas Chestang (1984) and Valentine (1971) pointed out the psychological difficulties of maintaining a positive self-image while having to integrate parts of the self identified with majority and oppressed groups. In addition, Chau (1989) has suggested that understanding how problems occur between two cultural environments, or *sociocultural dissonance*, can be most useful in cross-cultural social work education and practice.

An example of the political posture of not intervening at all is discussed by Good Tracks (1973). He pointed to the Native American principle of *noninterference*, that is, because traditional Native American societies were organized around voluntary cooperation, members would strictly subscribe to the idea of self-determination. He concluded that to the extent a Native American retains his or her culture, social workers may not be accepted or may need to take considerable time to earn trust, and many practice techniques may appear to be coercive.

Another concept used to understand culture's influence on human behavior is acculturation. *Acculturation,* or the degree to which a person subscribes to mainstream culture, may vary widely on a continuum from those most acculturated to those least acculturated. The extent of acculturation depends in part on such factors as the individual's degree of urbanization, the number of generations that have passed since the original family member came to the United States, the extent to which a person may prefer to keep linguistic and cultural differences, or political beliefs about the mainstream culture.

Over the past several decades it has become evident that *assimilation,* or the process of diverse racial and ethnic groups coming to share a common culture, an ideal of many new Americans, has a negative side. Namely, many immigrants did not want to become culturally indistinguishable from each other, to "throw off the cultures of their homeland as so much old clothing, that would no longer be needed" (Alba, 1985, p. 5). This realization is apparent, given the numerous discussions in social work journals about how to provide social work services within an increasingly diverse society and among immigrants to the United States who have arrived at different times and may have varying beliefs regarding their assimilation path.

An individual who is *bicultural* is able to move freely between his or her ethnic community and the larger culture. Bicultural theories suggest that socialization is a two-pronged process whereby an individual from an ethnic minority group is socialized in the values, perceptions, and normative behaviors of two cultural systems (Padilla, 1980). de Anda (1984) suggested that the concept of bicultural socialization helps explain cultural differences without suggesting one culture is better than another.

Clearly, more can still be learned about how the process of "stepping in and out of two discrete cultures" affects personal identity (Lukes & Land, 1990, p. 155). With the growing diversity of the U.S. population, many social workers will have to become multicultural or competent in dealing with differing cultures (Chau, 1991; Gomez, 1990). Social work practice in a multicultural society may assume a culturally relative approach to human behavior (Solomon, 1987). The *cultural relativity* school of thought emphasizes that behavioral norms do not need to be modeled on white mainstream standards. Rather, historical and life experiences of a particular ethnic or cultural group member are key influences on human behavior.

SOCIAL SYSTEMS: UNDERSTANDING FAMILIES, GROUPS, ORGANIZATIONS, AND COMMUNITIES

In addition to biopsychosocial factors, human behavior is a "function of families, groups, organizations, and communities" (Swenson, 1979, p. 215). This perspective is guided by the person-environment metaphor and the perspective that "every person is a member" (Falck, 1988, p. 30). Socialization, in which people learn to play certain roles over the life cycle, may reflect considerable variation between and within cultural groups, and occurs within the context of all environmental systems. Therefore, social work practice within a diversity framework must address the various societal institutions and community systems of which the client is a part.

Solomon (1976) proposed a perspective to explain relationships between and among ethnic groups and their political position vis-à-vis larger systems. She coined the term *ethnosystem* to describe "collective interdependent ethnic groups, with each group sharing unique historical and or cultural ties bound together by a single, political system" (p. 45). As part of Solomon's conception, the United States was viewed "as an open ethnosystem" in which there is a "continuous interchange of energy with successively more encompassing systems" (p. 46).

Solomon and her colleagues wanted to draw attention to how the differential deployment of resources to various ethnosystems places a heavier burden on minority group members (Bush, Norton, Sanders, & Solomon, 1983). They viewed differential power among groups and the struggle for scarce goods as the major reason for racial and ethnic stratification, or relative position in the U.S. power structure. Social workers increasingly asked how the pattern of underrepresentation of minority groups in the economic and political life of the United States and the ethnic, racial, and class stratification that resulted affected social work curricula and practice. As a result of the demand for more culturally sensitive services and curricula, a renewed educational focus gave more attention to cultural pluralism. That is, there was a stronger interest in affirming ethnic, racial group membership and helping clients maintain personal identity, values, and preferred behavior patterns, as well as communal social structure.

If social workers are to work effectively with client populations that experience the effects of discrimination and oppression, human behavior content for diverse practice must encompass information about societal institutions and community groups. Integrating content about institutional racism, sexism, and ageism has been strongly advocated (Allen & Burwell, 1980; Hopkins, 1980; Sanders, 1974). The need for such content is based on the long-standing philosophy that clinical social workers as well as community workers should act as effective change agents at the societal level. The role of change agent requires knowledge of group and institutional behavior, institutionalized inequalities, and advocacy skills (see Chapter 12). Over past decades, political advocacy related to institutionalized inequalities has increased the consciousness among faculty members of schools of social work about the need to reexamine issues of oppressed groups in the curriculum. Schools of social work incorporated courses on racism and sexism in the curriculum, and some educators suggested that the concept of power serve as the integrating framework for human behavior classes (Allen & Burwell, 1980; Lowenstein, 1976).

It was suggested that to be more effective in changing the lives of the traditionally less powerful clients, clinical social workers master knowledge of empowerment and advocacy techniques to redress societal inequities and more effectively intervene with clients who belong to negatively stigmatized groups (Pinderhughes, 1978; Solomon, 1976; Wilson, 1973). Discussion also occurred about whether social inequalities, and the manner in which social work services are designed and delivered, contribute to the pressure felt by minority group members to conform to the life-styles of the dominant culture.

Finally, schools of social work—staff, students, and faculty—were recognized as part of the body politic and societal thrust in which the movement toward greater cultural understanding occurs. Faculty members and students proposed that institutional inequities among racial and ethnic groups, social classes, and genders be addressed in social work courses, and that students come to understand the inherent racism and sexism built into societal institutions (Hopkins, 1980). For example, Mirelowitz and Grossman (1975) cautioned that student acculturation—in this case socialization to the professional culture of social work—should not mean that a minority student who learns certain aspects of the mainstream culture should have to give up features of his or her own culture. Because of such advocacy efforts, concern, and heightened sensitivity, schools of social work increasingly are offering learning opportunities for social work practice within a diversity framework.

The Social Work Interview:
Legacy of Carl Rogers and
Sigmund Freud ———————————————————— 3

Roberta R. Greene

*The concern of the social work interveiw is with the unique entity—the unique
individual, the unique group, the unique community.*

(Kadushin, 1972, p. 13)

Whether conducted with individuals, families, or groups, the social work interview is the most consistently and frequently used therapeutic practice
technique. Many of the ideas central to what constitutes an effective social
work interview are derived from human behavior theory assumptions of
Rogers and Freud. For example, the widely accepted practice principle—
tuning-in to client feelings—is based on Freud's assumption that the therapist's role is to interpret a client's hidden feelings to expand his or her self-
awareness; while the assumption that a cardinal feature of the effective
interview is establishing rapport is based on Rogers's concept that it is critical for the helping person to express empathetic understanding to promote
client self-actualization (Greene, 1991b; Raskin, 1985).

The purpose of this chapter is to examine how such assumptions "import-
ed" from Rogers and Freud and "amalgamated" into social work practice affect transcultural social worker–client interactions (Briar and Miller, 1971, p.
59). The chapter first outlines Rogers's and Freud's major premises about the
helping process, and explores how each's concepts about what constitutes
effective therapeutic techniques have shaped the interviewing process. The
chapter then examines whether these assumptions about the social work interview, both implicitly and explicitly stated in the social work literature, are
effective when applied in practice with diverse populations.

The Rogerian assumptions discussed in the chapter suggest that in an
effective interview the practitioner will affirm a client's worth and dignity,
support client self-determination, forge a therapeutic relationship, and communicate with empathy, authenticity, and genuineness. The Freudian or psychoanalytic assumptions explored suggest that the social worker should
listen to client feelings, interpret latent or hidden meanings, develop client
insight or understanding, assess client behaviors and motivation, and maintain professional authority and control in the interview.

THE SOCIAL WORK INTERVIEW

A social work interview is a communication process comprised of practice skills, guided by a theoretical orientation (Shulman, 1984). Theoretical orientations "shape what the practitioner tends to see, what he or she makes of it, and what he or she tends to do about it" (Greene and Ephross, 1991, p. 6). Theories of human behavior that are useful to social work practitioners "identify, describe, explain, and predict a world of stimuli and observations" in the practice role (Siporin, 1975, p. 101). That is, theories of human behavior must present assumptions suitable to explore the pertinent, and to translate a practitioner's observations into practice principles.

Two human behavior perspectives about such questions have dominated the social sciences and have been infused into social work thinking about how to proceed with interview practice techniques. Objectivist theorists assume that social phenomena have a real existence that is factual and can be studied through natural science research methods, and that underlying universal laws can be discovered. That is, psychological knowledge about the client can be discovered with the help of practitioner interpretation. Research and practice methodologies, for example in Freud's psychoanalytic approach, search for objective meaning based on regularities and laws among social or psychological phenomena—in this case how personality is determined during the formative years within the family triangle.

Subjectivist theories, as in Carl Rogers's humanistic approach, take the stance that social reality exists in or is a creation of human consciousness, and that people are proactive in its creation. The only reality then is in the person's consciousness. The client's social reality cannot be studied as such, but must be experienced with the client (Martin & O'Connor, 1989).

Both objectivist and subjectivist approaches have influenced social work practice skills. Practice skills refer "to the 'how' of helping, to purposeful, planned, instrumental activity through which tasks are accomplished and goals are achieved" (Siporin, 1975, p. 43). Of necessity, practice skills employed by the social worker must allow him or her to accomplish the best treatment interventions. Social work interviewing skills provide an enabling process with a recognized and agreed-upon purpose to help people resolve or cope more effectively with identified problems undermining social functioning.

Interviewing skills are professional behaviors or techniques, central to gathering information for appropriate assessment and intervention outcomes. Interview techniques structure the relationship between and among client(s) and the social worker, and organize the therapeutic tasks necessary to carry out an interactional helping approach.

In large measure, discussions in the social work literature reflect the view that, irrespective of theoretical orientation, "effective interviews conform to a general structure, manifest certain properties, and reflect use of the same skills by interviewers" (Hepworth & Larsen, 1987, p. 996). Common properties of the clinical interview discussed in social work practice methods texts tend to include establishing rapport, responding empathically, relating as a genuine person, starting where the client is, exploring problems and client meaning, structuring social worker responses, seeking concreteness in client problem identification, formulating treatment or intervention goals and negotiating contracts, and accomplishing client change-oriented skills (Briar, 1987; Meyer, 1973, 1987; Hepworth & Larsen, 1987).

Less frequently addressed in the social work literature is the need for social workers to adapt their interviewing techniques to different client contexts to better communicate across gender and culture. There is, however, a small body of literature that specifically addresses diversity and the interviewing process. For example, Shulman (1991) has pointed out that it is necessary to understand the impact of gender, age, education, and socioeconomic factors on the social worker–client interaction; Greene (1986), the importance of chronological age; Paviour (1988), the influence of race; Sotomayor (1977), the affects of language; Edwards and Edwards (1980), the importance of historical and cultural background; and Pinderhughes (1979), the impact of societal power issues.

The discussion that follows explores why the ability to conduct a skillful social work interview with diverse populations may require the selective and differential use of both human behavior theory and practice methods, and an evaluation of the effectiveness of person-environment interventions (Compton & Galaway, 1989). It is argued that the differential use of theory-informed practice with diverse populations is central to transcultural client–social worker encounters, and that such differential use of theory for practice allows help to be given and used within an age- and gender-appropriate cultural context.

ROGERIAN INFLUENCES ON THE SOCIAL WORK INTERVIEW: BASIC ASSUMPTIONS

One premise can be said to transcend all others in social work, and from it many secondary values can be derived: the individual human being has an intrinsic worth, dignity, and importance. (Briar & Miller, 1971, p. 33)

Valuing the Individual and the Right to Choose

Carl Rogers, the founder of the person-centered approach to counseling, has had a major influence on social work practice, so much so that many of his value assumptions have become tenets. Rogers is best known for his humanistic view that suggests people have intrinsic worth and a natural tendency toward growth that can be facilitated by a warm and caring practitioner-client relationship (Rogers, 1957, 1961). His belief in the intrinsic value of all human beings, fundamental to all democratic societies, accounts for the very existence of social work (Briar & Miller, 1971) (see Table 3.1).

Another value orientation derived from the humanistic school, and an integral part of the matrix of social work ethics and beliefs, is the right of client self-determination. The principle of the right to client self-determination suggests that social workers who serve as facilitators and assist clients in making their own choices and decisions provide clients with a positive mode of problem-solving experience.

Perlman (1965), a social work practice theorist, has provided a definition of client self-determination that speaks to its powerful force in social work practice:

> Self-determination, then, is the expression of our innate drive to experience the self as cause, as master of one's self. Its practical every day experience builds into [people's] maturation process because it requires the recognition of the actual, the consideration of the possible. . . . Self-determination is based upon a realistic view of freedom. Freedom, in essence, is the inner capacity and outer opportunity to make reasoned choice, among possible socially acceptable alternatives. (p. 421)

The right to self-determination has high priority in an effective social work interview (Hepworth & Larsen, 1987, 1990; National Association of Social Workers [NASW], 1978; Northen, 1982; Perlman, 1957). Nonetheless, client self-determination is usually not seen as unconditional, and sometimes is discussed as a right influenced or even restricted by certain situations and conditions, particularly those conditions considered immoral and/or criminal acts.

McDermott (1982) has raised thorny questions about the principle of a client's right to determination: Does the right to self-determination commit the social worker to support policies or decisions he or she may find unacceptable? Does the principle require the social worker to stand by idly while a client brings disaster upon himself or herself? McDermott goes on to answer these questions: A social workers can, without violating the principle of self-determination, attempt to persuade the client of the desirability of adopting or not adopting a particular course of action. However, the real threat in situations that limit the right to self-determination is using the helping relationship as an opportunity to manipulate the client or to coercively exercise illegitimate authority. "The more insidious powers of the 'hidden persuader' . . . threaten our liberty" (p. 87).

Table 3.1.   The Person-Centered Approach: Basic Assumptions

People are trustworthy, capable, and have a potential for self-understanding and
self-actualization.

Self-actualization is a lifelong process.

People develop and grow in a positive manner if a climate of trust and respect is
established. Individual growth is promoted through therapeutic and other types
of relationships.

Positive attributes of the helping person, including genuineness, acceptance, and
empathetic understanding, are necessary conditions for effective helping relationships.

Respecting the subjective experiences of the client, fostering freedom and personal
responsibility and autonomy, and providing options in therapy facilitate the
client's growth.

The helping person is not an authority. The helping person is someone, who
through his or her respect and positive regard, fosters positive growth.

Clients are capable of self-awareness and possess the ability to discover more appropriate behaviors. Clients, as do all people, have a propensity to move away
from maladjustment toward psychological health.

The practitioner should focus on the here-and-now behavior in the client–social
worker relationship. The content of the helping relationship also should emphasize how the client acts in his or her world.

Getting to know the true self is a major goal of the helping relationship.

The aim of the helping relationship is to move the client toward greater independence and integration.

Source: Greene, R. R. (1991a). "Carl Rogers and the Person-Centered Approach." In R. R.
Greene and P. H. Ephross (Eds.), *Human Behavior Theory and Social Work Practice*, p. 109.
Hawthorne, NY: Aldine de Gruyter.

At the same time, Abramson (1985) has suggested that there are four conditions in which a social worker should assume a paternalistic, or authority,
role:

1.   when a client is a child and lacks the capacity to make an informed
     decision;
2.   when the client is mentally incompetent and is unable to understand
     the results of his or her decisions;
3.   when the consequences of a client's act are far-reaching or irreversible
     such as in suicide; and
4.   when the temporary interference with a client's liberty ensures future
     freedom and autonomy.

The extent to which a social worker affirms a client's right to self-determination rests, in large measure, on the practitioner's perceptions of the helping role and the helping process (Hepworth & Larsen, 1990). For example,
does the social worker perceive his or her role as the provider of solutions?
Does the social worker erroneously perceive a particular client as a member

of a group—such as a member of an oppressed community—lacking in strength and problem-solving capacity (Solomon, 1976)?

In practice situations, the social worker may often face conflict between his or her social responsibility and a client's right to self-determination, for example, in the controversy concerning a mentally ill person's right to refuse treatment or a homeless person's right to refuse shelter. There also are some social work functions that carry legal authority that may limit client self-determination, such as protective services for children, the aged, and the mentally impaired.

Working with particular client populations may present ethical conflict and countertransference issues (see below) for social workers when client behaviors and practices differ from their own (Calenek, 1970; Maki, 1990). These conflicts may prevent a social worker from making "every effort to foster maximum self-determination on the part of clients" (NASW, 1978, p. 5). For example, in a discussion of the legal and ethical issues related to AIDS, Ryan and Rowe (1988) have pointed out that the stigma attached to the human immunodeficiency virus (HIV), the unfortunate negative perception of the client, and the conflict over the right of significant others to know, make the AIDS crisis a challenge to social workers to reaffirm their profession's traditional values of advocacy. Nonetheless, they believe respect for differences and a commitment to client options are necessary (Reamer, 1988; Ryan & Rowe, 1988).

The extent to which a client's right to self-determination is affirmed in the client–social worker relationship also is influenced by the helper-client power differential. A power differential between client and social worker can be brought about by differences in gender, "their respective cultural identities, and group connections" (Pinderhughes, 1989, p. 110). Pinderhughes has cautioned that because power is an important factor in minority relationships, a client's sense of powerlessness may be reinforced in the cross-cultural encounter more readily and frequently than expected. Therefore, practitioners must guard against putting the client in a one-down position and use their helping role to encourage and empower (see Chapter 12). Finally, she suggested that the ideal social worker–client relationship affirms self-determination and fosters growth because the relationship is based on a partnership of mutual respect in which both parties search for common solutions.

Establishing a Client–Social Worker Relationship: Empathy, Genuineness, and Warmth

Rogers (1957) hypothesized that clients experience significant personality change only within a warm and caring therapeutic relationship. In large measure, this assumption dominates the social work profession's helping process: Most social work theorists agree that the client–social worker relationship is central to the clinical social work process, and a positive opportunity for client change (Table 3. 2). In addition, empathy, warmth, and genuineness have come to infuse social work method and are called the "core conditions" of social casework (Fischer, 1978, p. 189).

Most practice methods texts discuss the therapeutic relationship as a communication based on the emotional interaction between people necessary to client self-development, growth, and problem-solving capacity (Kadushin, 1972; Northen, 1982; Shulman, 1984). For example, Biestek (1951) considered the client–social worker relationship a dynamic interaction and psychological connection between people that is "the soul of social casework" (p. 370). Hollis saw the relationship as the keystone of the casework process and basic to all treatment, while Perlman (1957) stated that "all growth-producing relationships, of which the casework relationship is one, contain elements of acceptance and expectation, support and stimulation" that are necessary for client change (p. 57).

Another key idea about the nature of the social work interview derived from the Rogerian perspective is that positive change will occur if the practitioner is *empathetic*—recognizes the client's feelings and experiences; accepts the client with *unconditional positive regard*—is warm and does not force conclusions on the client; and is *genuine* in his or her respect for the client—presents himself or herself as real (Tobin, 1986; Truax, 1966; Truax & Carkhuff, 1966). Communicating with empathy and authenticity and a nonjudgmental attitude have come to be considered the "necessary and sufficient conditions of personality change" (p. 164), and the "common sense" of therapeutic relationships (White & Watt, 1981, p. 257; see Greene & Ephross, 1991a, for a full discussion; see also Table 3.3).

At the same time, practice methods texts historically have recognized that it is necessary to specifically address clients' cultural background in the in-

Table 3.2.   The Rogerian Helping Relationship

Client	Social work therapist
Establishes self-trust	Values the client in a free environment
Is open to experience	Establishes a therapeutic climate
Is open to self-evaluation	Promotes client's self-exploration
Experiences freedom to grow	Provides genuineness, positive regard, and empathy
Moves to a new self-concept	Experiences a renewed sense of caring

Source: Greene, R. R. (1991a). "Carl Rogers and the Person-Centered Approach." In R. R. Greene and P. H. Ephross (Eds.), *Human Behavior Theory and Social Work Practice*, p. 109. Hawthorne, NY: Aldine de Gruyter.

Table 3.3.   Guidelines for the Social Worker Practicing in the Rogerian Tradition

---

Examine your own belief system. Review your attitudes about the self-worth of
   each individual's potential to use the helping relationship effectively.
Deliberate about whether you have the capacity and are able to promote an atmosphere of warmth and trust within the helping relationship.
Involve the client in a therapeutic relationship in which he or she takes the lead in
   describing his or her experiences and in expressing feelings.
Show respect for the subjective experiences of the client by echoing his or her concerns accurately.
Focus on the here-and-now experiences within the interview. Develop a process in
   which the client can learn that he or she can trust his or her own experiences.
Use interviewing techniques that express genuineness, empathy, and congruence.
Accept and interpret the client's life experiences that may stand in the way of his or
   her positive self-evaluation.
View the helping relationship as an opportunity to facilitate growth (for both client
   and therapist) and promote self-evaluation.

Source: Greene, R. R. (1991a). "Carl Rogers and the Person-Centered Approach." In R. R.
Greene and P. H. Ephross (Eds.), *Human Behavior Theory and Social Work Practice*, p. 109.
Hawthorne, NY: Aldine de Gruyter.

terviewing process (Mizio, 1972). For example, Perlman (1957) argued that
a person's behavior is both shaped and judged by cultural expectations and
the various roles a client plays. Kadushin (1972) cautioned that the social distance between client and social worker could be a barrier to communication, and that class, color, age, and gender "are some of the subcultural
differences which might separate interviewer and interviewee" (p. 220).
Northen (1982) suggested that a social worker must pay attention to the constellation of a client group and learn to work across ethnic lines.

Kadushin (1972) asked how the racial factor affected the social worker and
client in the interview. He suggested that racial differences between client
and social worker could be "an impediment to an optimal interview" (p. 231)
given the history of exploitive race relationships in U. S. society. However,
he did believe that cross-racial contact in the client–social worker interview
could be established by not being "color blind" or denying the real differences that need to be accepted through an open discussion of racial issues
(Block, 1968, p. 39, cited in Kadushin, 1972, p. 235).

There have been a number of theorists who have challenged the idea that
social worker empathy is an essential condition for successful therapy. For
example, Kadushin (1972) raised a question about how social workers who
share few of the client's life experiences can achieve empathetic responses
in the interview. He suggested that such empathy was possible only if the social worker accepted that he or she is likely to have little experience that may
lead to empathy, and therefore needs to be more ready to listen, and more
open to correction.

In specifically examining the interview element of empathy in psychotherapy with women, Miller and Stiver (1991) have proposed that people yearn for connections with others, yet tend to keep a large part of themselves "out of connection" (p. 1). According to Miller and Stiver, being out of connection, or not relating in a disclosing manner, occurs more frequently with women because women are socialized to appear less (sexually) available and more compliant. Therefore, for psychological growth to occur in the therapeutic relationship, mutual empathy and mutual empowerment must occur. The sense of *mutuality* in therapy, in their view, is based on a true sense of authenticity that allows for equally true engagement.

Pinderhughes (1979) has suggested that practitioners who wish to empathetically deal with clients from cultures other than their own must first address the power differential between client and social worker. She stated that the helping relationship is in itself a power relationship: "The expertise of the social worker and the neediness of the client place them in positions of power and lack of power, respectively" (p. 315).

In the helping encounter, both clients and practitioners bring experiences, feelings, and behaviors related to their social class, gender, age, ethnicity, or race, all of which are social markers related to power. Empathy, according to Pinderhughes, is the key ingredient that neutralizes the client's powerlessness.

Gibbs (1985) has suggested that achieving empathy in the social work interview is made difficult by the erroneous belief that all people are the same. This assumption that empathy is grounded in human sameness is often expressed in the social work literature. So too is the belief that specified social worker behaviors transmit universal messages with predictable and specified interpretations. The idea that all practitioners can learn to deliver the same interview skills in the same way, rather than adapt their techniques to different client contexts, may lead to what Bernardez (1982) has called "cultural countertransference" or unconscious assumptions about human behavior that are based on prevailing cultural beliefs (p. 8).

Kaplan (1990) argued a similar point: Assuming the client is the same as the practitioner, when attempting to be empathetic, can result in "a decidedly nonempathetic helping response, especially when the client is from a group that has been marginalized or demeaned by the prevailing culture" (p. 8).

From a cross-cultural point of view, the theoretical underpinning of the social work interview must assume knowledge of a client's culture to allow the social worker to develop different skills and strategies in the interview. For example, perhaps, the best known technique that does not apply across cultures is the maintenance of eye contact. For many American Indian clients, eye contact may cause uneasiness, and a method of looking elsewhere is recommended (Edwards & Edwards, 1980). Of course, to some extent, the practice of maintaining eye contact varies with the individual, often depending on his or her adoption of mainstream ideas and values. Therefore, it is always important to individualize the seemingly universal suggestion to maintain positive eye contact.

Edwards and Edwards (1980) have proposed that it is necessary to use culture-specific techniques to enhance the transcultural interviewing process. For example, they suggested that with many American Indian clients, when discussing issues related to someone close who has died it is useful to use a term such as sister, brother, father, and so on, rather than the person's name, because it is a violation of tradition to use a dead person's name. Such cultural sensitivity to clients who follow this tradition enhances the empathetic response of the social worker.

Scholars and practitioners who are exploring the utility of constructionist thought for social work practice have challenged the idea that the social work interview should focus on the core conditions (Duncan, Solovey, & Rusk, 1992, p. 35; see Chapter 7 on constructionist thought). For example, Duncan et al. (1992) argued that empathy, unconditional positive regard, and so forth, are not social worker behaviors, but can only be realized as client perceptions and interpretations, and an experience between people. Therefore, the core conditions would be experienced in a highly idiosyncratic manner according to the specific and unique meaning system of the client:

> Empathy [is] *not* . . . a specific therapist behavior or attitude . . . a means to gain a relationship. . . . Rather, empathy is therapist attitudes and behaviors that place the client's perceptions and experiences above theoretical content and personal values. Empathy is attempting to *work within* the expressed meaning system of the client. (pp. 34–35)

Bachelor's (1991) research on empathy found considerable variation in clients' interpretation of empathy, and concluded that it is not a universal construct, thus adding doubt to the value of a strict emphasis on skill building as a means to practice effectiveness. From this perspective, the goals of multicultural competence may be better served by learning experiences that focus on the skills of adaptive, reflective responses, by which—as Duncan et al. (1992) suggest—the social worker can "accommodate a wide variety of interpersonal styles and meaning systems" (p. 39).

Social work theorists have come increasingly to question whether there is a universal approach to helping and client change. Various theorists have presented the point of view that effective social work service across a diversity of populations involves identifying cultural factors that may be barriers to establishing rapport and effective communication in the social work interview. For example, such barriers may include a reluctance to reveal problems to others, to reflect on what may be perceived as personal inadequacies, or to acknowledge a history of discrimination and mistrust. Still other barriers to forming an effective therapeutic client–social worker relationship in the social work interview may include the cultural norm of not discussing family business with outsiders, and an inability of the client and social worker to discern the other's intended meanings (Hepworth & Larsen, 1987).

Green's (1982) model of cross-cultural social work attempts to address the limitations of the general features of the helping interview. Green has proposed that careful listening, openness and honesty, and an effort to gain rapport and develop empathy are not enough when interviewing minority or ethnic clients. He suggested that social workers must take a learning stance to understand client meanings so as to communicate with competence across cultures. He argued that a practitioner's caring response cannot be contrived nor may he or she rely solely on empathy and openness to get in touch with a client's feelings. Rather, the practitioner who is culturally competent must use ethnographic interviews to "comprehend what the client knows and how that knowledge is used in the mundane traffic of daily activities" (p. 74).

According to Green (1982), the ethnographic approach to the social work interview delineates culture-specific cognitive and behavioral structures to go beyond "global statements about helping and caring for others" (Green, 1982, p. 75). The goal of an ethnographic interview is to reduce practitioner ethnocentrism and to increase bicultural sensitivity (Spradley, 1979). To help the social worker appropriately assess client problems and provide effective social work interventions, this perspective on cross-cultural social work focuses the social work interview on "localized group-specific categories of how the world is organized to generate an insider's perspective" (p. 72).

Gibbs (1985) has authored a five-stage model of interpersonal orientation to treatment in which the client evaluates the social worker, while the social worker is attempting to establish a relationship and to assess the client's problems (see Table 3.4). The model, intended to overcome problems of misdiagnoses and early termination found among many black clients, explores and offers practice suggestions for the initial interviews that set the tone of the helping relationship and establish the boundaries of treatment. The focus of the model is on the content of verbal and nonverbal interactions between social worker and client, and the goals they agree need to be accomplished. Furthermore, the model examines practitioner behaviors, which are evaluated in each stage by the client according to his or her treatment priorities. The social worker dimensions of counselor competence are Rogers's warmth, empathy, congruence, and unconditional positive regard for the client.

Stage I of the model is the *appraisal stage,* during which the client sizes up the social worker, is generally aloof, and evaluates the personal authenticity of the worker. Stage II is the *investigation stage,* characterized by the client checking out the practitioner usually by challenging the social worker's qual-

Table 3.4.   A Model of Interpersonal Orientation to Treatment

Client evaluation stages (themes of evaluation)	Counselor behavior responses (dimensions of competence)
I. Appraisal ("sizing up")	I. Personal Authenticity ("genuineness")
II. Investigation ("checking out")	II. Egalitarianism (status equalization)
III. Involvement (social interactions)	III. Identification (positive identity)
IV. Commitment (personal loyalty)	IV. Acceptance (empathy, support)
V. Engagement (task involvement)	V. Performance (task performance)

Source: Gibbs, J. T. (1985). "Treatment Relationships with Black Clients: Interpersonal vs. Instrumental Strategies." In C. Germain (Ed.), *Advances in Clinical Social Work Practice,* p. 188. Silver Spring, MD: National Association of Social Workers.

ifications and background. Stage III, the *involvement stage,* proceeds when the client believes the social worker is "able to deal effectively with their differences," and begins a process of client self-disclosure. The relationship during stage III is based on a sense of perceived mutuality and positive identification. The client may ask the social worker to be involved in his or her community activity.

During stage IV, the *commitment stage,* the client expresses more personal regard for the social worker and is more active in the treatment process. This is the point that the client should recognize that the practitioner has demonstrated acceptance through empathetic and supportive behaviors. Stage V, the *engagement stage,* is the final stage of treatment, when the client and social worker engage in mutually defined tasks. The attention to tasks acknowledges the interpersonal competence of the worker.

Gibbs based her model on research that suggested that black clients tend to evaluate the interpersonal competence of the social worker in terms of

1. personal authenticity, or being perceived as genuine, "real," and "down-to-earth";
2. egalitarianism, equalizing perceived differences from an ethnic or socioeconomic background;
3. identification, resolving problems without pressuring clients to relinquish their sense of ethnic identity and cultural values;
4. acceptance, empathizing with the client to the extent that the client is provided a nonjudgmental attitudes and support; and
5. performance, cooperating in the treatment process.

Gibbs's model is illustrative of the idea that problems in cross-cultural communication can result from failure to personalize the client–social worker relationship. Rather, effective interviewing with diverse populations requires that the practitioner "treat a universalistic situation in a particularistic way" with interpersonal competence involving mutual trust (Gibbs, 1985, p. 191).

FREUD'S INFLUENCE ON THE SOCIAL WORK INTERVIEW: BASIC ASSUMPTIONS

[Interpretation] presents the client with a viewpoint discrepant from the client's own, the function of which is to prepare or induce the client to change in accordance with that viewpoint. (Claiborn, 1982, p. 442)

Listening to Client Feelings, Interpreting Meaning, and Developing Client Insight

Social workers' strong interest in Freudian explanations of human behavior dates back to at least the 1920s, and lasted through the 1950s and well into the 1960s and beyond (Baker, 1985; Briar & Miller, 1971; Greene & Ephross, 1991a). Among the most important assumptions that many social workers adopted from psychoanalytic thinking is the view that all behavior is determined in a purposeful and orderly way, and therefore can be explained (Freud, 1956). Other psychoanalytic principles adopted in social casework include a primary focus on clients' intrapsychic mental processes, and on their past experiences. Taken together, these assumptions led to an emphasis on the clinician interpreting psychological events, and helping a client develop insight (Briar & Miller, 1971;, see Tables 3.5 and 3.6).

Insight involved the therapist obtaining a client's essential history and discovering historical influences on present difficulties to achieve a curative effect. The social worker's purpose from a psychodynamic point of view is to uncover "discrepancies between statements and actions, gaps, silences, repetitions, and omissions, which are clues to a person's inner experience" (Siporin, 1975, p. 245). Interpreting the client's meaning from information presented in the interview often is viewed as the most important element of the social work helping process. The goal of the client–social worker relationship from this perspective is to help the client attain self-awareness through self-disclosure and social worker interpretation.

Because client self-awareness is generally seen as a key ingredient of mental health, social work practitioners have tended to view interpretation of client meanings as critical to the helping process. Some social work theorists

Table 3.5. Assumptions About the Psychoanalytically Oriented Helping Person

Examining and explaining the symbolic nature of symptoms is the path to reconstruction of past events, particularly childhood traumas.

Uncovering pertinent repressed material and bringing it to consciousness is a necessary ingredient in the helping process.

Expressing emotional conflicts helps to free the individual from traumatic memories.

Reconstructing and understanding difficult early life events will be curative.

Using the relationship of the helping person and client as a microcosm of crucial experiences is an important part of the helping relationship.

Developing self-awareness and self control are the goals of social work intervention.

Source: Greene, R. R., and Ephross, P. H. (1991a). "Classical Psychoanalytic Thought, Contemporary Developments, and Clinical Social Work." In R. R. Greene and P. H. Ephross (Eds.), *Human Behavior Theory and Social Work Practice,* p. 72. Hawthorne, NY: Aldine de Gruyter.

have contended that insight through interpretation "emphasizes a generic view" about a client's need to receive a "discrepant viewpoint," and that such insight "is the 'supreme agent' in the hierarchy of therapeutic principles" (Hepworth & Larsen, 1990. p. 542).

For example, in a 1958 article, Hamilton (1958b) contended that "caseworkers must sometimes bring to the attention of the client ideas and feelings, whether acceptable or not, of which he [or she] was previously unaware" (p. 26). Kadushin (1972) proposed that to achieve the purpose of the interview, it is necessary to "move . . . from a surface statement of the [client's] situation] to a more personal, emotional meaning of the content" (p. 165). In addition, Kadushin believed it important for the social work interviewer to distinguish between *clarification,* mirroring what the client has

Table 3.6. Guidelines for Psychodynamically Oriented Practitioners

Accept that all behavior has meaning and can be explained.

Engage in active listening to ascribe meaning to the material the client produces in the helping relationship.

Evaluate the relative outcomes of the psychosexual stages by observing and analyzing present derivative behaviors.

Assess the relative use and pattern of ego defenses. Weigh the flexibility or fragility as well as level of maturity of ego defenses.

Pay attention to your own motivations and feelings.

Allow the client to reflect on his or her feelings, thoughts, and behaviors in a nonobtrusive manner.

Provide interpretations of fantasies, feelings, and events described. Allow for feedback about the interpretations' efficacy.

Source: Greene, R. R., and Ephross, P. H. (1991a). "Classical Psychoanalytic Thought, Contemporary Developments, and Clinical Social Work." In R. R. Greene and P. H. Ephross (Eds.), *Human Behavior Theory and Social Work Practice,* p. 74. Hawthorne, NY: Aldine de Gruyter.

said and therefore is aware of, and *interpretation*, making explicit what the client is feeling but is unaware of.

Freud offered two concepts for understanding the client–social worker relationship as a here-and-now microcosm of past intrapsychic events: transference and countertransference. *Transference* was defined as the client's special interest or feelings about the practitioner brought into the clinical experience, but based on earlier authority relationships. *Countertransference* was defined as the social worker's reaction to the client based on past events or feelings that could interfere with therapeutic work.

Freud's belief that a client can be helped by reexperiencing past feelings within the therapeutic encounter is frequently expressed in social work practice texts (Shulman, 1981 1984). For example, Northen (1982) in her text on clinical social work practice stated that, although they may or may not be based on accurate perceptions, "feelings, attitudes, and patterns of responses are transferred from earlier relationships" into present situations (p. 42). She also made reference to the social worker being self-aware so he or she does not "transfer attitudes from his [or her] past onto the client " (p. 42).

Because transference and countertransference have been defined as a mixture of conscious and unconscious distortions of reality, social work practitioners have characteristically contended that these phenomena are obstacles to the helping process (Northen, 1982; Perlman, 1957). Over the years, however, the definition of countertransference has broadened and emerged as an experience in the therapeutic relationship that can make a positive contribution (Greene, 1986; Peabody & Gelso, 1982). Recent literature increasingly addresses countertransference issues in social work with various populations, including people who are terminally ill, mentally ill, members of countercultures, or who are homosexual (Buckingham & Rehm, 1987; Buckingham & Van Gorp, 1988; Dunkel & Hatfield, 1986). In addition, theorists have suggested that a key issue in working with the aged is an ability to recognize practitioner misconceptions and biases (Abramson, 1985; Butler & Lewis, 1973; Greene, 1986; Reamer, 1988; Sprung, 1989).

Dunkel and Hatfield (1986) have pointed out that social workers in health care have identified eight countertransference issues in working with persons with AIDs that, if understood, may enhance the treatment process:

1. fear of the unknown—the fear that the "true" means of transmission of HIV remain unknown;
2. fear of contagion—the fear that all precautionary measures have not been identified;
3. fear of death and dying—the fear of dealing with our sense of mortality;
4. denial of helplessness—gaining control through feelings of omnipotence or power;

5. fear of homosexuality—unresolved feelings about gays that ghettoize or marginalize the client;
6. overidentification—overinvesting time and energy in the client to the point of loss of objectivity;
7. anger—unconscious feelings that "blame the victim" for his or her "predicament"; and
8. need for professional omnipotence—the social worker as an authority who does not respect the client's right to human dignity and self-determination.

Paviour (1988) has stated that because mental health practitioners believe in an egalitarian society, they may not be aware of transference and countertransference problems. However, when the concepts of countertransference and diversity are considered together, a different dimension is added to the client–social worker encounter. By attending to countertransference, practitioners can deepen their understanding of diverse client groups (Palombo, 1985).

The idea that it is important for the practitioner to confront the client about underlying factors that contribute to his or her problem remains prevalent in the social work literature. While it is recognized that confrontation may jeopardize the social worker–client relationship, it generally is suggested that highly skillful confrontations to interpret client meaning, sometimes termed *additive empathy*, will contribute or add to a client's sense that the practitioner is helpful.

There has been considerable discussion about the place of interpretation as a primary technique in the social work interview. Although theorists from the existential, client-centered, and Gestalt schools of thought argued against interpretation as a therapeutic technique, most other theorists believe interpretation is a key therapeutic intervention. These theorists posit that interpretation, although varying in content with the theoretical orientation of the worker, offers a client a different point of view that prepares him or her for change (Claiborn, 1982; Hepworth & Larsen, 1987).

In his 1972 text, Kadushin contended that "the core of traditional casework derives from theoretical conceptions which have limited applicability to many lower-class clients. Traditional casework is more applicable to the neurotic, introspective, articulate client whose problems are primarily intrapsychic" (p. 229). On the other hand, some social work theorists have suggested that there is no empirical evidence that more disclosure, more self-exploration is more effective. There simply may be different types of communication. For example, Ryan (1985) has suggested that Chinese-American clients "cannot understand free association as a method of understanding" because they tend to believe that verbalization is a discipline, and language is to be used with precision. Chinese-American clients also may think it unaccept-

able to express inner conflict. Therefore, a social worker who "encourages
. . . self-expression may seem to a Chinese client to be leading away from
peace of mind" (p. 335).

Edwards and Edwards (1980) have presented another view about the importance of self-understanding and introspection. They pointed out that
many American Indian clients believe that people should be able to understand one another; therefore, constant questioning about past or present
events may not build a therapeutic alliance. From this perspective, it should
not be necessary for the client to explain to the social worker his or her problem with great detail. Rather, the professional person should be able to understand.

Sotomayor (1977) pointed out that any therapeutic relationship must take
into account "the intrapsychic meanings of ethnic sense of belonging and
identification, the meaning and utilization of cultural symbols . . . and the
various functions of language" (p. 203). How accurate client clinical assessments are across culture, class, and gender groups remains a serious concern. In large measure, research on this topic, although not conclusive, has
suggested the presence of bias. At the very least, social work's effectiveness
in cross-cultural social service delivery has not been empirically demonstrated (Chandler, 1980; Fischer & Miller, 1973; Franklin, 1985; Paviour,
1988).

Briar and Miller (1971) have contended that because insight attainment in
treatment became the primary goal of treatment under the Freudian-influ-
enced medical model, social workers had to face the issue of how to treat
clients and problems thought to be not suited for a psychoanalytic approach.
They go on to state that the primacy of insight-oriented therapy led to a three-
fold treatment topology—classical psychoanalysis, psychodynamically oriented social work, and supportive therapies—and that by definition these
three approaches "imply a value hierarchy" (p. 67). The value hierarchy, in
their view, involves issues of who is qualified to provide therapy of different
types, and who are considered "bonafide" clients for certain forms of treatment interventions.

Assessing Client Behaviors and Motivation

Members of the diagnostic and psychosocial schools of social work practice were particularly influenced by Freudian theory, and based many of their
classic texts on Freud's medical model, a model that emphasizes diagnosis,
treatment, and cure (Hamilton, 1958b; Hollis, 1964; Perlman, 1957). For example, Perlman (1957) stated that social work diagnostic interview includes
an exploration of the balance among *ego*, "the personality's problem-solving
apparatus" (p. 17), *superego*, "the personality's automatic punishment-or-re-

ward system" (p. 11), and *id*, the "life force" (p. 10). Perlman and others from the diagnostic and psychodynamic schools believed that the purpose of the social work interview was to assess and bring about a better relative balance among ego, superego, and id.

Kadushin (1972), who also proposed that the interview involved a diagnostic process, later stated that the social work interview is designed to keep the client focused on affective material, and to encourage the interviewee to reveal himself or herself. The social worker's role is to interpret affective materials, to help clients become more aware of their feelings, and to seek therapeutic change through the client–social worker relationship.

Many contemporary approaches to direct practice in social work incorporate the concept of study or assessment as the basis of intervention (Franklin, 1985). However, the emphasis on the accumulation of client data to form an assessment continues to come under question. Chandler (1980) has cautioned that social workers trained in diagnostic assessment and treatment should be alert to the "potential bias inherent in any one ethnocentric educational approach" (p. 348). Practitioners also need to be aware of biases in differential diagnoses and differential treatment regimens and be sure assessment and interventions are appropriate for a member of a particular ethnic population. Pinderhughes (1979) and Tidwell (1971) have questioned how the systematic approach to information collection followed in the diagnostic school was affected by political and power issues.

Finally, it is important to note that theorists are concerned that the helping process be based on client-practitioner shared meanings of events. For example, Lowe (1991) has cautioned that "numerous cases of ethnic differences in expectations of treatment can be traced to cultural distinctions embedded in belief systems and norms of culturally appropriate behavior" (p. 13). Sue and Zane (1987) have suggested that culturally sensitive assessment involves three major guidelines:

1. The social must define the problem in a manner that is consistent with the client's belief system.
2. Expectations for change must be consistent with the client's cultural values.
3. Treatment goals must be compatible with the client's perceived outcome goals.

Maintaining Professional Authority and Control in the Interview

Many social workers, particularly those identified with the psychodynamic school of thought, have adopted Freud's view that the course of the helping process is determined by the clinician. From this perspective, the social worker guides, structures, or, some might say, takes charge of the interview (Biestek, 1951). *Resistance* to social worker authority is defined as a normal reaction to the idea of being helped. Resistance also has been attributed to client effort to hold onto the familiar, a lack of client motivation or capacity, and client fear of change or the unknown (Strean, 1978). For example, Shulman (1984) has suggested that practitioners should expect that "problems with the authority theme [are] a normal part" of the helping process that present barriers to change (p. 88). On the other hand, Northen (1982) proposed that the client needs to come to understand the nature and extent of the worker's legitimate authority, and the worker needs to come to understand the client's need to control or to submit to the worker's authority (p. 205).

Verbal exchanges in which client self-disclosure and social worker interpretation set the context of the helping relationship have increasingly come under question. For example, Edelman (1982) has suggested that helping professionals may face clients who have reasonable grounds for resistance to control. He urged professionals to take care when rationalizing their authority and defining what they consider normal behaviors (see Chapters 5 and 6).

Ridley (1984) made a similar argument when he contended that individual verbal therapies, with their roots in Freud, often put clients in a paradoxical situation: Although client self-disclosure is generally considered necessary for successful counseling outcomes, there may be many complex intrapsychic, interpersonal, and sociocultural reasons that affect a client's willingness to self-disclose.

Because most therapy with black clients is conducted by white therapists, who are likely to inhibit self-disclosure in their black clients, Ridley argued that a "shared failure" may result (p. 1237). Some client reluctance to disclose personal information can be attributed to "playing it cool" or to a "healthy cultural paranoia." He also attributed many of such failures in disclosure to the ineffectiveness of the helping person who does not address the client's often negative interracial experiences in the therapy. In a similar vein, Edwards and Edwards (1980) have pointed out that many American Indian clients are suspicious of Anglo people in authority and approach many social workers with great caution. In addition, American Indian people often are taught to deal with problems within their own family and tribal settings.

Briar and Miller (1971) have argued against the use of unnecessary caseworker authority from another perspective. They put forth that a reliance on the view that the social worker is an authority in the relationship may lead to the client belief that the social worker has "magical powers" (p. 39). They went on to state that there are times when the misuse of the phenomenon of transference may "eventuate in raw coercion" and, at the very least, may raise a serious concern about how self-determination coincides with case planning (p. 40).

Finally, it is important to state that when the effectiveness of a particular therapeutic technique is examined, such as those used in interviewing, theorists usually discuss what clients are "good" or "bad" candidates for that particular method. The discussion tends to encompass information about how social worker or client blindspots inhibit goal attainment. Rarely does the discussion include the limitations of the theory or paradigm itself.

However, questions are increasingly being asked about the frameworks used as the theoretical underpinning for practice skills. Social work scholars continue to provide suggestions for an eclectic use of theory-informed practice skills necessary for social work practice with diverse populations. Practitioners are moving from traditional intrapsychic therapies to an eclectic, more systemic approach to intervention (DeHoyos, 1989; Ephross-Saltman & Greene, 1993). Many believe the move to a multitheoretical, multimodal approach to helping will not minimize the role of verbal techniques. Rather, an eclectic, more systemic approach may offer the potential of a variety of interventions including social environmental changes (DeHoyos, 1989; DeHoyos & Jensen, 1985; see Chapters 11 and 12 for a discussion of change in macrolevel systems).

Symbolic Interactionism:
Social Work Assessment,
Meanings, and Language 4

Roberta R. Greene and Joan Ephross Saltman

> *[Assessment is]* a differential, individualized, and accurate identification and evaluation of the problems, people, and situations and of their interrelationships, to serve as a sound basis for differential helping interventions.
>
> (Siporin, 1975, p. 224)

The next three chapters of the text focus on how human behavior theory guides the social work assessment process. Assessment is a social work procedure used to explore a client's or a client system's life situation or problem for purposes of selecting intervention strategies. According to Meyer (1993), assessment has the professional purpose of coming to know the client's own story. Northen (1987) has suggested that assessment requires the social worker to make a series of judgments about "the adequacy of [client] behavior" (p. 179). Assessment content, and whether or not a particular behavior is seen as appropriate, typically is based on the social worker's chosen theory base (Greene, 1986; Hepworth & Larsen, 1990). For example, the most frequently used theory to understand a client's stage of development is Erikson's Eight Stages of Development (see Chapter 5), whereas Parson's Role Theory often is employed to determine if a behavior interferes with one or several of the client's roles (see Chapter 6).

To achieve a sound assessment, social workers are concerned with assessing the person-in-environment and viewing the client within the context of his or her daily life (Meyer, 1993). Because of social work's diverse client constituency, and the rapid changes in life-styles and life conditions, determining the "adequacy of behavior" also requires the practitioner to have an understanding of how "socioeconomic status, race, and ethnicity affect psychosocial functioning" (Northen, 1987, p. 179).

Cross-cultural social work assessment must individualize clients by gathering culturally sound information and establishing shared meaning of issues and events. Symbolic interaction theory may be useful to the practitioner in obtaining such culturally sensitive information. Symbolic interaction theory explores people's participation in social groups and the way in which societies and their institutions develop as a result of the interaction of its members. "Symbolic interactionism emphasizes communication, its development, limitations, distortions, significance, content, and symbolic nature" (Ephross & Greene, 1991, p. 204). Therefore, it can be applied in client assessment to increase awareness of how cultural expectations may vary between and within any given culture.

Symbolic interaction theory not only explains how and why people and organizations communicate the way they do, but also lends itself to finding ways to intervene to improve communication. Because symbolic interaction theory strongly emphasizes the use of language as a tool for interaction, it is also useful in analyzing social worker–client encounters (Munson, 1981). Symbolic interaction theory also focuses on how the self emerges through social interaction and the way in which "normal" people function in day-to-day life. The theory, therefore, provides a means for understanding and incorporating information on cultural strengths in the assessment process.

Because symbolic interaction theory is organized around concepts that emphasize the significance of cultural symbols and explain the development of collective meaning in various cultural groups, this chapter addresses how the theory's major assumptions can be used to examine cross-cultural issues in social work assessment. The chapter also explores cultural differences in client help-seeking behavior and how language serves as a cultural product central to social worker–client communication processes.

The key symbolic interactionist assumptions explored in this chapter suggest that people differ largely because they have learned varying symbolic vocabularies for interpreting life experiences through social interaction. Principles examined in this chapter assume that (1) clients derive their meaning of life events through social interaction, (2) clients act toward things or events on the basis of the meaning they have for them, (3) behavior is symbolic and largely rests on linguistic processes, (4) the self is a social structure that arises through social interaction, and (5) client change results from the development of new systems of meanings through an interpretive process.

SOCIAL WORK ASSESSMENT

Emerging conceptual frameworks [for assessment] are more contextual, incorporating a rigorous examination of the complex interactions and interdependence inherent in person-in-environment configurations. Within a contextual framework, available data can be organized in multiple ways, offering alternative potential approaches to effective change. (Mattaini, 1990, p. 237)

All social work interventions begin with an assessment or an understanding of the client situation. Since as early as 1917, when Mary Richmond published her work *Social Diagnosis*, the general approach to social work practice has been to collect "the nature of social evidence" and interpret data that lead to the "social diagnosis" (Richmond, 1917, pp. 38–40, 342–363). Assessment aims to identify and explain the nature of a problem, to appraise it within a framework of specific elements, and to use that appraisal as a guide to action (Perlman, 1957). "Its purpose, whether the problem rests with an individual, family, group, or community, is to bring together the various facets of the client's situation" (Greene, 1986, p. 43).

Social work theorists have used various terms and procedures to define types of assessments. They generally have viewed a *psychosocial diagnosis* as an examination of the problem and a plan of action to solve it and a *clinical diagnosis* as a means of classifying a person by the nature of a particular illness. A *dynamic diagnosis* is an examination of the forces at play in the "person-problem-situation" (Perlman, 1957, p. 170). Ascertaining the beginning of a problem or its cause-effect development is called an *etiological* or *genetic diagnosis*. Other assessments contain predictive statements or enable the social worker to prescribe an administrative program.

Because of the strong association between the terms *diagnosis* and *illness*, for many social workers *assessment* has come to be the preferred term (Meyer, 1993; Northen, 1987). Unlike diagnosis, assessment requires that the social worker's identification of the problem include an evaluation of the interrelationship among biopychosocial variables. Assessment of an individual's biopsychosocial functioning involves getting to know the person—his or her motivations, strengths, weaknesses, and capacity to change. In addition, it is important that the social worker view the assessment as an opportunity to understand client potential and opportunities for growth.

Types of assessment vary. Some assessments are a statement of whether a client meets the normative behavioral standards of the community. Assessment can be seen as a product because the social worker often must provide a formal, written description of the client's difficulty, and a time-limited "snapshot" of a situation for agency purposes. Reports may encompass a statement of the problem, an assessment of the personality of the client, or a situational analysis. An assessment also may include a discussion of the client's social problem or an overview of the various social systems with which he or she interacts.

Social work practice methods texts often suggest that once the data are collected, it is the role of the social worker to analyze "the individual-group-environment gestalt" (Northen, 1987, p. 179). For example, Kadushin (1972) has suggested that, although client feedback is important, the diagnostic process is a social worker's mental process of applying theoretical generalizations to the data obtained and organizing and interpreting the data for valid inferences.

Increasingly of concern in assessment is the importance of the participation of the client in information gathering and analysis of the situation. For example, Prager (1980) has proposed that social workers often overlook the role of the client in formulating his or her own assessment. He noted that client input in most areas of professional practice is limited and that "help is still largely defined, planned, and evaluated for [clients] not by them" (p. 5).

The interest in client participation in, if not creation of the assessment recognizes the symbolic interactionist view that people are active shapers, if not creators of their life situation. Because assessment may be erroneously understood as solely an information-gathering activity, the idea that it also is based on a dynamic, individualized social worker–client relationship cannot be sufficiently underscored.

From the inception of the profession, social workers were cautioned that diagnosis can be an imposition "if it ignores the objective reality with which the person [client] is struggling" (Reynolds, 1951, pp. 130–131). In addition, social workers were advised not to conduct their client diagnoses as "strangers with alien interests, but [to weave] together the threads that both client and caseworker draw from life and work on together" (Reynolds, 1951, p. 109).

Although assessments may include such inputs as observations of nonverbal behaviors and interactions and reports from various collateral sources, from the symbolic interactionist perspective verbal exchanges of meanings between client and social worker are at the heart of the assessment process. From this view, "language is more than a means of communicating about reality: it is a tool for constructing reality" (Spradley, 1979, p. 17). Understanding a client's life meaning is an interactive process of interpreting, evaluating, and defining the situation until client and social worker arrive at a mutually shared orientation regarding person-in-the-environment interventions. In turn, *assessment* is the ongoing process of building mutual understanding between client and social worker that goes on throughout the treatment process to achieve viable, culturally sound solutions.

Finally, the assessment process is "the joining of art and science" (Meyer, 1993, p. 41). The idea that an assessment be viewed as both a theory-based science and an empathetic art is a dominant theme in the social work literature (Briar & Miller, 1971). Simon (1960) captured well the relationship between a humanistic and systematic approach to assessment:

> The use of a body of theory to organize, systematize, and rationalize a caseworker's knowledge, thinking, and action is ultimately liberating of the personal gifts that mark the artistic practitioner. Having at his [or her] command organized and systematic ways of thinking and doing, the caseworker is then

free to exercise the empathy and sensitivity, to admit his [or her] feelings, to take in the flavor and the uniqueness of the patient and his [or her] situation. (p. 25)

DEFINITION OF MEANING: BASIC ASSUMPTIONS

Symbolic interactionism sees meanings as social products, as creations that are formed in and through the defining activities of people as they interact. (Blumer, 1969, p. 5)

Blumer's Definition of Meanings

Developing Collective Meanings Through Interaction

Symbolic interaction theory has its origins in social psychology and considers behavior as resulting from the fact that people are social beings. Symbolic interaction theorists examine people's participation in social groups and the way in which societies and their institutions develop as a result of such interaction. In addition, symbolic interactionists examine how individuals learn to assign meanings to feelings, experiences, social forms, and structures as well as how families, groups, organizations, and communities develop unique sets of meanings through such social participation (Bruner, 1986, 1990; see Table 4.1).

Table 4.1. Basic Assumptions of Symbolic Interaction Theory

Humans are a self-conscious, reflective, thinking species.
Personality development is a process of learning to assign meaning to symbols. This learning process occurs through interaction with real and symbolic others.
Individual and groups meanings arise from human interaction.
Behavior is symbolic and largely rests on linguistic processes.
The self is a social structure that arises through social interaction.
The self is derived through taking the attitudes, perceptions, and actions of others toward oneself and one's own and internalizing their meaning.
Deviance is nonnormative behavior. Conceptions of deviance and norms are constructed by society.
The differences among people are largely the result of having learned different symbolic vocabularies for interpreting life experiences.
Change results from the development of new systems of meanings.

Source: Ephross, P. H., and Greene, R. R. (1991). "Symbolic Interactionism." In R. R. Greene and P. H. Ephross (Eds.), *Human Behavior Theory and Social Work Practice*, p. 109. Hawthorne, NY: Aldine de Gruyter.

Blumer (1969), an early symbolic interaction theorist, proposed that personal meaning is a social product (derived through social interaction). This premise of symbolic interaction theory suggests that if the social worker can understand the ongoing process of interaction between the client and the groups and social structures of which the client is part, then the social worker can begin to enter the client's world (Ephross & Greene, 1991). Because symbolic interactionists believe that an individual's personal meanings are a result of social participation in a variety of social groups and institutions, the social worker can only know another person in depth if he or she participates in the world as the client sees it.

Goffman (1959) also has proposed that people learn to perform their roles in various groups through the meanings they learn to attribute to situations. Through a process of internalization, a group's system of meaning becomes part of the thinking of its members. Because meanings may be modified or remain long after the dissolution of the group, the formation of group meaning is an ongoing process.

Culture and Meanings

Collective behavior is the term used to refer to the social aspects of behavior and the social context that gives behavior meaning. Because people participate in small groups, creating within them social ideals, values, and norms, symbolic interaction theorists suggest that individuals create cultures and the various social structures that compose society (Cooley, 1902).

Ethnic Membership

Ethnic membership is an example of a social group created through collective social interaction and participation. *Ethnicity* generally refers to shared social and cultural heritage of a group of people. Members of an ethnic group also may share ideas, perceptions, feelings, and behavior (Ho, 1992). To understand ethnicity, it is necessary to examine "the values, signs, and behavioral styles through which individuals signal their identity in cross-cultural encounters" (Green, 1982, p. 12).

Culture comprises the abstract values, beliefs, and perceptions of the world that lie behind people's behavior. These shared beliefs are not static; rather, they shape behaviors within a range of variation. The evolving interacting between and among people produces the orienting features of a particular culture or group membership.

Consideration of client culture is an important issue in social work assessment. Limited understanding of any individual's cultural meanings and thinking about his or her life situation may lead the social worker to culture-bound solutions. *Culture-bound thinking* refers to the formulations of ideas based on the assumptions about the world and reality from one's own culture only (Haviland, 1990). Pedersen (1976) has called a therapist lacking in cross-cultural sensitivity "the culturally encapsulated counselor" (p. 24), that is, a therapist who evaluates the client's living circumstances according to criteria more suitable to the personal or professional ideas of the counselor than to the day-to-day experiences of the client.

Social workers are increasingly borrowing techniques from ethnographers and ethnoarchaeologists, who study culture through informants who comment on the use of an artifact or validity of an interpretation of daily life events. In a recent study of Nubian culture, a culture that has often been misinterpreted, scholars may be embarrassed when not turning to living informants to comment on ancient relics:

> Shortly after the Oriental Institute's exhibition opened, [the curator] met Awad Abdel Gadir, [an African] teaching in Texas. He took her aside, pointed to a stone object and said politely, "that's not an incense burner. We have those in our village. It's a receptacle for a liquid offering." [The curator] changed the label. (Roberts, 1993b, p. 100)

Ho (1992) has proposed use of a transcultural framework to enhance the social worker's sensitivity during the problem identification phase of treatment (Table 4.2). A transcultural framework acknowledges between-group and within-group racial and ethnic differences and uses cultural or social mapping as a means of ascertaining a client's problem (Cochrane, 1979; Pendagast & Sherman, 1977).

Cultural mapping considers the client's cultural reality in problem specification and involves identifying and linking localized or culture-specific sources of the [minority] client's solutions in the therapy. Social mapping involves identifying and locating all ethnic groups in the area; describing the social organization of the community; describing the beliefs and ideological characteristics of the residents of the community; recording the patterns of wealth, its accumulation, and its distribution; describing the patterns of mobility, both geographical and social; and providing information on access and utilization of human services providers (Cochrane, 1979)

Ephross and Greene (1991) have pointed out that symbolic interactionism is especially useful for overcoming culture-bound thinking, which presents barriers to understanding between client and social worker. Such barriers that may be attributed to differences in meaning between client and social worker and may involve gender, age, sexual orientation, race or ethnic background, social class, or religion. For example, Lum (1986) has proposed that an ethnic-oriented assessment should aim for a psychosocial balance between objective, external factors of the community, and subjective, internal

Table 4.2. A Transcultural Framework for Therapy With Ethnic Minority Children and Youth

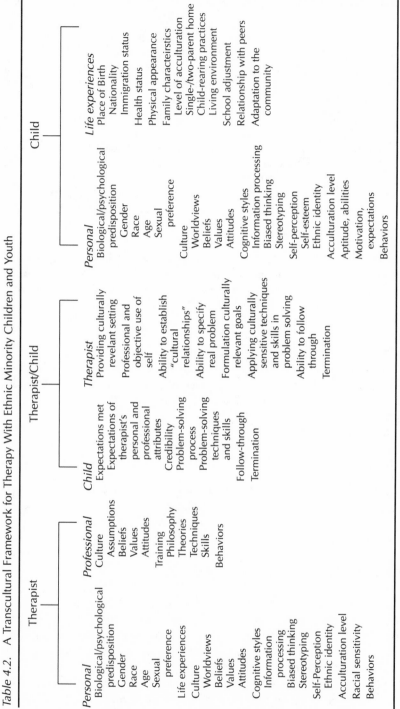

Therapist		Therapist/Child		Child	
Personal	*Professional*	*Child*	*Therapist*	*Personal*	*Life experiences*
Biological/psychological predisposition	Culture	Expectations met	Providing culturally relevant setting	Biological/psychological predisposition	Place of Birth
Gender	Assumptions	Expectations of therapist's personal and professional attributes	Professional and objective use of self	Gender	Nationality
Race	Beliefs	Credibility	Ability to establish "cultural relationships"	Race	Immigration status
Age	Values	Problem-solving process	Ability to specify real problem	Age	Health status
Sexual preference	Attitudes	Problem-solving techniques and skills	Formulation culturally relevant goals	Sexual preference	Physical appearance
Life experiences	Training	Follow-through	Applying culturally sensitive techniques and skills in problem solving	Culture	Family characteirstics
Culture	Philosophy	Termination	Ability to follow through	Worldviews	Level of acculturation
Worldviews	Theories		Termination	Beliefs	Single-/two-parent home
Beliefs	Techniques			Values	Child-rearing practices
Values	Skills			Attitudes	Living environment
Attitudes	Behaviors			Cognitive styles	School adjustment
Cognitive styles				Information processing	Relationship with peers
Information processing				Biased thinking	Adaptation to the community
Biased thinking				Stereotyping	
Stereotyping				Self-perception	
Self-Perception				Self-esteem	
Ethnic identity				Ethnic identity	
Acculturation level				Acculturation level	
Racial sensitivity				Aptitude, abilities	
Behaviors				Motivation, expectations	
				Behaviors	

Source: Ho, Man Keung. (1992). *Minority Children and Adolescents in Therapy,* p. 24. Newbury Park, CA: Sage.

reactions. Lum went on to state that "ethnic beliefs, family solidarity, community support networks, and other cultural assets are intervening variables" in the assessment process (p. 145).

Dieppa (1983) has cautioned that assessment of ethnic minority clients often tends to evaluate internal and external liabilities rather than include an identification of positive cultural strengths. Causative factors tend to be placed with individual and family psyche, and solutions are couched in terms of mental health treatment when they should, in Dieppa's view, include an understanding of oppressed populations and social problems within an ecological framework. Romero (1983) also argued that when assessing minority clients, practitioners need to understand "the socioeconomic stresses that are compounded by poverty, racism, oppression," and the lack of access to educational, legal, and health care systems (p. 91).

Pluralistic societies contain a diversity of subcultural patterns. Therefore, the social worker must be able to examine a client's reality from the client's point of view. Haviland (1990) defined *cultural relativism* as the thesis that, because cultures are unique, they can be evaluated or understood only according to their own standards and values.

Green's (1982) model of cross-cultural social work (see Chapter 1) is an example of a culturally relative approach. The model outlines why people may perceive and report their experiences related to stress and crisis differently based on social group membership. The model also recognizes that the experience of a problem or crisis is both a personal and a social event. In addition, language is important to the model because "it is the symbolic device by which the flow of that experience is categorized, labeled, evaluated, and acted upon" (Green, 1982, p. 28). That is, "language is the key component of any presenting problem" (p. 29; see Figure 4.1).

There are four components to Green's help-seeking model:

1. the client's recognition of an experience as a "problem"—the client's explanatory model of events complete with cultural themes;
2. the client's use of language to label and categorize a problem—the client's use of folk categories and knowledge in the communication;
3. the availability of indigenous helping resources in client communities and the decision-making process involved in the use of these resources—the client's "legitimate" help providers; and
4. client-oriented criteria for determining that a satisfactory outcome has been reached—goals of client interventions that are aimed at cultural standards of success.

Green's (1982) discussion of help-seeking behavior is based on the idea that there is a division between what the client knows and does in response to a problem and what the social work practitioner, who does not share the

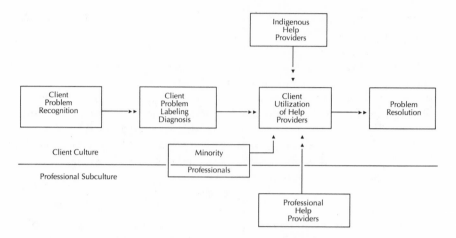

Figure 4.1. The help-seeking model in social services. With permission from Green, J. (1982), *Cultural Awareness in the Human Services*, p. 30. Englewood Cliffs, NJ: Prentice Hall.

client's cultural background, knows and does about the problem. The dichotomy between worldviews is related to contrary "stocks of knowledge" and perceptions and interpretations of events (Hayes-Bautistista, 1978, p. 85). Overcoming the disparity between these worldviews is the goal of the cross-cultural social work assessment process.

Religious Membership

Religion is another dimension of cross-cultural social work practice that has personalized and community-based meanings. Historically, there has been a lack of integration between religion and social work. In fact, many social workers have chosen to treat religion and religious issues as private concerns and not as concerns of the social work profession (Sanzenbach, Canda, & Joseph, 1989). There is a continuing debate among social work theorists about how to approach religion in social work practice. In recent times, social work has developed as a secular profession, and many social workers continue to think that religion is not integral to professional practice. Other social work theorists have pointed out that religious values are an important means of expressing the spiritual aspect of humans and need to be considered in clinical social work practice (Canda, 1989; Joseph, 1987; Sheridan, Bullis, Adcock, Berlin, & Miller, 1992; Siporin, 1986).

Social workers' and clients' religious values may impact on what takes place in social work practice whether there is an open awareness or not

(Canda, 1989). If client and social worker come from different religious backgrounds or orientations, language, both verbal and nonverbal, may have different connotations. Therefore, social workers need to be cognizant of the possibility that clients' religious beliefs and or practices and the meanings attributed to them might be central components to the exploration, assessment, and intervention phases of social work practice.

Lowenberg (1988) contended that there is no single social work response to religion. Rather, it is important for social workers to become aware of the place of religion in contemporary society and to explore its meaning for themselves and their clients. Imre (1971) argued a similar point. She stated that if a client wishes to discuss religion or if religious beliefs are important to understanding the client's situation, the social worker needs to affirm this aspect of the client's meaning.

From a symbolic interactionist client-centered approach, religion is an important, if not a neglected dimension of clinical social work practice. In addition, it is another aspect of human culture that significantly affects individual and collective behavior (Canda, 1989). Religion has been defined as "the communal expression of faith in institutional forms or the embodiment of a worldview and value system in the lives and practices of historical individuals and communities" (Joseph, 1987, p. 14). That is, the meaning of God and religion evolve in the lifelong development of the self in interaction with others.

The following case study illustrates that social work practitioners can play an important role in appreciating the behavioral implications of clients' religious diversity, as well as clients' specific religious traditions and perspectives. Symbolic interaction theory also can be used with individuals and groups of differing religious or cultural backgrounds to communicate more effectively.

Miss M., a 22-year-old, who described herself as a "culturally Jewish woman," decided to seek counseling at Jewish Family Services. She indicated that "she was having serious disagreements with her older brother since returning home from college." Miss M. also said that she could not understand why she was having this difficulty as she was enjoying her job as a computer programmer, getting along well with her parents, and was excited about her upcoming marriage to a man she had met in college.

The social worker, Mrs. S., a middle-aged Jewish woman with a strong religious identity, asked Miss M. about her engagement. Miss M. said she was engaged to Mr. B., a 23-year-old college-educated engineer, who was an observant Methodist and active in his church. Miss M. also stated that both families approved of the approaching wedding. When Mrs. S. asked Miss M. how she felt about an interfaith marriage, Miss M. insisted it was "no big deal." Nonetheless, when Mrs. S. suggested conjoint premarital counseling, Miss M. agreed.

During the counseling sessions, Miss M. acknowledged that as the actual date of the wedding drew closer, she was becoming increasingly anxious even though all the formal arrangements were made. At first, Miss M. and Mr. B. said they were reluctant to discuss religion as it "was not important in their marriage." When the social worker asked the couple what a counselor at a religious-based agency must think about an interfaith marriage, Miss M. and Mr. B. both agreed that the social worker "must disapprove." The social worker explained that she neither approved or disapproved, but hoped to help them explore their concerns. Gradually, the couple began to explore similarities and differences in expectations they each held for their marriage. They also discussed what it meant to come from different religious and cultural backgrounds, and in what ways these meanings might affect their married life. Both made a commitment to learn about each other's faith by reading books and attending classes.

From a symbolic interactionist perspective, exchanges of meanings are at the heart of the assessment process and necessary to the client–social worker relationship. As Schneider (1989) noted, "if one considers the concept of religion as a language, and understands that each individual was born of parents who spoke a particular religious language and passed this on, it is easy to see that the language may be different" (p. 49).

DEVELOPING THE SELF THROUGH INTERACTION

We see ourselves through the way in which others see or define us—or, more precisely, we see ourselves by taking roles. (Blumer, 1969, p. 13)

Establishing Personal Meaning

Symbolic interaction theorists believe that an individual's personal meanings are derived, modified, and refined as a result of social participation in a variety of social groups and institutions. Blumer (1969) argued that meanings are not imposed on people, nor is behavior simply a response to the environment. Rather, meanings arise out of social interaction as people confront and create the world around them. Each time an individual confronts the world, he or she must interpret it—through his or her unique set of personal meanings—so that he or she may act.

From the symbolic interactionist viewpoint, people live in a society characterized by symbolic interaction. The use of symbols enables a person to assimilate information about significant others. The use of symbols also allows people to take the role of others and to elicit from others the proper behavior. That is, how a person symbolizes his or her experiences leads to specific behavior in a given situation. This role-taking permits people to share the perspectives of others and leads to cooperative action (Knott, 1973).

The view of the self as based on shared, cultural linguistic labels and meanings has been expressed by Goodenough (1957), an anthropologist:

> A society's culture consists of whatever it is one has to know or believe in order to operate in a manner acceptable to its members, and to do so in any role that they accept for any one of themselves. . . . It is the forms of things that people have in mind, their models for perceiving, relating and otherwise interpreting them. (p. 167)

These symbolic interactionists' assumptions about the relationship between personal and social meaning further clarify Green's (1982) model of help-seeking behavior. The model recognizes that a crisis is both a personal and social event. It is personal because it is disruptive to the individual. It is social because a specific culture labels the experience in a particular fashion and thus confirms what corrective action should be taken. For example, Does a particular issue, event, or symptom require me to visit to the mental health clinic?

To symbolic interactionists, the personality, excepting only those idiosyncratic and unique aspects that each individual possesses, is built through interaction with others. Through the process of socialization into a culture and through primary group experiences, people learn how to behave and how to predict the responses of others (Blumer, 1969). Language, then, is the vehicle for learning a client's personal meanings and also "represents community practices" (Efran, Lukens, & Lukens, 1990, p. 30). Therefore, appropriately questioning the client and listening for his or her worldview is critical to the assessment process.

For example, Ryan (1985) has stated that many Chinese-Americans are still influenced by the teachings of Confucius, Laotze, and Buddha. Therefore, to achieve an accurate assessment and effective intervention, it is necessary for the social worker to understand how these influences may affect a client's way of life, thinking, and communicative behaviors. Confucius taught that correct naming, or labeling, is of extreme importance. If language is not used accurately or with precision, success cannot be achieved; that is, "verbalization is a discipline. Speech, the basic tool of the therapeutic and counseling process, is not something Chinese can use casually" (Ryan, 1985, p. 334).

Mead's Definition of Self

George Herbert Mead (1925) proposed that the "I"—referring to the spontaneous, impulsive aspects of self—and "me"—including the organized expectations of others—constitute the self. The *self* is "a social structure that engages in reflective activity, and emerges through the transfer of interpreted meanings (to and from others)" (Mead, 1934, p. 5). The largest portion of the self includes internalization of community and societal norms and standards, a sense of who one ought to be, and how one measures up to societal demands. The self comprises definitions of the life roles one plays—spouse, agency administrator, parent, for example—and how well one is playing those roles. The self also includes a picture of oneself as good/bad, attractive/ugly, and so forth (Ephross & Greene, 1991).

In this context, the attitudes of others, or the social "me," is a central force in shaping human behavior. Do I define myself in response to others? How do people experience themselves and others? What do people have in mind when they say "I" or "me"? These series of expectations for behavior become generalized into what Mead (1925) called the *generalized other*.

Social work theorists have applied the concept of the generalized other to examine the critical issue of character development in a hostile environment (Chestang, 1972). This issue recognizes that racism and discrimination, particularly in the form of institutional injustices, profoundly affect the lives of ethnic minorities through a socialization process by the majority group that devalues the individual. In such situations, "the inner forum of the person" may act to devalue the individual (Cottrell, 1969, p. 549).

Chestang (1972) has argued that institutionalization gives rise to disparities in human rights "gives rise to ego-syntonic [those compatible with self] feelings of distrust, suspicion, and rage . . . [that may result in a] diminished sense of self-worth, and low self-esteem" (p. 44). In a society that depreciates the value of the character of African-American children, Chestang maintained that children are "seduced" as they go through the process of "redefining the relationship between the environment and the self" (p. 47). That is, children may accept the negative attributions of self to make it in the majority society, often "sacrificing pride in victory" or "casting off a part of themselves" (pp. 47–49).

To be successful in a hostile environment, Chestang (1972) proposed that children must adapt to two systems: (1) the dominant or sustaining system that is the source of economic and political power and (2) the nurturing system—the family and community that provide comfort and strength. This notion of the dual perspective (Norton, 1976, 1978) offers a dynamic way of describing and working with minority clients to resolve dissonance between the sustaining and nurturing aspects of self.

Sotomayor (1977) also has traced critical aspects of self-development to "majority-minority of color group relationships in this country . . . [that produce] social stratification and conflict" (pp. 195–198). She suggested that the sense of belonging, critical in the development of the self-concept, becomes "blurred if one's language, cultural patterns, and ethnic experiences are not reflected and supported, but rather given negative connotation in the environment" (p. 196). She urged that the social and survival significance of language as a means of symbolic continuity be understood by human service delivery systems.

In a similar fashion, Jones (1979) has proposed that it is essential for social workers to use African-American norms and frameworks when assessing the attitudes and behaviors of African-American clients. By failing to examine these clients in relation to their own varied cultures, Jones asserted that professionals often arrive at distorted diagnoses. For example, Ladner (1971) proposed that child development needed to be understood in the context of the majority of Black children who have been unable to experience a "protected, carefree, and nonresponsible childhood" because of being raised in a hostile environment (p. 57).

Beverly (1989), in a discussion of treatment issues for black alcoholic clients, has suggested that social workers can better understand and appreciate the concept of the dual perspective—the ability to navigate, and negotiate life in two worlds (see Chapter 1)—by using symbolic interaction theory. He added that social workers need to understand a black client's sociohistorical experience to understand behavior in the context of the meanings clients attach to precipitating events. He cited the following case example in which the client can be helped by using a dual perspective to empower:

> If a black, alcohol-addicted client says, "I don't care how well I perform at work, it is never good enough to get a raise or a promotion," the practitioner must determine what the client is really saying. Is he or she saying that others have received raises and promotions for the same or less amount of work? Have there been other black persons with ability equal to the client's who have received raises and promotions? Does the statement reflect self-depreciation regardless of the client's effort? (p. 374)

MEANING AND THE LANGUAGE OF THE SOCIAL WORK PROFESSION

Human interaction is mediated by the use of symbols, by interpretation, or by ascertaining the meaning of one another's actions. (Blumer, 1969, p. 79)

Symbolic interactionists explore the functions of language in the socialization process. Most interaction, according to symbolic interactionists, occurs through the use of symbols, primarily language. Therefore, language is a communication vehicle between members of the group, and it establishes relationships and solidarity, is a "declaration of the place and psychological distance" held by the group's various members, and is used in the coordination of the activities of the group (Sotomayor, 1977, p. 198).

Language also is central to the social work process in interviewing, listening, recording, and understanding social worker–client communication. Because people have a capacity for language, they are self-aware and capable of self-reflection in the therapeutic encounter (Efran, Lukens, & Lukens, 1990). Although there are ways of communicating that are nonverbal, verbal communication between client and social worker is most often the primary helping tool. Symbolic interactionism offers a framework for examining the language of communication, its development, limitations, distortions, significance, content, and symbolic nature.

Language used in everyday speech as well as social work jargon may be viewed "as a potent force in our society that goes beyond being merely a communicative device. Language not only expresses ideas and concepts but may actually shape them" (Podair, 1967, p. 39). It has been hypothesized that language is not simply an encoding process but rather is a shaping force that predisposes people to act in a certain way. "Language is not separate from action—it is a particular form of action" (Efran, Lukens, & Lukens, 1990, p. 21). For example, a single Navajo verb contains its own subject, objects, and adverbs and can translate into an entire English sentence. Therefore, in the Navajo language, "words paint a picture in your mind" (Watson, 1993, p. 37)

Social work theorists have used symbolic interactionists' assumptions to explore how societies define what is deviant or what constitutes acts contrary to cultural norms—who may be labeled "sick" or "criminal." Goffman (1957) proposed that once a person was labeled and hospitalized as a "mental patient," changes occurred in the person's self. Goffman (1963) also contended that through the use of certain labels, people become discredited or discounted by others in society.

For example, many U.S. citizens have mixed feelings about providing financial assistance to the poor. On the one hand, they may think they have a moral obligation to help people less fortunate. On the other hand, they may share the widely held societal belief that the United States is a land of opportunity and that people can succeed by dint of hard work. As a result of this labeling process, welfare clients often are stigmatized and there tends to be a negative meaning attached to welfare programs, so much so that they are considered the last resort by many. Consequently, a large proportion of those eligible for welfare do not apply (Goodban, 1985).

Some theorists have stated that it is important to explore whether the classification of clients' problems can do an injustice to clients by focusing on social worker–oriented issues rather than client-oriented situations (Northen,

1982). This perspective suggests that classification can violate the principles of client individualization and self-determination.

Other theorists have argued that labels can become the instruments of social control. For example, Edelman (1982) has proposed that the client–social worker encounter, as a social situation, is affected by the political language of the helping professions. He cautioned that, although categorization of problems is necessary to science and indeed to all perceptions, it also is necessary to guard against the use of client labels or the description of treatment techniques as a means of political power and control. For example, to speak of "seclusion" or a "quiet room" rather than solitary confinement may mask the difficulties encountered by patients who are confined against their will.

Whorf (1956) has proposed that the way people think is largely determined by the words they use. From this perspective, if clients perceive verbal communication as abusive or evasive, it can be a serious barrier to a genuine helping relationship. At best, cliches, ready-made phrases, and technical jargon often can be perceived negatively (Bloom, 1980; Burgest, 1973). At worst, language may encompass derogatory terms or language habits that are "instruments of control devised to prevent or diminish communication and or conflict" (Baird, 1970, p. 265).

During the 1960s, concern about sexist language was underscored by the women's movement, and by the mid-1970s, public policy against sexist language was clear (Else & Sanford, 1987). Nonetheless, gender bias continues to be an issue in educational materials, such as college textbooks and professional journals. For example, Else and Stanford (1987) found that of 32 leading social work journals studied during a 2-year period, only 8 provided explicit instructions to authors regarding the use of nonsexist language in submitted manuscripts, and only 10 consistently implemented the standard.

The civil rights movement of the 1960s also brought attention to terms such as *cultural lag*—perceived "as racist jargon when applied to the inability of black families to use particular services of an institution in resolving its problems" (Burgest, 1973, p. 22). The civil rights movement brought about increased activism and a demand for community control to be accompanied by a "new set of verbal symbols . . . [and an] affinity for revolutionary rhetoric," such as symbolized in the speeches of Malcolm X (Tidwell, 1971, p. 61).

Edwards (1982) has provided another example of the need to use culturally appropriate language in the client–social worker encounter. He pointed out that, although the public use of first names when addressing an adult may be acceptable or cordial in many interactions between white people, in most social and professional interactions black adults prefer to be addressed by their last names. This practice defines the positive social value of the person and often indicates respect and self-worth (Goffman, 1967).

Sands (1988) has suggested that it was not until the 1970s that a body of literature sensitized social workers to the need to become more knowledgeable about how the diverse ethnic, occupational, and linguistic groups think and perceive reality. For example, Sotomayor (1977) discussed the role of language, culture, and ethnicity in developing self-concept. Bloom (1980) spoke of the "insidious, dangerous, and increasingly prevalent tendency of practitioners to use stale, sterile, hackneyed, obscure, and evasive language" (p. 332).

In addition, Draper (1979) has proposed that an understanding of the interaction between oppressed people and an oppressive society must consider the special coping capacities and resources necessary to survive and function in a hostile society. She applied this observation to the development of language usage among some African-Americans who use the adjective *bad* is used to mean *good.* She contended that this usage is a "behavior calculated to transform impotence into an active force" (p. 274). She argued further that statements such as "If you're black, stay back" are used to successfully "refer to the boundaries around social space exerted by whites" (p. 272).

Recently, Abramovitz (1991) suggested that stereotypical thinking about client groups that is part of social workers' daily parlance shapes the manner in which practitioners and policymakers are able to effect change. For example, social workers may think in value-laden terms such as broken homes for single-parent families or sexual assault for rape. Jones (1979) has pointed out that the term *culturally deprived,* coined in the 1960s by the dominant society in reference to low-income African-Americans and others, represents a devaluation of African-American culture.

Sands (1988) has suggested that social workers can learn valuable interviewing techniques through *sociolinguistics*—the study of the social context of language. According to this perspective, the client–social worker interview is an interactive process in which each participant brings and constructs a frame of reference to the situation that must be interpreted. *Ethnography*, a systematic means of documenting and understanding alternative realities, contexts, or cultures, has been suggested as another means of guarding against language bias in social work practice (Green, 1982). Ethnography is a tool borrowed from anthropology that offers listening techniques to uncover explanations of cultural differences and contextual meanings.

Kadushin (1983) and others have proposed that the interview be viewed as a "conversation" in which cultural meanings are explored (p. 13). Similarly, Green (1982) has suggested that the process of the social work interview allow the client to guide the social worker "through a cultural setting about which the worker is unfamiliar" by using statements such as, "I want you to tell me your story from your point of view" (p. 77).

Through the language of conversation, messages between client and so-

Table 4.3. Guidelines for Social Workers: A Symbolic Interactionist Approach

---

Acknowledge that clients have their own personal system of meaning derived through interaction with others and their environment.

Engage in active listening to ascertain the client's meaning of past experiences and present events.

Communicate an interest in understanding the symbolic meanings of the client. Choose your words carefully.

Let your client be your teacher as to the symbols and meanings in her or his world. Do not assume that your client's experiences are the same or mean the same as yours.

Reflect the meanings you have ascribed to the client to be sure you have understood correctly.

Assess with the client whether or not the client's personal meanings or his or her view of events contribute to the presenting problem.

Determine with the client if and how personal meanings of significant others and reference groups are understood and may contribute to his or her difficulties.

Share with the client your own meanings and interpretations of events.

Remember that the agency or the organizational structure in which you work has a system of meanings that contribute to the social worker–client encounter. Be aware that the way in which your client perceives the help available will affect the social worker–client relationship.

Learn to use nonverbal as well as verbal communication. Participate in the helping process.

Contract with the client to help him or her interpret events differently and to negotiate new meanings.

Source: Ephross, P. H., and Greene, R. R. (1991). "Symbolic Interactionism." In R. R. Greene and P. H. Ephross (Eds.), *Human Behavior Theory and Social Work Practice,* p. 109. Hawthorne, NY: Aldine de Gruyter.

cial worker become clarified. Clients become conscious of themselves and can consider the nature of their problems and their solution. Simultaneously, the social worker learns a new way of thinking about a client's world and how he or she operates in it (Table 4.3; see Chapter 7 for a discussion of constructionist theory).

Erikson's Eight Stages of Development: Different Lenses

5

Nancy P. Kropf and Roberta R. Greene

> *The phenomenon and the concept of social organization, and its bearing on the individual ego was, thus, for the longest time, shunted off by patronizing tributes to the existence of "social factors."*
>
> (Erikson, 1959, p. 18)

One of the most important professional judgments social workers are called on to make in assessment is whether a client's behavior is appropriate to his or her stage of development. The many questions to be addressed include ascertaining when and why a certain behavior began, how long it has persisted, whether the behavior is acceptable in a sociocultural group or related to a client's gender or ethnic background, and whether the behavior interferes with one or more of a client's roles (Northen, 1987).

The theorist who has provided one of the most widely used approaches to answering these questions and who made a major contribution to the conceptualization of a developmental approach to ego mastery is Erik Erikson. Erikson was one of the few great personality theorists (Carl Jung was another) to view development as lifelong (Hogan, 1976). Erikson proposed that development occurs in eight life stages, starting at birth and ending with old age and death. He viewed each stage of development as a new plateau for the developing self or ego to gain and restore a sense of mastery within the context of social factors (Greene, 1991b).

In contrast to Sigmund Freud, Erikson is noted for his attention to social phenomena (Erikson, 1974). To account for social forces, Erikson turned to social anthropology, ecology, and comparative education for social concepts. According to Greene (1991b), in keeping with his emphasis on the social world, Erikson reformulated the concept of *ego identity* to encompass mutuality between the individual and his or her society. He hypothesized that there existed a "mutual complementation of ethos and ego, of group identity and ego identity" (Erikson, 1959, p. 23).

An understanding of the natural, historical, and technological environment

75

was among the factors Erikson considered part of ego identity and necessary for a true clinical appraisal of the individual. Central to Erikson's (1964a) philosophy was the idea that a "nourishing exchange of community life" (p. 89) is key to mental health. "All this makes man's so-called biological adaptation a matter of life cycles developing within their communities changing history" (Erikson, 1959, p. 163).

Erikson restated the nature of identity, linking the individual's inner world with his or her unique values and history (Hogan, 1976). He proposed that membership identities, including social class, culture, and national affiliation, provided people with the collective power to create their own environment. Society—through its ideological frameworks, roles, tasks, rituals, and initiations—"bestow[s] strength" (Erikson, 1964a, p. 91) and a sense of identification on the developing individual. Social influences including economic, historical, and ethnic factors were stressed, as was the view that people are socialized positively to become part of the historical and ethnic "intertwining of generations" (p. 93).

Although Erikson has been credited with adding a much needed social dimension to the psychoanalytic perspective on clinical intervention, he also has been criticized for what some have called his white, heterosexual, male-defined life cycle of adult development (Berzoff, 1989; Gilligan, 1982; Kravetz, 1982; Schwartz, 1973). For example, social work educators such as Schwartz (1973) and Wesley (1975) have argued that Erikson's theory, widely read in courses in human growth and development, has contributed to sexism within the social work curriculum. Wesley (1975) noted that in *Childhood and Society*, Erikson (1950) devoted 17 pages to the development of the male adolescent and a single paragraph to that of the female. She contended that such bias contributed to stereotyped concepts of women.

Still other theorists have questioned whether Erikson's theory of development effectively captures the experience of racial and ethnic minorities (Foster & Perry, 1982; Logan, 1981). For example, Chestang (1984) proposed that although establishing a sense of identity is a basic human need, understanding the process and its dynamics among African-Americans requires further consideration of the special characteristics inherent in realizing racial identity. Theories of personality formation and development are increasingly taking into account differences in life span events and episodes (Boxer & Cohler, 1989; Cornett & Hudson, 1987; Sophie, 1986). In addition, nonstage theories of human development are increasingly discussed as an alternative, for example, Germain's (1992) ecological approach to development and Thyer's (1992a) behavioral perspective, which examines principles of social learning theory as an explanation for behavior (see Chapter 8). This reexamination of Erikson's approach is marked by an interest in developmental continuities for individuals in diverse populations. Such research is producing a contemporary study of the ecology of the life course (Boxer & Cohler, 1989).

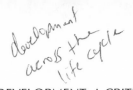
BASIC ASSUMPTIONS OF DEVELOPMENT: A CRITIQUE

Each successive step [in development], then, is a potential crisis because of a radical change in perspective. . . . Thus, different capacities use different opportunities to become full-grown components of the ever-new configuration that is the growing personality. (Erikson, 1959, p. 57)

Defining Life Span Development

Development across the life cycle is the focus of Eriksonian *psychosocial theory*, a theoretical approach that involves analysis of social and environmental factors that produce changes in thought and behavior. His primary focus was on the tendency of an individual's life to form a coherent, lifelong experience and to be joined or linked to lives of those in previous and future generations. This is known as a *life cycle approach* (see Table 5.1).

Erikson's perspective on development was derived from the biological principle of *epigenesis*, the idea that each stage depends on resolutions of the experiences of prior stages. Epigenesis suggests that "anything that grows has a ground plan, and out of that plan *parts* arise, each part having its *time*

Table 5.1. Eriksonian Theory: Basic Assumptions

Development is biopsychosocial and occurs across the life cycle.

Development is propelled by a biological plan, however, personal identity cannot exist independently of social organization.

The ego plays a major role in development as it strives for competence and mastery of the environment. Societal institutions and caretakers provide positive support for the development of personal effectiveness. Individual development enriches society.

Development is marked by eight major stages at which time a psychosocial crisis occurs. Personality is the outcome of the resolution—on a continuum from positive to negative—of each of these crises. Each life stage builds on the success of former, presents new social demands, and creates new opportunities.

Psychosocial crises accompanying life stages are universal or occur in all cultures. Each culture offers unique solutions to life stages.

The needs and capacities of the generations are intertwined.

Psychological health is a function of ego strength and social supports.

Confusions in self-identity arise from negative resolution of developmental crises and alienation from societal institutions.

Therapy involves the interpretation of developmental and historical distortions and the curative process of insight.

Source: Greene, R. R. (1991b). "Eriksonian Theory: A Developmental Approach to Ego Mastery." In R. R. Greene and P. H. Ephross (Eds.), *Human Behavior Theory and Social Work Practice*, p. 83. Hawthorne, NY: Aldine de Gruyter.

of special ascendancy, until all parts have arisen to form a *functioning whole"* (Erikson, 1959, p. 53). Erikson (1982) defined epigenesis as

> a progression through time of a differentiation of parts. This indicates that each part exists in some form before "its" decisive and critical time normally arrives and remains systematically related to all others so that the whole ensemble depends on the proper development in the proper sequence of each item. Finally, as each part comes to its full ascendance and finds some lasting solution during its stage, it will also be expected to develop further under the dominance of subsequent ascendancies, and most of all, to take its place in the integration of the whole ensemble. (p. 29)

Personality development, then, is said to follow a proper sequence, emerge at critical or decisive times in a person's life, progress over time, and be a lifelong integrative process. However, epigenesis, the assumption that future functioning is determined by history and biology, has met with criticism. Feminist scholars have taken exception with the view that gender determines successful functioning. They contend that while women's development is different than men's, its uniqueness does not make it inferior (Gilligan, 1982; see Chapters 6 and 12 for a further discussion).

Personality Development in Eriksonian Theory

From an Eriksonian epigenetic perspective, personality develops through a predetermined readiness "to interact with a widening social radius, beginning with the dim image of a mother and ending with mankind" (Erikson, 1959, p. 54). The healthy personality begins to develop in infancy. Over time, the child, "given a reasonable amount of guidance, can be trusted to obey inner laws of development, laws which create a succession of potentialities for *significant interaction* with those who tend him" (p. 54).

Erikson argued that identity not only emerges in stages but also involves restructuring or resynthesis. The view that personality development involves new configurations at different life stages is called *hierarchical reorganization.* This is the concept that development over time is not only linear but also has changing structures and organization that permit new functions and adaptations (Shapiro & Hertzig, 1988). Through a series of psychosocial crises and an ever-widening circle of significant relations, Erikson (1959) believed the individual develops "a new drive-and-need constellation" and "an expanded radius of potential social interaction" (p. 21).

Although Erikson proposed that individuals have a readiness to interact with a widening circle of other people throughout their lives, he emphasized that psychological individuation is paramount. Feminist scholars and others have taken exception to this view of ideal adult development (Berzoff, 1989; Gilligan, 1982). For example, feminist scholars contend that women's experience of connectedness (including mothering, nurturing, and caretaking) should be valued as the catalyst for self-development (Bricker-Jenkins, Hooyman & Gottlieb, 1991; Van Den Bergh & Cooper, 1987; see Chapter 12).

In addition, Ho (1992) has suggested a transcultural framework for examining development. He cautioned that practitioners can misconstrue closeness between family members, particularly mother and child, among many Latinos or Asian-American families. Similarly, among many minority adolescents, autonomy is not determined solely by moving out of the home. Rather, it is expected that family members will continue to live in extended households.

Critique of Life Stage Models of Development

Erikson's (1959) most important and best known contribution to personality theory is his model of eight stages of ego development. In this life cycle approach, he proposed that development is determined by shifts in instinctual or biological energy, occurs in stages, and centers around a series of eight psychosocial crises. As each stage emerges, a psychosocial crisis fosters change within the person and in his or her expanding interconnections between self and environment. Crises offer the opportunity for new experiences and demand a "radical change in perspective," or a new orientation toward oneself and the world (Erikson, 1963, p. 212). The result is an "ever-new configuration that is the growing personality" (Erikson, 1959, p. 57).

Erikson emphasized that one stage of development builds on the successes of previous stages. Difficulties in resolving earlier psychosocial issues may foreshadow further difficulties in later stages. Each stage of development is distinguished by particular characteristics that differentiate it from preceding and succeeding stages (Newman and Newman, 1987). The notion that development occurs in unique stages, each building on the previous one and having its own emphasis or underlying structural organization, is called *stage theory* (Figure 5.1). Erikson argued that personality is a function of the outcome of each life stage. The psychological outcome of a crisis is a blend of ego qualities resting between two contradictory extremes or polarities. This means an individual's personality reflects a blend of ego qualities such as trust or mistrust.

Social workers and other human services professionals refer to several theories of personality development that are based upon assumptions of sequential, universal stages. In addition to Erikson, other well-known stage theorists include Sigmund Freud, Heinz Hartmann, Margaret Mahler, Jean Piaget, and Lawrence Kohlberg (Germain, 1991). Although stage theories con-

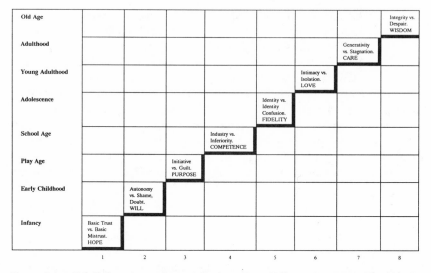

Figure 5.1. Erik Erikson's psychosocial crises. From Erikson, E. (1982). *The Life Cycle Completed,* pp. 56–57. New York: Norton. Reprinted with permission.

tinue to be used by practitioners, their utility and universality are being increasingly questioned.

As stated in Chapter 4, on symbolic interaction, social work assessment is used to explore needs and resources as a process to select interventions and treatment modalities for a client. From a practice perspective, a person's progression throughout life may be evaluated by the normative (and therefore desirable) standards proposed by Eriksonian theory. As with other stage or phase theories, the perspective of normative patterns of development and transition implies that a different progression is undesirable, involves unresolved conflicts and issues, and is deviant. Interventions by the practitioner become attempts to assist a client with fitting into the stages or resolving previously unresolved internal issues.

Unfortunately, the use of a model where stages are mastered in a linear sequence does not consider cultural variations in life-style decisions and behaviors. If practitioners are uninformed about influences of gender, racial or ethnic, religious, sexual orientation, or cohort variations in clients' development, decisions about treatment approaches may prove to be inappropriate or even harmful.

The critique of stage theories, including Eriksonian theory, is related to the assumptions of fixed sequence development. For example, the identity development of gays and lesbians has been found to be different from heterosexuals, as well as to have intragroup variations (Boxer & Cohler, 1989;

Sophie, 1986). The whole concept of timing of events, both in the individual's personal history as well as his or her sociocultural setting, has an impact
on the progression and mastery of developmental tasks (Germain, 1991; Sophie, 1986). As Boxer and Cohler state (1989), "It is precisely this social definition of the course of life which transforms the study of the life span or life
cycle into the study of the life course" (p. 320). The question then becomes
whether any fixed, determined sequence of life tasks adequately addresses
an understanding of human development during changing cultural, social,
and political eras.

EIGHT STAGES OF DEVELOPMENT: DIVERSITY PERSPECTIVES

*The ego is learning effective steps toward a tangible collective future, that is
developing into a defined ego within a social reality.* (Erikson, 1959, p. 22)

Erikson outlined eight states of development spanning birth through death.
This section summarizes each of the stages and discusses the associated development tasks. An additional component is a brief critique based on individual and cultural group differences in development is presented for each
stage. Cultural influences on issues related to various stages are examined,
and the concept of mastery of developmental tasks is explored.

Stage 1: Basic Trust Versus Basic Mistrust

Erikson (1959) believed that "enduring patterns for the balance of basic
trust over basic mistrust" are established from birth until about age 2 (pp.
64–65). He viewed the establishment of trust as the "cornerstone of the
healthy personality" and the primary task during this first stage (p. 58).

The resolution of each psychosocial crisis, according to Erikson, results in
a basic strength or *ego quality*. He indicated that the first psychosocial
strength that emerges is *hope*, the enduring belief in the attainability of pri-
mal or basic wishes. Hope is related to a sense of confidence and stems primarily from the quality of maternal care a person receives. Although Erikson
focused on the development of healthy personalities, he acknowledged that
the resolution of each crisis produces both positive and negative ego qualities. He identified a tendency toward *withdrawal* (detachment) from social
relationships as the negative outcome of the first life crisis. Erikson proposed
that tendencies later in life toward low self-esteem, depression, and social
withdrawal are indications that there may have been difficulty during the first
developmental stage. In working with clients who have these behaviors,

practitioners need to become knowledgeable about the history of their relationships. Clients with difficulties in these areas may internalize their anger
or employ strategies to avoid engaging with others.

Chestang (1972) has argued that Erikson did not sufficiently address the
consequences of injustice, inconsistency, and feelings of impotence on personality development. He suggested that character development of members
of groups who are treated differently by virtue of their living in a hostile environment must be examined in the context of institutional disparity. Chestang went on to suggest that a deficit model, or one viewing an individual's
adjustment as pathological, is not an acceptable assessment when societal
structures have impeded development through "excessive shaming," and
"repeated environmental assault" (pp. 46–48). Rather, it is necessary to ask
how an individual's personality has adapted or transcended these provoca-
tions.

Stage 2: Autonomy Versus Shame

Autonomy, or a sense of self-control without loss of self-esteem, involves
the psychosocial issues of holding on and letting go. On the other hand,
shame, the feeling of being exposed or estranged from parental figures, involves a child's feeling that he or she is a failure and, as a result, his or lack
of self-confidence. A successful resolution of the psychosocial crisis of autonomy versus shame results in the positive ego quality *will*, or the unbroken
determination to exercise free choice. Will's antipathic counterpart is *compulsion*, the repetitive behavior used to restrict impulses. Compulsion is the
negative result of autonomy versus shame.

In this stage of development, independence or separation is the desired
outcome. For Erikson, male identity formation is an antecedent to intimacy
in relationships with others. However, more recent research has shown that
women's development is more relational and less individualistic than that of
men. As McGoldrick (1989) argued, the major theories of human development have viewed concerns about relationships with others as a weakness
of men rather than a strength of women. In the past few decades, theories
have emerged that specifically recognize and value the different patterns of
women's development (Gilligan, 1982; Miller, 1976). These theories focus
on the importance of attachments in women's development and the importance of relationships throughout life.

The emergence of female voices in life span development has challenged
assumptions of earlier theorists. In theories that bring an analysis of a
strengths perspective to women's development, the ability to maintain attachments to others is seen as positive and functional. Women's ability to be
connected has the goal of sustaining and affirming creativity and coopera-

tion in family life (Berzoff, 1989). Miller (1984) suggested that the capacity to adapt to others is central to being empathetic. A reconceptualization of attachments in a feminist framework implies that relatedness, not merely autonomy, is a desirable state.

Stage 3: Initiative Versus Guilt

During the stage of initiative versus guilt, as a result of being willing to go after things and to take on roles through play, the child develops a sense of purpose. However, if he or she is overly thwarted, a feeling of *inhibition* or restraint prevents freedom of thought and expression from developing.

Erikson echoed Freud when he stated that girls "lack one item: the penis; and with it, important prerogatives in some cultures and classes" (Erikson, 1964b, p. 81). As is typical of Erikson, he identifies the source of the inequality he notes not in some form of biological determinism, as did Freud, but rather to the inner workings of certain societies. Erikson (1963) stressed that, at this stage, the child engages in an active investigation of his or her environment, and the family remains the radius of significant human relations.

However, Erikson departed from traditional psychoanalytic thought when he proposed that, during this stage, children are more concerned with play and with pursuing activities of their own choosing than they are with their sexuality. Some theorists (Gilligan, 1982) have taken issue with Erikson's concepts relating play activity to biologically based "masculine and feminine imitative" (Erikson, 1959, p. 82). For example, in research at a playground, Lever (1976) noted that boys fought over the rules of a game, whereas girls tended to leave the game when disputes arose. She interpreted this finding as showing that girls quit the game to sustain their friendships. In addition, Ho (1992) has pointed out that because play content, feelings, and fantasies vary from group to group and within different societies, practitioners need to be cautious about applying one set of norms when working with young children and their families. Part of the assessment process needs to include investigation of the meanings and outcomes of children's play, and specifically the private meanings held by the client.

Stage 4: Industry Versus Inferiority

This life stage occurs between ages 6 and 12 years. Classically trained psychoanalysts believed that this is a time when the sexual drive lies dormant (or is sublimated) and children enjoy a period of relative rest, known as the latency period (Corey, 1986). Erikson (1959) broke with psychoanalytic thinking by suggesting that the central task of this time is to achieve a sense of *industry*. Developing industry is a task involving "an eagerness for building skills and performing meaningful work" (p. 90). The crisis of industry versus inferiority can result in a sense of competence or a blend with its opposite, inertia (a paralysis of thought and action that prevents productive work). Success at creating and making things together with one's neighbors and schoolmates is a critical task in the child's expanding physical and social world at this time (Erikson, 1982; Newman & Newman, 1987).

Attitudes toward productivity may vary among and within cultures. For example, Sue and Sue (1990) discuss the importance of tribal allegiances for many American Indians, whose identity and security are entwined with their tribal affiliation. Productivity is valued as a communal good and less as a reflection of individual success. This concept also is different from the cultural values of Native Australians. In their social order, a rite of passage to manhood is the "walkabout," which is the practice of being alone in the environment, demonstrating one's ability to survive independently in one's world (White & Epston, 1990). In the social work assessment process, the strategies and symbolic rituals that accompany a sense of industry must be examined with the particular client.

Stage 5: Identity Versus Identity Confusion

From 12 through 22 years, the adolescent develops into the young adult. The central task of this stage, according to Erikson (1963), is to form a stable identity, which he defined as "a sense of personal sameness and historical continuity" (p. 153). *Identity*, which involves the establishment of personal identity, autonomy from parents, acceptance of one's sexual preference, and commitment to a career, also depends on social supports that permit the child to formulate successive and tentative identifications. This process culminates in an overt identity crisis in adolescence. During adolescence, an individual struggles with the issues of how "to be oneself" and "to share oneself with another" (Erikson, 1959, p. 179). The peer group becomes the critical focus of interaction.

The person who forms a relatively healthy identity views the world of experience with a minimum of distortion and defensiveness, and a maximum of mutual activity. *Fidelity*, or the ability to sustain loyalties, is the critical ego quality that emerges from this stage. *Identity confusion* is based on a summation of the most undesirable and dangerous aspects of identification at critical stages of development (Newman & Newman, 1987). Severe conflicts during this stage can result in *repudiation*, or a rejection of alien roles and values.

Erikson (1964a) viewed identity as "a new combination of old and new identification fragments" (p. 90). He believed that identity is more than the sum of childhood identifications. The individual's inner drives and his or her endowments and opportunities, as well as the ego values accrued in childhood, come together to form a sense of confidence and continuity about "inner sameness" and "one's meaning for others" (Erikson, 1959, p. 94). Absorption of personality features into a "new configuration" is the essence of development during this stage (Erikson, 1959, p. 57). Erikson proposed that identity formation is a lifelong developmental process. Therefore, the ability to retain one's belief in oneself as well as one's life-style and career (often a focus of therapy) can be enhanced throughout life.

Erikson (1959) developed the concept of identity crisis:

> Every person and every group harbors a negative identity as the sum of all those identifications and identity fragments which the individual has to submerge in himself [or herself] as undesirable or irreconcilable or which his [or her] group has taught him [or her] to perceive as the mark of fatal "difference" in sex role or race, in class or religion. (p. 20)

Identity crisis among adolescents is frequently explored in the literature. The task for the practitioner is to evaluate how the adolescent perceives and internalizes the images that confront him or her. In forming an adult identity, adolescents may struggle with images that are negatively portrayed, such as overtly masculine lesbian women or feminine gay men. In addition, Ho (1992) expressed concern that attitudes of young Asian-Americans toward themselves self often are negatively influenced by a society in which the media constantly bombard them with the superiority of Western values. In addition, there has been increasing concern about the role of educators who do not positively reinforce feminine identity, which contributes to a negative identity formation among young women, particularly with regard to self-esteem (American Association of University Women, 1991).

There also is a suggestion in the literature that identity formation for African-American adolescents "may be more problematic because of negative messages they receive from the dominant society" (Gibbs & Moskowitz-Sweet, 1991, p. 580). Billingsley (1968) has pointed out that such negative messages make child raising or "socialization doubly challenging, for the family must teach its young members how to be human, but also how to be Black in a White society" (p. 28).

Stage 6: Intimacy Versus Isolation

Erikson's sixth stage involves a mature person's ability to form intimate relationships. This occurs between the ages of 22 and 34 years. Corresponding to Freud's genital stage, the stage of intimacy versus isolation focuses on the psychosocial modality of "being able to lose and find oneself in another" (Erikson, 1959, p. 179). The radius of significant relations expands to include partnerships in friendship and love and encompasses both cooperative and competitive aspects. *Love,* or a mutual devotion that can overcome "the antagonisms inherent in a divided function," is the emerging ego strength (Erikson, 1968, p. 289). Shutting out others, or *exclusivity,* is a sign that an individual has not been successful in reaching intimacy (Newman & Newman, 1987).

Erikson (1968) subscribed to Freud's view that the criterion for defining a mature person is the ability "to love and work" (p. 289). Erikson also agreed with Freud that *intimacy* includes mutuality of orgasm with a loved partner of the opposite sex, with whom one shares mutual trust and the continuing cycle of work, recreation, and procreation. However, he also perceived intimacy as being more than sexual gratification, but as also having an interest in another's well-being as well as in intellectually stimulating interactions. On the other hand, Erikson (1959) suggested that the psychoanalytic perspective on mature generativity "carries a strong cultural bias," and that various societies might define the capacity for mutual devotion differently (p. 102).

Erikson's sixth stage relates to the intimate social relationships that develop during early adulthood. However, this assumes that opportunities, structures, and resources are available that promote interaction and intimacy. His stages also suggest that relationship skills develop during certain chronological age ranges. Both of these assumptions do not consider the life course development stages of people with developmental disabilities.

The ability to enter into adult relationships and roles is a result of a person's social skills and the availability of social opportunities (Pridgen, 1991). Therefore, social functioning is not solely an individual process but depends on the opportunities that exist in a particular environment. Communities may be structured in a way that promote or inhibit a person's ability to function adequately. As Germain (1991) put it, competent communities are those that are structured to promote functioning of all members.

One group that has historically lacked social and vocational options is people with mental retardation. Because of the limited opportunities afforded them, their ability to work, love, and hold adult family roles has been compromised. Rather than providing increased opportunities for people with disabilities, many communities restrict individuals with mental retardation from social participation through segregated work and living environments (DeWeaver & Kropf, 1992; Seltzer, Seltzer, & Litchfield, 1982).

The limited options for adult work roles for people with mental retardation have been a major employment barrier. In the past, people with such challenges have been segregated from nondisabled adults in sheltered workshops and day activity programs. This type of separation has had the effect of isolating people with disabilities. Currently, supported employment programs are demonstrating that they are a viable method of providing competitive employment for people with disabilities in integrated work settings (Moon, Inge, Wehman, Brooke, & Barcus, 1990). The additional support this type of program provides is essential, because many people with mental disabilities have lacked other opportunities to learn skills necessary to be successful in a workplace environment with nondisabled peers.

Lack of opportunity also affects the ability to form more intimate relationships. Erikson (1959) defined intimacy as the ability to be lost in another person. However, intimacy issues for people with mental retardation have been a source of controversy and concern (Abramson, Parker, & Weisberg, 1988; Howard, Lipsitz, Sheppard, & Steinitz, 1991). Historically, society has not allowed sexual expression among people with mental disabilities and their intimate relationships have been discouraged and suppressed.

Despite many barriers to intimate relationships, some people with mental retardation do become parents. Part of the intimacy versus isolation stage of development is the desire and ability to have children. Most parents who have mental retardation are individuals functioning in the less severe ranges of disability (Schilling, Schinke, Blythe, & Barth, 1982). However, even more functional parents with disabilities report little preparation in assuming a parenting role. In addition to possible inadequate socialization, these mothers and fathers may lack other psychological, social, and environmental resources that can enhance their caregiving ability (Whitman, Graves, & Accardo, 1989). To be successful in their roles, many parents with mental disabilities need ongoing educational and support, which is not provided by many families or service providers.

Stage 7: Generativity Versus Stagnation

This stage occurs in adulthood between ages 34 and 60 years, and is concerned with "establishing and guiding the next generation" (Erikson, 1968, p. 290). The psychosocial crisis centers around "the ability to take care of others" (Erikson, 1959, p. 179). The radius of significant relations extends to dividing labor and sharing households. Broadly framed, generativity encompasses creativity through producing a family; mentoring a student,the colleague, or friend; and engaging in a career and in leisure activities.

Generativity versus stagnation involves the ability to take care of others; the inability to care for others sufficiently or to include them significantly in one's concerns results in the negative ego quality, *rejectivity*. What is commonly called a midlife crisis may actually be an inability to satisfactorily resolve Erikson's stage of generativity versus stagnation.

The concept of generativity is currently being reexamined. Generativity has been expanded to include activities external to the family that are more diffuse (e.g., mentoring, and craft development). For example, Sands and Richardson (1986) have suggested that "women in their middle years are at a crossroads in their developmental histories" (p. 36). These researchers contended that women often find themselves sandwiched between the needs of their elderly parents and their teenage or young adult children. Therefore, practitioners are often working with middle-aged women who are frequently involved in the demands of caretaking even as they are reassessing their interpersonal relationships, their physical well-being, and their work and achievements.

Another example of the reexamination of Erikson's concept of middle adulthood is Cornett and Hudson's (1987) examination of middle-aged gays. Their discussion of generativity explored whether gays are able to successfully achieve a state of generativity, because most gays have no offspring. They propose that generativity can be attained through alternative avenues, such as careers, hobbies, voluntary activities, and relationships with cohorts of younger gays. Cornett and Hudson argued that gays can be involved in promoting and guiding younger generations through means other than actual parenthood. They cited contributions by brilliant, productive, and creative middle-aged gays through the ages, such as Socrates, Walt Whitman, and Tennessee Williams. The histories of these great men point to the need of the practitioner to explore alternative options with clients. A feeling of generativity is not simply caregiving for blood-related family members.

Stage 8: Integrity Versus Despair

The final stage, which is concerned with late life events, begins at about age 60 years and last until death. The issue of this psychosocial crisis is how a person is able to grow older with integrity in the face of impending mortality. *Integrity* is achieved by individuals who have few regrets, who have lived productive lives, and who cope as well with their failures as they do with their successes. The person who has successfully achieved a sense of integrity appreciates the continuity of past, present, and future experiences. He or she also comes to accept the life cycle, to cooperate with the inevitabilities of life, and to experience a sense of being complete. *Wisdom,* or the active concern with life in the face of death, characterizes those who are relatively successful in resolving this stage.

Erikson's notion that one stage of life is intimately related to all the others comes full circle at the end of life. His view that the needs and capacities of the generations intertwine is reflected in his statement that the development of trust in children depends on the integrity of previous generations: "Healthy children will not fear life if their elders have integrity enough not to fear death" (Erikson, 1950, p. 269).

Despair, on the other hand, predominates in those who fear death and who wish life would give them another chance. The older person who has a strong sense of despair feels that life has been too short and finds little meaning in human existence, having lost faith in himself or herself and others. The person in whom despair predominates has little sense of world order or spiritual wholeness (Butler, 1969). Disdain, or a scorn for weakness and frailty, characterizes those who are relatively unsuccessful in resolving integrity versus despair.

Antonovsky and Sagy (1990) "rejected the Eriksonian notion of stages that are epigenetically determined, universal, and clearly demarcated age wise" (p. 367). They also proposed that Erikson did not give ample attention to the tasks of the later years of life. They questioned why there is no further development during almost 40 years of the life cycle—from the time an individual emerges from the stage of generativity versus stagnation until he or she enters the stage of integrity versus despair. They then suggested that Erikson's formulations be used to examine how a life cycle transition is characterized by a number of major life tasks. They also differentiated between tasks and outcomes of a given stage; for example, the successful outcome of the crisis of integrity versus despair is integrity. However, it is possible to conceptualize a process of personal needs and social demands that may arise during this stage, such as retirement transition and a concern for maintaining one's health. Finally, Antonovsky and Sagy proposed that the exploration of psychosocial developmental tasks within a historical context, as suggested, allows for an enriched cultural-specific understanding of adult human development.

DIFFERENTIAL ASSESSMENT AS A FOUNDATION FOR INTERVENTION

Although norms are necessary, rapid changes in life-styles and the conditions of life make it difficult for workers and clients to assess the adequacy of functioning, as do the varied cultural backgrounds of clients. (Northen, 1987, p. 179)

In social work practice, the assessment phase includes collecting information on a client's functional status. This process also involves making sense of this information by understanding it within the framework of a theoretical perspective. Although Eriksonian theory provides a life stage perspective on development, what would be considered successful mastery of the life stages may be different among various cultural groups and among dif-

ferent people. As discussed in the previous section, gender and disability status—and often cultural characteristics—have an impact on progression
through the eight stages proposed by Erikson.

In social work, the value placed on individualism and autonomy has had
a major effect on the profession's knowledge base. The effect of this individualistic paradigm can be seen in various aspects of assessment and treatment.
Even the terminology used in professional practice reflects a desired state of
autonomy—for example in the term *codependency* for women with addict-
ed partners, or *welfare dependents* for women who use public assistance programs. Practice interventions often have a goal of helping people separate
from others. This could encompass helping a family secure a group home
residence for a relative with a disability, assisting a couple through divorce
mediation, helping older workers with retirement planning, or helping a
mother on public assistance find job training.

The way social work has been taught is not immune from the effects of paradigms built on values of individualism. Back in the early 1970s, schools of
social work were admonished for teaching sexist content in the curriculum
(Schwartz, 1973). In more recent years, issues related to assessment of members of various groups (e.g., elderly people, people with disabilities, gays and
lesbians) have continued to surface in the professional literature (DeWeaver
& Kropf, 1992; Kropf, Schneider, & Stahlman, 1993 Newman, 1989).

On the surface, progress appears to have been made in representing the
experiences of diverse groups of people because content on race, ethnicity,
and gender is now a mandated part of the social work curriculum. However, others proclaim that an additive model is insufficient to address the fundamental problems of "doing social work" based on an individualistic
model. Some in the profession advocate a paradigmatic shift that includes a
focus on relatedness and interdependence rather than on autonomy and individualism (Falck, 1988; Kravetz, 1982; Tice, 1990).

As suggested by feminist scholars, practice needs to move beyond a separation model. The assessment process must include a focus on helping
clients in various life situations with the transitions they face. Instead of "letting go," however, assessment and treatment may have the goal of helping
clients "loosen" relationships, as in the case of a family investigating residential placements. When relationships must be terminated, as in the case
of retirement from a job, social work assessment must also be prepared to
help clients who have lost relationships "grab on" to new ones, such as
through joining a senior citizen's group in the community. Berzoff (1989) suggested that a more relational model of practice would move into a modality
of working in group settings instead of having an emphasis such as the current one on individual models of treatment (Table 5.2).

The functional status of a client involves more than understanding about
that individual's behavior. Considerations of environmental influences need

Table 5.2. Guidelines for the Eriksonian-Style Practitioner

Understand that your client is engaged in a lifelong process of personality development in which the practitioner can be instrumental in promoting growth.

Engage the client in a self-analysis, which results in a developmental history.

Distinguish with the client his or her relative successes and difficulties in resolving psychosocial crises.

Determine areas of development that have led to a distortion of reality and a diminution in ego functioning.

Interpret the client's developmental and historical distortions. Ask for client confirmation of your interpretations.

Develop the client's insight and understanding about unresolved normative crises and their historical implications.

Identify ways in which the client can use his or her ego strengths to cope more effectively with his or her environment. Explore how these coping strategies can be put into action.

Clarify how and in what ways various social institutions support or fail to support the client's psychosocial well-being.

Seek means of enhancing the client's societal supports.

Promote the client's developing a new orientation to his or her place in the social environment.

Source: Greene, R. R. (1991b). "Eriksonian Theory: A Developmental Approach to Ego Mastery." In R. R. Greene and P. H. Ephross (Eds.), Human Behavior Theory and Social Work Practice, p. 102. Hawthorne, NY: Aldine de Gruyter.

to be included in the assessment process, such as opportunities and resources that do not exist for certain groups of clients. For example, throughout their lives, people with mental retardation have limited social support networks (Malone, 1990). Furthermore, adults with mental conditions often express a desire to make more friends and meet new people (Flynn & Saleem, 1986; Mest, 1988; see Chapter 11 for a discussion of social support networks). In the assessment process for clients with mental retardation, community-level factors can have an important influence on an intervention plan. The focus of the intervention may move from an individual to a system change direction, which is more inclusive of all people regardless of personal characteristics such as age, race and ethnicity, gender, disability status, sexual orientation, or religious affiliation.

Role Theory and Social Work Practice   ————————   **6**

Kathryn H. Thompson and Roberta R. Greene

Humans are never just individuals trying to meet their own needs. They are social in nature and live out their lives in the context of social systems and their constituent roles. The meeting of individual needs is intimately caught up in the dynamics of the system as a whole.

(Longres, 1990, p. 45)

Role theory provides a set of constructs for understanding human behaviors that arise out of life in the human group. It perceives human behavior as a pattern of reciprocal relationships in which there are a set of culture-specific attitudes, beliefs, values, and expectations regarding how people should conduct themselves in a particular situation. The concept of role addresses how people learn what behavior is expected, permitted, or prohibited within their families and social groups and explains human behavior as flowing from internalized social prescriptions, motivated by the nature of group identification on the one hand and bounded by status assignment on the other.

Role theory came to the fore in social work practice during the 1960s and early 1970s, when there was renewed interest in environmental factors that influence personality (Davis, 1986; Ephross-Saltman & Greene, 1993; Stein & Cloward, 1958). According to Hamilton (1958a), social workers' increased attention to the concept of social role represented a "revolution" in the social sciences and a return to a stronger focus on the social perspective on behavior (p. xi). Writing at the zenith of the social work profession's strong interest in intrapsychic processes as the explanation for human behavior, Hamilton believed role theory would offer social and cultural insights that would no longer "restrict the social worker to a consideration of how the client feels about his [or her] situation," but would allow the professional to "be equally attuned to the effects on the client of ethnic, class, and other significant group determinants of behavior" (p. xi).

The construct of role also was proposed as a way of "studying and describing the interaction of two members of a social group as they adjust to each other within a social system," thereby permitting an analysis of diverse interpersonal systems (Turner, 1974, p. 319). Social workers were urged to use role analysis to better understand and treat marital difficulties, child-rearing issues, and workplace concerns. Because role theory explores the changing societal context in which behavior is defined and explains how individual behavior is influenced by the social environment, it was argued that it contributes to an understanding of the personal and social dimensions of behavior across culture and gender.

Theories that attempt to explain how group norms and values are established, how groups achieve a division of labor, and what contributes to systems maintenance are of strong interest to social workers (Longres, 1990; Strean, 1974). Therefore, it is not surprising that concepts of social role were viewed as making an important contribution to understanding human behavior and the social environment, and the theory was infused into several social work practice models (Hollis, 1964, 1977; Perlman, 1968). Since the 1970s, however, researchers have reexamined role theory, particularly the underlying assumptions about gender roles, family definitions, and hierarchical structures within families that are based on role relationships (McGoldrick, Anderson, & Walsh, 1989). Feminist scholars specifically have been concerned that role theory has not appropriately addressed questions about gender roles and family structure and that role theory has been used uncritically to maintain systems within which devalued and inferior roles are ascribed to women.

This chapter explores the perspectives of social role theory for culturally sensitive and gender-sensitive social work practice. It specifically applies social role concepts to the assessment process and the client–social worker interaction. Applications of social role constructs to human behavior and the implications of these for devalued social roles and groups in our society are discussed (Table 6.1).

ROLE THEORY: A PERSON-IN-ENVIRONMENT PARADIGM

Individuals are connected to social systems through the roles they occupy in them. Roles are at the same time an element of the individual and an element of a social system. They represent the joint boundary between the two, the point at which person meets environment. (Longres, 1990, p. 41)

Role theory provides conceptual tools for understanding the social dimensions of individual and group behavior (Ackerman, 1954). Although role theory examines the attitudes and behaviors expected of people in a particular position, it holds that others' expectations always impinge on the expectations of self. The concept of social role then serves as a link for understanding an individual's emotional life, behavior, and place in society.

Table 6.1.   Role Theory: Basic Assumptions

1. Certain behaviors are prescribed (by us and by other elements of our social system) relative to our position within that system.
2. Every role involves both our own expectations and abilities and one or more others.
3. The notion of role expectation implies that there are certain social norms that set the outside limits for congruent, nonconflicted interactions, and transactions between positions within the system and between systems.
4. There are emotionally charged value judgments to how people carry out their roles both on the part of the person occupying the role position and others.
5. Social functioning may be seen as the sum of the roles performed by a human system (Boehm, 1959a, pp. 95–97).
6. The concept of role, role functioning, role expectations, and role transactions may be used to increase the knowledge based used for the assessment of the problem situation. Role failure and/or role conflict will tend to follow:
   a. The loss or absence of resources necessary to a system's ability to perform a role well.
   b. When systems are thrust into new roles without knowing the role expectations.
   c. When there is a role expectation on the part of interacting systems.
   d. When there is a conflict of role expectations within the cluster of roles carried by one system.
   e. When there is ambiguity on the part of the systems as to role expectations.
   f. When the individual as a system, or as a member of social system, is [disabled or challenged] in physical, intellectual, or social capacities demanded of the role.
   g. When high feelings or crisis situations suddenly and without warning disrupt previous effective role patterns (Perlman, 1962, pp. 17–31).

Source: Compton, B., and Galaway, B. (1989). *Social Work Processes,* pp. 131–132. Chicago: Dorsey. Copyright 1984 by The Dorsey Press. Reprinted with permission.

Because roles are simultaneously "an element of the individual and an element of a social system," the concept of role exemplifies the person-in-environment paradigm (Longres, 1990, p. 41; see Figure 6.1).

Role theory has primarily focused on the "downward" impact of societal influences on individuals, families, and subgroups; yet individuals impact society through their daily role performance as both carriers and harbingers of societal change (Kluckhohn & Strodtbeck, 1961, p. 38). For example, in discussion of the implications of changing gender roles on family structure, Lipman-Blumen (1976) proposed that the concept of role cannot be understood without considering socioeconomic and political factors that shape society. At the same time, the individual and his or her "changing sex roles are a sound barometer of a more pervasive change within a society" (p. 67).

Because cultural relativity is inherent in role theory, the phenomenon of cross-cultural role conflict can be understood. Hence, role theory directs attention to the way that values govern a particular family and its country of

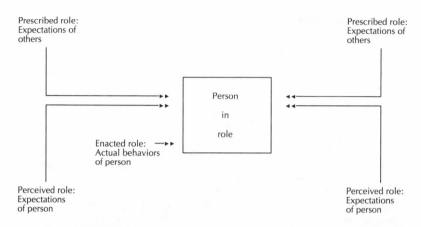

Figure 6.1. Definitions of role. A person's role in any situation is defined in three ways: from the perspective of the expectations of others for people in that role (the prescribed role), the expectations of the person taking the role (the perceived role), and that person's actual behaviors (the enacted role). Source: based on Deutsch, M., and Krauss, R. M. (1965). *Social Psychology,* pp. 175–177. New York: Basic Books.

origin when conceptualizing role behaviors. For example, traditional Asian/Pacific clients have been heavily influenced by Confucian philosophy and ethics, "which strongly emphasize specific roles and the proper relationships among people in those roles" (Ho, 1987, p. 25). The perception that the wife is assigned to a low status in the family structure, and role expectations of a parent-child relationship are well defined are specific Confucian values that may often conflict with values in mainstream American society. Therefore, Ho has suggested that for today's Asian/Pacific clients, practitioners must determine whether the family members were born in their native country or in the United States as well as family members' level of education and income. This information can provide a rough gauge of the degree of the clients' acculturation and assimilation (see Chapter 8) and, consequently, of the possible cross-cultural role conflict within the family, between the family and their current American environment, and between the social worker (and agency) and the family or its individual members.

Role performance, though, should not be described in a binary (either/or) fashion (Thorne & Yalom, 1982). Categories such as gender, race, and class may be too simplistic (Piven & Cloward, 1971; Frazer & Nicholson, 1990). For example, what is considered "masculine" behavior is a generalization that often requires overconformity and ignores the existence of a continuum of acceptable behavior for either gender. Although prescriptions of society are powerful factors contributing to human behavior, they do not subsume the multiple, diverse contributions of simultaneous roles that people enact. These broad categories blur the distinctions among role prescriptions that arise from the individual's particular locale and simultaneous membership in multiple roles in terms of gender, race, and class. "Since most people in pluralistic societies participate simultaneously in more than one reference group [a group whose values guide one's actions], the picture becomes more complicated" (Shibutani, 1961, p. 275).

Tice (1990) argued that the very use of dichotomous (role) categories are themselves oppressive. For example, feminists have suggested that gender role descriptions convey "the sense of roles being fixed and dichotomous as well as separate but equal" (Hare-Mustin, 1989, p. 72). This approach also implies a harmonious balance in roles, and hence may obscure conflict and power differentials (Gottlieb, 1987; Valentich & Gripton, 1984). Practitioners should neither focus on whether to ignore or address role differences in social work practice nor on the reality that the construction of gender opposites in therapy can be dangerous. Rather, "to see both sides of a problem is the surest way to prevent its solution, because there are always more than two sides" (Hare-Mustin, 1989, p. 69). Instead of creating false dichotomies, Hare-Mustin suggested the construction of client-practitioner reality within the therapy, which considers the social, economic, and political context and the inequalities of power that accompany class, race, gender, and age. Sands and Nuccio (1992) specifically urged feminists to speak of a *particular* woman, rather than the universal woman. Such advice is compatible with that of contemporary social constructionists, who emphasize the subjective meaning attached to the individual's perception of the role prescription. Social constructionists also renew concern that the complex meaning of events and behaviors needs to be understood from a client-centered perspective (Scott, 1989; see Chapter 7).

Types of Roles

Role theory holds that all organized groups have a division of labor; the delineation of these labor roles establishes the status structure, for which reciprocal roles, in turn, are defined:

> It is the relation of the individual's perception of his [or her] own role to its perception by others that largely determines the nature of his [or her] social functioning. Status is a "structural" term indicating the individual's location in a given framework or hierarchy of positions; role is a "functional" concept, indicating how the individual is expected to behave in that status. (Linton, 1936, p. 171)

All individuals are simultaneously engaged in a multiplicity of roles (e.g., career woman, wife, mother, group spokesperson, daughter, friend, sister, activist, student, and teacher). Individuals enact multiple roles both within as well as across several categories; moreover, they show idiosyncratic variations in their commitments to each role, and those commitments also vary across time for the same individuals. Multiple role engagement creates opportunity for role conflict between different simultaneously enacted roles and for role strain, but it also creates opportunity for stress-buffering effects of one role to offset stress-creating effects of another role (Billings & Moos, 1982).

One way to summarize the various types of roles is with regard to the levels of group organization to which they apply: Some roles are specific (l) to the microlevel of family and a circle of close friends; (2) to the mesolevel of community and other nonfamily small groups or organizations; (3) and to the macrolevels of national (or global) organization. In addition, still other roles may be thought of as "cross-cutting" the micro-, meso-, and macrolevels; these cross-cutting roles are triggered by the given personal biological characteristics of the person such as gender, race, and age) and by group process dynamics such as scapegoat, caretaker or leader (see Figure 6.2).

Undoubtedly, much of the attractiveness of role theory to social scientists has been its applicability to macro- (organizational) as well as micro- (individual) phenomena. For example, a given social structure may be viewed as a system of role behaviors. To the extent to which individuals in a society enact normative role behaviors—that is, fulfill their socially obligated behaviors—social structure is maintained (Merton, 1957a, 1958; Parsons, 1942). An application of this assumption of role theory provided Max Weber (1958a,b) and others with the conceptual tools for explicating an organizational model known as bureaucracy. Key to their concept of bureaucracy was rational role assignment, based solely on technical qualifications (Merton, 1957b), disciplined engagement in prescribed roles by occupants, and a resulting status structure that avoided role confusion, ambiguity, and conflict (Reissman, 1958).

Just as the organizational theorists have drawn from role theory to develop models of organizational behavior, those theorists interested in personality development have used role theory concepts as explanatory vehicles. To better understand behavior, Hollingshead and Redlich (1958a,b) joined social role and social stratification concepts: Their research attempted to link social class with incidence of mental illness. Similarly, Davis and Havighurst (1958) and others (Aronson & Overall, 1966; Mayer & Timms, 1969; Rebecca, Hefner, & Olishansky, 1976) proposed an association between social class, color differences, and child rearing.

However, such linkage of cultural demands, behavioral traits, and adherence to roles has since been seriously questioned, especially the validity of trait theories founded on social class of family of origin in the United States.

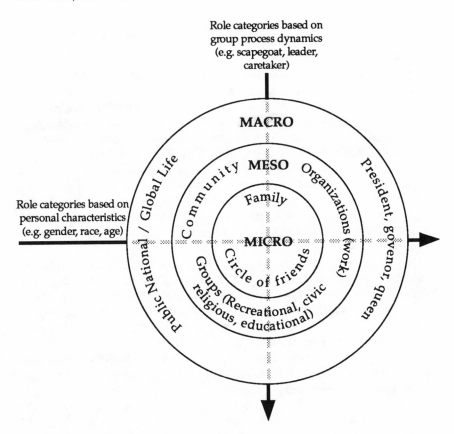

Figure 6.2.   Types of roles: levels and categories.

Since the democratization of higher education, which resulted from the GI Bill following World War II, role expectations are at least as profoundly shaped by the person's educational attainment as the family of origin (Coleman and Rainwater, 1978). Moreover, Green (1982) challenged the categorical approach to ethnicity based on these early writings and suggested that the process of interaction between and within groups be the focus of attention.

Because roles are interrelated, what constitutes a claim for one party is an obligation for another. Longres and Bailey (1979) contended, for example, that female liberation must consider male liberation. Role expectations, therefore, are influenced by the interactive contexts in which people find themselves. An individual's role must be viewed in reference to other roles, usually those that are paired, such as parent–child or client–social worker (Figure 6.1).

Role Variations and Changing Role Expectations

Early contributors to role theory observed that although "roles are cultur-ally determined patterns of behavior, [and the] culture sets the limits of vari-ation of roles, . . . alternative roles may be available in a given culture" (Sutherland and Woodward, 1940, pp. 250–253). Symbolic interactionists who studied role performance (Mead, 1934) proposed that social position, role, authority, and prestige were derived from how people behaved toward one another; thus the fit of societal members is not predetermined (Blumer, 1969). That is, behavior cannot be understood by simply examining "status positions, cultural prescriptions, norms, values, sanctions, role demands, and social system requirements" (p. 7). Rather, behavior must be understood by examining social interaction (social role performance) and the meaning that people attribute to it (perception and values attached to social role perfor-mance).

Stigmatized roles are an outcome of social interaction, and consist of "dis-credited," "tainted," or "discounted" attributes (Goffman, 1963, p. 3). Plac-ing an individual in a stigmatized role is understood as a means of creating social distance and justifying social control (Wolfensberger, 1972). Stigma-tized individuals—for example, those who may have a mental or physical disorder, be imprisoned, be unemployed, or be a member of a particular race or religion—are characterized as possessing "an undesired differentness from what the group anticipated." This stigmatization could be used to oppress or usurp power from those individuals (Goffman, 1963, p. 5).

Role expectations vary not only in culturally relative and culturally dis-tinctive ways but, within a given culture, with regard to their clarity and rigid-ity. When societies (or communities) are relatively stable, a person's status is relatively clear, with limited tolerance for variation. In a rapidly changing so-ciety, there is less consensus over rights and duties of these various positions, and the avenues of advancement or variation are not so clearly marked. When rigidly held role prescriptions are challenged by large numbers of peo-ple—as occurs in periods of rapid social change—reactions are stimulated to reaffirm the "old order" and considerable social conflict surrounds role prescription.

Lipman-Blumen (1976) cautioned that "there is nothing intrinsically neg-ative about changing roles" (p. 67). For example, the increase in female-headed households and greater labor force participation of women signal changing roles for men and women in our society; although the valuation of these changes may differ widely among different members of the society, the changes themselves are inherently neither good nor bad.

Nonetheless, the impacts of rapid social change in the United States on the emergence of social conflict over role prescriptions confront people daily. During recent decades, demographic, socioeconomic, and political circumstances have dramatically changed this society. These changes, coupled with political events such as the civil rights movement, the war on poverty, and the women's movement, have brought about a serious reexamination of fundamental beliefs, values, and standards for social behavior. As a result, many of the ground rules for how people behave and express their needs have become ambiguous, if not challenged outright. According to Martin and O'-Connor (1989), the phenomenon of ambiguous roles is so common that the "hegemony of a few values, norms, and mores that formerly constrained the actions of family, neighbor, friend, and stranger has given away to a variety of competing standards" (pp. 5–6).

Normative expectations, or common understandings for role behavior, depend, among other things, on gender, age, and class (Davis, 1986). *Sex typing*, a process through which a culture socializes male and female children into masculine and feminine adults, is a key example of how culture prescribes behavioral norms for what is appropriate behavior. Bem (1974, 1981, 1987) has argued that because each person's culture implicitly and explicitly communicates that gender is one of the most important categories in social life, children develop a "spontaneous readiness to impose a gender-based classification system on social reality, a spontaneous readiness to see reality as carved naturally into gender categories" (1987, pp. 264–265).

Standards for what constitutes appropriate emotional behaviors are evaluated and constructed socially (Shields, 1987). In a study to explore the social meaning of emotional behavior, Shields found a double standard for how people viewed emotionality. For example, in the case of anger, different criteria were applied in evaluating anger displays in men than in women.

Such examples illustrate the power of gender role stereotypes in U.S. society. Each gender is evaluated differently on the basis of social norms or beliefs about what is appropriate behavior for men and women. Long ago, Florence Kluckhohn (1953) noted:

> The role of the woman in the United States is as little understood for its variant character as are some of the differences in social classes. Although it is frequently stated that the feminine role is poorly defined and full of contradictions, it has not been noted that the behavior expected of women in the wife-mother role is relative to value orientations which are markedly different from the dominant American values that are so well expressed in the man's occupational role. (p. 356)

Bem (1974) has suggested that people be viewed as possessing varying combinations of behavior that may be thought of as masculine or feminine. Alternatively, Rebecca, Hefner, and Oleshansky (1976) proposed that the sweeping societal changes in roles for men and women suggest a model of gender role transcendence. *Transcendence* is "an atmosphere in which

choices are no longer traced even to the concepts of masculinity and femi-
ninity" (p. 162).

Hare-Mustin (1989) pointed out that in the 1950s, when family therapy began, the family was different than in subsequent eras—people married
younger, had larger families, and fewer women worked outside the home.
These societal conditions became equated with gender role stereotypes that
account for much of the polarity and inequality between the two genders and
that often underpin the theory base that is currently used in the clinical hour.

Theorists concerned with women's issues have called for a reexamination
of the assumptions about women's work and family roles (McGoldrick, Anderson, & Walsh, 1989). Because of changing gender/sex, racial/ethnic, gen-
erational, and occupational roles created by society, social work theorists
have questioned how newly sought identities and role definitions affect social work practice (Berlin, 1976a,b; Chafetz, 1972; Fischer, Dulaney, Fazio,
Hudak, & Zivotofsky, 1976; Kravetz, 1976; Schwartz, 1974; Thomas, 1977).
For example, Hopkins (1973) argued that social work agencies need to review their policies that support or negate the social role prescription for
"manhood" for African-American men. In addition, Hanson (1980) pointed
out that with urbanization over past decades, American Indian women have
experienced difficult transitions as they move from the role of homemaker to
breadwinner. Hanson added that these changes have created a demand for
more active participation of American Indian women in all phases of life that
needs to be appreciated by social service providers.

APPLICATIONS OF ROLE THEORY TO SOCIAL WORK PRACTICE

*The utilization of role theory in the study phase would inevitably induce the
worker to investigate what demands for social performance are being made on
the client, by whom, and in what social context* (Strean, 1974, p. 329)

Role theory has been used in social work assessment and intervention to
better understand clients' many roles, their prescribed patterns of behavior,
and the valuation of associated gratification and stress that may affect social
functioning of individuals, families, groups, communities, and organizations
and the client–social worker relationship.

Assessment

From the role theory orientation to client assessment, social workers attempt to understand the client's perception of her or his various roles, and to

discern the impacts of role expectations arising from the client's original and current ethnic group, religion, social class norms, and community norms that impinge upon the client's ideas, feelings, and behavior (Strean, 1974). Role analysis requires that social workers obtain a full picture of the client's person-environment context; hence social workers may comprehend the complexities and ramifications of the client's presenting problem.

In addition, a role analysis includes all the social role demands that contribute to the client's social functioning. For example, it includes the fact that a woman is a wife, a mother, a daughter, and a worker and that she is expected to be a wife, mother, daughter, and worker in highly particularized ways, shaped by the past as well as current context and reference groups. It includes attention to how these multiple roles interact with each other; with other ascribed roles (such as race, gender, class, age); with the client's location in a particular time and culture; and with roles prescribed to others with whom the client is in reciprocal role relationships. Included in a comprehensive role assessment must also be a refined knowledge of the normative role expectations specific to the client's geographic locale, which in turn further texturizes each role expectation/enactment. Hence role analysis requires inclusion of socioeconomic, cultural, and biopsychological data (Hamilton, [1940] 1951).

Several dimensions of social role may be considered in a comprehensive social work assessment approached from the perspectives advanced by role theory:

1. *Assessment of role competency as the basis for determining social functioning.* Examination of role competency provides for assessment specifically focused on social functioning and thereby is especially beneficial for social work practice. Table 6.2 provides guidelines for assessing role performance of clients. Adapted from work by John O'Brien and Ron Gerhard in 1978, these guidelines offer an approach to client assessment that examines competency in various social roles as the centerpiece of evaluation in a mental health system.

> Assessing role performance emphasizes the client's current behaviors and opportunities to interact. Such goal directed behaviors are related to fundamental social needs and expectancies. Most adults have (or need opportunities to have) primary connections in a number of the following role areas:
>
> In the immediate household and with extended family,
> With their spouse or life-partner,
> With child(ren),
> With friends,
> With neighbors and community groups,
> With associates on a job
> With other teaching and helping persons/agencies. (p.16)

Table 6.2.   Role Theory: Practitioner's Guide to Assessment

Various role behaviors may be identified as associated with competent social role functioning by adults within the context of the sociocultural milieu in which the client lives
and the reference groups with which the client is identified. While these will therefore
vary relative to the relevant sociocultural characteristics of the person-in-situation, the
following roles and role behaviors (not in any order of priority) are generally considered as associated with competency in social role performance in American society:

Household/family member
   Persons who live alone or with others perform many of the following role behaviors: household upkeep and cleaning; shopping for, planning, and preparing
   meals; laundry, ironing, mending; tending to yards; scheduling and contracting
   with others for maintenance of property and furnishings; decorating and purchas-
   ing furnishings and equipment; managing finances; utilizing the property and
   conducting activities within the household according to the norms of the immediate neighborhood and laws of the community.

Self–health care
   Social role competency in this role is enacted on two levels:
   (1)   Competency is reflected in the ability to self-monitor one's health status and
         practice good principles of self-care. For example, the following competen-
         cies will be noted: Daily self-care such as bathing, and care of hair and
         teeth; dressing according to the season, weather, and immediate environ-
         mental conditions; carrying out a routine of regular exercise appropriate to
         one's age and health status; eating nutritious meals and appropriate quanti-
         ties of food at appropriate intervals; moderation in use of alcohol and avoid-
         ance of drugs not prescribed by one's physician; appropriate use of first aid
         materials and procedures; engagement in safety procedures (e.g., buckling
         the seatbelt in a car and attending to safety precautions in transportation, in-
         cluding avoiding activities such as picking up hitchhikers, walking alone in
         dangerous areas and/or when others are not about).
   (2)   Competency is also reflected in the ability to negotiate the arrangements for
         medical assistance. These include: making and keeping medical appoint-
         ments; following through on medical directions (e.g., securing and taking
         prescribed medications according to directions); filling out forms for finan-
         cial payment of medical services; staying abreast of medical benefits and
         making arrangements for changing and applying for those as appropriate;
         and, in some cases where the labyrinth of paperwork and interpretations of
         rules governing coverage are so complicated, making arrangements for an
         expert to manage these affairs.

Worker/wage earner
   A central role in American society for all adults, competency in the role of work-
   er/wage earner includes: development of knowledge and skill for doing selected
   work, finding opportunities for being hired for that work, and negotiating the ap-
   plication/hiring process for employment; carrying out the expected responsibilities of the position in a way that meets the normative expectations within the
   work setting; engaging in interactions, communications, and appropriate acts of
   mutual aid with colleagues and bosses; engaging in appropriate social activities
   with others in the work setting (e.g., going out to lunch, planning and participating in a retirement party). Some work requires that the person be more proactive

(continued)

Table 6.2. (*Continued*)

in developing relationships with work peers; for example, the solo entrepreneur, a telecommunicating secretary, or private practitioner in a solo or small group practice will have much less opportunity for contact with peers engaged in similar work than in a large central office, plant, or agency. Hence, greater social competency in the interpersonal aspects of the work role are required for the more isolated worker who must reach out and proactively develop a work-related social network.

Friend

Indicators of social role performance in the role of friend include: satisfactory interactions with males and females; maintenance of regular contacts and interactions with a number of adult friends outside the family; activities of a reciprocal nature—e.g., planning and engaging in celebration of important events in the lives of others such as birthdays, holidays, and anniversaries, and planning and engaging in ongoing social activities with other adults; giving and receiving help in times of stress/need.

Spouse/life-partner

Role behaviors include competencies in: interpersonal communications; planning and participating in shared activities; planning and participation in shared responsibilities; sexual interactions; giving and receiving mutual aid and support; and many of the competencies noted above for the friend and household/family member roles.

Parent

Clients in parental roles must carry out responsibilities appropriate to the need of the child(ren) and conduct interpersonal communications and interactions consistent with community norms for parent roles. For example, competent role performance includes requirements to: provide a safe physical and interpersonal environment appropriate to the age of the child(ren); provide appropriate structure for the child(ren)'s age-appropriate activities; assist the child(ren) in effective engagement in age-appropriate child roles (e.g., dress, play, learning of problem-solving skills, coaching re appropriate social interaction); teach and model skills for living and culturally expected future role performance; communicate values of the social group to which the client belongs; demonstrate affection, concern, and caring in culture and age-appropriate ways.

Neighbor/community member

The ability to participate in the life of the social group in the immediate environment of the person's residence indicates social role competency as a neighbor/community member. Among the behaviors related to this role might be: sharing resources (e.g., tools, garden vegetables or flowers) with neighbors; participation in mutual aid (e.g., babysitting, taking in the mail for neighbors on vacation, cooking for a sick neighbor); participation in social and political efforts of interest to the neighborhood (e.g., banding together with others in rent control efforts in a building or to affect a zoning change in the immediate neighborhood). Assessment of social role performance in this role should attend not only to the types of activities but to the extent to which the person is engaged with people and issues in immediate proximity to her/his residence and/or extending from that immediate cluster to a wider and wider community (e.g., coalition of neighborhoods, city, state)

(*continued*)

Table 6.2. *(Continued)*

Educational consumer

Adults improve their social functioning through lifelong learning and engage-ment in informal and formal learning projects. Social role competency as an edu-cational consumer is reflected in: skilled use of educational resources in the person's community (e.g., library, public lectures/presentations, museums); plan-ning for and engagement in travel; enrollment in sponsored educational pro-grams (e.g., YWCA programs, university degree and nondegree programs); subscribing to and reading newspapers and magazines; watching educationally informative programs on TV.

Public services consumer

Many clients must develop considerable competencies as consumers of human services. These are similar to those noted under the role of self–health care and under the role of educational consumer, except these are applied to programs with a specific service needed for maintenance of many of the other social roles noted above. Examples of these competencies include, in addition: practical knowledge of the benefits offered by different programs and how they relate to one's needs; skill in locating these programs, inquiring about their applicability to one's situation, applying for service; making appointments or securing applica-tions and documents; providing information as needed to secure benefits; engag-ing in professional interviews through which service may be dispensed; following through on required activities to maintain services; when fees are charged, providing for financial arrangements to meet those; when needed, filing complaints and appeals related to the provision of services.

Citizen

Social functioning in this role is closely related to aspects of the neighbor/com-munity member role but implies broader participation in the society than just at the immediate neighborhood or community level. In addition to the competen-cies already noted, this would include: keeping informed of sociopolitical ideas, policies, events; participating in social action and political activities; voting; en-gaging in discussions with others concerning broad social issues and concerns; contributing money to social/political causes; volunteering to provide service in social programs.

Whenever possible, asking open-ended questions to assess role performance is rec-ommended. For example, in asking clients what a typical day (weekend, week) is like (at home, at work, etc), clients often signal the presence or severance of friend-ships or attachments to other support systems. Specific leads may then be followed in the context of the client's reported recollections.

Source: Adapted and expanded from original materials prepared for mental health workers in the Georgia Mental Health Institute Consortium by John O'Brien & Ron Gerhard, 1978, Atlanta.

2. *Assessment of the impacts of multiple roles and expectations on so-cial functioning.* Because roles prescribe the daily interactions between persons, social workers can also use role analysis to better understand how a client is meeting his or her needs in "a complex of roles" (Anderson & Carter, 1984, p. 53). For most people, engagement in multiple and varied roles—assuming that enough of these roles are in statuses valued by their so-

cial group and society as a whole—characterizes the "good life." Barriers to role taking or competency may be evaluated as an entree to understanding the discontinuities in the person-environment fit.

3. *Assessment of the stressors arising from role conflict as an approach to evaluating social functioning.*   Two contradictory sets of prescriptions for an individual's role performance, requiring that the person respond simultaneously to incompatible expectations, inevitably causing the person to violate someone's expectations, creates considerable tension. Parsons (1951) proposed that having conflicting sets of legitimized role expectations is an obvious source of strain and frustration, causing difficulty at the personality level (for the individual) and with the interaction system. During the following years, feminists maintained that the expectation that women will simultaneously be "feminine" and "act just like a man" in the workplace holds great potential for role conflict (Freeman, 1984; Hooyman & Cunningham, 1986).

4. *Assessment of the impacts on role performance arising from role overload on social functioning.*   The concept of *role overload* refers to occasions when a person must perform a series of roles that are not necessarily in conflict but are more demanding than she or he can handle. Single mothers in the United States, increasingly living with their children in conditions of poverty, comprise a large group of people in contemporary American society who are especially vulnerable to role overload. Likewise, single fathers, a small but growing client population and albeit with substantially greater financial resources with which to purchase auxiliary services, experience similar difficulty with simultaneously maintaining successful role performance as they juggle child care and home management with wage-earning responsibilities.

5. *Assessment of consequences for individuals and families generated by discomplementarity in family roles.*   Role theorists are interested in how family members enact numerous roles on a daily basis, all of which are played out with other family members. These theorists propose that a process of defining the rights and duties associated with family membership and deciding what is desirable in a particular family results in a complicated pattern of role relationships. Understanding mutually dependent and reciprocal roles and how and whether there is a harmonious fit is the key to understanding the family unit (Parsons, 1964; Parsons & Bales, 1955; McGoldrick, 1990). Concerted or joint action is facilitated when people play conventional or well-established roles and share the way in which roles are defined. As long as people agree about the claims and obligations that constitute their respective parts, role reciprocity or cooperation is maintained (Shibutani, 1961). This, however, does not mean that all role occupants equally prosper or benefit (McGoldrick, 1989).

Because the concept of role complementarity emphasizes the mutual meeting of needs through social interaction in small groups, it has been used in the assessment and intervention processes in family-focused social work practice. In fact, family interventions may be viewed as an attempt to modify and enhance family role performance and has been integrated into social systems thinking (Greene, 1986; Martin & O'Connor, 1989; Strean, 1974). However, role complementarity may fail for a variety of reasons: cognitive discrepancy, when one or both parties involved in the relationship are not familiar with the role requirements; discrepancy of goals, situations in which the immediate or ultimate goal of a role is unclear; allocative discrepancy, which involves questions about how a role is to be allocated or who has the right to a specific role; instrumental discrepancy, in which the technical equipment, physical facilities, or instrumental prerequisites for role performance are unavailable; and discrepancy in cultural value orientations, in which there are differences in cultural values about the performance of the role (Spiegel, 1968).

Cross-cultural research has suggested that there may be great differences in how families enact roles (Ho, 1987; Tseng & Hsu, 1991). Among the differences that lead to differential assessment and intervention are family value systems, sociopolitical histories, role definitions and structures, communication patterns, and relative acculturation to U.S. culture. These differences also affect who a family turns to for help, how a family defines their problem, and their specific help-seeking behaviors and expectations (see Chapter 8).

An extensive body of literature also has addressed the issue of role complementarity from a feminist perspective. For example, Boss and Thorne (1989) suggested that practitioners need to rethink the notions of family balance and role complementarity. Social workers must recognize that families exist in a larger societal, sometimes disruptive context; that conflict may coexist with equilibrium or balance-seeking activities; and that power distribution in families is unequal. For example, it is not professionally ethical to encourage maintenance of homeostasis within families in which there is a battered wife, or "in which one parent is locked in an alcoholic pattern of self-destruction and the other into martyrdom" (p. 87). McGoldrick (1989) even argued that until the difference in economic power (usually in favor of the husband in a couple) is addressed with practical steps that equalize access to financial resources, it is not professionally ethical to engage the partners in marital counseling.

Redefining Family Roles

Sociologists who examine how groups achieve consensus and shared values, and how social systems meet their needs and goals as well as maintain

relatively harmonious functioning are called *structural functionalists* (Merton, 1957a,b; Parsons, 1954, 1964). In their study of human affairs, structural functionalists emphasize an examination of the social system as a whole (see Chapter 8), as well as the component parts—the persons or groups of persons who interact and mutually influence each other's behavior within that system. From this perspective, "the behavior of the system and its components [or role performances] is determined by the total system's needs and goals" (Anderson & Carter, 1984, p. 4).

Parsons (1954), a major functionalist theorist, developed a framework for family functioning that greatly affected social work practice. He focused on how the family functioned and maintained itself as a unit based on the role assignment of its members. His portrayal of the family made from the 1940s to the 1960s, generally emphasized a married couple and their children or the nuclear family, and was defined as having two major functions: (1) socializing children, or imparting societal values and beliefs, and (2) maintaining the emotional health of family members. He also viewed age and gender as critical organizing features of the family that translated into two dichotomous roles: (1) the male *instrumental role*, which focuses on getting things done by earning a living outside the family, and (2) the female *expressive* role, which emphasizes nurturance and caretaking inside the family. The conceptualization of the stay-at-home mother and a breadwinning father became known as "the normal family" (Boss & Thorne, 1989, p. 79):

> The wife/mother is excluded from the struggle for power and prestige in the occupational sphere. . . . It is of course possible for [her] to follow the masculine patterns and seek a career . . . in direct competition with men of her own class [but] this could only be [accompanied by] profound alterations in the structure of the family. (Parsons, 1964, pp. 258–259)

Feminists scholars and others have challenged these gender-based role definitions (Adamek, 1982; Lipman-Blumen, 1976). For example, Romero (1977) suggested that such a conception of what is considered masculine or feminine is a gender bias that permeates the social work knowledge base and therefore affects research and practice. Jackson (1977a,b), a pioneer in the family therapy movement, replaced the concept of gender roles with that of family rules. *Family rules*, which are the implicit or explicit norms that organize family interaction, function to maintain a stable system, sometimes limiting expression of a family member's behavior. However, rules are not necessarily stereotypes, cultural preconceptions, or a priori categories about proper role behavior. In addition, Jackson argued for a theory of marriage that focused on the interactional and collaborative aspects of the relationship (see Chapter 9 for a discussion of family interventions).

Social work theorists also have questioned whether the practitioner's theoretical orientation has influenced attitudes toward women (Davenport &

Reims, 1978). For example, Boss and Thorne (1989) criticized structuralist theory for perpetuating stereotypes and inequality as well as jeopardizing counseling and therapy outcomes for women. They credited Jackson (1977a,b) with advancing the family therapy field through his implication that each spouse enters a marital relationship as an equal partner with freedom to define any rules. Boss and Thorne (1989) also proposed that both instrumental and expressive tasks—not roles—have to be carried out in families, and that both males and females should learn how to handle all family tasks.

The structuralist view of role definition also was challenged because it presented an idyllic view of a family unencumbered by multiple demands, or issues of power and conflict. For example, Sherman (1976) spoke to the social work therapists "tensions, awkwardness, and internal conflicts," because as practitioners they are "caught in a time of transition in contradictions, or incongruence, between conflicting pressures in our body politic, our economy, and families [producing] changes in socially expected behavior" (p. 94). He pointed out that as a man, he did not stand aside and observe. Rather, he was involved in the changing gender roles in a way that he needed to understand in order to be an effective practitioner.

Practitioners have worked to change what many believe to be an outdated and romanticized view of the family. This view of the family did not recognize or legitimate a range of family structures, including situations of single women and men, single-parent families, extended families, lesbian and gay households, child-free heterosexual couples, elderly unmarried couples, and elderly communities (Boss & Thorne, 1989).

At a time when long-standing assumptions about the family are being challenged, Walsh and Scheinkman (1989) call for practitioners to reexamine the gender dimensions in models of family therapy. They propose that the target of the reexamination should be the assumptions about the role of gender in family functioning and in problem development and maintenance as well as how gender is considered in therapeutic objectives. In order to address gender issues, they believe that "models of change need to be accompanied by models of family functioning, relative to varying economic and cultural contexts and fitting the particular developmental tasks and environmental demands" (p. 38).

THE CLIENT–SOCIAL WORKER RELATIONSHIP: CLARIFYING RESPECTIVE ROLE EXPECTATIONS

An understanding of role conflict, in the client, in the worker-client relationship, often in the practitioner's own roles, is especially important because of the strains such conflict can create. (Hamilton, 1958a, xiii)

One of the most important tasks specific to the study or assessment phase is clarification of respective role expectations. Role theory postulates a set of expected behaviors patterned with a partner in a reciprocal relationship. From the perspective of role theory, the client–social worker relationship is considered to be "paradigmatic treatment" in which the treatment situation "becomes a model [or representation] of the world, a stage on which all possible dramas and roles may be played out" (Nelson, Nelson, Sherman, and Strean, 1968, p. 123). Both client and social worker occupy many roles or social positions. By examining the client–social worker relationship as a social system comprised of complementary roles, the social worker can better understand that no role exists in isolation. Understanding role performance of both the client and the social worker, then, is critical to the helping process (Coleman & Nelson, 1957).

Furthermore, the role of the social worker is prescribed by expectations of others, how the social worker perceives the role, and how he or she enacts the role. Therefore, the practitioner must not only consider the role expectations of clients, but must become aware of his or her perceptions, behaviors, feelings, and "special vulnerabilities" arising from role expectations the social worker brings to the therapeutic encounter (Greene, 1986, p. 215).

Social theorists have suggested that when an individual enters the presence of another person, she or he attempts to acquire as much information about the other as possible. Such information helps a person *define the situation*, that is, the person's behavior is not a response directly to environment, but "constitutes a succession of adjustments to interpretations of what is going on" (Shibutani, 1961, p. 41). "Information about the individual helps to define the situation, enabling others to know in advance what he [or she] will expect of them and what they may expect of him [or her]" (Goffman, 1959, p. 1). People move into each situation with general ideas about how to orient themselves in that situation. For example, as clients approach the reception desk of a social agency for the first time, they will bring with them a particular notion of how to behave in their role.

According to Davis (1986), the literature contains considerable information documenting the differences in role expectations between what "good" clients and "good" social workers do. This lack of congruence between social worker and client expectations regarding their respective roles may jeopardize the help-seeking/help-rendering transactions or interfere with "starting where the client is."

During the late 1960s and 1970s, several researchers found that practitioner failure to clarify mutual role expectations led to discontinuance from therapy (Aronson & Overall, 1966; Perlman, 1968; Rhodes, 1977). Client dissatisfaction arose when clients and social workers had substantially different perceptions of the therapist's activities. Clients often were unaware of social workers' approaches to problem-solving; social workers tended not to carefully explore client requests carefully, and, in the contracting procedures, the therapist's ideas overshadowed those of the client. From this perspective, barriers between client and social worker resulted because client expectations were not clear to social workers, and clients were not fully aware of the social worker's expectations (Perlman, 1962).

Client dropout, or premature termination of service, is frequently attributed to failure to negotiate a mutually agreed-upon set of expectations for social worker–client interactions in the initial assessment phase (Turner 1974). Turner contended that the role prescribed by many social workers for assessment may be unacceptable to the client. Among other things, social workers may expect clients to involve themselves in the relationship, attend regularly scheduled appointments, reveal secrets, and listen to the social worker's supportive and clarifying remarks. Clients may "fail" in their *role complementarity*, the fit of roles, because they may be unfamiliar with the role they are expected to assume, they may not possess the necessary skills for the role, they may refuse to accept the role because the role described by social workers does not fit with their idea of the role, and there may be a discrepancy in the cultural value orientation between clients and social workers (Greenson, 1955; Turner, 1974).

To assist in overcoming these difficulties, Hepworth and Larsen (1990) have proposed developing a process of educating clients to more appropriate role behaviors and clarifying the roles of both clients and practitioners. This mutual client–social worker discussion of role expectations and goals— *role induction*—is achieved by determining the client expectations, explaining the nature of the helping process, and defining the client–social worker relationship as partners seeking a common solution (Hepworth and Larsen, 1990). For example, Tsui and Schultz (1985) emphasized the relevance of explaining to Asian-Americans why social workers ask questions to ascertain information about mental health problems:

> The therapist must explicitly educate the client about the purpose of questions regarding clinical history, previous treatment information, family background, and psychological stressors. The linkage of these issues to their current symptoms is not clear to many Asian clients. Many Asian clients conceive of mental distress as the result of physiological disorder or character flaws. This issue must be dealt with sensitively before any sensible therapeutic work can be effected. (pp. 567–568)

Practice models and assumptions about appropriate client goals are affected dramatically by the degree and speed of societal change. Because of the changing standards for role behavior, the social work profession has a reexamined of many of its theoretical approaches as well as challenges to its traditional methods of social services delivery. Social work practitioners have been asked to respond to these societal changes and the role stereotyping and ambiguity associated with role performance (Goldner, 1989; Hanson, 1980; Hopkins, 1973).

For example, Berlin (1976a) questioned how women socialized for "dependent" and "self-effacing" roles could better be helped by social workers in direct practice (p. 492). Thomas (1977) inquired if therapists could be helpful to women if practitioners subscribed to gender stereotypes regarding "so-called appropriate behaviors, lifestyles, and roles" (p. 449). In a study of social work with wealthy clients, McKamy (1976) explored whether effective services could be delivered if the client and social worker come from different socioeconomic statuses and do not share similar role expectations for social work treatment. Mosteller (1963) observed that the similarity between the worker's and client's commitment to upward mobility was more significant than similarities in their social class of origin in predicting successful outcomes of social work service for clients.

The role concept, then, has allowed social work theorists such as Hollis (1964) to conceptualize the client–social worker relationship as a set of mutual expectations:

> Where the caseworker . . . is dealing with a client from an ethnic background not completely familiar to [the caseworker], certain questions should inevitably occur to him [or her]. What, for example, is the client's image of the agency, in view of his [or her] ethnic background? [The client] may be culturally oriented to see the agency as distant and authoritative, as in the case of the Spanish-American, or as an opponent he [or she] must pressure, cajole, and match wits with. What may seem like a manipulative quality in a client may turn out to be simply a natural tendency carried over from previous experience and having little bearing on [the client's] basic personality (Stein & Cloward, 1958, p. 5)

This quote illustrates both the contributions and limitations of role theory as applied to practice. Role theory draws the social worker's attention to cultural expectations but simultaneously leads to overgeneralized and stereotyped assumptions about the client; on the one hand, it calls for the suspension of the social worker's assumptions about behavior based on her or his own role expectations of the other but leads her or him to other assumptions that may be equally inaccurate, although based on role prescriptions normative to the client's cultural origins.

How an applicant undertakes the role of client does not clarify how the social worker utilizes knowledge of the client's role-embedded context in cross cultural social work. By becoming more aware of the client's reference groups, the social worker may more readily understand the client's social standards (expectations of how a role should be played), likely reference group sanctions, and a preference for some values and behaviors (Strean,

1971). Yet, simultaneously, social workers must be alert to the clues from clients regarding individual differences from the norms of the reference group, the degree of identification with the norms and the group, and potential conflicts arising from a clients' efforts to manage an array of role expectations that may be in conflict with their current statuses or family and culture of origin. Practitioners must also examine these issues for themselves.

Roots of role performance standards and expectations primarily lie in the larger social systems, which often have tremendous investment in how a particular role is carried out and in role assignment itself. Goffman (1959, 1967) and Wolfensberger (1972) have drawn attention to the way in which the sick role, for example, is enhanced by medicalization of differences; psychopathology provides the categories for human behavior at variance with the social norm. Labels arising from medical categories, then, are treated as though they are realities rather than social constructions. This serves society by containing and segregating social deviants, protecting and preserving the system of statuses and power represented by the normative in the status quo.

Strean (1974) has suggested that the psychoanalytic concept of transference be viewed from a role perspective. *Transference* is the "client's efforts to induce the [social] worker to abandon his [or her] chosen role of either helper, explorer, or environmental manipulator and instead project roles of parent, sibling, etc." (p. 334); see Chapter 3 for a discussion of transference). Greene (1986) also has contended that understanding the client–social worker encounter as a pattern of reciprocal roles allows social workers to communicate more effectively and to address distortions in the communication process. Such an interactional view recognizes the potential for certain client groups to evoke countertherapeutic responses. That is, certain client groups, such as the mentally or physically disabled or the aged may be more likely to elicit problematic responses from a particular social worker. These responses may be understood as a divergence in role expectations or role enactment between therapist and client (Greene, 1986).

Overall, social role theory is conceptually fertile, spawning constructs for both assessment and change strategies. Application of this theory is especially germane in the quest for effective cross-cultural and gender-sensitive social work practice.

A Constructionist Approach With Diverse Populations   7

Robert Blundo, Roberta R. Greene, and Paul Gallant

*Man is an animal suspended in the web of significance he himself has spun,
and culture is the name given to this web of meaning.*

(Geertz, 1973, p. 4)

Social constructionists are part of the postmodern movement, which devalues the search for universal laws and theories, emphasizes localized experiences, and recognizes differences (Fraser, Taylor, Jackson, & O'Jack, 1991; Sands & Nuccio, 1992). Social constructionists suggest that local or personal understandings help reduce stereotypes and promote firsthand understanding. Furthermore, they believe that personal meanings and views of social reality grow out of interaction and discourse in daily life experiences (Gergen & Gergen, 1983). These theorists also recognize that individual and family meanings are "socially constituted within the context of the present sociopolitical juncture" (Lowe, 1991, p. 47). Therefore, social constructivist therapies have the potential "to relate to themes of justice, poverty, gender, politics, and power" (p. 47). Social constructionists also contend that their interest in multiple perspectives emphasizes communal belief systems, an emphasis that is useful in clinical practice (Lax, 1992; McNamee & Gergen, 1992).

The social constructionist concept of culture is the expression of historically shared meanings of a community of people. The meanings emerge within the context of human interaction and are continually transformed during that transaction. Culture does not exist as an entity, even though people often speak of culture as if it had a permanent and unchangeable form. A social constructivist perspective recognizes "cultures as texts . . . [which therefore are] differently read, differently construed, by men and women, young and old, expert and nonexpert, even in the least complex societies" (Keesing, 1987, p. 161).

Culture thus is not recognized as a monolithic stereotype of groups of people. Attempts to draw broad cultural pictures of peoples does injustice to any particular individual who does not match this stereotypical version of a culture. For example, although it might be said that Puerto Rican people inhabit the world of two spiritual belief systems—the Roman Catholic Church and *Botanicas*, that is the practices of visiting the *espiritistas* (spiritist mediums) for health and personal problems—it cannot be assumed that every individual would use either belief system as other members of their community might (Delgado, 1977; see Chapter 11 for a discussion of natural healers). Social constructionists recognize the importance of social workers being aware of these beliefs and values especially in terms of the particular meaning for the client. Depending on the significance of either system, social workers would be able to acknowledge and work with these values and beliefs in support of the work in which they and their clients are engaged.

SOCIAL WORK INTERVENTION: CHANGES IN SCIENTIFIC PARADIGM

Science is the constellation of facts, theories, and methods collected in current texts (Kuhn, [1962] 1970, p. 1).

This chapter is the first in the text to emphasize the use of human behavior theory to guide social work intervention with diverse populations. Interventions in social work generally are thought of as social treatment—a process in which the social worker uses selective methods and techniques to enhance social functioning. These interventions may encompass forming supportive relationships, exploring and clarifying feelings, confronting issues, educating, or mobilizing and restructuring support systems (Northen, 1982).

To understand the use of social constructionist theory as a guide to social work practice and its particular approach to intervention, it is first necessary to understand social work's interest in science and the scientific method. Thomas Kuhn ([1962] 1970) suggested that the history of the philosophy of the social sciences is marked by the reconstruction of prior theory—the reevaluation of prior fact—and therefore is "an intrinsically revolutionary process" involving changes in underlying scientific paradigm (p. 7). Because any particular scientific approach is taken for granted, changes in underlying paradigm are indeed revolutionary. For example, Copernicus destroyed time-honored ideas about terrestrial motion; Newton did the same in his explanation of gravity; and Einstein rewrote the laws of classical physics.

The social and psychological sciences have undergone a similar change process. The history of the social work profession's relationship to the philosophy of social science centers around a theoretical approach to questions such as: What is social reality like? How do people come to know about this reality and how is this knowledge transmitted? What is human nature basically like? What methodology do people use to study or observe social reality? (Burrell & Morgan, 1979; Martin & O'Connor, 1989).

Two perspectives on how to answer these questions have dominated the social sciences and have been infused into social work thinking. Burrell and Morgan (1979) suggested that most social sciences are either subjectivist—claiming that human consciousness exists primarily in the mind—or objectivist—believing that it has a real concrete existence. As an expression of Western culture and the era of science, social work presently reflects the faith in progress through systematic observation and analytic reasoning that, for example, has occurred in the study of the physical world and the technologies of medicine. Much of social work rests on the belief that through the discovery of "objective" facts and universal laws, technology will be designed to take care of personal and social ills.

Bertrand Russell (1956) expressed this belief in the possibilities of science and technology when he proclaimed that the social sciences would discover the mathematics of human behavior as precise as the underlying working of machines. The rationalists and empiricists proposed this fundamental belief that truth is based on reason and logic. The study of humankind was to be scientific and could thus be understood in the same logical terms as mechanical devices (Priest, 1990; Russell, 1956).

A steady commentary within social work has been concerned with the development of the knowledge base of social work, that is, the perspective through which the profession conceives the relationships of persons and their worlds. Much of this work has been a part of a controversy over the implications of positivism or the scientific method and possible alternative perspectives (Bateson, 1979; H. Goldstein, 1981, 1986c; Gould, 1984; Gottschalk & Witkin, 1991; Heineman, 1981, 1982; Haworth, 1984; Imre, 1982). For example, Bernice Simon (1970) expressed concern that social work lacked the conceptual tools to produce a fundamental knowledge base encompassing the complexity of "man [sic] in movement with life" (p. 367). Germain (1970) asserted that this problem was a consequence of "our language, cultural habits of thought, and schooling," which prevented social workers from seeing the world in other than linear cause-and-effect ways (p. 19). Constructionist and feminist theorists particularly addressed the issue of linear cause-and-effect thinking and questioned the notion of objective discovery and reductionistic cataloging of the human condition and clinical intervention. Instead, they proposed a different concept of reality: one based on the context and meaning for both clients and social workers (Bicker-Jenkins & Hooyman, 1986; Hare-Mustin, 1990; Ruckdeschel, 1985; Saleebey, 1989, 1992; Scott, 1989; Tice, 1990; Weick, 1981, 1983, 1987).

Clearly, the mechanistic metaphor of objectivism has dominated the social sciences and social work. As a consequence, constructionist theorists believe that social work has reduced the complexity of persons living out their lives to either their intrapsychic malfunctions or social and societal causes. For example, Rodwell (1987) claims that general systems theory is an example of objectivist thinking, which assumes that scientific inquiry can produce a body of universal assumptions and facts that, in turn, facilitate and explain all human behavior. The consequence, according to constructionists, is that the environment may be seen as a separate entity that acts on the person or is acted upon by the person in simple linear, billiard-ball fashion. The scientific method goes a step further and assumes that the unique complexity of any single person can be discovered through scientific study.

Constructionist theorists have tended to criticize the use of such classifications, categories, theories and treatments (Gergen, 1982, 1985; Mahoney, 1991; Weick, 1983). Constructionists suggest that a fundamental reality cannot exist independently of the complexity of people's lives. In addition, constructionists have moved away from the objectivist's idea that the social worker is an expert who has access to universal truths through which he or she interprets and intervenes in the life of the client. Although values, beliefs, and sociopolitical and ethical issues are assumed to be eliminated from the objectivist process of discovery through use of proper scientific control (Hudson, 1978, 1982), constructionists believe such values are at the heart of the helping process. Constructionist reject the premise of objectivity because they believe that it forgoes the diversity of individuals, families, and communities, and the interweaving of a particular gender, race, religion, age, socioeconomic position, sexual preference, and life experience is thereby lost.

The emerging alternative perspective to the notion of objectivity and scientific inquiry within social work has been referred to by such labels as naturalistic, qualitative, heuristic, ethnographic, hermeneutic, phenomenological, postmodern, postpositivist, and constructivist or social constructionist. Although this new body of work has reflected differing emphases, these emphases have had in common a more dynamic and nondeterministic way of thinking of the complexity of human life (Fisher, 1991). For example, Ann Weick (1983, 1986) and Dennis Saleebey (1989, 1992) have based their work on the fundamental notion that human behavior cannot be isolated into component parts and predicted.

Howard Goldstein (1981, 1983, 1986b, 1990a,b) also has proposed an orientation toward social work knowledge that is concerned with the constructs with which individuals define their place in the world. He has suggested that the client's conceptualization of his or her life is contained within "the private metaphors and symbols used by the mind to explain the world as it is perceived" (p. xi). This is the basis for "starting where the client is," that is, for understanding the client's unique version of the world and his or her place in it. In addition, Carolyn Saari (1986a,b, 1991) and Joseph Palombo (1992) incorporated a similar concept of meaning-making within human interaction into psychoanalytic and object-relations-oriented clinical theories.

However, there is not a single theory of constructivism or social constructionism conceived by one individual or academic discipline. It was not until recently that various theories and conceptualizations started to coalesce into patterns of ideas shared by members of different disciplines. As understood presently, this perspective represents a convergence of theories, concepts, and research from many areas of study (linguistics, sociology, anthropology, cognitive psychology, ethnology, philosophy, hermeneutics, neurobiology, developmental psychology, epistemology, and biology).

Mahoney (1991) has proposed viewing these diverse ideas as a "family of theories about mind and mentation," which share three basic commonalities, in that they

> (1) emphasize the active and proactive nature of all perception, learning, and knowing; (2) acknowledge the structural and functional primacy of abstract (tacit) over concrete (explicit) processes in all sentient and sapient experience; and (3) view learning, knowing, and memory as phenomena that reflect the ongoing attempts of body and brain to organize (and endlessly reorganize) their own patterns of action and experience. (p. 95)

The constructionist perspective taken by Mahoney (1991), Guidano (1990), Hayek (1978), Weimer (1977), and others considers a personal reality to be a "co-creation" of the person and his or her social and physical worlds. The basic sense of a person's being emerges from and is an expression of his or her unique individual history within the context of the community of others and the physical world.

This brief overview of the kinds of contributions to this family of theories— social constructionism—demonstrates the diverse nature of the development of constructionist thought. Presently, emphasis is on viewing language use in the context of social interaction, including the interaction of social work intervention. The concern is with how, through language, each person weaves a unique narrative or story about his or her life in the context of others and societal constraints (Sarbin, 1986). For example, anthropologist Clifford Geertz (1973) presented culture as a social system of shared symbols or language that provides the context for meaning and structure.

Given these increasingly popular ideas, social work must consider a fundamental shift in thinking about what intervention entails and its implications for the diversity of individuals and groups with which social work is concerned. The following provides the basic premises that underlie a social constructionist perspective of social work intervention and issues of diversity.

BASIC ASSUMPTIONS

The First Wave in psychotherapy was pathology-based. The Second Wave was problem-focused or problem-solving therapy. The Third Wave was solution-focused or solution-oriented. The Fourth Wave is what is emerging now. Only no one has a good name for it yet. (O'Hanlon, 1993, p. 3)

The social constructionists' approach to social work practice draws on a multifaceted conceptual base that addresses how people think about and organize their worlds (Berlin, 1980; Fisher, 1991; Mahoney, 1988). In general, social constructionists tend to make four assumptions:

(1) The manner in which people study the world is based on available concepts, categories, and scientific or research methods; these categories are a product of language.

(2) The various concepts and categories that people use vary considerably in their meanings and from culture to culture as well as over time

(3) The popularity or persistence of certain concepts and categories depends on their usefulness, rather than on their validity; ideas tend to persist because of their prestige or congruence with cultural values.

(4) The way in which people describe or explain the world is a form of social action that has consequences; for example, the consequences of theories built on male experiences may deny women's values and processes (Gergen, 1985; see Table 7.1).

Social constructionists have proposed that no final, true explanation of the world, or client lives, can be found (Sluzki, 1990). Rather, there are multiple realities, and the purpose of inquiry is to gather conceptualizations of these realities manifested and considered in the social worker–client encounter. These constructs reflect the context of the lives of both client and therapist. Jenkins and Karno (1992) noted that "cross-cultural psychiatric literature of the past several decades has documented substantial cultural differences in conceptions of psychosis, display of emotion, behavioral rules and norms" (p. 19). For example, the importance of the concept of *confianza* (trust) and the interpersonal space that reflects respect for some Puerto Rican clients must be understood by the social worker (Morales, 1992). Understanding must encompass an appreciation and recognition of communal processes and not classify client issues in an oppressive or pejorative manner (Fruggeri, 1992).

The social constructivist perspective asserts that people are active creators of their experience and not merely passive recorders of an external world. The world does not consist of things out there to be passively seen, experienced, and learned. The experience of "out there" is the result of a person's biological structure "bringing forth a world" (Maturana & Varela, 1987).

Table 7.1. Constructivist Theory: Basic Assumptions

People, as biological organisms, manifest a biological imperative to differentiate and categorize the stimuli they receive.

People actively construct or create meaning over time through interaction with other people and action with the environment.

Language is a particular form of action. Through language, people are able to contemplate and self-evaluate events and construct personal meanings.

People are able to consider alternative meanings because those new versions of reality are less disruptive to their sense of personal integrity.

Emotions and cognition are interrelated manifestations of personal meanings in the context of the person's life and the moment.

The construction and reconstruction of the core of personal meanings is experienced by the person as a sense of self.

The sense of self is reconstructed as the core of meanings or life narrative is rewritten.

The formation of meaning and the use of language are a form of communal action. Therefore, people develop systems of meanings called culture. A sociocultural system is a meaning-processing system through dynamic social exchange.

From this perspective, there is no such thing as a single or universal view of reality, but a reality constructed as an outcome of the biological structure and as a manifestation of a person's system of beliefs and social context at the moment (Watzlawick, 1984). Within the uniqueness of personal constructs it must be recognized that "phenomenological day-to-day [contexts] of race, language, class, gender, and age" emerge in each individual's recognition of himself or herself and the individual's relationship with his or her world (Rivera & Erlich, 1992, p.7). Both social worker and client reflect in their actions the diversity of their respective experiences.

From their beginnings, people act on the world, creating distinctions out of the enormous complexity of biological stimuli its structure is capable of organizing. These distinctions and classifications that emerge from people's actions are known as knowledge (Efran, Lukens, & Lukens, 1990; Maturana and Varela, 1987). Knowledge and meaning participate in the emerging patterns of experience as they form the forever-evolving perspective or core meanings from which the sense of order and consistency of one's own self and world are created and maintained. A person construes himself or herself in the world in a particular way by selectively attending, perceiving, interpreting, and integrating stimuli as meanings are generated consistent with the evolving core of meanings. This core is the emerging sense of self in the world. It is within the context of this most central and dominant core of meanings, as the individual's personal reality is constructed, that thoughts, affect, and behavior arise. A fundamental consequence of this biological imperative is that each individual occupies a unique reality reflecting his or her own biological propensities, history of personal experience, and the myths and traditions of community.

Biological Propensities

Each person comes into the world with unique sensitivities or tempera-ments (von Glaserfeld, 1984; Markus, 1977; Nisbett and Ross, 1980; Pepi-tone, 1949; Schacter, 1964; Weimer, 1977). People are biologically "wired" differently (Mahoney, 1991). For example, one child may sleep through the night, respond with an inviting smile, and act at ease with contact, whereas another child may awaken during the night, act fretful or cry, and stiffen when approached. The parent or caretaker will have his or her own interactional style that will result in a unique encounter between him or her and the child. A particular caretaker may respond to the first child with satisfaction and in-timacy but respond to the second child with less satisfaction and connect-edness. Thus the biological disposition may set the possibilities for the experience between the caretaker and each child, and the consequence will be a part of the evolving relationship between them and, later, others (Guidano, 1991).

In addition to caregiving behaviors, Tiefer (1987) has suggested that hu-man sexuality is another behavior that can be examined from a social con-structionist perspective. She contended that a universal norm or single social-historical context cannot be used to define or understand human sex-uality. Rather, biological sexuality is the necessary precondition to a set of potentialities transformed by societies.

History of Personal Experiences

Humans cannot know the world except through the self-referential con-text of perceived distinctions or meanings (Guidano, 1991). It is through the "eyes" of constructed meanings that each person views himself or herself and the world. Meanings are founded on the distinctions each person makes of the stimuli he or she engages. As a consequence of the embedded nature of constructs in language and discourse, people take for granted the reality of the world as differentiated and expressed in language and thus perceived (Stewart, Franz, & Layton, 1988). It is difficult for people to imagine it other-wise. It is on the bases of meanings attached to these perceived differences that decisions are made and actions are taken that affect people. A signifi-cant example is a person's skin color. Rivera and Erlich (1992) provided a poignant example of the strength of constructs in limiting understanding and of their power to act on others:

Middle-class Asians, Latinos, or African Americans are still viewed as minorities because of a most easily identified characteristic: skin color. Good clothes and an elegant briefcase are not much help when you need a cab in the middle of the night in Chicago or Washington, D.C. (p. 6)

In a similar manner, a person can experience a complex social occurrence from his or her unique perspective and interpret its meaning differently than anyone else. The history of personal experiences evolves over time, creating a perspective of idiosyncratic expectancy based on the accumulated picture of one's self in relation to the world, that is, a perspective that should reflect the diversity of an individual's personal life history. The basic concepts that account for these processes and their consequences are meaning, language and narrative, mind and knowing.

Meaning

A fundamental premise of constructivist thinking is the idea that people construct meaning out of the jangle and dissonant cords of stimuli impinging at every moment (Gordon, 1964; Mahoney, 1988). Meaning denotes the implications, effect, tenor, and intent of its referent. In this sense, meaning represents a form of distinction (see Chapter 4 for a discussion of symbolic interactionism). Meaning thus represents a person's ability to separate out and characterize the world. In this way, the person structures his or her world and attributes significance to the makeup of that structure. Meaning making represents a fundamental process by which people engage in and experience their existence in the world. Kelly (1955) observed that "man [sic] creates his own way of seeing the world in which he lives, the world does not create [perceptions] for him" (p. 12).

Language and Narrative

Meanings about the self in the world occur through language—any means of conceptualizing, representing, and communicating experience. Metaphorical representations expressed in narrative form provide the means for organizing and structuring the person's life experience in language (Polkinghorne, 1988; Sarbin, 1986). The story a person constructs about his or her existence provides that person with a coherent understanding or meaning of his or her life as lived and a context from which to view the present and future.

Schank and Abelson (1990) suggested that these stories or scripts are means of coherently organizing experience into personally meaningful conceptualizations of one's life. The person approaches the world through the eyes of the organization of previous experiences expressed in the form of the metaphorical narrative. A story or script is thematic in that it contains not only content but a relationship between the details. In this way, a story acts as the context for understanding a familiar situation by recalling similar content and understanding novel situations by matching both details and the thematic nature of the story.

Lakoff and Johnson (1980) stated that people will

> define [their] reality in terms of metaphors and then proceed to act on the basis of the metaphors. [They] draw inferences, set goals, make commitments, and execute plans, all on the basis of how [they] in part structure [their] experience, consciously or unconsciously, by means of metaphor. (p. 158)

Consider, for example, the emergent shift in African-American conceptualization of understanding self in relation to an oppressive society, which has been reflected in the change from the use of *Negro* to *black* and later to *African-American*. These were not merely changes in words used but changes revealed through the experiences of resisting oppressive and discriminatory practices. These metaphors represent an emergent meaning out of a people's experience and provide a way of considering oneself in relation to others on one's own terms.

Mind and Knowledge

The biological process we call *mind* fills in and elaborates on the sensations available to people. The mind enables a person to maintain a sense of consistency and steadiness in the midst of the shifting and changing world (Guidano, 1987). People are continually involved in the process of creating notions about their world to anticipate and predict its circumstances. According to Popper (1959), a person survives as a result of his or her ability to solve problems. The person can be thought to be continually constructing and reconstructing theories about his or her world (Weimer, 1977).

In turn, the theory or theories of the world form the context from which a person selects in order to see and interpret his or her world. From this perspective, knowing the self and the world is acting on the sensations encountered at any particular moment (Maturana & Varela, 1987). The person knows by organizing the stimuli based on their previous organizations, stories, or scripts within the context of the moment.

Myths and Traditions of the Community

Language expresses the mind's construction of a person's life in the world. Language is a communal act and reflects both human biology and the communal relationships between persons. People are born physically helpless and dependent on a caretaker, who in turn has come of age within a community of other people with whom he or she shares a language. Through relationships, an infant acquires not only the means of using the caretaker's language but the meanings embedded in that language. Language expresses the myths and traditions of the family and community of which the growing child is a part. As a result, language provides individuals with the means of organizing the world and their relationship with others in terms of the experiences of their shared community. These shared experiences, values, and beliefs of the community, present and past, are contained in the language and in the stories or traditions used by the person to understand himself or herself and the world in which he or she lives.

Each person is continually constructing a life narrative reflective of both his or her own unique life experiences and the prevailing theories about possible lives that are a part of that person's communal traditions (Bruner, 1987; Schank & Abelson, 1990). Each person lives a life that is original and yet is within the broadest boundaries of the community of shared possibilities of a life to be lived. Although the context of an individual's life or culture can thus constrain change, people also bring about change through social discourse and a reconstruction of ideas and beliefs (Gelfand & Fandetti, 1986; Malinowski, 1954; Myerhoff, 1978).

CHANGE AND INTERVENTION

The narrative view holds that it is the process of developing a story about one's life that becomes the basis of all identity and thus challenges any underlying concept of a unified or stable self. (Lax, 1992, p. 71)

The Self and Change

The social work profession's attempt to understand the consequences of the practitioner intervention or client change has had at its core the traditions of a mechanistic scientific theory. This perspective assumes that there is a reality that can be objectively measured, tested, and verified independent of the observer and context. Underlying varied methodologies and techniques is the assumption that interventions are concrete entities that somehow exist independently of a particular encounter or context. Problems exist as if they are entities to be discovered, identified, and measured through objective investigation and testing. Once a problem is objectively studied and understood, then the correct solution can be applied.

Schon (1983) has referred to this basic premise as the myth of technical rationality. A consequence of this scientific perspective is that it fails to provide a body of knowledge for understanding the processes involved in what transpires during the encounter between the social worker and client (Gordon, 1983; Stiles, 1988). Schon's (1983) work has demonstrated that expert technical understanding—that is, methodology—can result in misunderstanding the essence of the client's situation. It is the contention of Rice and Greenberg (1984b) that this "preoccupation with the role of the therapist and theoretical orientation used has led to . . . losing sight of the mechanisms of change with the client. It is the client who changes" (p. 18). To understand the change processes, social work must concern itself with the client.

A consistent theme in the literature is that change necessitates transformations of meaning about the self and the world, although the theories of explanation and methodology differ. For example, Rogers and Dymond (1957) described change as the "emergence into awareness of new perspectives of self" (p. 425). Sanville (1987) contended that change is the creation and re-creation of the self throughout one's life, and intervention is the vehicle for freeing this process in the client. In her text on clinical social work treatment, Saari (1986b) stated that intervention involves the client's "organizing of old meanings into newly constructed consciousness [or] new meanings" (p. 27).

Significant changes within the person are the consequence of transformations in the fundamental core of meanings about the self in relationship to others and within the context of one's life. The person experiences himself or herself to be the same person in encounters from day to day and over a lifetime. At the same time, the context of that person's life is in constant flux as each forthcoming encounter has yet to be experienced. To alter the fundamental core of meanings is to alter the person's felt experience of what it is to be his or her self and to be in his or her world. Alternative versions of how a person should be or how that person should live a life challenge the individual's experience of a sense of self and reality.

Language is not only a means to change: It is the means by which persons categorize, explain, and predict their world. Therefore, from this point of view, the client's hesitation, reluctance, or uncertainty to take on the social worker's perspective is not resistance, but client maintenance of the continuity of experience.

Language also is an action and, in many instances, contains power differentials between people. For example, Elliot Liebow's (1967) work *Tally's Corner* challenged the dominant culture's belief that the poor demonstrated an inability to defer gratification. Although viewed as an important sociological "fact," Liebow demonstrated that this statement does not reflect the issues of poverty or the lives of these particular people. Rather, this sociological language of the dominant culture blames the poor for their plight.

In fact, according to Lee (1980) language used by social workers can be an aggressive and demeaning act toward their clients. She commented that "how we talk and think about a client or, perhaps more importantly, a 'class' of clients, determines how we act toward the client" (p. 580). It is not unusual for social workers in community mental health settings to use their professional jargon in referring to clients who do not cooperate with the rules and process of treatment. Such clients often are described as "resistant," "uncooperative," "not ready for treatment," or "borderline," as seen in the following case study:

> During a clinical conference in a mental health clinic in a large city in the Northeast, social workers were insistent that a particular female client was definitely a passive-dependent personality and resisting treatment because she would not recognize the importance of taking specific assertive actions the social worker had decided were needed. All the social workers at the meeting knew that these actions were the "healthy" thing for her to do and concurred with her pathology. Then, one social worker pointed out that she was from a small rural town in the South and had lived there for 30 years before moving. This social worker, having lived in a town similar to that of the client, pointed out that the client and her family might view what was being asked of the client as being "uppity" and therefore unacceptable. The social worker was able to identify this issue with the client and their work took a different turn. Later, the client talked about her sessions, and confided that she had felt both pressured and stuck during the earlier part of their work together.

It is evident from this discussion that it is not only the client's construction of meaning but the social worker's personal and professional meanings that must be revealed if a truly collaborative exchange is to occur.

Interventions: Changed Meanings

White and Epston (1990) noted that "persons who seek therapy frequently experience an incapacity to intervene in a life that seems unchanging; they are stymied in their search for new possibilities and alternative meanings" (p. 36). An acceptable outcome of intervention would be the generation of alternative narratives that "enable [a person] to perform new meanings, bringing with them desired possibilities—new meanings that [the person] will experience as more helpful, satisfying, and open-ended" (p. 15).

According to Shafer (1983), psychoanalysts are "people who listen to the narrations of analysands and help them to transform these narrations into others that are more complete, coherent, convincing, and adaptively useful than those they have been accustomed to constructing" (p. 240). That is, therapists coauthor a new version of the original story, also known as restorying. The social worker's role is to ask questions that bring forth "alternative landscapes" and facilitate the "reauthoring" process (White, 1993, p. 41). All interventions are a variation on this process.

The social constructionist approach requires that practitioners adopt a "not-knowing position" (Anderson & Goolishian, 1992, p. 29). A practitioner must be diligent about his or her own assumptions about the client. Although the social worker must be aware of preconceived theoretical positions, he or she should rely on the client's views and explanations. This perspective is particularly congruent with James Green's (1982) model of cross-cultural practice. Practitioners may not place people in predetermined social categories, but must take the stance of learner to achieve cultural congruence with clients.

The constructivist perspective views intervention, then, as an opportunity for the social worker and client to explore together the narratives the client has evolved to give meaning to his or her life. The social worker must appreciate that his or her own understanding about the client reflects personal narratives or contexts. It is through language that collaboration is expressed in personal meanings and exchanged in conversation. From this perspective, intervention is not a treatment as much as it is a dialogue in which multiple meanings are shared and from which cultural meanings are drawn from both client and social worker. Change, then, is a rewriting of the personal narrative so that a person sees himself or herself and the world from a different perspective.

At times, the client seeks assistance because he or she has identified a personal struggle ensuing from living, for instance, a bicultural life. Such was the situation for a 20-year-old Puerto Rican woman attending college. She had attempted to come to terms with her family and their opposition to her decision to move out of the neighborhood and start a career. The issue was not one of autonomy and individuality, which the dominant culture had decided was the "natural" order of things, nor was it what was best for her or who was right or wrong. Rather, the struggle was how to maintain what was important to her about her family and culture and, at the same time, express different values she had come to embrace while growing up in the United States. Issues of dating, marriage, and living on her own were only a few with which she had to come to terms in her efforts to maintain good relations with her family and also live a life that differed from her family and community's expectations. The issue for the social worker is that of appreciating and understanding the client's struggle in the language of the client. In this example, the social worker participates with the client in rewriting her cultural history as she has lived it and as she may live it in her life.

Restorying People's Lives

Social constructionists have suggested that it is important to value a client's experiences "without trying to rid clients of those [seemingly negative] experiences directly" (O'Hanlon, 1993, p. 14). The focus is on client ideas, beliefs, frames of reference, and language, and how these relate to the presenting issue. Clients are urged not to blame themselves, but to change their stance toward the problem (Anderson, 1991; Auerswald, 1986; Durrant & Coles, 1991; H. Goldstein, 1986a, 1986b).

One way of restorying, that is, developing new meanings, is through deconstruction (Derrida, 1976, 1978). *Deconstruction* is a technique in which the practitioner disrupts typical frames of references, listens for multiple meanings, and reconstructs new meanings (White, 1993, p. 34). Feminist therapists Hare-Mustin and Marecek (1988) have contended that practitioners must challenge dominant norms related to gender through nontraditional forms of intervention such as deconstruction. In addition, Laird (1989), a family-focused theorist who wrote about restorying women's self-constructions, contended that, generally, women's stories have not been told by women but have been defined by men. The deconstruction of and retelling of women's lives is at the heart of the feminist movement (see Chapter 12). Similarly, Taggart (1989) argued that the struggle by women to define themselves has been held back by "the standard theories [that] routinely construct" the female position (p. 100). He believed that limited socially constructed knowledge about women, particularly women's roles in families, needs to be addressed in family therapy approaches (see Chapter 9).

An example of deconstruction is a cartoon of the Holocaust drawn by Spiegelman (1991) entitled *Maus*. In the cartoon, in which the Nazis are portrayed as cats and Jewish people as mice, Spiegelman shocks the reader out of any sense of familiarity with the events described. Instead, he approaches the unspeakable through the diminutive; thus, externalizing events generates what might be thought of as "counter-language" (White, 1993, p. 39).

Knowledge and Power

Client stories, generally, tend to be directed by the knowledge of the dominant culture and may describe oppressive experiences (Polanyi, 1953; White, 1993). The way in which such knowledge is construed may give some individuals and groups power to dominate others (Foucault, 1965, 1978, 1980). According to Poster (1989), "to begin a discourse is to enter into a political world" (p. 50). One such argument about the political nature of knowledge concerns the revised third edition of the *Diagnostic and Statistical Manual of Mental Disorders* (DSM-III-R) published by the American Psychiatric Association (1987). Carolyn Cutler (1991) contended that DSM-III-R reflects the differential power-based relationship between the social worker and the client. She states that this differential relationship is "based on the clinician's desire to see clients as other than themselves" (p. 157). Consequently, the client so labeled often becomes depersonalized and powerless (Rosenhan, 1984).

Tomm (1990) argued against pathologizing people through labeling and segregating, whereas Armundson (1991) has suggested that when considering classification and or labeling of clients, practitioners remember that "'truth' is often historical, that social practices evolve and that psychology and psychiatry ride on the back of, rather than stand apart from, culture" (p. 30). For example, use of the term *learning disabled* invites a person who is so labeled to view himself or herself as less than whole, and avoids an examination of contextually oriented interventions (Stewart and Nodrick, 1990).

How a practitioner defines truth or insight supports particular social/political arrangements (Efran, Lukens, & Lukens, 1990; Kleinman, 1973). When knowledge is seen as universal or essential, it can be institutionalized in oppressive ways (Lowe, 1991). The practitioner listens within his or her own "convictions, and puts them in a cultural context. . . . [Therefore, the helping process always] stems from the therapist's personal history, cultural context, and theoretical orientation" (Cecchin, 1992, p. 93). Hence, therapists must "become responsible for their own actions and opinions . . . to dare to use their resources to intervene, to construct rituals, to reframe situations, behaviors, and ideas for both the client and themselves" (pp. 92–93).

For example, de Amorin and Cavalcante (1992) used a combination of constructionist narrative and puppet drama to counter the stories of stigmatized individuals—developmentally disabled adults—who faced myths of deficiency:

> Using a social constructionist perspective in our work we have encouraged persons labeled as "developmentally disabled" to reconstruct their personal narratives, socially re-examining the misconceptions and/or myth-conceptions that have caused their segregation. (p. 149)

The Social Worker's Role

Constructionist theory is not a theory of universal stages such as Erikson's (1974). Stage theories are considered static insofar as they tend to represent the attitudes and beliefs of a culturally derived way of conceiving of human development at a particular time in social history. On the other hand, constructionist theory does not impose a cultural- or temporal-bound model of human development. Rather, the theory provides the social worker with a seemingly homogeneous group (ethnic, religious, geographical, political, and so forth), that is, a means to understand a *particular* individual within his or her sociocultural context (Table 7.2).

The social worker listens to the client's story with curiosity and openness, acknowledges his or her own assumptions and beliefs, and attempts to refrain from quickly interpreting the client's story. In addition, the social worker does not assume that he or she knows what the client means. This form of sensitivity protects the social worker from potentially stereotyping the client's culture. This intervention approach stems from the perspective that any time practitioners set up predetermined assumptions about a group, they are evaluating those particular clients on the basis of an artificial stereotype—not all Italians are the same, not all blacks are the same. Familiarity, even if based on the latest descriptions of a particular culture, holds the danger of becoming a template by which clients are measured.

Table 7.2. Guidelines for Social Workers Using a Constructionist Approach

The social worker takes a stance of unconditional respect for the uniqueness of each client and the context of the client's life. The social worker recognizes that both he or she and clients respond to situations in idiosyncratic ways that reflect their experiential history, biological propensities, and the community of shared meanings embedded in the language of their day-to-day life.

The social worker makes an effort to be aware of his or her preconceived ideas (both personal and theoretical) about who the client is, what the problem is, and how the client should be helped, and refrains from imposing those ideas on the client. The social worker takes the stance of open curiosity and interest in the client's life narrative and the issue as perceived by the client.

The social worker acknowledges that the context of the therapeutic setting by its very structure and procedures reflects the values and beliefs of the community sanctioning the work to be done.

The social worker respects the client's personal reality and the maintenance of this reality as a means of strengthening the integrity of his or her sense of self and the world as the client knows it.

The social worker appreciates that the issues will be resolved as a result of a collaborative understanding, shared meanings, and the generation of alternative meanings. The social worker does not support unjust and prejudicial interpersonal or institutional actions. In these instances, the social worker seeks alternative meanings to alleviate a negative condition.

Therapy involves an ongoing exchange of client–social worker meaning that shifts as new information is added. Meaning is generated through this communication.

To help people with interpersonal functioning, it is important to assist them to take the perspective of the other person.

The process of social work interventions is to provide a situation conducive for alternative meanings to be shared, understood, and used by the client and the social worker. Client-defined problems can be resolved as alternative meanings or perspectives emerge.

Constructionists appreciate differences, but in terms of the particular meanings expressed by the clients. Contained in the meanings is a particular person's experience with gender, race, socioeconomic and religious background, and so forth, experience within the context of all levels of social structure: family, neighborhood, community, region, and country. Understanding client meaning also includes understanding the client's relationships with other groups and social systems.

The social worker starts where the client is—remains open to the client's story. In addition, the social worker is a collaborator, learning anew with each client what it is like to be, for example, *this* African-American male, *this* American-Indian female, *this* southern white female, *this* northern Jewish male, or *this* white Methodist male. The uneasy task is to initially take a learning stance with the client rather than portraying oneself as an expert who knows all about diversity and what the problem is. This task can be uncomfortable until the practitioner recognizes that it is his or her responsibility to hear the client's story. The social worker's ability lies in enabling the communication to inform him or her about who the person is and how the person understands himself or herself in the particular context of systems or community. The collaboration continues as the social worker and client reassure themselves that there is a mutual level of understanding of how the client lives his or her life, and what work might need to be done to meet the client's needs.

Overall, social constructivism addresses the fundamental issue of diversity as it is expressed in the life of a particular person or group of persons with whom the social worker is engaged. It is diversity as it is lived, reflecting the temporal and contextual meanings for a particular client or client group. Social constructivism recognizes that the agency, its structure, and its organizational values and goals may not necessarily reflect the needs of the client. Agencies, policies, and theoretical perspectives reflect the value-laden social scripts of how to get help and where to get help. The structures of time, physical setting, and proper procedures all represent a fundamental belief in what is the "normal" or "right" way to live a life. Those who are a part of the dominant culture or those who successfully function within that culture do not recognize the embedded values as anything but reality.

Social constructionist perspectives challenge the social worker to move away from the comfort of knowing and from technique to join with clients in discovering meanings and beliefs that the social worker, client, or both have assumed to be the only way to live. Diversity is an important and compelling example of the significance of differences. As each person respects another's version of life, he or she can recognize that there are multiple perspectives by which one can live.

Social Learning Theory:
Empirical Applications to
Culturally Diverse Practice ⎯⎯⎯⎯⎯⎯⎯⎯⎯⎯⎯⎯⎯⎯⎯⎯ **8**

Bruce A. Thyer

> *A very large part of the social environment we call a culture consists of descriptions of contingencies of reinforcement in the form of advice, maxims, instructions, rules of conduct, the laws of governments and religions, and the laws of science. With their help, members of a group transmit what they have learned to new members.*
>
> (Skinner, 1985, p. 294)

This chapter discusses social learning theory, an objectivist theory that emphasizes the application of universal (scientific) principles (see Chapter 7 for a discussion of subjectivist and objectivist theory). This perspective emphasizes that the practitioner need *not* apply (social learning) behavioral theory differentially, but can achieve effective interventions if the theory's practice assumptions are sensitively and accurately undertaken. This chapter takes the perspective called behavior analysis or radical behaviorism. Other behaviorists, such as those espousing cognitive-behavioral theory, may emphasize other learning mechanisms (e.g., Blechman, 1984) and may contend that the behavioral approach is not as value-neutral as is presented.

The application of the principles of social learning theory to the field of social work is almost three decades old. The earliest behavioral article authored by a social worker appeared in 1965 (Staats & Butterfield, 1965), and the earliest book was published in 1967 (Thomas, 1967). Since that time the field of behavioral social work has expanded enormously. Social learning theory is now a preferred orientation for a large minority of social workers (cf. Jayaratne, 1980), and the approach is well represented in professional curricula (Thyer & Maddox, 1988), textbooks (Thyer, 1985), and journals (Thyer, 1981).

The social learning theory foundation of behavioral social work has produced an approach to understanding human behavioral development and diversity of expression that is characterized by an empirical approach to research, largely (although not exclusively) quantitative in orientations and committed to understanding objective relationships between human beings and their psychosocial environments. This empirical orientation has proven to be professionally productive: Well over 50% of the controlled outcome studies with positive results that have appeared in the social work literature have been based on social learning theory (see Reid & Hanrahan, 1982; Thomlison, 1984; Rubin, 1985; MacDonald, Sheldon, & Gillespie, 1992).

That the behavioral approach is represented in professional training and practice and is relatively well documented as efficacious for a wide variety of problems addressed by social workers seems reasonably established. The purpose of the present chapter is to illustrate the congruence of the behavioral approach to delivering effective social work services to culturally diverse client groups.

BASIC ASSUMPTIONS

Men act upon the world and change it, and are changed in turn by the consequences of their action. Certain processes, which the human organism shares with other species, alter behavior so that it achieves a safer and more useful interchange with a particular environment. . . . If by chance the environment changes, old forms of behavior disappear, while new consequences build new forms. (Skinner, 1953, p. 1)

A Person-in-Environment Perspective

It is not well recognized that behavioral social work's learning theory foundations have given rise to an approach to practice that is almost exclusively oriented toward the *person-in-environment* perspective that has long characterized the field of social work. For example, compare the above quotation from Skinner with a description of the ecosystems perspective, which aims at:

building more supportive, helpful and nurturing environments for clients through environmental helping, and increasing their competence in dealing with the environment through teaching basic life skills. (Whittaker & Garbarino, 1983, p. 34)

We could also compare Skinner's view with that of Germain, promoter of the ecological approach to working with clients:

[P]eople use an almost infinite variety of *learned* capacities to reach and sustain an adaptive balance between their needs and goals and the properties of the environment. (Germain, 1981, emphasis added)

The human being and the environment reciprocally shape each other. People mold their environments in many ways and, in turn, they must then adapt to the changes they created. (Germain, 1992, p. 407)

The similarities are striking.

A behavioral analytic perspective on human development is a viable alternative to traditional stage theories. Rather than postulating a hierarchy of stages in cognitive-moral-behavioral-development, behavior analysis attempts to explain the emergence of differential human capabilities and expressions in terms of the operation of various forms of empirically supported learning theories. These mechanisms of learning are said to apply to all cultures and races and to men and women equally. The psychosocial environments in which they operate may considerably vary, but the fundamental mechanisms are understood to remain the same.

The Role of Biological Factors

The biological differences that imperfectly distinguish various cultural and ethnic groups obviously arise from genetic factors, but a given person's genetic endowment is itself the function of many generations of natural shaping by the environments in which human beings have lived (see Skinner, 1966, 1975). Indeed, recent developments in the field of sociobiology suggest that aspects of *behavior*, not just physical features, may be genetically mediated (see Reynolds, Falger, & Vine, 1986). Extensions of the influence of biological factors are also being made into the realm of those behaviors giving rise to what we call ethnicity (see Chapman, 1993). Although it is clear that nurture has a role as well as nature in accounting for cultural diversity, from the perspective of social learning theory, most cultural differences are not intrinsic to people but to the different environments in which they live and from which they learn. For example, most of those things that make a Black child culturally Black, a Latino adolescent Latino and so forth, are learned (at least in part, if not in toto) via respondent and operant conditioning, and by imitating peers and caregivers. Children's acquisition of language, be it English, Spanish, or any other language, is largely acquired via reinforcement and modeling (see Whitehurst & Valdez-Menchaca, 1988). Whether one jogs down the street in a warmup suit or wears name brand sneakers, is seen as largely acquired through similar processes.

Elaborations of the principles of social learning theory are widely available in the social work and non–social work literatures (e.g., Thyer, 1987a, 1988, 1991, 1992a; Wodarski & Bagarozzi, 1979; Fischer & Gochros, 1975; Ferster & Skinner, 1957; Malott, Whaley, & Malott, 1991) and will not be extensively reviewed here. Table 8.1 provides a summary of the major as-

sumptions of behavioral social work as they apply to practice with culturally diverse clients.

Mark Mattaini, a social worker in practice in New York City, has prepared
a Behavior Code, a set of guidelines to personal comportment to be followed
by members of the Walden Fellowship he has established, a combination human service agency and cultural think-tank (see Mattaini, 1991). Two of the
items found in this evolving Behavior Code include the following:

1. People's actions are lawful and shaped by personal history and biology; all
   persons, therefore, deserve equal respect regardless of behavior. This is true
   regardless of race, sex, age, ethnicity, class, religious or sexual preferences,
   educational level or disability.
9. Cultural practices emphasizing mutual respect and cooperation generally
   produce greater overall satisfaction and reinforcement than do those based

Table 8.1.   Basic Assumptions of Behavioral Social Work with Culturally Diverse
      Clients

---

1. Human behavior consists of everything that a person *does*. This includes observable behavior as well as private events such as thoughts and feelings, and
   all those phenomena called *cognitive* and *affective*.
2. Human behavior is, to a very large extent, learned.
3. There are three major biological processes by which persons learn: respondent
   conditioning (e.g., Pavlovian), learning from past consequences that have followed behavior (operant conditioning), and learning by imitating others (modeling). These three processes comprise the mechanisms of social learning
   theory.
4. The underlying biological processes by which people acquire behavior are
   similar across racial, cultural, and ethnic groups, by gender, social classes, and
   all other methods of categorizing human beings. Social learning theory is a
   useful framework for explaining human differences, across individuals, groups,
   families, and societies.
5. Similar learning *processes* taking place in different environments, within a individual's life span, within a cultural environment, and across the history of the
   human race (via genetic mediation), have given rise to the diversity of expressions we call the human experience.
6. Assessment of clients involves an analysis of past and present learning experiences that may be responsible for giving rise to problematic situations. By definition, social learning theory takes into account the person-in-environment.
7. Behavior social work intervention involves providing a client with
   remedial/corrective learning experiences, and/or the restructuring of the client's
   psychosocial environment so that adaptive behavior is promoted and maladaptive behavior is weakened. There is an explicit preference to use reinforcing
   contingencies rather than punishing ones.
8. Behavior social work practice is embedded in traditional social work values of
   respect for individuals, maximizing client autonomy, and working toward the
   elimination of racism, discrimination, and social injustice.

---

on oppression, competition or coercion; therefore acting for the common welfare is generally valuable.

Although clearly derived from social learning theory, these elements of Mattaini's Behavior Code would seem highly relevant to social work practice in general, and to practice with culturally diverse client groups in particular.

Definitions and Mechanisms of Behavior Change

One definition of behavioral social work is the following:

> Behavioral social work is the informed use, by professional social workers, of interventive techniques based upon empirically-derived learning theories that include but are not limited to, operant conditioning, respondent conditioning, and observational learning. Behavioral social workers may or may not subscribe to the philosophy of behaviorism. (Thyer & Hudson, 1987, p. 1)

The foundations of social learning theory were originally developed outside the field of social work, primarily through the work of experimental psychologists, but the last three decades have seen ample evidence that the principles of learning established in the experimental laboratory with other organisms are isomorphic with those operating with human beings (cf. Ribes, 1985). That humans present vastly more complex elaborations of behavior is undeniable, but it seems clear that to a very large extent our comportment develops through the three learning mechanisms described in the above definition.

Respondent conditioning is the most fundamental learning mechanism shared by humans and other animals. Shown to occur in all animal species ever tested, including single-cell organisms, even individual nerve and muscle cells are capable of respondent learning (e.g., Walters & Bryne, 1983). Pavlov and his associates demonstrated how a neutral stimulus, if presented one or more times immediately prior to the occurrence of an event (unconditioned stimulus) that produced an innate reflexive response (unconditioned response), the previously neutral stimulus could come to elicit a similar response. After such conditioning trials the neutral stimulus that now elicits such responses is called a *conditioned stimulus* (CS) and the largely involuntary response to the CS is called a *conditioned response.* The types of bodily responses involved in such conditioning processes are called *respondent behaviors,* and the learning process is called *respondent conditioning.* It appears that significant components of human sexual behavior, emotional reactions, and even glandular secretions can be modifiable through the processes of respondent conditioning. The capacity for such learning in human is present at birth (e.g., Lipsitt & Kaye, 1964) and even, remarkably, in utero (e.g., DeCasper & Spence, 1986).

The second major form of learning addressed by social learning theory (actually the dominant one) is called *operant conditioning*, which examines how the *consequences* that have *followed* a behavior in the past come to influence its present occurrence. This is a completely different mechanism than respondent conditioning, which focuses on how stimuli that occur *before* a behavior come to elicit relatively simple reflexive acts. In the operant model developed by Skinner and others, the consequences that follow a behavior can take four major forms: something good is presented (positive reinforcement), something bad is taken away (negative reinforcement), something bad is presented (positive punishment), or something good is taken away (negative punishment). Reinforcement (both positive *and* negative) tends to strengthen behavior, whereas punishment tends to weaken it. Building upon these conceptually simple operations, a vast edifice of operant theory has been established, strongly supported by empirical research, which addresses most of those human activities we call voluntary behavior (the term *operant* is derived from the fact that our behavior can be said to operate upon our psychosocial environment). Virtually all animal species have been shown to acquire new behavior or to modify existing repertoires through operant learning processes, a capacity that seems to be present in humans even at birth (e.g., Siqueland & Lipsitt, 1966).

Learning via *imitation of others* (also called *modeling*) is a third important mechanism of learning. The capacity for imitation appears to be present in humans at birth (e.g., Field, Woodson, Greenberg, & Cohen, 1982) and has been demonstrated in other animals (Fiorito & Scotto, 1992; Whiten & Ham, 1992). The development and maintenance of complex imitative repertoires seems strongly mediated by operant factors (e.g., does the modeled behavior produce rewarding or punishing consequences?) and is held to account for much of an individual's acquisition of culturally and gender-specific behaviors (see Perry & Bussey, 1979). The innate capacity for imitation is itself strongly affected by the consequences of one's own modeled behavior. A child who imitates a peer and obtains reinforcement for this is simultaneously strengthening two repertoires: the particular behavior that was imitated, *and* the generic likelihood to model others. Over the time course of childhood development, most individuals develop strong imitative skills, skills that are durable in part because of the sometimes inconsistent occurrence of being rewarded for imitation. By adolescence and often earlier, generalized imitation will persist for quite some time even in the absence of reinforcing consequences.

The focus of social learning theory on these three processes for developing and changing behavior does not deny the possible relevance of other factors. Rather it represents a parsimonious determination to explore as fully as possible the possible role of environmentally mediated learning *prior to* developing accounts based on other mechanisms. This is similar to other fields, such as genetics. Geneticists examine the influence of chromosomal factors in their accounts of the development of the human body and its actions. They largely ignore operant factors occurring during a person's life, possible psychodynamic influences, drug ingestion, and so forth. Nevertheless, genetics is seen as a credible field whose findings are accorded respect. To have a clearly defined focus is scientifically acceptable, and the focus of behavioral social work is on how the environment gives rise to behavior via learning processes. No other explanatory principles are necessarily deemed to be unimportant. This focus upon learning mechanisms that are based on the transactions occurring among persons and their environments is obviously congruent with central themes adopted by the field of social work and represents one manner of operationally defining the historic person-in-environment perspective of our field.

PRACTICE ASSUMPTIONS

Behavioral social work does not strongly rely upon traditional theories of human development in attempting to understand culturally diverse clients. This is justified because the validity of traditional stage theories is increasingly coming into doubt (see Baer, 1970; Brainerd, 1978), and because of the growing evidence that they may fail to capture cultural diversity issues related to development (cf. Germain, 1987). Similarly, traditional practice wisdom and contemporary research about culturally diverse groups is being questioned. For example, it appears that most applied research on African-American women has involved limited or nonrepresentative samples (cf. Wyche, 1993). Most studies that examine racial differences highlight between-group differences, ignoring the fact that within-group variation is typically very large, and that various racial groups more often than not share far more features in common than differences (cf. Zuckerman, 1990). A similar caveat has emerged from meta-analyses of research on purportedly significant gender differences in cognitive functioning (see Hyde, 1990). From a social learning perspective, a middle-class white adolescent may have more in common with a middle-class black teenager than with a poor white youth from Appalachia.

Social learning theorists do recognize that differences among clients exist, and that these differences need to be assessed and taken into account when practicing with persons from culturally diverse backgrounds (e.g., Hunter & Kelso, 1985; Wilson & Calhoun, 1974; Goldstein, 1974). For the behavioral social worker, effective culturally diverse practice *does not* consist of as-suming that skin color or ethnic heritage exerts a predictable influence on one's role as a client. Rather, it consists of some traditional social work prac-tices such as conducting individualized assessments, attempting

- to leave behind preconceptions of what people should be like, based on their race or gender
- to take what clients bring to the practitioner in a non-condemnatory way
- to respect clients' views
- to try and conceptualize the problem in a manner consistent with so-cial learning theory and to translate this conception to the client in a manner he or she can understand
- to propose, based upon empirical research if such exists, one or more courses of joint action
- to develop a means to assess client change in a manner that is accept-able to the client, and is at the same time reliable and valid
- to alter treatment plans as the client and/or data indicate modifications are needed
- and to recruit significant others into treatment as needed to help ensure the maintenance and generalization of meaningful change.

The above is not meant to disregard those cultural differences that may ex-ist between clients, but is intended to emphasize that such differences need to be revealed through individualized assessment, rather than assumed to ex-ist by the social worker. For example, behavioral researchers have undertak-en systematic assessment of the components of assertive behavior as relevant to Black clients (Keane, St. Lawrence, Himadi, Graves, & Kelly, 1983) in the hope of developing assertiveness training that is more relevant to Blacks. It is also important to consider that persons from differing cultural groups may find certain behavioral interventions less acceptable than others. For exam-ple, selected behavioral methods of reinforcement and punishment for use with children may be more compatibly taught to parents from some back-grounds than others. Accordingly, Heffer and Kelley (1987) carefully ascer-tained the acceptability of such procedures for use by parents of different races and income levels.

Behavioral social workers make no pretence that the behavioral approach is value free (see Skinner, 1971) or can be applied across the board with dif-ferent persons, regardless of their individual likes and dislikes or learning his-tories. But it is sufficiently flexible that a skilled social worker, drawing upon an informed knowledge of social learning theory, is in a good position to de-vise an interventive program that takes into account such individual differ-ences and that will be of benefit to the client.

PRACTICE ISSUES AND EMPIRICAL SUPPORT

One operational definition of a social worker's skills in culturally diverse practice is his or her ability to effectively help clients from varying cultural backgrounds. The behavioral social worker does not see a practitioner's choice of theory, purported cultural sensitivity, knowledge of unique family systems, etc., as important as answering the query: What evidence is there that your client's situation improved? The social worker capable of providing such evidence has, ipso facto, demonstrated his or her capacity to effectively work with culturally diverse clients. On the other hand the "culturally sensitive" social worker could nevertheless provide services that are not helpful to minority or oppressed clients.

Advocates of social learning theory argue that it is one conceptual framework that has demonstrated not only its potential but its actual applicability to many of the practice issues of concern to social work and, just as importantly, has demonstrated its effectiveness across many culturally diverse groups. There is a large body of literature (see Table 8.2) that discusses various culturally diverse groups, studies selected practice problems/issues, and describes the use of social learning theory to help ameliorate these problems.

The examples listed in Table 8.2, which are from a far more extensive list than can be cited here, run the gamut from uncontrolled case studies to well-designed large group experiments. Books have been written pertinent to some culturally diverse groups [e.g., Turner and Jones (1982) in practice with African-Americans and Blechman (1984) in practice with women]. Review articles have been published about behavioral practice with other groups, such as American Indians (Renfrey, 1992). In addition, a number of descriptive articles that have been published illustrate the applicability of social learning theory to culturally diverse groups, as in Ardilla's (1982) work with Latin Americans and Das et al.'s (1980) report on behavioral social work in India. Cottraux, Legeron, and Mollard's (1992) recent book contains entire chapters devoted to the state of behavior analysis and therapy as presently practiced in the Czech and Slovak Republics, Hungary, Poland, and Estonia. As the following case illustrations suggest, behavior social work has been used successfully employed with selected culturally diverse clients.

Case Illustration with American Indians

American Indians are at high risk to abuse drugs and alcohol. Early intervention seems indicated to help *prevent* such problems from developing. Drawing upon a social learning theory base, social workers devised a behavioral skills training program designed to teach American Indian youth ($N = 102$, 49% female, average age 11.3 years) methods of coping with environmental stressors and peer pressure, which can lead to drug use, to promote self-esteem and ethnic pride, and to develop increased knowledge of the ill effects of substance

Table 8.2.   Selected Examples of Using Social Learning Theory in Helping
Culturally Diverse Client Groups with Selected Problems

Cultural/racial group	Problem/issue addressed	Supportive citation(s)
African-American children	Classroom learning	Jones (1982) Edgar & Clement (1980)
African-American & white children	Promoting racial integration	Hauserman et al. (1973)
	Reducing racial prejudice	Spencer & Horowitz (1973)
African-American male adolescents	Improving job performance	Pierce & Risley (1974)
	Pregnancy prevention	Schinke & Gilchrist (1978)
African-American parents	Parent training	Dangel & Polster (1984)
	Child abuse	Wolfe et al. (1982)
African-American adults	Community problems	Saafir (1982)
	Substance abuse	Jenkins et al. (1982)
	Sexual dysfunction	Wyatt et al. (1976)
Inner-city minority youth	Delinquency, school dropout, unemployment	Blechman (1992)
African children	Classroom misbehavior	Saigh & Umar (1983)
Mexican-American youth	Promoting reading	Staats & Butterfield (1965)
Mexican-American women	Assertiveness	Boulette (1976)
Mexican and Costa Rican youth	Child behavior problems	Acosta & Evans (1982)
Cuban youth	Prosocial behavior	Ginsberg (1989)
Spanish children	Enuresis	Caceres (1982)
Korean adult	Interpersonal anxiety	Kim (1979)
Gays	Assertiveness	Duehn & Mayadas (1977)
	High-risk sexual behavior	Kelly et al. (1989)
Lesbians	Sexual dysfunctions	Nichols (1989)
Elderly	Increasing social support	Pinkston & Linsk (1984)
	Promoting safety belt use	Thyer et al. (1991)
	Urinary incontinence	Schnelle (1991)
Visually impaired persons	Motor skills	Correa et al. (1984)
	Social, living, and academic skills	Van Hasselt (1987)

(continued)

Table 8.2. (*Continued*)

Deaf children	Promoting reading	Wilson & McReynolds (1973)
American Indians	Mutism	Conrad et al. (1974)
	Preventing substance abuse	Schinke et al. (1988)
Asian-Indian transsexuals	Gender role and identity	Khanna et al. (1987)
Women	Rape victims	Foa et al. (1991)
Children from Appalachia	Behavior problems	Wahler & Erickson (1969)

abuse. Using a no-treatment control group design and random assignment, treatment was delivered by one American Indian research staff member and one respected indigenous community leader (who knew the subjects well). The two groups of youth (treatment and no-treatment) were similar at pretest on all outcome measures. Posttreatment (six months later), those youth receiving the training (anonymously) reported fewer instances of using alcohol, marijuana, or inhalants. The program was highly rated by the youth on measures of sensitivity to American Indian culture, applicability to daily living, and effectiveness. Three-fourths said they would recommend the program to their friends and siblings (see Gilchrist, Schinke, Trimble, & Czetkovich, 1987).

Case Illustration with an African-American Client

Dr. Zev Wanderer, an Israeli social worker temporarily practicing in the United States, was consulted by Mr. M., an African American stockbroker in his midthirties. Mr. M. had recently changed his position from accountant to stockbroker, but was troubled by disabling fears elicited by making "cold calls" to prospective clients. These fears assumed the proportions of a social phobia and significantly inhibited his ability to earn a living. He put off making calls, and his quavering voice did not lend itself to customer confidence. Based upon prior empirical research demonstrating that specific phobias of this type respond well to a program of prolonged therapeutic exposure to anxiety-evoking stimuli (see Thyer, 1987b), Dr. Wanderer proposed such a program to Mr. M., after giving him a case conceptualization and rationale for such treatment, based on social learning theory. Mr. M. agreed, embarked upon the treatment program with the social worker, and had his difficulties substantially alleviated within six sessions lasting a little over a month. Moreover, he was taught self-treatment skills that enabled him to autonomously deal with any relapses. Such relapses had not occurred at 9-month follow-up (see Wanderer & Ingram, 1991).

Case Illustration with Single African American Mothers

Richard Dangel and Richard Polster were social workers in practice in Texas who developed a systematic parent training program based on social learning theory for use by single mothers (and by two-parent families) to help solve complex child management problems and to promote healthy child development.

Their program was explicitly designed to reflect the concerns of diverse ethnic and socioeconomic populations and was centered around 14 instructional booklets and 22 color videotape lessons. Training focused on teaching the parents skills in using the principles of social learning theory in an effective manner, with lessons devoted to using praise and affection, rewards and privileges, planned ignoring, time out, and other techniques. Apart from training in general principles, individual booklets dealt with specific problems such as lying, stealing, hyperactivity, communication, nutrition, temper tantrums, arguing, homework, school problems, mealtime behavior, sexual curiosity, and other potential problem areas. Following extensive pilot testing, this self-paced program, called WINNING! was used with over 2,000 families, involving white and African American parents, single mothers, Latinos, and people with diverse income and educational backgrounds. Many participants were recruited from a black inner-city government-subsidized housing project. Data collected pre- and posttraining, and involving validated self-report *and* systematic direct observations taken in the parents' homes, showed significant improvements in the parents' use of selected parenting skills, *and* in the behavior of the children and youth. Consumer satisfaction ratings indicated the high level of acceptability of the WINNING! program. The program is highly cost effective, with 9 of 11 parent trainers being M.S.W. students requiring only about 20 hours of training themselves in the WINNING! program in order to be able to deliver it effectively. Over 40 agencies in 16 states have adopted the WINNING! program (see Dangel & Polster, 1984, for additional details).

CRITIQUE AND LIMITATIONS

In discussing the real and potential limitations of utilizing social learning theory in social work practice with culturally diverse clients, the one limitation that strikes the author most forcibly is the extent to which this approach continues to fall prey to misconceptions about the nature of behavioral practice. As outlined in Thyer (1991), our literature continues to perpetuate the myths that behavioral social work ignores client affect and cognition, being focused solely on modifying publicly observable behavior; that social worker–client relationship factors are of limited interest; that symptomatic relief only is sought, with no attention to the true "causes" of client problems, and so forth. The perpetuation of such misconceptions likely accounts for the limited dissemination of this approach within professional social work.

A second limitation, shared with colleagues from other theoretical orientations perhaps, is the temptation to apply techniques in a rotelike manner. For example, if parents complain of their child's refusal to go to school, then it may erroneously be quickly concluded that parent training in reinforcement techniques is needed to bring junior into line, and factors such as junior's being afraid of neighborhood bullies may possibly be overlooked.

While it is important to consult the available empirical research literature in devising projected treatment plans, such information needs to be integrated into the context of the practitioner's overall assessment of a client's environmental situation and available behavioral repertoire. A DSM-IV diagnosis, while possibly important, is often an insufficient basis to decide upon a given course of treatment.

A third limitation is that the study of the principles of social learning theory and of the practice techniques comprising behavioral social work could consume an entire M.S.W. training program (see Thyer & Wodarski, 1990). This is a conceptually rich orientation, which has generated literally hundreds of interventive methods, each with its own degree of empirical support and applicability to clients from culturally diverse backgrounds. The design and content of most M.S.W. programs does not allow for mastery of this content. As a consequence, social workers are often not aware of the remarkable degree of empirical support that this approach to practice has garnered, and are poorly trained in the skillful delivery of behavioral interventions.

Another limitation is the spotty nature of the supportive research on social work practice. Some methods have been but weakly investigated. Accordingly, it would be considered sound practice for a social worker to regularly and systematically empirically evaluate the effectiveness of their own practice using these methods, perhaps by employing single-system research designs (see Thyer, 1992c), or through simple group evaluation methods. This, of course, is merely sound social work practice, but it is a form of practice that is more often honored in word than in deed by practitioners of all theoretical orientations.

Social learning theory is itself an evolving body of knowledge. The traditional distinctions between respondent and operant conditioning have been called into doubt by some researchers, and it may emerge that learning via imitation is a complex form of operant conditioning as opposed to a conceptually distinct mechanism. Fifty years ago the field now known as social learning theory did not exist. It is to be hoped that 50 years hence the present formulations will have been replaced by a conceptual framework that captures even more of nature's truth and that yields ever more effective methods of social work practice. In the interim, it must be acknowledged that the present framework is an incomplete one and that many areas of social work practice, particular those dealing with culturally diverse client groups, lack a strong foundation of empirical support for the application of behavioral methods. Recognition of this fact should not obscure the impressive achievements that have been made to date in this area, but rather should serve as a stimulus for further conceptual and empirical progress.

Although the principles of respondent, operant, and observational learning are held to be uniform across culturally diverse clients, empirical research examining the influences of variables as income, race, or education has lagged (cf. Heffer & Kelley, 1987). One authority on behavioral practice with women clients (Blechman, 1984) has made the following point:

> When I first wrote about behavior modification with women, I made much of the value-free technology of behavior modification. Both time and Alan Gurman have changed my mind. From the vantage point of the woman consumer,behavior modification is no more value free than any other form of psychological or medical intervention. The egalitarian argument that the basic mechanisms do not differentiate between the sexes has a fatal flaw. The same mechanisms operate between two different psychosocial environments, one male, one female. For better or worse, the world treats women differently from men. (p. xii)

SUMMARY

Social learning theory has much to offer social work in terms of helping members of our profession offer culturally sensitive and effective interventive services to diverse client groups. The theoretical foundation of behavioral social work is strongly supported by empirical research, and numerous replication studies across clients representing various cultures, races, ethnic backgrounds, nationalities, sexual orientations, and other aspects of diversity suggest that this approach produces positive benefits generalizable to various clients groups. A social learning theory perspective on diversity issues suggests that cultural/ethnic differences arise through the operation of common learning processes occurring within the context of differing psychosocial environments. No particular group is held up as normative standard, and an individual's behavior can only be properly understood when examined within the context in which it developed. By viewing client problems as arising from past and/or present environmental learning experiences and as a function of various physical, social, and psychological resources, an inherently nonpathological, respectful, and optimistic perspective arises from which to promote positive changes.

A Systems Approach: Addressing Diverse Family Forms

9

Roberta R. Greene and Karen Frankel

> *Families [are] small, open systems, deeply affected by their internal, interpersonal dynamics and by the many aspects of the external environment with which they interact.*
>
> (Chilman, Nunnally, & Cox, 1988, p. 8)

This chapter outlines the basic tenets of general systems theory as well as key concepts from select schools of family therapy. It then critiques how these assumptions and concepts have been used to serve diverse family forms. It specifically emphasizes human behavior principles that explain differences in family culture, composition, and developmental processes. The chapter also examines the literature that takes issue with the family systems perspective assessment and intervention techniques, particularly the application of the family systems perspective in certain family therapy approaches (Boss & Thorne, 1989; Hare-Mustin, 1989).

In the past three decades, the structure and the functioning of American families have undergone rapid and far-reaching changes (Billingsley, 1987). Given these changes, a range of definitions regarding what constitutes a family has emerged, "from the traditional family, a nuclear unit comprised of blood relatives, to the self-defined family unit comprised of individuals bound together by emotional relationships" (Greene & Ephross, 1991, p. 32). Social workers are increasingly practicing with single-parent households, lesbian couples, remarried and two-career families, commuter families, step or blended families, gay partners, among others.

In addition to variant family forms, social workers are serving ethnic minority families more and more. Although a family's culture influences how the family defines a problem and the way in which the family tends to seek help, the literature on family-centered approaches mainly uses a frame of reference centered around the white, middle-class U.S. family (Ho, 1987). Only recently have ethnic differences been considered when developing therapeutic models (McGoldrick, 1982; McGoldrick, Preto, Hines, & Lee, 1991). Ho (1987) has suggested that this insensitivity is often a problem because "some of these therapeutic approaches diametrically oppose indigenous cultural values and structures of ethnic minority families" (p. 8).

Social workers must not only understand the role of culture and ethnicity in family life, but must be prepared to understand the developmental histories of client families (Pinderhughes, 1982). For example, Noble (1988) pointed out that an African-American family cannot be understood without addressing its African roots, the history of institutional racism, and the way in which "the family unit is embedded in a network of mutually interdependent relationships with the African-American community and the wider (white) society" (p. 48). On the other hand, Ho (1987) has proposed that practitioners need to use cultural mapping to ascertain acculturation differences among recently arrived immigrant families, immigrant-American families, and immigrant-descendant families. To provide effective services to diverse families, social workers must be armed with human behavior theory that can address each family's "persistent system of rules, predominant themes and patterns of behavior, and particular pattern of adaptation and change" (Hartman & Laird, 1983, p. 105).

Research has suggested that failure to address families in a value- and culturally sensitive manner often leads to ineffective service (Doherty & Boss, 1992). For example, as a result of their research with the National Chicano Research Network, Rothman, Gant, and Hnat (1985) found that failure to identify family cultural characteristics in the design of intervention strategies resulted in less effective service delivery. They urged that research be used more extensively to derive culturally sensitive family social work techniques.

Although there is a considerable body of theory that informs family-focused social work practice, in many instances, general systems theory has been used to better understand the reciprocal interactions among a system's members in many types of systems (Hepworth & Larsen, 1990; Minuchin & Montalvo, 1971). Because general systems theory is a highly abstract model, it is viewed as well suited for explicating the value orientation, culture, and developmental stage of a particular family (Greene, 1986; Hearn, 1969; Herr & Weakland, 1979; Lewis, 1980; Rhodes, 1977, 1980). For example, Greene (1991d) believes that systems theory's broad universal principles suggest the inclusion of cross-cultural content and have the potential to offer culture- and gender-fair assessment and intervention techniques. She argued that it is particularly useful in understanding the evolution of a culture and in appraising transactions between different cultural systems, thus permitting an understanding of various family forms.

BASIC ASSUMPTIONS: A CRITIQUE OF UNIVERSALITY

In family groups, all members influence and are influenced by every other member, creating a system that has properties of its own and that is governed by a set of implicit rules, power structure, forms of communication, and ways of negotiating and solving problems. (Hepworth & Larsen, 1990, pp. 256–257)

General systems theory is a comprehensive model for analyzing the interaction and relational qualities between and among the components of a system. Its assumptions serve as a working hypothesis for explaining, predicting, and controlling phenomena. General systems theory, which came to the fore in the late 1960s and early 1970s, provides a multicausal context for understanding human behavior, emphasizes the interdependence and interactions among people, and considers the many systems in which people interact (Janchill, 1969; Leighninger, 1977; Petr, 1988). The theory is a means of conceptualizing the mutual interrelatedness of individuals-families–social groups–communities-societies. Systems theory is a way of thinking in an organized, integrated way about the interactions among systems members (Table 9.1). A *social system* is a defined structure of interacting and interdependent persons that has the capacity for organized activity. As a social system develops over time, it takes on a unique character. Because of the high degree of interaction and interdependence among systems members, systems theory proposes that a change in any one member of the system affects the social system as a whole.

Systems theory also suggests a number of concepts that may be applied to diverse family forms. Perhaps its most important assumption is that each family has its own interlocking network of relationships with discernible structural and communication patterns. Minuchin (1974) defined a family as a system that operates though repeated transactional patterns of how, when, and to whom members relate: "Family structure is the [resulting] invisible set of functional demands that organizes the way in which family members interact" (p. 51).

Another major assumption is that because each family has a history of working together and maintaining homeostasis, its structure, energy exchange, and *organization*—or its system of relationships—vary. Through repetitive exchanges, each family develops distinctive patterns of *roles*, that is, differentiation of members by tasks. These patterns provide the family with cognitive maps about how to interact in reciprocal roles such as mother/daughter or husband/wife (Greene, 1991d; see Chapter 6 for a discussion of role theory).

Over time, family interaction also produces subsystems, components of a system that are themselves systems. Parental, sibling, or spouse family sub-

Table 9.1. Systems Theory: Basic Assumptions

A social system comprises interrelated members who constitute a unit or a whole.

The organizational "limits" of a social system are defined by its established or arbitrarily defined boundaries and identified membership.

Boundaries give the social system its identity and focus as a system.

A systems environment is an environment that is defined as outside the system's boundaries.

The life of a social system is more than just the sum of its participants' activities. Rather, a social system can be studied as a network of unique, interlocking relationships with discernible structural and communication patterns.

There is a high degree of interdependence and internal organization among members of a social system.

All systems are subsystems of other (larger) systems.

There is an interdependency and mutual interaction between and among social systems.

A social system is adaptive or goal oriented and purposive.

A change in any one member of the social system affects the nature of the social system as a whole.

Transactions or movements across a social system's boundaries influence the social system's functional capacity and internal makeup.

Change within and from outside the social system that moves the system to an imbalance in structure will result in an attempt by the system to reestablish that balance.

Source: Greene, R. R. (1991d). "General Systems Theory." In R. R. Greene and P. H. Ephross (Eds.), *Human Behavior Theory and Social Work Practice*, p. 236. Hawthorne, NY: Aldine de Gruyter.

systems, for example, tend to follow an observable pattern based on the family's needs and culture. Family interactions also create a hierarchy; thus, family systems practitioners may proceed with the assumption that all families will have a power structure or a means of distributing power in particular circumstances. Observations of family hierarchies suggest how one member of the family influences the behavior of another and how family decisions are made.

All families also have *rules*—implicit and explicit agreements about duties, rights, and range of appropriate and acceptable behaviors. Social workers can come to understand a family's rules because they are reflected in a family's *communication patterns*, the flow of information within and from outside the system. For example, Hepworth and Larsen (1990) argued that because a major theme in many cultural groups is a pattern of discouraging open communication, practitioners must seek culturally sound ways of gaining pertinent information.

Energy, which deals with a system's capacity to act and maintain itself, is another important property of a social system. Energy is a family's power to organize itself—to keep itself in working balance—and its ability to obtain sufficient resources from its environment. Social workers, who hope to see a family become more adaptive, often set goals with families to obtain needed resources. The more adaptive systems use energy well and are able to keep relatively organized through effective communication, thus obtaining sufficient resources from the surrounding environment.

When energy is insufficient and communication poor, tension on the family's internal organization results. The literature suggests that these families are relatively dysfunctional, apt to be inflexible, less open to other social institutions, and therefore less effective (Goldenberg & Goldenberg, 1991). Families that are relatively functional tend to be well organized, have effective communication, and allow for the development of individuals.

However, what constitutes functional and dysfunctional behavior is debatable. Hepworth and Larsen (1990) suggested that practitioners must view functional and dysfunctional behavior within the context of a family's culture. This concept, known as *cultural relativity*, means that behavior found unacceptable in one culture may be perceived as acceptable in another. On the other hand, some theorists believe that "there is indeed psychopathological behavior" and that a universal standard can be set (Trepper, 1987, p. xi).

Although the family systems perspective is often characterized as neutral, the approach has been criticized for placing insufficient attention on factors of culture, class, ethnicity/race, gender, or age. The remainder of the chapter examines this contention.

FAMILY-FOCUSED SOCIAL WORK INTERVENTIONS AND DIVERSITY

Family-centered practice is a model of social work practice which locates the family in the center of the unit of attention or field of action. (Germain, 1968, p. 14)

Social work practice with families dates back to the inception of the profession. Today, most social work practice is family centered and reflects involvement with the family therapy movement, which has strong ties to general systems theory (Greene, 1986). Family-centered social work, part of direct practice in social work that emphasizes adaptation among individuals, families, and groups and their environments, has come to include a broad spectrum of services and methods of intervention, such as marital and family therapies, problem-solving guidance, environmental intervention, and advocacy, as well as homemaker service, financial relief, or other tangible assistance (Erickson, 1987; Greene, 1986; Meyer, 1987).

A major general systems theory theme in most family approaches is that in attempting to alleviate family difficulties, social workers attend to the impact of one family member's behavior on another. Generally speaking, family-centered interventions are indicated when the family is unable to perform its basic functions. Practitioners also address how a family changes and use interventions designed to modify those elements of the family relationship system that are interfering with the life tasks of the family and its members.

Most family-centered social workers share the view that if an individual changes, the family context in which he or she lives also will change, and vice versa. Hence, the ultimate goal of most family-centered social work is to enhance social functioning of all persons (Greene, 1986). Family-focused interventions tend to recognize that one family member's symptoms or problems usually bring a family for help, and so the focus of family approaches is altering family relationship patterns.

From a systems perspective, a problematic behavior is seen as not exclusively influenced by personality and past events. Rather, behaviors are influenced by current patterns of interaction between family members and between the family and its environments. Family theorists suggest that when problem behavior persists, the resolution of the problem usually requires an appropriate change in behavior within the family system of interaction (Hartman & Laird, 1987; Herr & Weakland, 1979).

Family social work, then, may be defined as an interactional process of planned interventions in an area of family dysfunction. The family is a self-regulating or rule-governed group with fairly consistent patterns over time. Interventions are aimed at the system as a whole, with the family's structure, organization, development, and openness to its environment as the targets of intervention. General systems theorists argue that the impetus for change rests with the family members, particularly in making adjustments in their present daily lives (Hartman & Laird, 1987). The idea that the family comprises individuals who make up an entity, system, or group that is capable of solving its problems is at the center of general systems interventions.

The degree of emphasis on these general systems principles varies within major schools of family therapy (Skynner, 1981). The different methods of family treatment form a treatment continuum. At one end of the continuum, the concept of the family emphasizes emotional or affective relationships within the system. The therapist promotes health and growth through insight-oriented techniques and uses transference for therapeutic goals (Ackerman, 1972; see Chapter 3 for a discussion of transference). At the other end of the continuum, therapists aim to intervene in the structure and communication patterns of the family to improve an area of family dysfunction. The focus of family therapy, then, is to alter the structure of the family group and the functions, or roles, of individual family members (Bowen, 1971; Minuchin, 1974).

The selection of family therapy techniques is influenced by the social worker's personal style and theoretical beliefs, characteristics of the family system, personalities of family members, developmental stage of the family, nature and severity of the presenting problem, particular family members present, and desired therapeutic goals (McLeod, 1986). Variation exists in family-focused social work and family therapy approaches, styles, and techniques as well as settings and specific client groups. Intervention goals also differ in emphasis and include restructuring the family (Minuchin, 1974), resolving intergenerational conflict (Bowen, 1971), renegotiating roles (Satir, 1967), and improving communication (Haley, 1976).

As social workers increasingly serve families of diverse forms and cultural backgrounds, it is imperative for them to sensitively and selectively use family-focused interventions and address family patterns and belief systems (Anderson, 1991; Boss & Weiner, 1988; Hepworth & Larsen, 1990; White, 1986). A number of theorists have suggested that general systems theory has brought social work practice to a more value-free, if not more universal, orientation (Berger & Federico, 1982; Janchill 1969; Meyer, 1973). Social workers have a framework for understanding the cultural context of how client families seek help. For example, Ziter (1987) offers a culturally sensitive problem-centered systems model that encompasses empowerment and bicultural concepts for working with black alcoholic families. Bryant (1980) proposed that the systems treatment approach be modified to serve inner-city families. Furthermore, Red Horse (1980a) has discussed systems theory as a means of understanding the family structure and value orientation in American Indian families. When there is a difficulty, many American Indian families prefer to use natural helping systems (Lewis, 1980; see Chapter 11 for a discussion of natural helping systems). In addition, many Puerto Rican families, according to Mizio (1974), must be understood within a "network of ritual kinship whose members have a deep sense of obligation to each other for economic assistance, encouragement, and support" that often conflicts with the idea of the nuclear family unit (p. 77). Mizio also found systems theory useful in understanding the family's position vis-à-vis other societal systems.

In contrast, some theorists argue that a general systems approach in family therapy has neither sufficiently made room for social justice and individual choice nor challenged the status quo (Brown & Slee, 1986; Goldner, 1988; Grunbaum (1987; Hoffman, 1990; Sider & Clements, 1982; Taggart, 1985; Thorne & Yalom, 1982). For example, in a discussion of the problem of gender in family therapy, Hare-Mustin (1986, 1989) contended that the use of systems theory in family therapy has led to a microscopic examination of family interaction but ignores societal changes and the concern for equality within the family. She suggested that practitioners who consider differentiation and negotiation as the most important intervention goals ignore "differences in power, resources, needs, and interests among family members" (p. 69). That is, practitioners alter the internal functioning of families, without proper concern for political, economic, and social contexts (Jacobson, 1983).

In addition, Hoffman (1985, 1990) proposed that practitioners should not act as experts who assess and describe family problems. She and other constructionist theorists (White, 1986) contend that giving people negative causal explanations of their problems serves only to maintain the family's problem and maintain negative power relationships (Bateson, 1972). Instead, constructionist theorists suggest that descriptions of a family's problematic behavior should be co-constructed *with* the family, pay ample attention to subjective ideas, and explore alternative courses of action. This alternative approach to intervening in circular, patterned cycles of events is known as *second-order cybernetics* and is increasingly used in family treatment (Hoffman, 1992; Madanes, 1981, 1990, 1991; see Chapter 7 for a discussion of constructionism).

Margolin (1982) stated that family therapy has different, if not more complex, ethical questions than individual psychotherapy, such as: Who is the client? How is confidential information handled? Does each family member have an equal right to refuse treatment? What is the role of the therapist vis-à-vis conflicting values of family members? (p. 608). Ryders (1987) took the point a step further and argued that family therapists often bury their value stances in the jargon they use to describe families, such as "dysfunctional" or "marital satisfaction" (p. 136). Aponte (1985) stated that values are central to family therapy. He proposed that a practitioner's "values are integral to all social systemic operations and therefore at the heart of the therapeutic process. . . . Therapists do not have a choice about whether they need to deal with values in therapy, only about how well" (p. 337).

Although family therapies may "appear to transcend the atomic individual," they are nonetheless "part of the American culture" or part of the mainstream of mental health practice (Doherty and Boss, 1992, p. 613). Therefore, the various family therapies follow other clinical professions and tend to ignore larger social, cultural, and political issues. According to Doherty and Boss, family therapy has tended to make family problems private matters rather than public concerns. How much should issues in the larger social sphere, such as gender and culture, be included in setting goals of therapy? To what extent should differentiation of self be considered a universal life goal suitable for therapy?

In another critique of the family systems perspective, Hare-Mustin (1978) suggested that "when we alter the internal functioning of the family without concern for the social, economic, and political context, we are in complicity with the society to keep the family unchanged" (p. 68). Likewise, Aponte (1979, 1987) argued that the relationship of societal forces to intrapsychic or mental distress has not been sufficiently addressed. Families may differ in terms of income, employment opportunities, and degree of discrimination.

Inattention to the effects of such strains on family structure often is a barrier to family-centered interventions. To be effective, a family systems perspective must consider ethnicity and socioeconomic influences on family lifestyles as well as the way in which gender shapes role expectations, experiences, goals, and opportunities within the family (Goldenberg & Goldenberg, 1991).

The family therapy field is highly abstract and insufficiently self critical (Weiner & Boss, 1985). Failure to be self-critical, according to Bernal and Ysern (1986), has led to the implicit acceptance of several social and political assumptions about the nature of U.S. society, including the structures of injustice and the way such exploitation harms families and the "normative endorsement of the nuclear family and its traditional sex roles" (p. 131). In this vein, the following section outlines key systems concepts and discusses how these concepts have been applied to address diverse family forms.

CULTURE AND THE FAMILY

Ethnicity and family life are two concepts which . . . go hand in hand. They are so entwined that it is very difficult indeed to observe the one or even to reflect it seriously without coming to grips with the other. (Billingsley, 1976, p. 13)

For social workers to provide culturally sensitive assessment and treatment for families with ethnic and cultural backgrounds different from their own, it is necessary to understand the cultural aspects of family systems (Tseng & Hsu, 1991). As family members interact with each other and the environment, they develop a set of shared meanings that serve as a social foundation for their culture (Chess & Norlin, 1988). *Culture* refers to a group's way of life: those elements of a people's history, tradition, values, and social organization that become implicitly or explicitly meaningful to the participants (Green, 1982).

The family is often viewed as the basic sociocultural institution through which culture is transmitted. Culture is said to shape the cycle of growth of family systems members as well as the group's culture. Within the contexts of its members, the family maintains itself throughout its life by adhering to its own values and beliefs (Kluckhorn, 1951). Culture, then, is "the symbolic image of [a family's] purpose that its members carry around in their heads" (Polsky, 1969, p. 12).

Castex (1993) cautioned, though, that ethnic groups are not static and must be understood as evolving interactional units that change over time. She warned that practitioners must shy away from the notion that there is a list of ethnic traits to describe any one family. This approach increases the risk of stereotyping and avoiding the effects of power relations on group behavior.

In a similar vein, Germain (1991) argued that social workers must be self-aware so that they can be more sensitive to the differences in behavior, expectations, and attitudes of diverse families. However, practitioners must be careful to distinguish between the general cultural traits, values, and norms attributed to a group, such as those found in some anthropological texts, and the unique features of a specific family group. Green (1982) proposed an ethnographic approach to understanding specific families as a method of culturally sound understanding (see Chapter 4 for a description of this approach).

In a book dedicated to presenting a conceptual framework for family therapy with ethnic minority families, Ho (1987) outlined the major features of culturally sensitive family therapy with ethnic minorities. Ho proposed that cross-cultural family practice

- recognizes that some of the assumptions of a particular human behavior theory may be antithetical to a particular cultural orientation
- uses theory-based practice differentially
- considers the family's sociopolitical history and present situation
- is congruent with the family's belief system and ethical and value orientation
- is accepting of the way in which a particular family defines its problem and expresses help-seeking behaviors
- identifies and works within a particular family's form
- is based on a culturally sound examination of family structure and communication patterns
- may, at times, be delivered in other than the English language or by a social intermediary
- recognizes the way culture shapes individual and family life experiences as well as developmental transitions
- is sensitive to the influences of culture on a family's role differentiation and process of self-definition
- selects skills and techniques differentially to achieve congruence with a family's culture
- uses a multisystems approach
- uses natural support systems and helpers, such as healers and religious leaders
- selects goals culturally congruent and mutually satisfactory to the family's goals
- is open to the family's ideas about what is effective for them.

Class and ethnicity often are distinguished from culture. Social class is based on differences in wealth, income, occupation, status, community power, level of consumption, and family background. Because people may belong to various social classes, ethnic groups, and cultures, seemingly similar groups may vary. For example, Logan (1990) cautioned that black culture should not be seen as "an 'underclass' world view, [that is,] that poverty and black culture are not to be viewed interchangeably" (p. 25). Rather, the issue of distinguishing class and culture is related to the controversy of why a group has a particular social and/or economic status (Franklin, 1988; Freedman, 1990b; see Chapter 12 for a discussion of power factors in social work practice). Ethnicity, or the behavioral and cognitive participation in the symbolic communication of a group, usually involves a common language. Many ethnic groups or subcommunities, each with its own common history, ancestry, and status, or power position, exist in U.S. society. The idea is increasingly proposed that the United States is a multicultural society, a society in which "ethnic identities are not amalgamated . . . [but] should remain a mosaic of separate, diverse, and equally proud identities" (Longres, 1990, p. 78).

However, "a member of an ethnic minority is inevitably part of two cultures" (Ho, 1987, p. 15). *Biculturalism*, in which a person participates in two cultural systems, often requiring two sets of behavior, usually involves two distinct ways of coping with tasks, expectations, and behaviors (Chestang, 1972). Within a family, there may be discrepancies in acculturation (how much a person takes on the "mainstream" culture) among family members. For example, in Asian/Pacific families, children, in contrast to their parents, tend to be more receptive to Western culture. When children may be more open to ideas of individualism and sexual freedom than are their parents, family dysfunction may occur (Ho, 1987).

Therapists need to be sensitive to the cultural transitions and cognitive changes that are often made as newly immigrant families become oriented to life in the United States. Matsuoka (1990) pointed out that there usually is a culture conflict when people migrate from one culture to another or when individuals in a pluralistic culture move from their ethnic community into the mainstream environment. He suggested that because there has been differential acculturation among Vietnamese refugees, there may be disruption in traditional age-related family roles. Given the large numbers of immigrants to the United States who may seek assistance, many social workers will need to understand these possible cultural disruptions (Bromley, 1987). Clearly, culturally appropriate methods are needed, particularly for refugees in crisis or for those for whom the "very concept of 'social work' does not exist" (Queralt, 1984; Timberlake & Cook, 1984; Weiss & Parish, 1989).

Shon and Ja (1982) outlined seven factors that may alter a new immigrants family relationships and structural patterns and, for which many families seek help: (1) cultural shock and disbelief at the disparity between what was expected and what actually exists, (2) disappointments at what exists, (3) grief at the separation from and loss of what was left behind, (4) anger and resentment, (5) depression because of the current family situation, (6) some form of acceptance of their situation, and (7) mobilization of family resources and energy.

STRUCTURAL ISSUES AND DIVERSE FAMILY FORMS

Family structure and lifestyles vary, especially at this time in society when a variety of family forms is becoming more common. . . . Each of these family forms has its own particular strengths and vulnerabilities. (Chilman, Nunnally, & Cox, 1988, p. 9)

Roles

Socially recognized family roles tend to be those explicitly and implicitly defined by culture. For many decades, general U.S. society conceptualized the family as comprising a husband/father who worked to support the family, a wife/mother who raised the children full-time, and their biological, dependent children (Parsons & Bales, 1955; see Chapter 6 on role theory). These roles generally were associated with traditional family functions, which included the legitimation of mating and sexual reproduction; the socialization of all members, particularly children; the economic maintenance of the group; the division of domestic labor; and the transmission of culture (Germain, 1991).

However, there is increasing confusion about the way in which roles are defined as well as about the evolution of family organization, form, or structure. This confusion stems largely from changing roles and forms of the U.S. family (Longres, 1990). For example, Pavalko (1986) contrasted the traditional family, with its clear role and power definitions, with the equal-partner marriage, a more democratic family in which there are shared authority, resources, decision-making, and child rearing.

Practitioners must be aware that personal and family definitions vary widely (Duberman, 1975; Tseng & Hsu, 1991). For example, Hepworth and Larsen (1990) cautioned that each culture has different role expectations and distribution of labor in the family, particularly concerning male and female roles. Therefore, social workers must assess the extent to which there is a "goodness of fit" between individual roles and the need of family members (p. 289).

Hepworth and Larsen (1990, p. 288) also suggested practitioners should ask several questions in making an assessment:

- To what extent are role assignments in the family made on the basis of gender rather than factors such as abilities, interests, and available time of individual members to perform various roles?
- How clearly are roles defined in the family?
- How satisfied are marital partners with their prescribed roles, and to what extent is each willing to consider adjustments when dissatisfaction is a key in family problems? How flexible is the entire family system in readjusting roles in response to everyday pressures and changing circumstances?
- How adequately do spouses perform in their designated roles as marital partner and parent?
- To what extent are pressures and stresses in the family caused by role overload, a state of affairs when marital partners play too many roles at home and at work for the time and energy they have available?

Differences in Family Definition Based on Structure

The family as a social institution exists in all societies. The U.S. Bureau of the Census (1988) defined *family* as "a group of two or more persons related by blood, marriage, or adoption and residing together in a household" (p. 5). This view of the nuclear family has been idealized by mid-twentieth-century sociologists (Martin & O'Connor, 1989). However, social scientists have increasingly called into question the idea that the nuclear family is universal (Longres, 1990: Visher & Visher, 1987, 1988; Westcott & Dries, 1990; Woodman, 1981).

There have been numerous approaches to the study of the family and topologies of family forms. Sociologists and anthropologists have distinguished between various family systems, relating to such parameters as marriage forms (the number of spouses a person has at one time); choice of mates (the choice of partners inside or outside one's own kin group); descent system (the rights and obligations as seen in male kinship connections, female kinship connections, or both); postmarital residence choice (the patterns of residence based on whether it is a new place of one's own or near the husband's or wife's family); or household structure (persons who share living quarters and family functions).

Families also may vary according to how they allocate authority, power, and decision-making, whether customarily relegated to the males, females, or both (Tseng & Hsu, 1991). In addition, family patterns must be understood in relation to historical, political, and economic variables (Billingsley, 1968; Franklin, 1988; Frazier, [1939] 1966; Herskovits, [1941] 1958). For example, to understand current African-American families, according to Dodson

(1988), it is necessary to examine multiple factors, such as the influence of African culture, the inherent strength of family networks, the oppressive racial conditions of American society, and the social class differences between and within groups.

Franklin (1988) contended that the strong family tradition among blacks survived "the slave system, then legal segregation, discrimination, and enforced poverty, and finally, . . . racially hostile governmental and societal practices, policies, and attitudes" (p. 25). On the other hand, Sudarkasa (1988) argued that to understand the African-American family, it is necessary to avoid false dichotomies concerning explanations of black family organization:

> Just as surely as Black American family patterns are in part an outgrowth of the descent into slavery, so too are they partly a reflection of the archetypical African institutions and values that informed and influenced the behavior of those Africans who were enslaved in America. (p. 27)

She suggested that Western or European cultures tend to follow conjugal patterns of family organization—affinal kinship created between spouses, whereas African families have traditionally been organized around consanguineal cores, biologically based kinship that is rooted in blood ties formed by adult siblings of the same gender.

Indeed, "American family life is taking different forms" (Longres, 1990, p. 199). Such forms may include serial monogamy—repeated marriages one at a time after divorce or widowhood, the one-parent family, stepfamilies or reconstituted families, cohabiting couples, and gay and lesbian couples. Although Longres (1990) chose not to use the terms *family* and *marriage* when referring to gay and lesbian couples, implying that such couples should not be judged by heterosexual norms, other theorists have used a systems definition. For example, Harry (1988) proposed that gay and lesbian families be defined as "a homosexual person tied by affectional and/or erotic needs to either another homosexual person or to children with whom they may cohabit" (p. 97).

Despite this definitional confusion, the state of the American family continues to be a social and political issue. Although in the late twentieth century traditional nuclear families are in the minority, much of the literature on family interventions still has assumed that the term *family* refers to the heterosexual nuclear unit of mother, father, and children, or the heterosexual single-parent family (Crawford, 1987). During the 1970s, when the conceptualization of family treatment approaches was under way, Minuchin (1974) characterized the "American family, like American society, . . . as under attack and in a transitional period" (p. 50). His comments foreshadowed many of the social and economic realities that would shape the need for new family structures that had not yet appeared or been sufficiently recognized.

Family Boundaries and Family Forms

From a family systems perspective, a *family* may be defined as "two or more people in a committed relationship from which they derive a sense of identity as a family" (Chilman, Nunnally, & Cox, 1988, p. 11). Hartman and Laird (1984) defined the family as consisting "of two or more people who have made a commitment to share living space, have developed emotional ties, and share a variety of family roles and functions" (p. 30). These definitions are broad enough to include many nontraditional family forms. Each family unit, then, has its own identity and focus as a system, distinguishable from other social systems by its *boundaries*, or organizational "limits." Boundaries are the permeable limits of a system that define who is inside or outside the system or who participates, and how.

From a systems point of view, people who join together and acknowledge family membership constitute a family and become the unit of social work attention. In addition, people within the systems boundaries have specific functions and roles or behavioral demands. Systems theory definitions are said to offer a means of understanding a family's cultural values, assessing their unique form, structured pattern of relationships, and communication style, as well as specific needs for intervention. For example, to achieve culturally sound social work practice with American Indian families, Red Horse (1980a) asserted that the role of the elders needs to be understood and the three-generation family-kinship network must be addressed. However, although there are choices among approaches to the definition of family, according to Hartman and Laird (1983), "all probably [fail] to encompass adequately the rich pluralism of [U.S.] racial, cultural, and ethnic diversity and the wide variety of lifestyle choices" (p. 27), such as the family forms of lesbian couple and single parent.

Lesbian Couple

One example of a different family form is the lesbian couple, with or without children (Poverny & Finch, 1988; Roth, 1989; Roth & Murphy, 1986; Shernoff, 1984). The literature increasingly offers research and theoretical constructs about the pattern of developmental processes and coherent personal identity of persons with a homosexual orientation (DeVine, 1984; Herdt, 1992; McWhirter & Mattison, 1984). However, most of the literature on family interventions assumes the family is a heterosexual unit.

Theorists who have offered suggestions for family therapy with lesbian couples have suggested a redefinition of the family to include factors such as continuity of commitment by members over a significant time, mutual obligation, economic and domestic interdependence, and performance of daily family functions (Poverny & Finch, 1988). Definitions are seen as having important implications for policy and practice.

From a systems perspective, the broader definition suggests that practitioners aim to understand the way in which lesbian couples tend to be oppressed by general society. Crawford (1987) contended that negative conceptualization of the family in a homophobic environment can adversely affect treatment with lesbian families and contribute to their stress and isolation. She also proposed that this societal oppression makes the family building process for lesbians more difficult than for the heterosexual family. Harry (1988) also contended that foregoing concealment by homosexual couples may be "fraught with dangers" and may produce "permanent or long-term rejection" (p. 98).

When practitioners examine their own notions of the family and expand their definitions, they are better able to identify significant members of the client system as well as the issues they face (Crawford, 1988). Practitioners who are conversant with a systemic approach to helping lesbian families have suggested that problems be explored in such a way as to expand the family's ideas and beliefs about themselves, thereby seeking a greater number of possible solutions. For example, those lesbian couple systems that are more closed to the outer environment can achieve more support, or lesbian couples may explore how their connections with families of origin may be enhanced (Crawford, 1987).

Single-Parent

Single-parent families represent one of the most significantly increasing family forms (Westcot & Dries, 1990). Despite the increasing number of one-parent families over the decades, family therapists have not focused much attention on this form; instead, the literature has concentrated on the parental or marital subsystem, the parent-child subsystem, and the sibling subsystem. (Westcott & Dries, 1990). Kissman (1991) has urged that social work with single-parent families "redefine the boundaries of 'functional' family norms," and not use "negative comparisons with 'intact' families" (pp. 23–24).

Family therapy is a psychotherapeutic approach that concentrates on changing interactions between family members and between families and other interpersonal systems in a way that improves the dynamics of the family, the subsystems, and individual members (Wayne, 1988). Although this definition does not preclude work with single-parent families, it does not focus on the particular needs of families, such as the way in which single-parent status was acquired, for example, a child born to a single woman, divorce, death, or abandonment by a parent (Morawetz & Walker, 1984). Nearly a quarter of the nation's unmarried women become mothers. The social and political explanations for single parenthood are beyond the scope of this chapter, and are a matter of heated debate among social scientists. However, recent U.S. Census Bureau statistics indicate that practitioners should avoid stereotypical conclusions. For example, there is a sharp change in demographics from a decade ago with the number of never-married mothers doubling among white, college-educated women (Deparle, 1993)

Nonetheless, most single parents face social stigmatization because they are seen as having a "broken home." Therefore, it is even more important for therapists not to view the single parent as having an emotional disability because he or she is living in a nontraditional family. If this stereotyping occurs, the treatment adds to the problem-generating cycle. In addition, the family therapy focus frequently is not on stressors, for example, child maladjustment due to death or divorce of one parent, grief, loss, guilt, visitation rights, parenting functions, financial matters, and social life issues (Korittko, 1991).

Feminist-based social workers have argued that practitioners need to take a more holistic view of single-parent families (Becker, 1989; Bricker-Jenkins & Hooyman, 1986; Kissman, 1991; Miller, 1987; Van Den Bergh & Cooper, 1985) and recognize and address single-parent families' strengths (Boulette, 1976). They have contended that interventions with single-parent families across the life cycle can be linked to important feminist social work tenets of networking, awareness, support, and self-help.

Furthermore, theorists who have discussed the phenomenon of single parenthood in the African-American community have suggested that, although the level of poverty among single-parent families is of great concern, to enhance quality of social and economic opportunity, social workers need to understand the social and cultural context of early childbearing (Dore & Dumois, 1990; Logan, Freeman, & McRoy, 1990). One such exploration is a seminal study by Stack (1974), who lived for several years in a low-income black community in the midwestern United States and described that community's adaptive response to child raising. Stack's study discussed the community's cultural value of the inherent worth of each child as well as the way in which black fathers remained connected to their children through kinship networks.

A 1987 report designed to explore the needs, life strengths, and stresses of families headed by women supported this view (Miller, 1987). The study examined the life strengths of women who were poor, minorities, and from urban areas. The most striking outcome was that a vast majority of the women said their families were stronger (60%) or as strong (25%) as other families. The most important strength these single parents identified was strong helping networks with relatives, friends, and neighbors.

As in other family treatment approaches, applying a systemic perspective to family therapy with single-parent families means viewing symptoms other than in linear cause-and-effect terms (McLeod, 1986). Rather, systemic family therapists may conceptualize problems by looking at the family system to include the nuclear family, and also the larger system including extended family members and friends (Madanes, 1991). Sider and Clements (1982) have suggested that therapists decide at what level or levels of system to intervene, because there are times when intervening at one systems level may interfere or alter the functioning of the system at another level. In addition, problems encountered by clients may result from relationships in their families of origin (Minuchin, 1974). Therefore, therapists must look at the larger kin network.

Minuchin's approach, called *strategic family therapy,* appears to be the most popular with single-parent families (Grief, 1987). By engaging in direct teaching with the family using techniques such as role-playing, teaching of communication skills, discussion of limit setting, and assertiveness training, family members learn to relate differently to one another and gain insight into their own behavior or role in the single-parent family system.

Another family treatment approach, Bowen's (1976, 1978) *extended family systems therapy,* has been used to establish a supportive social network for low-income single-parent families. This network includes family, former spouses, mother's siblings, mother's parents, friends, and relatives (Speck & Attneave, 1971; Westcot & Dries, 1990). Reciprocal support of a social network helped single parents function at a more optimal level. Another structural family therapist has instructed therapists to assist fathers in improving their adjustment as single people (Grief, 1987). Social workers might provide vocational counseling for finance and employment issues or discussions to help families adapt to different life schedules, might involve former spouses with children in discussions regarding boundaries, and might develop viable boundaries of parent-child subsystems.

Although the family therapy literature offers established systems of family therapy, it does not make a clear enough distinction between transitional single-parent systems and those more stabilized into a single-parent family unit. Therapists who are working with single-parent families, therefore, must look at different strengths and risks of each family to develop the kind of therapeutic intervention that fits each individual family (Miller, 1987).

DIVERSITY OF FAMILY DEVELOPMENTAL TASKS

The family is a social unit that faces a series of developmental tasks. These differ along the parameters of cultural differences, but they have universal roots.
(Minuchin, 1974, p. 16)

General systems theory has served as a conceptual model for examining the family group as a developmental unit (Rhodes, 1977, 1980). The developmental approach to the family suggests that the family unit passes through normal, expected life stages that test the group's adaptive capacity, usually in terms of landmarks such as marriage, as well as bearing, raising, and launching children. Each change brings about a new set of circumstances to which the family must adapt (Greene, 1986). Rhodes (1980) suggested that the family is a social system that evolves over time, with shifts in family composition at different points in the life cycle. However, failure to meet life transitions may lead families to seek mental health services (Minuchin, 1974).

The stages of the life cycle have tended to be defined for "intact nuclear families in contemporary Western societies" (Tseng & Hsu, 1991). The stages have tended to include the unattached young adult, the formation of the dyadic relationship, the family with young children, the family with adolescents, the family launching children, the family with older members, and the family in later years (Carter & McGoldrick, 1980; Friedman, 1980; Goldenberg & Goldenberg, 1991; Rhodes, 1980). Some theorists, though, have addressed how the structure and development of the family may vary with diverse needs and interests. For example, Groze and Rosenthal (1991) described the adaptability of families who have adopted special-needs children; Hersh (1970), the changes in family functioning following placement of a mentally challenged child; and Kuhn (1990), the normative family crises of confronting dementia.

Roth (1989) has cautioned that although all couples are unique, lesbian couples have no markers of critical developmental events, such as the change in status from dating couple to married couple. The addition of children further complicates separation and differentiation from their families of origin as well as presenting issues of public acceptance. Because rituals and ceremonies are central features of family life, these situations often produce stress for the lesbian couple.

Lesbian families "are discovering new territory" in regard to children (Crawford, 1988, p. 6). Because of homophobia and secrecy about sexual orientation, historically lesbian couples often have kept the true nature of their emotional bond from their children (Dahlheimer & Feigal, 1991). However, lesbian mothers increasingly share in their children's social growth and development, such as attending their children's school events. Nonetheless, Crawford (1987) has proposed that further recognition of lesbian mothers—often caught between two worlds, and not fully acknowledge in either—is needed.

Studies of the family life cycle also should consider the effects of cultural variables such as social class, ethnicity, and religion (Falicov & Karrer, 1980). When applying this perspective to family assessment, it therefore would be more appropriate to think of several "typical" family life cycles. For example, although women play a central role in families, the idea that women may have a "life cycle apart from their roles as wife and mothers" (McGoldrick, 1989, p. 200) is fairly recent.

These family life cycles vary among families of different cultural backgrounds, according to Tseng and Tsu (1991):

- In addition to marriage and the bearing and rearing of children, there are many other milestone factors relating to family system and structure. These factors may include the pattern of getting married, ways to bear and adopt a child, and cohabiting members in the household, all of which affect the total configurational pattern of the family life cycle.
- Due to numerous variations (such as differences in premarital experience, patterns of childbearing, the life span of parents, and the structure of the household), the rhythm of family development may vary, the transition between phases may be clear-cut or blurred, and each stage may be short, long, or even absent.
- Associated with the different cultural implications of critical issues concerning developmental milestones (such as the formal marital union, dissolution of marital relations, launching of children from the home, and widowhood), the impact of such milestones of family development on the family members has different meanings and effects. Therefore, it is necessary to examine the meaning of family development in the context of cultural background. (p. 46)

Family developmental patterns also may be affected by the geographical origin and birthplace of its members and where they are in the cycle of acculturation to mainstream U.S. society. Ho (1987) proposed that practitioners need to be aware that behaviors differ depending on whether a family and its members are foreign-born or native-born and the degree to which they are bicultural. He suggested that the process of immigration and cultural transition has delivered a severe blow to many Asian/Pacific American families. Therefore, practitioners may need to assist with factors including economic survival, American racism, loss of extended family and support system, vast cultural conflicts, and cognitive reactive patterns to a new environment.

With African-American families, the life cycle unfolds within a context of culture and significant life events, a process social workers must understand (Freeman, 1990). In addition, social workers must acknowledge the differences and similarities in the life cycle of black families and in that of other minority and majority families. According to Freeman, black families make three major adaptations that result from a history of oppression, institutional racism, and a general degree of economic deprivation: (1) fluidity of roles, (2) the value placed on education, and (3) the dual perspective. She traced the fluidity of roles observed in many black families to the African family patterns of extended families, joint decision-making, ownership of property, and the socialization of children by the extended family group. This pattern of including "pseudo-family members and other relatives in family roles continues among many black families today" (p. 57). The value of education also is linked to external conditions that often thwart gainful employment. Barriers to education may lead many African-American youths to feel that they have missed the opportunity to better their life. Furthermore, the dual perspective, a conflict between expectations of the larger society and those of one's own group, has a strong impact on the life cycle of the black family (Logan, Freeman, & McRoy, 1990). Black parents frequently must struggle with how to socialize children to have a positive self-image, maintain their cultural strengths, and meet general societal expectations. Social workers perhaps are more likely to ensure culturally specific interventions across cultures when using a strengths perspective.

SOCIAL WORK INTERVENTIONS ISSUES WITH DIVERSE FAMILIES

Social work practice is guided first and foremost by a profound awareness of, and respect for, clients' positive attributes and abilities, talents and resources, desires and aspirations. (Saleebey, 1992, p. 6)

Assessment: A Strengths Perspective

Social work theorists have long sought a strengths perspective (Freedman, 1990a,b; Saleebey, 1992). The practitioner who uses a strengths perspective examines each family's particular attributes and needs, respects a family's cultural patterns, and avoids using negative labels. Poor and many minority families face economic and social stressors. Many families may be "crushed by the effects of poverty, and a legacy of racism" (Aponte, 1991, p. 24). Dodson (1988) has argued that to achieve a strengths perspective with the black family, an acceptable conceptualization of the family, one that suggests that family patterns possess a degree of integrity, must be made.

Goals of Family Intervention

The goals of family intervention vary with the conceptual approach. For example, the structural approach to family intervention is based on the idea that the family "is more than the individual biopsychodynamics of its members" (Minuchin, 1974, p. 89). Families are viewed as social structures with behavioral patterns discernible to social workers. Each person in a family is seen as carrying out multiple roles based on what that particular family expects, permits, or forbids (Jackson, 1965).

This school of thought, which emphasizes family roles, was influenced by sociologists who believed roles are assigned on the basis of legal or chronological status and gender (see Chapter 6 on role theory). In this traditional view, males are seen as the more aggressive wage earner, the female as the more expressive and nurturing figure. For example, Minuchin (1974) stated that by joining the family to make a structural diagnosis, the practitioner observes how family members relate. Questions of concern include: Who is the family spokesperson? If the father is acting as spokesperson, what does this mean? Is the mother "ceding her power temporarily to the father because of some implicit rule about the proper role of men"? (Minuchin, 1974, p. 89).

The observation of the family by structural family therapists results in a family map that serves as an organizational scheme to understand and to set therapeutic goals. According to structural theorists, no family model "is inherently normal or abnormal, functional or dysfunctional. A family's differentiation [is thought to be] idiosyncratic, related to its own composition, developmental stage, and subculture" (Minuchin, 1974, p. 95). Practitioners also accommodate a particular family's style and affective range.

Family-focused therapies also emphasize the differentiation of self, which refers to a family's ability to accept and encourage its members to be autonomous. Several schools of family therapy suggest that practitioners explore how much "connectedness" or "separateness" each family member has achieved (Hartman & Laird, 1983). Yet feminist theorists have suggested that concepts often addressed in family therapy, such as separateness, power, and control, negate female values of intimacy and connectedness (Germain, 1991; Hare-Mustin, 1978).

In a similar vein, Falicov and Karrer (1980) indicated that, in contrast to Anglo-American values, identity seeking or "finding oneself" often is not a primary concern of Mexican-American young adults. Forming a marital system with common goals and negotiated values usually has precedence over the impetus for individuation. Likewise, Ho (1987) pointed out that because most Asian/Pacific American families do not stress individuality, and members expect parents, grandparents, and extended kin to be part of shaping their lives, this principle is ineffective. Therefore, it is important for social workers to remember that there needs to be an eclectic selection of techniques that are congruent with the client system's culture (Red Horse,1980b).

The Role of the Social Worker

Social workers in family-focused interventions generally use techniques that restructure dysfunctional family interaction patterns (Table 9.2). Perhaps the most debated technique to achieve this end is the use of the paradoxical intervention. Through paradoxical interventions, practitioners explain a family's problems in counterintuitive ways, deliberately escalate the symptoms of a member, or redirect symptoms into new or different contexts [for example, "I want you and your mother to plan four eating binges this week" (Doherty & Boss, 1992, p. 618)].

Concerns associated with the use of paradoxical interventions include manipulation, client self-determination, and client control and empowerment. For example, Haley (1963) discussed whether the helping person should be directive and how much control truly rests with the practitioner or the client. He concluded that the use of any technique is a matter of the practitioner's awareness or ignorance of what he or she is doing. Therapists have universal influence on a client no matter the school of thought or nature of intervention—practitioners always are given authority and power by society and clients to solve problems.

Other theorists have argued that the "manipulative" nature of paradoxical

Table 9. 2. Systems Theory Guidelines for Assessment and Intervention in Family Social Work

---

Assume the family is a system with a unique structure and communication patterns that can be examined. The purpose of assessment is to work with the family to determine what is bringing about its dysfunction.

Define the boundaries of the family system by working with the family to ascertain membership. Observe functions and behaviors, and be cognizant of cultural forms. Assess the properties related to relative openness or closed boundaries by observing and asking about the extent of exchange the family has with larger societal systems.

Determine how well the family system fits with its environment. Review what additional resources need to be obtained or accessed to improve the family system–environment fit.

Develop a picture of the family structure through an understanding of its organization. Explore socialization processes, how subsystems are created, the nature of their hierarchy(ies), and the way roles are and continue to be differentiated. Learn from the family how its culture influences organizational structure.

Examine the family's communication patterns. Follow the transfer of information and resources in and between the system and its environment. Assess the relative nature of the system's feedback processes. Determine how this relates overall to patterns of interaction. Ask if the family can describe its rules. Work with the family to identify dysfunctional triangulation in communication. Ask family members about their specific cultural communication clues.

Determine how responsive the family is to stress. Work with family members to identify elements in their structure and communication patterns that contribute to entropy, synergy, or achieving a steady state. Explore ways the system can decrease stress and move to a new level of adaptation, possibly by restructuring.

Source: Greene, R. R. (1991d). "General Systems Theory." In R. R. Greene and P. H. Ephross (Eds.), *Human Behavior Theory and Social Work Practice*, p. 256. Hawthorne, NY: Aldine de Gruyter.

interventions may be a deception for the purposes of control (Collier, 1987). Weiner and Boss (1985) contended that this use of power or control is particularly harmful when the clients may be in socially disempowered situations, such as woman-headed and minority families.

The extent to which individuals are seen as relatively autonomous persons or strongly connected to their family is a major theme in family-centered approaches (Green & Hansen, 1989). Possible conflict exists between individual and family goals, as well as the potential for practitioner gender bias in therapy. Because the pursuit of family-level goals may conflict with individual goals, different family members are unlikely to equally benefit from therapy (Hare-Mustin, 1980). In addition, because women tend to struggle with personal growth in addition to roles as caretakers, they may need help in therapy in balancing their own personal needs with those of family members (Gluck, Dannefer, & Milea, 1980).

When attempting to resolve whether a clinician's loyalties are to the individual or the group, there are general culture differences (Freymann, 1974). Western medicine has tended to view responsibility to the individual as greater, whereas Eastern cultures have tended to place the practitioner's first responsibility to the group. Sider and Clements (1982) have addressed the problem of how practitioners resolve the issue of loyalty and ethics when choosing among therapeutic modalities and techniques. They suggested that, although the resolution of this dilemma is difficult, the practitioner make explicit statements to the family about possible conflicting loyalties.

THE FAMILY AND OTHER SOCIAL INSTITUTIONS

[The focus of family-centered practice is the] family-environment interface, as the social worker and family examine the fit or lack of fit between the family and its "surround." (Hartman & Laird, 1987, p. 582)

Studies of human development are increasingly using an ecological systems approach that examines how intrafamilial processes are influenced by the external environment (Auerswald, 1971; Bronfenbrenner, 1986; Germain, 1991). Although the family continues to be the principal context for human development, it is recognized that development is affected by the "other environments" with which families interact. For example, even though children may never physically enter a work setting, their psychological development is affected by work settings in which their parents spend their lives.

Culturally sensitive social work practice with ethnic and racial minorities often uses an ecological systems approach involving and accessing other social systems on behalf of the family (Aponte, 1987; Ho, 1987; Sotomayor,

1971; Wright, Kail, & Creecy, 1990). This approach examines the family within the context of the wider social context in which families must interact. The family–larger systems interface often involves work systems, school and religious institutions, and health care systems. For some families, it may include welfare agencies, mental health clinics, or criminal justice systems such as courts (Imber-Black, 1991).

Many theorists have suggested that it is important for practitioners to conduct a family–larger system assessment when engaging in family systems interventions (Hartman & Laird, 1983; Ho, 1987; Imber-Black, 1991; Speck & Attneave, 1973). This process examines the interdependence between people and resources, and may be achieved through pencil and paper simulations or ecological mapping. Both techniques involve asking the family to describe and draw a simulation of their interaction with other social systems, such as educational, religious, health, recreational, political, and economic systems. It also may include asking the family about the agencies and institutions with which they are involved as well as which members are most likely to seek outside help. By examining the macrosystem for possible definitions of the problem and solutions, the practitioner is better able to effect change (see Chapter 11 on natural support networks).

Language is another particular family and ethnic group feature that becomes even more important when moving outside the family's boundaries. For bilingual people, for example, the choice of language in certain circumstances has symbolic meaning (Draper, 1979). Practitioners who do not speak the same language as their client family may want to consider collaborating with a natural or community helper.

Many minority group members hesitate to seek mental health services from formal agencies. Instead, they may rely heavily on the mutual aid of extended family members and religious leaders (Pinderhughes, 1983). Often natural helpers may be asked to work in conjunction with social workers. For example, a family-centered approach that is endemic to Native Hawaiian culture, called *ho'oponopono,* is a spiritual family conference that works to assess, prioritize, and resolve a problem (Mokuau, 1990). *Ho'oponopono* serves as a means of affirming native Hawaiian culture and history.

Finally, family functions, such as participation within society, need to be examined in light of institutional racism. Because societal institutions promote the "melting pot concept" with its "individualistic, competitive achievement" many Mexican-American families, whose values are in conflict, are excluded from full participation (Sotomayor, 1971, p. 317). For such reasons, the ecological-systems approach that views a family's social supports as "an inextricable component of an overall helping strategy" may provide the most inclusive model (p. 318).

Small Group Theory and Social Work Practice: Promoting Diversity and Social Justice or Recreating Inequities? 10

Charles D. Garvin and Beth Glover Reed

> *The constructed patterns of social relations among a set of interactants can be thought of as micro-level social structures . . . [which] include patterned differences that emerge among interactants in power and prestige, influence, the organization of speaking, nonverbal behavior, situated identities, and social and emotional behavior.*
>
> (Ridgeway, 1992, p. xi)

The profession's interest in practice with groups, and what may be termed *small group psychology*, dates back to the earliest period of social work history (Richmond, 1922). This treatment intervention usually is preferred when the client is seeking help coping with issues of social functioning and can benefit from mutual sharing of experience and small group communication. Because interaction in groups has the potential to enhance social competence, many human service agencies offer a variety of group modalities (Northen, 1988).

To establish the theoretical base for group work, social group workers adopted human behavior concepts from several perspectives including field theory, social exchange theory, psychoanalytic theory, and general systems theory (Garvin, 1991). Most social work practice with groups uses the intersystem approach, which takes into account "both the members and the process that operates within the group and in the environment" (Northen, 1988, p. 20). This chapter explores how generic principles apply across the diversity of clients social work serves, and the context within which social workers work.

Small group theory has the potential to contribute greatly to social work conducted with people who experience social oppression because of their gender, ethnicity, sexual orientation, age, or other characteristics. There are several reasons for the value of small groups in this respect. One is a "strength-in-numbers" perspective through which group members can work together to change oppressive social conditions. Another reason is that oppressed people may not recognize the sources of their oppression; they may internalize aspects of the societal assumptions about their group or experience a lack of power. They also may unconsciously blame themselves for some circumstances they experience within society and its components. In addition to learning through group experiences how to change social conditions, these individuals can also be empowered as they begin to think and understand things differently while taking control of their own group. This shift in understanding is often called *consciousness-raising* (Brodsky, 1973; Freire, 1973), which is an important component of working toward empowerment (Gutierrez, 1990). One of the ways people strengthen their social identities is through group experiences with others who share the same identity. A group also represents a social microcosm in which people from different backgrounds or genders can learn to resolve intergroup and intragroup conflicts and power issues if these dynamics are identified and addressed.

Groups also can be vehicles for learning about one's culture (in homogeneous groups or through explaining oneself to others in heterogeneous groups). They also can help group members to identify and resist (when appropriate) the interactional dynamics, language, and other aspects of the group that reinforce and recreate what some researchers call micro-inequities—those interpersonal actions and assumptions that both reflect and perpetuate larger patterns of macroinequities (see Chapter 6 on role theory and Chapter 12 on power concepts).

KEY CONCEPTS

Because it is difficult to condense a complex literature into a short chapter, concepts and illustrations that could be broken out in a longer discussion are interspersed throughout the chapter. Some of the relevant dimensions are noted below so that the reader can recognize them. If these concepts (and other knowledge and skills related to diversity) are not incorporated into group work practice, group processes may actually obscure and perpetuate patterns of inequities and miscommunication within the group.

One important element is the composition of the group, or its relative *homogeneity-heterogeneity*. Groups can be comprised of people who are similar on a dimension of concern (e.g., all women, all African-Americans, or all gays or lesbians); who are selected to represent different characteristics (e.g., a group comprised of women and men in equal numbers), or who randomly represent differences on some characteristic. Each of these compositions will present opportunities and challenges with regard to promoting diversity and social justice through social group work practice.

Multiple dimensions of diversity coexist within each group (e.g. gender, ethnicity, social class, religion, sexual orientation). Also, at least two different sets of factors are relevant for most topics of concern in this chapter:

1. those that contribute to *differences* (e.g., cultural norms, patterns of socialization, interaction styles), and

2. those that arise from past and present patterns of oppression, discrimination, and privilege, and that are often recreated in group interactions, factors often described as markers of *status* (Berger et al., 1977; Berger & Zeiditch, 1985).

All of these are present in every group, although the leader and/or members will often focus on one at a time, or be more sensitive to one element or set of processes, and may not recognize or care about others. In general, learning to recognize and understand many aspects of diversity and oppression at work in a group is important to prevent group experiences from inadvertently disadvantaging some of its members. Working to create group norms and a climate that provides some *sociocultural safety* (usually some assurance that differences will be respected and a commitment to identifying and addressing potentially disadvantaging dynamics) will be important, especially for those who are culturally different from the majority of group members, or have experienced oppression on some dimension that is relevant in the group.

Experiencing discrimination related to an attribute that is devalued in mainstream society can help a person to recognize and empathize with the discrimination of others, whether it arises from the same or another attribute. Some individuals, however, have difficulty recognizing or empathizing with forms of discrimination they have not experienced personally, and may resent it when a group member makes comparisons among different forms of oppression. People who experience significant societal barriers related to one or more social status dimensions usually have some attribute that is culturally valued and advantages them in interactions and in access to societal resources and rewards.

In general, people are less able to recognize and accept the ways in which they are *privileged*. For instance, a white woman may recognize patterns of gender discrimination, but not recognize the benefits she derives from being white and heterosexual (McIntosh, 1992). An African-American or American Indian may focus on racism, but not perceive or accept the limitations that gendered dynamics pose for women. Different cultures and subcultures also are more or less tolerant of people with differing cultures.

In addition, group members as well as group workers often do not see how they apply their own *cultural standards* to others, because they may accept these as universal standards of appropriate behavior and not just as a cultural variation. Group workers also are likely to recognize *individual prejudice* much more readily than they do the ways that bias is structured into policies, practices, and norms about social interactions (*institutionalized racism*) (Feagin & Feagin, 1986). Because what occurs in groups reflects societal patterns, incorporating activities that can educate group members to recognize these larger, institutionalized patterns is important so they can resist unwarranted self-blame if they are negatively affected by institutionalized dynamics, and can realistically assess their abilities if they are advantaged by these processes. This recognition also is important if people are to work to change institutionalized patterns.

A social worker also must learn to apply a *transactional understanding of culture* within group work. This means that one person's behavior in and perception of a situation is at least partially determined by the situation and the characteristics of those with whom the person is interacting. How, how much, and how quickly a person communicates with and trusts a group worker also are influenced by the race, gender, and other characteristics of the worker. In addition, many people have learned to operate within many cultural contexts, and adopt whatever style protects or advantages them the most, especially if their trust level is low. They may need to learn to put some of their usual interactive patterns aside if they are to benefit or contribute optimally within a group.

Since dynamics related to power, structural power, and *monoculturalism* within a group are often unseen by group members, especially those who occupy more societally valued positions, a group worker must strive to be conscious of group members' behaviors as well as his or her own.

Social work theories used in social work with groups (and in other forms of practice as well) are also relevant to diversity and oppression issues. The person-in-environment concept should allow social workers to look not only at individual problems but at the social forces that produce them. Consequently, targets of change often must include aspects of the individual environment. The group member has several levels of social organization to consider, including the group itself, the organization with which the group is affiliated, the community where the organization is located, and the larger society. If the group worker helps a group examine interrelationships among these factors, the parallel forces in each of these entities (such as the mechanisms that perpetuate a culture's racism and sexism) are likely to be perceived by group members as they extrapolate from group experiences embodying these forces to larger systems outside the group.

Other theories used by group workers that are explored in depth throughout this chapter can be useful for understanding and working with diversity issues. Small group theories and concepts drawn from sociology, psychology, political science, and anthropology, as well as from the experiences of social workers, direct our attention to phenomena such as subgroups formed of people with similar cultural and/or gender affiliations, power differentials among these subgroups, and the norms that are held in common (as well as those that are in conflict) by people with similar identities. Group workers also use concepts regarding social roles, socialization, negotiation, decision-making, conflict resolution, social cognition, and social learning, and each has implications for working with issues of diversity.

FEMINIST PRINCIPLES

Feminist principles also are relevant and emphasized in this chapter. Many feminist authors represent multiple types of feminism at different stages of development, articulation, and transformation (Butler & Wintram, 1991; see Chapter 12 for a discussion of feminism). An elaboration of these concepts goes beyond the scope of this chapter, and they are discussed more fully elsewhere (Reed & Garvin, in press). However, the feminist principles drawn upon include the following:

1. Social justice and social change are major goals in feminist practice.
2. Feminist values, theory, and knowledge should be the basis of action. These values emphasize women's strengths within a critique of societal assumptions about women and gender, traditional gender role options, and the ideology and institutions that perpetuate women's lesser access to social resources and lower status in the social system (see Chapter 6 on role theory).
3. Group workers should engage group members in ongoing self-reflection and consciousness-raising, particularly regarding power issues, gendering processes, and the social context.
4. Group workers should use the processes of praxis, that is, regular reflective cycles between action and theory.
5. Group workers should recognize that the personal is political, which means that everything that occurs at the personal level is related to societal factors, that personal change should occur within an understanding of the societal and cultural context, and that women's lower social status has both psychological and sociocultural effects that must be addressed.
6. Group workers should help reconceptualize and reexamine power, especially as power is used in oppressive ways.
7. Process and product are equally valued. This means, for example, that in group situations both the attainment of the purpose of the group and the processes occurring among members are of equal importance.
8. Group workers should incorporate regular and continuous mechanisms for examining gendering practices and other culturally based assumptions operating within the group.
9. Group workers should reduce the use of false dichotomies and pro-

mote understanding of the relationships among often dichotomized categories. Examples from groups are the dichotomies between the individual and the group and between the process and the outcome.

10. Group workers should rename and interrogate the meaning of words and symbols because the definitions used in the group and the choice of language affect individual and group thinking (see Chapter 7 on social construction).

11. Group workers should examine and strengthen relationships among women that have been disrupted by sexism.

12. Group workers should discover and use multiple ways of learning and knowing within the group.

13. Group workers should seriously and regularly encourage group members to attend to all sources of oppression.

Many aspects of culture and discrimination other than sexism have been incorporated within these principles. Systematic application of such guidelines will greatly strengthen a practitioner's ability to identify and monitor the impact of differences and oppression and to catalyze empowering processes within groups.

The remainder of this chapter begins with a discussion of the small group literature that informs understanding about issues of diversity in groups. Group work practice derived from this literature as well as from the authors' professional experiences is then described. The chapter concludes with a discussion of future issues that should be addressed as social workers strive toward a practice that is fully oriented to issues of diversity.

GROUP PURPOSE AND OPPRESSION

Although the mechanisms and consequences of patriarchy are experienced by women in many different ways, women's groups provide a shared means of becoming conscious of the nature of that material and ideological oppression. (Butler & Wintram, 1991, p. 8)

All social workers need to consider group issues with respect to the consumers of their services, whether or not these social workers directly interact with specific groups. This is because all individuals belong to groups that heavily influence them and that they, in turn, influence. For example, a social worker seeking to help an adolescent drug user at various times had to consider the adolescent's interaction with her peer group, classroom, neighborhood, and family.

When the above client was invited to join a treatment group and a self-help group, the social worker at times focused on these other group experiences. Because the client was a Latina, each of these groups had to be understood in terms of their impact on her particular sense of ethnic identity, her gender, and her socialization as a Latina in her neighborhood in a diverse southwestern city. Within the self-help group, the client also expressed her desire to find ways to combat her experiences with racism and sexism.

In addition, much of social work practice occurs within group contexts (e.g., therapy groups, self-help groups, and support groups, committees, boards, reference groups, families, and social action groups (often related to a social movement). These groups all have some dimensions in common as well as ways in which they differ. They differ in the extent to which they are created to help people with individual problems or to accomplish a specific task (e.g., to raise funds, plan an event, or recommend a decision to the larger organization). Social workers often put together a particular type of group of clients to catalyze and support specific kinds of change and development among members.

All of these groups can be examined in terms of the diversity issues discussed here as well as in terms of small group theories. The practitioners' roles differ somewhat, however, based on whether they are defined as therapists, chairpersons, staffers, or members. The tools used in the group to plan activities and make decisions may also differ. And finally, members enter in different kinds of groups with varying expectations as to how a group will function and what their role will be in each.

BASIC ASSUMPTIONS OF SMALL GROUP THEORY

The helping group is the most important core characteristic of social work practice. . . . It is the membership dimension of the human condition, in the most general sense and in social work in particular, that clarifies the match of personal problem with public concern. (Falk, 1988, pp. 62–63)

A *small group* has been defined as "two or more persons who are interacting with one another in such a manner that each person influences and is influenced by each other person" (Shaw, 1976, p. 11). Shaw also viewed the small group as having no more than 20 members. This number is arbitrary but indicates an approximate size beyond which the properties of the small group begin to include those found in larger entities.

Several significant concepts within group theory can be relevant for examining issues of diversity. One of these is *group purpose,* which is the function to be fulfilled by the group. Does this purpose address the issues of diversity that are relevant to the particular group, especially if the group is composed of oppressed individuals or contains some mix of individuals who have been oppressed for various reasons? Another is *group goals,* which are the desired outcomes of the group's activities and are related to group purpose. To what degree does a group's goals relate to the kinds of oppression that its members experience?

In building a viable group, *cohesiveness*, which refers to how much the members are attracted to the group, becomes relevant. Group members' attraction to a group is often related to such diversity issues as whether the group will be composed wholly or in part of other persons like themselves and whether psychologically safe space develops for particular members. The degree to which the group recreates gender, cultural, and other dynamics that may be oppressive to some members while being advantageous to others will also affect a group's cohesiveness. In what ways are diversities among members affecting cohesiveness?

Group task, which group workers often refer to as *program*, consists of the activities which members engage in together. Is the group attending to the ways that some tasks are preferred or rejected by people from different cultural groups or of either gender? And are members of various groups bringing different assumptions and working styles to the tasks?

Group structure is the pattern of interaction among members, such as who speaks to whom and who fulfills what roles. Some group theories stress *status structures* and their development, that is, stable differences in the power and influence among group members. Is the group addressing the ways that status characteristics outside the group influence how people are perceived within a group, paying special attention to power and influence structures within the group and challenging those that appear to recreate gender- and race-based inequities as well as other societal injustice within the group? Gender, ethnic, and other diversity factors are also strong determinants of the structure of every group (e.g., when men sit with men and women with women).

Group process is how the group changes from moment to moment or over longer periods of time. Processes such as decision-making or the unfolding of a conversation among several people are also strongly affected by culture, gender, and other status issues. Is the social worker attending to these aspects of group processes? For instance, men or women communicate quite differently in every culture (e.g. Tannen, 1990). People with higher status often talk more and express themselves differently than do those with less status, and there are also marked differences across cultures as well. A number of the feminist principles cited earlier have implications for understanding and working with such processes.

Some basic assumptions derived from small group theories were originally developed for an earlier work (Garvin & Ephross, 1991) and presented in tabular form. A modification of the earlier table, in which a column has been added to identify some of the diversity issues related to each assumption, is presented in Table 10.1. The following section discusses research studies from which these additional assumptions were derived.

Table 10.1. Basic Assumptions of Small Group Theory: Relationship to Issues of Diversity

Basic assumptions	*Relationship to diversity issues*
The human personality develops, grows, changes, and is modified in and through interaction with other persons, largely carried on in small groups.	These interactions are strongly affected by a group member's gender and cultural identities, as well as by the identities of others in the group.
The roles, statuses, and experience that people have in one group can become part of the person and be carried over into other groups by the person. Perceived roles and statuses outside the group affect status within the group.	The roles and statuses of people are strongly affected by their early group experiences. These experiences are typically with people from an individual's own culture. The ways that a culture treats gender and other status characteristics have effects on later group interactions. Also, assumptions within the larger society about gender, race, ethnicity, and other status characteristics lead to higher and lower status being ascribed to members. This affects assignments of status within the group.
The influence of peers in groups can affect people's understanding, attitudes, feelings, and behavior in powerful ways.	The ways that peers in groups behave, perceive, and react to each other is strongly influenced by the cultural and gender identities and characteristics of the group's members.
Mental and social health have to do with actions and experiences, not just with analysis and introspection.	The events that occur in the group are affected by the racial and gender characteristics of the group. These events comprise the actions and experiences that contribute to mental and social health. Consequently, an effort to improve mental and social health through groups must attend to these compositional factors.
Joining together to accomplish group purposes is one of the major ways in which problems are solved in a democratic society and, at the same time, one of the ways in which people can find meaning and purpose in their lives.	The ability of the group to solve problems will be strongly determined by the cultural and gender makeup of the group. How the group goes about solving problems is also shaped by these factors.
Sharing mutually meaningful experience in small groups is one of the most effective ways people create bridges of understanding and learn to work together across obstacles of	The ability of diverse people to share these experiences depends on the creation of group conditions in which such people are not hindered from such sharing by virtue of power dif-

(continued)

Table 10.1. (Continued)

Basic assumptions	Relationship to diversity issues
differences in age, race, ethnic background, religion, social class, condition of physical or mental disability, gender, political beliefs, sexual orientation, or any other expression of human diversity.	ferentials, dysfunctional hierarchies, lack of trust, or the type of group composition in which individuals are "tokens" or present in such small proportions as to experience a lack of support and empathy.
It is more useful to approach helping people to grow and change from an assessment of their individual and collective strengths than from a focus on their weaknesses.	This recognition of strength must be driven by a recognition of the strengths of each culture and gender represented in the group.
Through its problem-solving process and/or program development, each group develops its own structure, communication patterns, and culture.	The group culture often modifies but does not obliterate the structure, communication patterns, and culture that people bring to the group from their culture and gender experiences outside the group. Without active attention to gender issues and oppressive dynamics, groups will recreate structures and processes that perpetuate inequities.
Groups move through a life cycle as events unfold over time.	In ways that are not yet fully understood, the group's development is affected by the gender and culture of the members.
Because groups are a microcosm of society, group members often express beliefs and values of the broader culture.	An important aspect of this broader culture is its condition with regard to issues of diversity.
Being a contributing member of social groups and enjoying the rewards of participation is linked to adaptive functioning.	The support an individual has for contributing to the group will be affected by the conditions present in the group related to diversity issues.
The purpose of social work practice with groups is to promote, enhance, or restore social functioning.	Social functioning consists in part of a person's ability to develop to his or her full potential *as a member* of the larger set of people with whom the person shares culture, gender, and common fate. Thus, social work practice with groups must be a practice that focuses on the empowerment of people who are disempowered because of their culture, gender, or in other ways through which their diversity is manifested. Also, the group

(continued)

Table 10.1.   (Continued)

Basic assumptions	Relationship to diversity issues
	worker must be sensitive to the different ways of characterizing social functioning in various cultures or the group worker will create or exacerbate culture conflict.
Being in a group with people similar to oneself is a powerful way to identify societal contributions to personal experience, rather than perceiving that experience individualistically.	This recognition is often defined in groups as consciousness-raising and is an important component in undercutting internalized oppression and victim-blaming dynamics. Processes of privilege can also be identified in this way, but with more difficulty.
Groups provide structures for people to pool information and skills, set priorities, develop and implement plans, coordinate activities, and support each other in work on tasks. Groups are important components in social change, policy development, and administrative work.	Attending to diversity and status dynamics within these groups makes it more likely that task work will also empower members, providing opportunities to increase members' knowledge of disempowering dynamics and factors that block progress toward social justice.

GROUP CONDITIONS AND ISSUES OF DIVERSITY

From a mental health perspective the small group, in acting as a conduit between the ethnic and the dominant communities offers belonging and counters alienation. Identification with the ethnic community can be a force in sustaining and rebuilding interpersonal security and self-realization. (L. E. Davis, 1984, p. 2)

To discuss research as well as theory related to group work and issues of diversity, the discussion has been organized around a number of group conditions. These include group composition, group processes, and leadership.

Group Composition

The issues that have been explored with regard to group composition relate both to client preferences for the characteristics of other group members as well as to the impact of different compositional patterns on the group. There is some evidence that whites have negative feelings toward groups in which they are a minority (Brayboy, 1971). On the other hand, African-Americans may have mixed feelings about being in groups solely comprised of

African-Americans, perhaps because of concern over the status of the group or the likelihood that members will only talk about racial issues (Davis & Proctor, 1989; Davis, Sharfstein, & Owens, 1974).

Davis and Proctor made an important contribution to the understanding of attitudes toward racial composition in groups when they reported on the result of an experiment in which responses of African-Americans and whites to the composition of simulated groups were noted. The conclusions have been summarized as follows:

> Results from the study indicate that blacks and whites do differ significantly in their preferences for the composition of these groups. Blacks selected approximately equal numbers of blacks and whites, while whites selected group compositions more consistent with black-white representation in society at large (e.g., 20% black, 80% white). Hence, group leaders may experience some difficulty composing a racially heterogeneous group that is to the satisfaction of both blacks and whites. (Davis & Proctor, 1989, pp. 90–91)

Composition issues become even more complex when one considers groups that include Latinos and Latinas or Asian-Americans. Each of these groups consists of individuals from different countries and cultures who do not necessarily identify with others who share these broad designations (Bilides, 1990; Davis & Proctor, 1989; Ho, 1984; Tylim, 1982).

A practice issue closely related to group composition is whether groups that are racially heterogeneous can be effective tools for changing racist attitudes of group members. According to Davis and Proctor (1989), there is evidence both for and against this proposition, but they suggested that groups that are effective in this respect consist of members who have something in common, such as socioeconomic status.

An important issue is whether or not social workers should seek to create groups that are entirely made up of individuals who share key characteristics, for example, a similar ethnic background. Some of these individuals may have undergone socialization experiences that led to negative self-evaluations (Solomon, 1976). Chau (1989) considered group intervention with members who share cultural characteristics as an important tool in raising ethnic consciousness and enhancing ethnic identity.

Group compositional issues are equally important with regard to gender, although Martin and Shanahan (1983) cited evidence "that interventions on the part of a group leader or experimenter can successfully counteract many otherwise undesirable effects of a group's given gender configuration" (p. 20). Some of the imbalances that occur between women and men in mixed groups, however, are often not recognized by either leaders or group members and are difficult to change because they have multiple causes.

Martin and Shanahan (1983) noted that the theoretical model most frequently used to explain male and female differences in groups is a "status characteristics/expectation states" model:

> This model directs attention to status and situational rather than personal factors to account for male-female differences. Gender is viewed as a *diffuse*, as opposed to specific, *status characteristic* which is "defined" in the broader society (external to the group) and which entails "expectations" (from both self and others) for normatively appropriate behaviors in social contexts. The term diffuse means that expectations for behavior associated with gender status (i.e., male or female) are "known" by most societal members and, lacking evidence to the contrary, are assumed to be widely applicable. They are, therefore, "brought into" most social situations. (p. 22)

Martin and Shanahan used this model to posit, for example, that males are more likely to be viewed by society as task leaders and often as being more competent and influential than women (see chapter 6). Men will therefore act this way in groups unless interventions are used to deal with such behavior.

Another model drawn upon by Martin and Shanahan (1983) was a "structural/numerical proportions" model (p. 23), which explains various group conditions according to the relative proportions of males and females in the group. For example, when most group members are men, they are likely to see the small number of females in the group as representative of all women rather than as individuals.

Martin and Shanahan (1983) found empirical support for other propositions:

1. Females are negatively evaluated in all-male groups and in groups in which they are a small minority.

2. The quantity and content of verbal interaction in groups varies by group gender composition and by gender of participant. Many specific findings are summarized by Martin and Shanahan. For example, women talk less and are talked to less in mixed groups than in all-female groups; men in all-male groups tend to focus on competition and status topics, whereas females in all-female groups focus on personal, home, and family topics.

3. Females are perceived less positively than males, even when equally "influential."

4. Solo or token females in otherwise male groups tend to fare poorly.

5. The research on all-female groups presents many inconsistencies, such as how effective they are compared with mixed groups. This inconsistency may be related to the interaction of group composition with other variables, such as type of task.

Martin and Shanahan (1983) indicated a number of ways of overcoming the effects of gender composition in mixed groups. These include legitimizing the right of the female to assume influence, recognizing the competence of females, and facilitating ways that women can demonstrate their motivation to assist the group in accomplishing its task. Because these dynamics are less disruptive when group composition is more balanced, another intervention is to create groups in which the proportion of men to women is equal. When logistics allow, the best intervention may be to allow time for single- and mixed-gender groups to meet over the course of a particular set of tasks, since experiences in each type of group help members to recognize how they behave differently in different group composition situations (Bernardez & Stein, 1979).

Contrary to women's experiences, the influence on men of membership in mixed groups is generally positive. In such groups, men tend to be less competitive and behave less stereotypically in other ways. However, Martin and Shanahan (1983) noted that in all-male groups, the facilitator may "wish to affirm the appropriateness of intimacy, closeness, and self-revelatory norms in the group and to discourage excessive competition, disagreement, and conflict" (pp. 29–30).

The reviews and studies cited here focus primarily on race or primarily on gender. As yet, few studies have taken into account the multiple dimensions that people bring to group interactions, many of which are linked to status and interactional differences. As shown in the next section, race, gender, sexual orientation, class, and other factors interact in ways that are not yet well understood. Often one dimension will acquire more salience in a group and become a major organizing influence within it; but many other factors may also be operating strongly. If their effects are not noticed, they can be badly misinterpreted. Whether and how it is useful to name and address the impact of multiple dimensions is not clear, and may vary with the purpose, time frame, and cohesiveness of a group.

Group Processes

One aspect of group process that is affected by diversity is what kinds of relationships people form in the group. In the Davis (1979) research cited earlier, the investigator found that in more intimate and smaller groups, African-Americans preferred having more same-race members than in larger, less intimate groups. This was not found to be true for white members. Davis and Proctor (1989) also cited evidence that small numbers of minority group members within a group do not have major effects on group processes, but larger numbers are more likely to be perceived as a threat (p. 103).

On the other hand, when whites are in the minority in a group, this strongly affects the racial consciousness of the whites who choose to associate only with other whites. Davis (1981) explained this finding by suggesting that whites are so accustomed to being in the majority that they develop an uncomfortable psychological state when this is not the case; he termed whites under this circumstance a "psychological minority" (p. 103). Because nonwhites are typically outnumbered in mixed groups, when they constitute more than 10 to 20% of a group they possess more influence and power and feel more like what Davis termed a "psychological majority" (p. 103). Another process variable relates to the amount of communication within a group. African-Americans tend to speak less in mixed groups than do whites and typically address their remarks to the whites. Davis and Proctor (1989) see this as being related to the status of members as they are affected by larger societal expectations. They also note that the studies that led to these conclusions were conducted before the black protest movements of the late 1960s. Changes have been taking place in these communication patterns, and they cited several sources to support this conclusion (Adams, 1980; Winter, 1971).

Davis and Proctor (1989) also reviewed group studies involving members of other ethnic groups. They found some reluctance on the part of Chicano and Chicana members to speak freely in mixed groups, which they attributed to the formality of the Mexican-American culture as well as certain family communication patterns. Issues arising from differences in societal status are also likely to be relevant. Davis and Proctor also found evidence that expectations about self-disclosure often create difficulties for Asian-American group members; such self-disclosure is in conflict with cultural norms about appropriate behavior outside the family.

In reviewing the literature on the influence of gender on group processes (Dion, 1985; Shaw, 1983; Reed & Garvin, 1983), Davis and Proctor (1989) concluded that males tend to be more competitive and verbally domineering in groups than females. Females, in turn, resist being dominated in this way. On the other hand, males are also more competitive in all-male groups than in mixed-gender groups. All-female groups seem to form through women identifying their similarities with one another, instead of developing norms about conflict and creating status hierarchies (see Chapters 9 and 12 for a discussion of hierarchy). These groups may then have difficulties dealing with differences and conflict, since conflict threatens a group cohesiveness that was developed without norms for addressing differences. All-women groups can benefit from early skill-building activities and norms that validate the usefulness of differences and conflict (Hagen, 1983).

Davis and Proctor's review also found that males performing competitive tasks have a stronger motivation to win than females, whereas females are more concerned with social and ethical considerations. There is also some evidence that women are more likely than men to comply with group decisions after they are made. Davis and Proctor (1989) concluded a detailed discussion of many other findings by noting that such matters are changing: "gender status effects may be becoming less problematic" (p. 232).

Leadership

Many interesting questions arise regarding diversity and group leadership. Do leaders from various backgrounds lead groups differently when the groups are composed differently? Are leaders perceived differently by group members based on their race and gender? Do leaders of various racial and gender backgrounds have different leadership styles? An even more complex set of questions suggests that the processes and structures of groups are shaped in part by members' expectations of and reactions to the personal characteristics—race, gender, and so forth—and not the behavior of the "leader." Leaders with different characteristics may have to behave differently to be effective, because the groups they lead develop different characteristics and may react to similar leadership behaviors differently.

Davis and Proctor (1989) cited literature suggesting that maintaining informality of style without sacrificing respect is important in leading groups composed of minority members in order to increase rapport. This is a statement derived from practice and not a research finding; these authors acknowledged there is little research on racial differences in leadership style. Nevertheless, they cited evidence that "group members have reported perceiving racially dissimilar group leaders as being more threatening, less positive, and potentially more punitive than a same-race leader" (p. 99). Moreover, they quoted from a management study (Richards & Jaffee, 1972) in which white members rated black group leaders as performing more poorly than white leaders, and in which whites were found to be less cooperative with black supervisors than they were with white supervisors.

Much more research has sought to relate gender to leadership rather than race. Davis and Proctor (1989) cited Lockheed and Hall (1976) regarding generalizations from the studies on mixed-gender groups. These included beliefs such as men are more active (i.e., initiate more verbal acts) than women; men are more influential than women (i.e., their opinions carry more weight); and men initiate more acts in the "task" category, whereas women initiate more in the social-emotional category.

There is clearly an interaction between group composition and leadership, as additional studies show:

> Females leading a group composed of males were observed to behave in a more "task-oriented" fashion. Similarly, male leaders with predominantly female groups were reported to behave in a more "social-emotional" fashion. (Davis & Proctor, 1989, pp. 234–235)

An important issue that is often neglected in research is how leadership styles develop over the life of the group. Davis and Proctor (1989) cited studies that indicate that between initial and final group sessions, some of the leadership style differences related to gender become less significant (p. 237). A study by Reed (1979) suggested that judgments about individual competence eventually override the initial gender-based assumptions about status.

Overall, Davis and Proctor (1989) found no evidence that there are differences between men and women in terms of their competence as group leaders, although woman leaders are often devalued. However, differences were found in the perceptions members had of male and female leaders as well as in leader-member interactions. These differences were found in groups comprising different proportions of men and women, in groups with different kinds of tasks, among members with more or less traditional attitudes regarding gender differences, and among groups that differed in the degree to which their activity was structured. These findings suggest that perceptions of leader behaviors are determined in complex ways related to the interactions of the personalities involved as well as to a variety of contextual factors. A few studies have found that other aspects of the group are also affected by the leader's gender; for instance, in one study, members sat closer together or were allowed less personal space in groups with women leaders (Giesen & McClaren, 1976).

Recent studies focusing on gender have applied multiple theoretical perspectives and methodologies to bear on complex human interactions and small groups. One set of studies focuses explicitly on the impact of complex defined social roles (Eagley, 1987). Another continues a focus on inferred status characteristics but broadens measures to include analysis of language, group culture, member interactions of various kinds, and multiple measures of structures and processes (Ridgeway, 1982). The implications of such research for social work practice are not yet clear, although studies continue to demonstrate the multiple ways that both micro- and macroinequities are created and recreated through interpersonal interactions, the use of language, and within-group structures and processes. Without rigorous and ongoing attention to these dynamics, social work in groups may perpetuate the very dynamics group leaders wish to change.

Discussions of race and gender differences in leadership typically treat these variables as if they were independent of each other. In contrast with this, the authors were part of a team that conducted an experiment to examine the interplay of race and gender in perceptions of leaders and various other group dimensions (Brower, Garvin, Hobson, Reed, & Reed, 1987). The experiment involved 32 four-person groups, each comprising 2 male and 2 female white college students. The groups were divided into 4 categories of 8 each, led by black female, white female, black male, and white male leaders. The leaders were trained through the use of a script to intervene identically with the groups because it was the intent of this experiment to identify the impact of the leader's race and gender rather than actual differences in leadership style.

The results of this experiment clearly supported the hypothesis that the effects of group leaders' race and gender cannot be inferred from an examination of leader race and gender studies separately. These results also supported the conclusion that male and female participants see the behavior of these leaders through different lenses. Though all of the findings from the study cannot be presented here, six findings are listed to illustrate the complex interactions between race and gender of group leader and gender of group member:

1. White male group members were less comfortable than white females in black-led groups.

2. Members had their most positive reactions to the group when the leader was the same gender as themselves.

3. Members evaluated leaders who were the same gender as themselves more positively than leaders of the other gender.

4. White males in white-led groups saw their leaders as being less involved than did white men in black-led groups.

5. In a number of ratings, members of groups with white female or black male leaders perceived their experiences similarly, but their ratings differed from those members whose groups had white male or black female leaders.

6. Groups used planning time quite differently in the various leadership conditions; only the groups with white male leaders used all of the allotted time.

GROUP WORK PRACTICE ISSUES RELATED TO DIVERSITY
AND OPPRESSION

The practice of social group work has succumbed to the pressures for containment and management of symptoms and to the definition of participants (clients) not as equal partners and members in a common endeavor but as somehow damaged and defective beings. (Lewis, 1992, p. 273)

This section presents an approach to work with groups that focuses on the issues of diversity in groups and that draws on the small group literature cited previously regarding these issues. The purposes of such an approach were discussed at the beginning of this chapter with respect to the strength-in-numbers phenomenon, as well as in terms of the goals of empowering group members, strengthening identities, and resolving intergroup conflicts (Table 10.2).

The first guideline for diverse group work practice is to help the group to become a system of mutual aid, that is, a system in which the members are committed to helping one another accomplish their individual as well as collective goals. A diversity approach recognizes that there may be barriers to the evolution of a mutual-aid system because of differences among members, similarities that obscure differences, or power and privilege differences that are not addressed.

These differences may prevent members from developing a sense of caring for each other or may even be the source of conflict among them. On the other hand, such diversity *can* help group members to create a strong mutual-aid system because of what they can bring to each other through their varying perspectives. For example, a group was composed of men and women who had problems in coping with their current life situations because of their recent divorces. The men and women initially found it hard to empathize with one another's situations because of the different issues facing men and women who get divorced. In addition, conflicts emerged in the group between the men and women members as each gender charged that the other had the greater advantage after divorce. The group social worker assisted the members to forge a strong bond among them as she helped them to see how much they could learn from each other, based on what they had in common as well as from insights into the other gender's experience. Attention to race, ethnicity, and class differences elicited additional insight.

In a task group, awareness of cultural and status differences also requires careful and recurring attention to group processes. Addressing these dynamics in a task group may be more difficult if members don't understand how it can positively help their work on the task: Do the norms allow everyone to participate in styles that are comfortable for them? Is influence within the group being shaped by status characteristics that have little to do with knowledge of the task and its concurrent responsibilities? Are members with different status characteristics being recognized and respected? Does the pace of the group allow more quiet and reflective members (those whose cultural norms define interrupting and competing for airtime as disrespectful) to participate? Does a member's choice of words reflect gendered and ethnically shaped assumptions?

The practice guidelines presented in Table 10. 2 are used somewhat differently based on whether the group is in its beginning, middle, or ending phase. The following discussion presents some of the issues that arise for the social worker who is sensitive to diversity issues at various stages of group development.

Table 10.2. Guidelines for Social Workers: A Group Work Approach

Guideline	*Diversity principle related to guideline*
Help the group become a system of mutual aid.	Overcome barriers to becoming a system of mutual aid based on diversity and similarities that exist among group members. Help members to see how their ability to help one another can transcend their differences.
Help the group members determine their individual goals, the goals of the group, and the relationship between these.	Help members select goals for themselves and their group that are not limited by societally imposed restrictions and forms of social oppression. Facilitate a process of consciousness-raising so that members determine these goals in the light of an enhanced awareness of the reality of oppressive social circumstances.
Assess and work with the individuals in the group, the group as a whole, and the environment, as well as the interactions between and among these.	Determine how the interactions within each system level as well as among system levels are either enhanced or hindered by social oppression and diversity.
Help the group function with increasing autonomy over time.	Help the members individually and collectively to become empowered and to overcome barriers to empowerment based on social oppression and negative reactions to diversity.
Help the members to determine and carry out individual and group tasks and activities.	Determine the cultural and gender meanings of tasks. Help in the selection of individual and group tasks that are not limited by culturally imposed restrictions rooted in racism, sexism, and other sources of oppression.
Develop and help the members to develop a picture of the group's structure and processes and the nature of its development as a system over time.	Determine how these group conditions are affected by sources of member diversity and differences in status. Help the members to work toward group conditions that support and enhance empowerment consistent with their cultural and other characteristics.
Make use of group processes to help the group accomplish its purposes.	Help members to fully explore the ways that their interactions are affected by their diversity so that this diversity leads to the most creative solutions to individual and group concerns and problems.

Beginning Stage

As stated in a chapter entitled "Working with Oppressed People in Groups" (Garvin, 1987), a number of tasks must be accomplished before the first meeting. First, the planning for the group ideally should be done jointly with those who will actually become members of the group or with those whose backgrounds are similar. This process is an important part of the goal of empowerment, as it may in some circumstances be contrary to this goal to call together a group of people who are expected to take charge of their individual and group destinies when someone else who has little in common with them has at first taken charge. Also, when members bring different styles and experiences of being empowered to such groups, they will not begin on a level playing field. The agency worker, together with these individuals, can undertake a *needs assessment.* in which other potential members indicate what they may need from the group. For example, in one situation, an agency, based on this kind of assessment, provided family-type group programs for Latino and Latina residents rather than programs that separated family members.

In certain instances, it is not feasible to engage in this kind of planning. This is the case when the group worker becomes aware of individuals who are oppressed by their social circumstances but the only feasible initial contact with them is the offer of a group service. This is typical of the practice reports included in several recent volumes on group work with individuals experiencing oppression (Chau, 1991; L. E. Davis, 1984; Lee, 1988). Even though their participation in early planning is not possible, from an empowerment point of view, the social worker should quickly communicate to the members that they will have a major say in determining how they will use the group. Some examples of this are the following: members of an African-American women's group who decided to use their group to form a tenant's organization (Lewis & Ford, 1990); members in a group of low-income minority girls who decided they wanted to focus on boy-girl and parent-teenager problems (Parsons, 1988); and members of a drop-in group for homeless women who wanted to focus on how to take better advantage of health facilities.

The staff who will work with the group as well as other key agency personnel should acquire information that they may not already possess about the cultural background of the group members or create a group norm that legitimizes learning about the cultural influences affecting each group member. This information will help group social workers and other staff to be sensitive to cultural issues as they assist the members in structuring the group and its activities appropriately (Garvin, 1987; Garvin & Seabury, 1984).

Key informational terms include the following:

Communications relates to the ways the group members use language, including employing rules about who speaks to whom and about what. The nature of colloquial speech used by group members and whether they can communicate in a language other than English are also relevant. Another issue is how hierarchy within or outside the group affects what members say. Feminist perspectives also recognize that speech can be used in oppressive ways, such as when masculine pronouns are used to refer to women or when male communication norms and styles dominate the group.

Habitat refers to how members think about as well as how they use physical space. This has implications as to where members prefer to hold meetings and how they decide to arrange the meeting space. Members from an ethnic group will have feelings about holding meetings in a facility that few (if any) members of their cultural group use. Certain rooms within a facility might have negative associations based on gender meanings. Some locations will not be barrier free or appropriately equipped for people with disabilities. Even decor may seem more comfortable for some groups rather than others.

Social structure relates to both the social divisions within the oppressed group as well as those between the particular group and the larger society. Some examples of this are the number of different groups classified as Latino and Latina and the attitudes they hold toward each other; the ways that some institutions discriminate against women as reflected in their structures (e.g., a board of directors that is all male); and the various life-styles in gay culture (e.g., those who cross-dress, those who emphasize leather in their dress). Group workers must consider these issues in composing groups and in understanding phenomena such as how coalitions and conflicts emerge in groups and the effects they may have.

Socialization relates to how the individuals associated with oppressed or privileged groups enter into social roles and learn to cope with role requirements. Processes such as how men and women learn gender expectations and the rites of passage in ethnic communities are pertinent. Sometimes group workers help members to learn more about and connect more strongly with their communities. An example of this was a project at the University of Utah to enhance the cultural awareness and identification of American Indian female students (Edwards, Edwards, Daines, & Eddy, 1978). At other times, the group worker helps the members to alter socialization patterns, such as working with women who want to relinquish some roles or change behaviors that have been traditionally assigned to their gender. A good example of this is the work of Haussmann and Halseth (1983) with a group to reexamine women's roles as a means of decreasing depression in women. In task- or social change–focused groups, members' socialization may help or hinder their ability to work on particular tasks.

Economy refers to how the group is affected by the economic institutions and practices of the larger society as well as the internal economic outlook within the oppressed group. For example, related issues include the kinds of occupations chosen by (or imposed upon) members of the group as well as the unequal distribution of societal resources among ethnic groups and between men and women. Group members who have had economic advantages as a result of their group memberships and societal status also need to recognize these processes that advantage them rather than attributing their success entirely to their individual achievement. Group members can be helped to see the connections between "personal troubles" and successes and these social issues.

Beliefs and sentiments refer to the philosophies, ideologies, norms, values, and myths found within groups. These are incorporated into the religion, folklore, literature, sayings, music, and poetry that members of groups see as their cultural heritage. These can be used by group workers to help the group to become an emotionally safe place for various members, to illuminate issues, and to teach new ways of coping.

Once the group members have convened, beginning activities include determining what the individual and group goals are or how a group wants to define and work on its tasks. This also requires the members to assess their situations as they relate to these goals. A value that is often proposed during these processes in groups made up of people from oppressed minorities is that individual and group goals should be chosen in relation to their impact on others who are similarly oppressed. For example, when women, African-Americans, elderly people, or members of any oppressed group become symbols of how open the opportunity structure of the society has become skewed, this can then be used to deny opportunities to others. This is often referred to as *tokenism,* and its effects can be insidious.

The social worker must also become skillful in assessing and helping members to assess their circumstances in light of cultural variables such as the ones listed here. This culturally based assessment should emphasize strengths and not just list deficits. An example of this was an African-American teenager who had joined a group to help him to succeed in school. The following were some of the strengths that were identified through the use of the concepts just described:

> Under the category of communication, for example, the social worker noted that the new member was highly capable of proposing solutions to his difficulties and to accepting suggestions if the social worker did not (as his teacher did) demand "correct" speech (as she defined it) from him. The social worker noted with regard to habitat that the teenager was more comfortable discussing these issues in the informal atmosphere of the group room than in the classroom. Regarding social structure, she discovered that the member was a very valued member of his family who had high expectations of him that he hoped to meet. Under the category of socialization, the social worker learned that the

teenager wanted to occupy a position of respect in his church and he related that to his desire for school success. With regard to economy, she was told by the teenager that he was aware of the educational limitations that had been placed on his parents, and he wanted to devote his energy not only to overcoming these barriers for himself but also for others. Finally, under the category of beliefs and sentiments, this group member had just finished seeing the television series "Roots," and he identified with African-Americans' many generations struggle against injustice—something he had thought about as he watched the story unfold.

It is also important for group members to assess their environments, especially as this increases their awareness of sexism, racism, and other forms of oppression that constitute barriers to accomplishment of their goals. They can then strategize how to overcome (or in some cases circumvent) these barriers. They can also decide how and when to take risks. Members of oppressed groups know that there are opportunities to be taken advantage of but also (at least in the short run) dangers to be faced.

Middle Stage

During this phase, members work to attain their individual and group goals. An important part of work with oppressed people to help them become empowered is to increase their *critical consciousness*. This term is adopted from the writings of Paulo Freire, a Brazilian educator who has had a significant impact on the thinking of a number of group workers concerned about empowerment issues (Freire, 1973). Critical consciousness refers to an understanding of the forces that maintain an individual's oppressive social circumstances. Freire called a well-developed critical consciousness a *critically transitive consciousness,* which he defined as follows:

> The critically transitive consciousness is characterized by depth in the interpretation of problems, by the substitution of causal principles for magical explanations; by the testing of one's "findings" and by openness to revision; by the attempt to avoid distortion when perceiving problems and to avoid preconceived notions when analyzing them; by refusing to transfer responsibility; by rejecting passive positions; by soundness of argumentation; by the practice of dialogue rather than polemics; by receptivity to the new for reasons beyond mere novelty and by the good sense not to reject the old just because it is old— by accepting what is valid for both old and new. (p. 18)

Group workers have used a number of techniques that increase the critical consciousness of members. One is to help the group's members review their life stories to see how past experiences have contributed to ways they have devalued themselves (see chapter 7). Another is to assist members in examining their current interactions with people who do not share their oppressed status to see if these interactions help maintain their sense of powerlessness. An important concept in this respect is *false consciousness,* which indicates that a person accepts the values of oppressors in ways that prevent him or her from achieving personal goals.

People who have written about consciousness have tended to focus on one or perhaps two dimensions. For Freire (1973), the dimension is most often class; for those concerned about racism, race and ethnicity have been the primary emphases. Among feminists, an emphasis on gender has often obscured other important sources of oppression (Hooks, 1984). It is important that those concerned about diversity and social justice identify and address the multiple ways that individuals are disempowered and help them examine sources of privilege as well. Otherwise, various groups will compete with each other rather than recognize common mechanisms of oppression, key differences, and ways they may contribute to the oppression of others while working toward their own empowerment.

Values clarification can also contribute to empowerment. This approach helps members to identify the values that guide their actions and to modify or reaffirm these values in ways that enhance their potential for effective action on their own behalf. An example of a values clarification exercise is to choose a relevant statement (e.g., "financial assistance to poor people should be limited in duration") and to ask members to rate the degree they agree or disagree with it. Members are then grouped alternatively with others who agree or disagree and are asked to discuss their own views.

Consciousness-raising in itself does not adequately prepare members to work for social change. They must also learn appropriate skills. One important skill is *assertiveness,* which means that an individual has the right to express her or his needs, wishes, and feelings in ways that do not deny others the same right. Many women have been punished for being assertive; consequently, specialized assertiveness training programs have been developed for women (MacDonald, 1982). However, different cultures vary widely on the value assigned to assertiveness. In some, deference to wisdom and the good of the group is more highly valued than individual assertiveness.

Other skills that are imparted to members in such groups include how to confront others constructively; how to express anger, support, or affection judiciously; and how to communicate information effectively. It may also be appropriate in some situations for a group member to be able to defend his or her rights aggressively and to create alliances with others who can be helpful in this respect. Educating members in the use of legal processes may also be necessary.

It is vitally important for oppressed people to be able to negotiate effectively. In their authoritative book on this subject, Fisher and Ury (1981) offer many ideas that can be used to help people in groups enhance their ability to attain their goals. The successful negotiator bargains in ways that focus on "interests" rather than "positions." An interest is what each person seeks to gain from an interaction, whereas a position is a specific "solution" that one party to the negotiation defends. For example, an employee's interest was to receive better pay; his position was to be promoted to a specific job. His employer's wish to have employees compensated in an equitable manner is an interest; whereas a decision to restrict the person in question to a specific salary is a position.

Fisher and Ury (1981) present useful information on how successful negotiators separate relationship issues from substantive ones, help each party accurately perceive the other's circumstances and reflect on one another's feelings, and then look for innovative solutions. These skills can be taught to group members in group sessions through simulations or enactment of actual situations.

This discussion is not meant to imply that groups sensitive to issues of oppression and diversity may not also help members in ways that any other group work approach might. As Garvin (1987) stated elsewhere:

> Someone who is oppressed may need help to improve the quality of his or her relationships, reduce a feeling of depression or anxiety, or raise a sense of self-esteem. While becoming an active social change agent (and we hope achieving some success) may ameliorate these problems, this is not inevitable. The agency, however, that offers treatment to oppressed people will be unlikely to emphasize pathology or view the coping behaviors of oppressed people as signs of "illness." (p. 296)

A group that focuses on empowerment is likely to undertake social action activities. Still another useful activity is for members in such groups to network with others who have similar concerns. The group worker can assist members in improving their networking skills through calling mass meetings, visiting other groups, advertising, and using the media to locate such people. The group worker also can sponsor a group or refer members to an action-oriented organizations.

Termination and Evaluation

Groups focused on issues of diversity may continue to meet as self-help groups after they have made optimum use of a group worker. The group worker, in those circumstances, should help prepare the group for this transition. This includes assisting the members to find answers to the following five questions:

1. What will be the nature of formal leadership in the group? If it will be leaderless, how will responsibility be assigned for notifying members of meetings, arranging for space, and so forth?

2. What are the initial plans for meeting places and times?

3. If the group needs help, such as consultation, in the future, how will it be obtained?

4. What problems in functioning does the group anticipate? Can solutions be proposed at this time?

5. Do the members want training in group leadership skills? Who will provide this?

The members should consider evaluating the group experience as a means of reinforcing gains made and of identifying techniques used that they may want to use again in the future. Some evaluation techniques that have been used successfully in such groups include completing an assertiveness scale if relevant (Gambrill & Richey, 1975), role-playing situations in which group members' competence is assessed by other members, performing self-evaluations on self-esteem (Fitts, 1965; Gergen & Morse, 1967; Kelly, 1955), or creating ways to evaluate successes and problems in reaching task goals. The social worker must be cautious that the scales chosen are not culturally biased.

Measures of identity can be created in which members indicate their feelings about their status as part of an ethnic group, as female, as gay or lesbian, and so forth. Members can also determine if they are achieving a critical consciousness by discussing whether, when facing oppression, members analyze the social forces at play, perceive who benefits from the oppression, and examine the consequences of the oppression for themselves.

PRACTITIONER ISSUES

Knowledge about the range of values held by persons within our American culture and its many subcultures may help social workers to separate [their] values from those of others. Understanding and coming to terms with the values of his [or her] own important reference groups is necessary for anyone who hopes to understand the values of other people. (Northen, 1988, p. 54)

To be effective in working with diverse members in a group, social workers must address their understanding and awareness of many issues. Clearly, one of these is how they react in groups of people who are similar to or different from themselves. When the other members are similar, do they as group workers present themselves as superior because of their professional status or their presumption that they no longer have to deal with the issues that the group members face? When the group members are different, do they as group workers feel either superior to or intimidated by the members? In either of these circumstances, it is best if group workers acknowledge that they themselves are still struggling at some level with the issues being dealt with in the group.

Developing one's cultural competence—continuing exploration of the group worker's own background and resulting interpersonal style, assumptions about appropriate behavior, intellectual competence, and effective ways of working—is especially critical (Green, 1982). Group workers must not only focus on ways they have been oppressed but must also examine ways in which they have been privileged—which is much more difficult (McIntosh, 1992). It is especially important to identify ways the group worker tends to slip into dynamics and behaviors he or she wants to avoid, and to empower group members to assist the social worker in recognizing less than useful patterns. One way to do this is to create circumstances in which group members can point out how the group worker's behavior may be creating difficulties or affecting them in ways that are not useful.

Another constellation of issues concerns the level of knowledge the group worker possesses—not only about the cultures represented by members of the group, but also about the processes that people engage in when confronted by diversity. The group worker does not have to be an anthropologist who specializes in specific cultures. However, he or she has to know some anthropological techniques to learn how people view, have been molded by, and seek to adapt, resist, or modify cultural conditions. This is in some ways a lifelong endeavor, but it is also an extremely rewarding one. Learning to recognize how language, assumptions, and group processes reflect cultural forces and gender issues is also a never-ending set of tasks, because subtle manifestations tend to develop when obvious ones have been eliminated. Power and status differences are constantly recreated as well, unless group workers and members are diligent in identifying and pursuing the mechanisms that perpetuate them.

In conclusion, the United States is growing more diverse, with often divisive polarizations and misunderstandings among its many ethnic groups. As a nation, we must find more ways to use all of our human resources. Social work, other helping professions, and people in general must succeed in developing knowledge and skills for working in multicultural groups, promoting social justice, and acknowledging and addressing the forces that perpetuate sociocultural inequities, whatever their sources. Work in groups provides an important arena for developing and applying this knowledge.

In addition to continuously updating and deepening self-knowledge and skills in cultural processes, cross-cultural communication, and the re-creation of microinequities, attending to diversity questions probably also requires increasing one's skills in bringing to the surface and using differences, conflicts, and intergroup issues. Some of what occurs between members is not personal but plays out tensions structured in the larger society, and must be addressed as societal representations. Thinking of the small group as a coalition of members with alliances to key identified groups in society is a way to accomplish this goal.

Working With Natural Social Networks: An Ecological Approach

11

Judith S. Lewis and Roberta R. Greene

> *The ecological focus on universal life processes reminds social workers that supporting people's strengths and reducing environmental barriers to growth and adaptation are their foremost concerns.*
>
> (Germain, 1981, p. 331)

The ecological approach to social work practice examines conditions that support or interrupt the balance or goodness-of-fit between people and their environments. This approach to intervention is increasingly popular because it directs the practitioner to elements in the client's social environment that "may occur naturally, as in an extended helping network of family and friends," who may have the potential to assist the targeted client (Whittaker, 1983, p. 29). Recognition that transactions between individuals and their environments can enhance or interfere with life situations, and thereby be a source of support or stress, is an important principle in social work with diverse populations. It is a particularly useful premise because it suggests the social worker needs to explore the "opportunity structures of the society [that] may be closed to particular groups by virtue of race, class, sex, and age" (Germain, 1979, p. 7).

According to Maluccio (1979), from the ecological perspective, the focus of intervention is on identifying, supporting, and mobilizing the natural resources of the client. The environment is a full-fledged interventive tool, rather than an ancillary means of interpersonal helping; that is, people's social networks are viewed as a mutual-aid system and affective resource (Gitterman & Shulman, 1986).

This chapter examines how the basic assumptions of the ecological perspective on human behavior have been applied in social work practice with diverse natural social networks. Evidence for such interventions is drawn from the social work literature on work with various client populations; particular attention is paid to factors of race, culture, gender, class, and age. The major assumptions of the ecological perspective are presented and their meaning for diverse populations discussed. The chapter concludes with a discussion of questions and challenges related to the historic social work commitment to improve client environments.

BASIC ASSUMPTIONS: THE ECOLOGICAL PERSPECTIVE

By offering the opportunity to relate to others and to exchange resources and social support, social networks have the potential for contributing to growth and adaptation. (Greene, 1991c, p, 282)

Drawing on concepts from ecology, general systems theory, ego psychology, anthropology, role theory, stress theory, and other bodies of knowledge, the assumptions of the ecological approach to human behavior provide a knowledge base for practice that addresses the "degree of person-environment fit, the reciprocal exchange between person and environment, and the forces that support or inhibit that exchange" (Greene, 1991c, p. 262). According to Germain (1979), people's needs and problems are viewed as located in the interface between person and environment, and interventions are aimed at ameliorating maladaptive transactions within this life space (Table 11.1).

A major appeal of the ecological perspective is its relevance for the enhancement of both the psychological and social life of the client as well as the environmental conditions and situations within which clients function. Ecological approaches emphasize the connections among individuals at various systems levels. For example, Bronfenbrenner (1979) conceptualized the nature of the ecological environment as "a set of nested structures, each inside the next, like a set of Russian dolls" (p. 22). The model also may be visualized as ever-widening concentric circles of environment that surround the individual, moving from the nearest to the remotest.

Bronfenbrenner (1979) has described four systems levels (see Figure 6.1):

(1) the *microsystem*, which comprises a pattern of activities and roles and interpersonal face-to-face relations in the immediate setting, such as the family;

(2) the *mesosystem*, which encompasses the linkages and processes occurring between two or more settings containing the (developing) person, such as the school and the family;

(3) the *exosystem*, which encompasses the linkages and processes that occur between two or more settings, at least one of which does not ordinarily contain the developing person, such as the workplaces of parents; and

(4) the *macrosystem*, which consists of the overarching patterns of a given culture, or broader social context, such as an ethnic group system.

Table 11.1.   The Ecological Perspective: Basic Assumptions

The capacity to interact with the environment and to relate to others is innate.

Genetic and other biological factors are expressed in a variety of ways as a result of transactions with the environment.

Person-environment forms a unitary system in which humans and environment mutually influence each other (form a reciprocal relationship).

Goodness-of-fit is a reciprocal person-environment process achieved through transactions between an adaptive individual and his or her nurturing environment.

People are goal directed and purposeful. Humans strive for competence. The individual's subjective meaning of the environment is key to development.

People need to be understood in their natural environments and settings.

Personality is a product of the historical development of the transactions between person and environment over time.

Positive change can result from life experiences.

Problems of living need to be understood within the totality of life space.

To assist clients, the social worker should be prepared to intervene anywhere in the client's life space.

Source: Greene, R. R. (1991c). "The Ecological Perspective: An Eclectic Theoretical Framework for Social Work Practice." In R. R. Greene and P. H. Ephross (Eds.), *Human Behavior Theory and Social Work Practice*, p. 271. Hawthorne, NY: Aldine de Gruyter.

Natural Social Networks

From an ecological perspective, social networks are a "significant variable in the life space of people, [and] behavior from the ecological perspective needs to be understood as a function of families, groups, organizations, and communities" (Swenson, 1979, p. 215). Using the concept of network as an analytical tool focuses attention on real relationships between people in a way that suggests both useful information and appropriate intervention for social workers (Collins & Pancoast, 1976).

A voluminous literature on social support and social networks, particularly in the field of anthropology, has emerged over the past two decades. Berkman (1983) defined *social support* as "the emotional, instrumental, or financial aid that is obtained from the social network" and a *social network* as "the web of social relationships that surround a person" (p. 747). This interest in social support and networks was prompted by landmark studies in the 1970s that found strong connections between social support and physical and mental health (Berkman & Syme, 1979; Lin, Simeone, Ensel, & Kuo, 1979; Nuckolls, Cassel, & Kaplan, 1972). Social support and social network are two distinct concepts, although they are sometimes mistakenly merged as social support networks, for example (Lewis, 1993). Social networks are referred to as "natural" when they are formed spontaneously without involvement from professionals. Natural helpers, found at many levels in the community, may be friends, neighbors, relatives, clergy, shopkeepers, or others who are in helping roles by virtue of their place in the community, personality traits, or occupation (Kelley & Kelley, 1985).

Practitioners often examine a client's social network characteristics, which include size, frequency of contact, density—the extent to which people in one's network know and have contact with each other, reciprocity, durability—the length of time one has known those in one's network, intimacy, and proximity—the geographic distribution of those in one's network (Berkman, 1983; Ezell & Gibson, 1989; Hirsch, 1979; Kaufman, 1990; Wellman, 1981). An individual may not necessarily perceive interactions with his or her social network as supportive. In attempting to establish a balance between professional and informal support to clients, the social worker needs to examine major network characteristics, particularly in relationship to family, friends, neighbors, or other types of network members (Froland, 1982).

Collins and Pancoast (1976) devoted an entire book to the application of the natural social network concept as a useful way for social workers to gather information and ideas about interventions by studying people's natural ways of forming helping relationships. Collins and Pancoast introduced a consultative model for social work practice with natural social structures that emphasized the importance of "an ecological impact study" before taking any action that could disrupt the balance of natural systems. Though diversity was not a major focus of the book, some projects from the 1970s involved work with social networks with various diverse populations, illustrating the many contexts within which the model could be applied.

In an era of scarce resources and erosion of public support for many human services, some have argued that natural social networks could be used to supplant formal services (National Commission on Neighborhoods, 1979; President's Commission on Mental Health, 1978; *Wingspread Report*, 1978). However, evidence currently suggests that natural social networks seem to work best when undergirded by the support of basic formal services (Pancoast & Collins, 1987). However, the nature of the relationship between formal providers and natural helpers is a delicate one that requires social workers to exercise great care so they do not usurp the position of the natural helper.

Culture and Natural Support Systems

An ecological view of human behavior assumes the importance of cultural context as it shapes behavior and is shaped by people (Germain, 1981; Devore & Schlesinger, 1987b). For example, Ho (1987) proposed that it is important to use an ecological-systems framework when working with ethnic minorities. To be sensitive to the client's cultural background, social workers should direct intervention efforts to multivariable systems and make use of natural systems and life experiences of ethnic minority clients.

Consideration of extended family structure is another factor that needs to be considered in social work interventions with ethnic minorities. For example, Reiss (1981) pointed out that Asian/Pacific-American families usually expect to resolve their life problems within a tightly organized social support network. Not giving ample attention to this commonly found feature of the culture may bring about a lack of acceptance of the social worker.

When considering work with natural social networks in contexts different from those familiar to the social worker, a host of other issues must also be considered. For example, the perception that a person needs help or support, and from what source, can be very much influenced by one's cultural background or social class. In Vietnamese and American Indian cultures, for example, a family member's emotional or social problem is thought to be the family's responsibility; in those cultures it is inappropriate to seek help from outsiders, particularly formal service providers (Land, Nishimoto, & Chau, 1988; Lewis & Ho, 1975).

The literature suggests further questions relevant for work with natural social networks among diverse populations (Devore & Schlesinger, 1987a; Whittaker & Garbarino, 1983). They include the following:

- How is the need for help defined by various client groups and to whom do people turn for help?
- How are the relative merits of formal versus informal help viewed by different client groups?
- What role does discrimination and the use of power play in clients' decisions about the need for help and help seeking, and in client–social worker determinations about options for intervention?
- What are the various sources of informal help that are used by different segments of the population?
- How does the use of formal or informal help affect the sense of autonomy and competence among diverse groups of clients?

Natural Social Networks as Buffers Against Oppression

The ecological perspective is concerned with societal power relationships and redressing inequities, including those associated with age, gender, sexual orientation, physical or mental disability, and race and ethnicity (Germain & Gitterman, 1987). Ecological theorists suggest that environments need to be more nutritive or supportive and offer a goodness-of-fit between minority individuals and their environment. They also are concerned with how minority Americans are devalued and the effect this devalued status—

and the accompanying social injustice and discrimination—has on development (Draper, 1979; Ho, 1992; Pinderhughes, 1983).

Theorists have long questioned whether social support systems have the potential to be buffers against societal oppression (Jackson, McCullough, & Gurin, 1988; Logan, Freeman, & McRoy, 1990). Martin and Martin (1985) traced the historical roots of the helping tradition among black families, concluding that the formerly strong tradition of natural helping among African-Americans had been devastated by overwhelming social and political change, including the Great Depression, northern migration, and the gradual adoption of a patriarchal and capitalistic value system. The revival of a strong helping tradition would require the institutionalization of race consciousness, a goal that in their opinion had yet to be realized (Martin & Martin, 1985, p.96).

Despite Martin and Martin's rather discouraging conclusion, there is evidence that the church and extended family networks still provide important sources of support among African-Americans (Devore & Schlesinger, 1987a; Martin & Martin, 1985; McAdoo, 1978; Stack, 1975). Although the realities of institutional racism and discrimination, including racism and discrimination within formal service systems, have necessitated the creative use of helping networks among African-American families, overburdened natural networks have their limits (Garbarino, 1983; Solomon, 1976). Wolf (1985) reported on a study about the implementation of an indigenous volunteer support program in a midwestern urban black neighborhood. Unfortunately the study did not focus on the racial context; rather, it concluded that volunteers who provided the most service to the people they were helping tended to be those who resisted the push toward professionalization of their role. These findings add to the evidence that unintended consequences may occur when social workers attempt intervention in natural social networks.

Although social networks among African-Americans today may be somewhat different in nature and scope from the predepression years (Martin & Martin, 1985), clearly the long tradition of self-help is still alive (McAdoo, 1978; Taylor & Chatters, 1986). However, questions remain: Without changes that address the most basic inequities faced by African-Americans, how effective can natural social networks be? Can social workers use an ecological approach with natural networks among African-American clients without acknowledging a responsibility for involvement in broad societal change as well?

Social Supports and Economic Well-Being

Ecological theorists argue that goodness-of-fit can be strongly, if not primarily, influenced by abuses of power by dominant groups that prevent equal access to housing, health care, education, and economic distribution. Germain and Gitterman (1987) suggested that the negative person-environment fit resulting from the misuse of power impairs human growth and development. They argued that, although interpersonal counseling may be helpful, such life stresses are created by society and therefore must be solved at the societal level.

Although the social work literature related to social class and ecologically oriented practice with natural social networks is limited, it does contain intriguing findings that have important implications for practice. With some consistency, the literature challenges the romantic notion that the lower classes take care of each other through strong social networks (Auslander & Litwin, 1988; Camasso & Camasso, 1986; Fischer, 1982).

For example, Auslander and Litwin (1988) compared 3 income groups from a large data sample on 9 measures of different social network characteristics. As hypothesized, they found that the poor had smaller and fewer available social networks, although those networks did not provide a lower degree of satisfaction. The poor lacked financial and other resources for mobilizing larger and more varied networks. The authors concluded that the poor were "people with heavy burdens, small circles of support already fully tapped, and few additional resources from which to seek informal help" (Auslander & Litwin, 1988, p. 237). The findings indicated that social workers must carefully assess network resources with different client populations and also must avoid generalized assumptions about the ability of natural social networks to meet human needs.

Camasso and Camasso (1986), in their study of social support as a mediator of psychological distress among medical assistance recipients, found that when there is an imbalance of needs and resources, people become less willing to help. For example, when people feel threatened by the neediness of others or vulnerable to exploitation by others, their efforts to enhance neighborhood support might fail (Camasso & Camasso, 1986; Garbarino, 1983). In addition, enhancing natural social networks is insufficient: "[E]fforts also must be made to modify established social structures and processes that generate stress (e.g., unstable employment, poverty, residential mobility, crime)" (Camasso & Camasso, 1986, p. 388).

Promoting Self-Sufficiency Through Social Networks

The ecological perspective suggests that individuals develop life problems when there is "a lack of good fit between the coping capacities of the person and the qualities of the impinging environment" (Swenson, 1979, p. 233). Moreover, social support networks as informal helping can function analogously to formal social welfare services on behalf of the client (Pancoast and Collins, 1987). Whittaker (1983) captured this idea well in his statement that

a good deal of what ails the human services at present will be greatly improved
by an infusion of ordinary lay people—friends, neighbors, kinfolk, and volunteers—doing what they do best: providing support, criticism, encouragement,
and hope to people in distress. (p. 43)

Whittaker suggested that social workers use a blend of formal and informal services to enhance person-environment fit and promote self-sufficiency. The elderly are an example of an underserved population in the
traditional mental health system for whom formal and informal services have
been used (Kimmel, 1990). Elderly persons, particularly women, are often at
risk for social isolation and in need of various supports to maintain independent living (Goldberg, Kantrow, Kremen, & Lauter, 1986; Lewis, 1993). Perhaps, in part, for these reasons, the elderly are the focus of much literature
on natural social networks, although the social work literature does not necessarily reflect this focus as clearly.

Gerontology is a multidisciplinary field. Early papers in the social work literature on natural social networks and the elderly focused on issues such as
differing needs for social support (Pilisuk & Minkler, 1980), various sources
of and deficits in social support (Goldberg et al., 1986), correlations between
social support and health (Gallo, 1982), historical patterns in social support
among certain ethnic groups (Metress, 1985), and the functions of social support in age-homogeneous versus age-heterogeneous living areas (Siegel,
1985).

Within the past several years, the social work literature on gerontology has
related more to examining or evaluating specific practice interventions involving the elderly and their social networks (Feingold & Werby, 1990; Kaufman, 1990; McDermott, 1989; Seltzer, Ivry, & Litchfield, 1987; Seltzer,
Litchfield, Lowy, & Levin, 1989). For example, Seltzer et al. (1987, 1989) reported results of a longitudinal study involving family members as case managers for elderly clients in a collaborative effort between formal and informal
social networks. In that experimental study, one group of family members
received training in case management and a control group did not. As predicted, trained family members performed significantly more case management tasks than those in the control group ($p < .001$). However, at 2 year
follow-up, there were no significant differences between the groups, and the
control group members had increased their level of case management functioning to that of the experimental group. The two factors that family members felt most supported their roles as case managers were their own contacts
within the formal service network and the support they received from other
family members and friends (Seltzer et al., 1989). The findings highlighted
the importance of social work support of natural social networks.

In an interesting case study in a housing complex for the elderly, Feingold
and Werby (1990) described a well-designed component of a program (a din-

ner plan) that neglected to ensure choice and control by the residents. Such a seemingly minor rule as assigned seating, for example, ignored residents' desire to choose their own dinner companions, that is, to benefit from their own natural networks. Clearly, natural social networks are important among the elderly, even in sheltered settings where residence itself implies some loss of autonomy.

The ecological perspective also emphasizes the innate capacity to interact with others and to strive for competence. One study that examined this premise described a program called a residents' rights campaign (McDermott, 1989). The program was designed to empower the nursing home residents to regain control over their lives and foster bonding among them. Findings indicate that even 1 year after the formal program had ended, residents continued to meet together, and levels of sociability, activity, and motivation remained high. The study findings are consistent with those of other studies in that "long term benefits of choice depended on the ongoing opportunity and ability to exert control" (McDermott, 1989, p. 156; see also Schultz, 1976). Unless there is continuing support for independence and connectedness among residents, the benefits of programs such as the residents' rights campaign are short lived.

Kaufman (1990) presented a model that case managers who are developing long-term care service plans for functionally impaired elderly persons can use to assess social networks. In addition to expressing the need for understanding the various structural and interactional characteristics of these social networks, he presented guidelines to case managers for evaluating relevant values and attitudes of their clients. For example, understanding feelings about dependence or independence, familial obligations and expectations, and the role of government and formal organizations in meeting people's needs can greatly influence help-seeking and service use behaviors (Kaufman, 1990).

Although the research cited seems to have contributed to further specification in the thinking about ecological practice with natural social networks among the elderly, there still is a great need for expansion of this knowledge, particularly as it relates to diverse groups of elderly such as racial and ethnic minority group members (Gibson, 1987; Sokolovsky & Vesperi, 1990; Taylor & Chatters, 1986), the very old, and elderly persons who are homosexual (Goldberg et al., 1986).

Empowerment Through Social Networks

The ecological perspective suggests that client empowerment is a critical approach to social work practice. Social networking among women as a means of empowerment has been a strong theme in the feminist literature of the past 2 decades, as evidenced in social work by the emergence of the *Journal of Women and Social Work, Affilia,* and the National Association for Women in Social Work, for example. The social work literature on social network as a component of help for women includes models of practice with battered women (Wood & Middleman, 1992), rural women (Olson, 1988), homeless women (Hagen & Ivanoff, 1988), and lesbian alcoholics (Schilit, Clark, & Shallenberger, 1988). Although none of these studies focused primarily on natural social network interventions, they all addressed the importance of natural social networks as part of the empowerment process essential to women's growth and development.

Recently the popular media have paid attention to natural social networks among men, although this topic apparently is not reflected in the social work literature. An ecological social network approach with men might be efficacious in number of practice areas: single fathers, men with AIDS, and young men at high risk for criminal behavior.

What conclusions can be drawn from this summary of the social work literature on ecological practice applications using natural social networks and diverse client populations? Is there sufficient evidence that the ecological perspective provides a way to use natural social networks in helping diverse groups? What have social workers learned from these applications to date? What other questions about this approach remain? What are the challenges ahead for the profession if application of this approach with diverse populations is to progress and benefit clients?

PRACTICE APPLICATIONS WITH DIVERSE CULTURAL GROUPS

It is conceptually useful to think of interventions in two main areas: those which engage existing networks and seek to enhance their functioning, and those that create new networks, or "attach" a formerly isolated person to a network. (Swenson, 1979, p. 225)

The ecological perspective on human behavior offers a positive view of capabilities. It strongly emphasizes the importance of client empowerment as a vehicle for strengthening competence in affecting the goodness-of-fit between self and the environment at all systems levels. In the ecological practice approach the social worker and client are viewed as partners in the process of assessing transactions with environmental systems to seek solutions that positively affect the client's life situation. Social workers must be prepared to honor clients' perceptions of the meaning of their life situations and environmental demands, and be open to a creative search for a broader range of interventions (Table 11.2).

Table 11.2. Guidelines for the Ecological Approach to Social Work Intervention

View the person and environment as inseparable.

Be an equal partner in the helping process.

Examine transactions between the person and environment by assessing all levels of systems affecting a client's adaptiveness.

Assess life situations and transitions that induce high stress levels.

Attempt to enhance a client's personal competence through positive relationships and life experiences.

Seek interventions that affect the goodness-of-fit among a client and his or her environment at all systems levels.

Focus on mutually sought solutions and client empowerment.

Source: Greene, R. R. (1991c). "The Ecological Perspective: An Eclectic Theoretical Framework for Social Work Practice." In R. R. Greene and P. H. Ephross (Eds.), *Human Behavior Theory and Social Work Practice,* p. 293. Hawthorne, NY: Aldine de Gruyter.

The ecological perspective has provided the foundation for well-known practice models such as the life model (Germain & Gitterman, 1980) and the competence-based approach to practice (Maluccio, 1979). From the life model perspective, the social worker's purpose is to strengthen adaptive capacities of individuals and influence environments so that transactions are growth promoting (Germain & Gitterman, 1980). The competence-based model also defines problems in transactional terms, that is, person-environment fit, and focuses on the "purposive use of life experiences as interventions" (Greene, 1991c, p. 292).

Despite efforts to develop theoretical frameworks and practice models that allow for a more comprehensive and inclusive view of human behavior, much work remains to be done when it comes to effective use of those frameworks and models across cultures, genders, ages, and social classes, etc. (Ephross-Saltman & Greene, 1993). For example, Gould (1987) critiqued the life model for social work practice—a model based on the ecological perspective. She suggested that the model presents an overly optimistic view of societal problems and that "the life model's conception of goodness-of-fit encourages a falsely optimistic belief in the potential of the system to respond positively and the ability of the profession to produce such a response" (p. 349).

Instead, Gould proposed a conflict model in the context of a feminist perspective that would allow for conflict as a necessary ingredient in institutional reorganization without negating the person-in-environment paradigm. Especially in the case of disenfranchised groups, it is unduly optimistic to assume that the "needs of individuals and the needs of society can be met simultaneously" (Gould, 1987, p. 348). The unrest resulting from conflict may in fact lead to greater long-term benefits. Conflict, then, is not viewed in negative terms, but as a functional regenerative force.

Gould is one of many social workers who have stressed the primary importance of making sociostructural change before a goodness-of-fit between clients and their environments can be reached (Brooks, 1974; Glasgow, 1972; Martin & Martin, 1985; Queiro-Tajalli, 1989). Although this line of reasoning does not seem incompatible with the ecological perspective, it is a reminder that clearly understood goals and values are important when attempting to assess and intervene in the situations that are problematic for clients.

Earlier reports focused on the necessity for better understanding of cultural differences for effective practice with social networks (Delgado, 1977; Lewis & Gingerich, 1980; Lewis & Ho, 1975; Montalvo, 1974; Starrett, Mindel, & Wright, 1983). However, more recent studies have presented models for preventive and interventive practice with natural social networks among various cultural groups (Berthold, 1989; Kelley, McKay, & Nelson, 1985; Land et al., 1988).

Great interest in studying natural social networks among minority groups may be attributed to the fact that these populations have been underserved in the American mental health system. Social workers and others (Devore & Schlesinger, 1987a; Sue & Zane, 1987) have attempted to identify the barriers inherent in our formal helping systems as well as the values, beliefs, needs, and natural helping systems of these underserved groups.

Social workers also are concerned with finding ways to enhance growth and development of natural helping networks among refugee groups struggling with adjustments to a new culture. Land and her associates (1988) surveyed a group of Vietnamese-Chinese refugees awaiting resettlement, and presented a service model that recommended ways to build and sustain natural social networks within a continuum of services.

Social workers using an ecological perspective are aware of respecting the client's own experience and acting in an advisory rather than a directive role with natural social networks. On a larger systems level, Kelley, McKay, and Nelson (1985) elaborated on an ecological approach to practice with indigenous Native American agencies, using an "Indian crisis house" as the focal setting. The non-Indian social worker was viewed as a "facilitator-mentor" and used such principles as mutuality and empowerment to achieve cross-cultural communication and maximize autonomy and competence among indigenous staff.

Natural helpers can contribute to mental health in many ways, which may vary considerably depending on culture. For example, Berthold (1989) discussed the use of spiritist mediums among Puerto Ricans and the ways social workers can use an understanding of the practice of *espiritismo* [a psychodynamic model of mental health care delivered by a socially designated healer; see Frank (1963) and Garrison (1977)] practices in a collaborative and respectful manner. In addition, Ho (1987), who argued that therapists should not hesitate to consult spiritual leaders when the need arises, discussed the vital role of the medicine person, shaman, or spiritual leader in Native American culture. Although these writings presented social network interventions at a variety of systems levels, they indicated a progression in the literature toward more specific methods of applying an ecological perspective and social network knowledge to work with diverse populations.

The social work literature on the ecological approach to working with natural social networks among diverse client populations prompts a number of observations and provocative questions for the profession. The ecological framework for practice logically incorporates social systems such as natural networks that exist across a broad range of client groups. Although some evidence points to attempts to operationalize this approach with the elderly and diverse cultural groups, with few exceptions such as Seltzer, Litchfield, Lowy, and Levin's (1989) experimental study, for example, the profession seems stalled in its efforts to move forward. Much of the literature has concentrated on identifying characteristics of social networks among various groups (Camasso & Camasso, 1986; Delgado, 1977; Ezell & Gibson, 1989; Gallo, 1982). There currently is a need, though, to formulate and test practice models that will help social workers build a stronger knowledge base to guide them in the use of this theoretical framework.

Although the ecological perspective and the models that have evolved from it are relatively recent, and proven practice models take time to develop, it seems reasonable to expect more advanced progress. What explanations, then, might exist for this state of affairs? Perhaps social workers just need more time to learn how to apply ecological concepts in real practice situations with diverse client systems (Germain, 1981). Also, social workers are still learning about characteristics and needs of the many diverse groups practitioners serve. However, there are three other possible explanations.

First, when the recent resurgence of interest in natural social networks occurred, some social workers hoped that they would be able to meet the needs formerly addressed by formal services that were being downsized. Perhaps when it became apparent that "informal helping networks [offered] no easy solution to the crisis in public support for basic human services" (Pancoast & Collins, 1987, p. 181), some momentum for the development of this practice approach was lost.

Second, as Gould (1987) and others have noted, effective application of the ecological approach, particularly with disadvantaged client groups, may not be possible unless social workers become more actively involved in broad sociostructural change efforts. Although there are advocates for such action, it is hardly an agenda item of the highest priority for the profession. Although the professional code of ethics addresses the social workers' responsibility for social change efforts on behalf of disenfranchised clients, the profession itself is embedded in a system that both creates and perpetuates social problems with which social workers are concerned.

Third, although there is expressed interest in addressing social problems inherent in the societal system, social workers may resist becoming too serious about acting on those concerns for fear that their own security may be jeopardized in the process. Undoubtedly, social workers have not escaped the well-publicized national climate of self-interest and lack of community so prevalent in the 1980s.

Perhaps the social work profession needs to grapple with these difficult issues before social workers are able to move ahead and commit themselves to the development of the ecological approach to working with natural social networks among diverse groups of clients. However, social workers have a great deal of knowledge about social networks gleaned from their work on the front line. Undoubtedly, systematic documentation will advance practice models that guide practitioners in an ecological approach with social networks with diverse client populations.

Power Factors in Social Work Practice

Roberta R. Greene

> *[Social workers can not ignore] the consequences of negative valuations directed toward members of stigmatized groups . . . and the relationship between power, powerlessness, and the processes of human growth and development.*
>
> (Solomon, 1976, pp. 13–17)

Although social workers tend to view themselves as egalitarian change agents, they also are susceptible to the sociohistorical issues of power, racism, and privilege of the general U.S. society. As members of society and an institutionalized professional group, as well as agency representatives, social workers are intimately involved in the dynamics of power issues (Burghardt & Fabricant, 1987; Pinderhughes, 1983, 1989; Scott, 1971; Solomon, 1976, 1982, 1991).

At the same time, a continuing and unifying theme in the historical development of the social work profession has been its interest in and concern for social equity and quality of life. In addition to its interest in the well-being of individuals, families, and groups, the social work profession has been committed to meet needs and provide opportunities for at-risk and oppressed populations through social reform. Social workers have long held the belief that it is important to help people exert their influence to obtain basic resources, such as housing, food, and clothing. Social workers also have seen the need to bring about the type of change involving social, structural, and institutional factors that produce stress, such as unemployment, poverty, and discrimination (Chandler, 1986).

Therefore, it is not surprising that there has been a search for human behavior theories that address the concept of power and for practice strategies of empowerment. Lowenstein (1976) was among the earlier proponents of addressing the functions and consequences of unequal power relations in human behavior classes. She urged that the Freudian concepts be reinterpreted as a power struggle and that the concept of power be introduced in all courses on human behavior. Max (1971) contended that because power "is located or latent in every level of society," social workers need to understand power theory and strategies of institutional change (p. 321).

This chapter examines theoretical assumptions related to the concept of power derived from general systems theory, ecological theory, and feminist theory. The chapter specifically explores human behavior power concepts that discuss the client–social worker relationship as a microcosm of societal power issues and relates social work practice to traditional power structures both within the profession and society. It discusses ways that social workers can become more effective in recognizing and dealing with their own biases rooted in power statuses and offers strategies for bringing parity to the helping relationship.

THE CONCEPT OF POWER

Power as a concept has been applied universally to all forms of human behavior—not only to explain intergroup behavior but also to explain dyadic relationships and individualistic behavior. (Wilson, 1973, p. 15)

Several concepts developed in the social sciences have set the stage for how the construct of power has been addressed by social work theorists. Power has generally been perceived as a complex phenomenon that is exercised at the individual, interpersonal, and societal levels. It is seen as central to a person's sense of mastery, competence, or psychological well-being, to the capacity to produce desired effects on others, and to the status and roles assigned within a group and within the larger society.

Because of its focus on communities of people in different economic circumstances and social classes, Marxian theory has influenced social work's perspective on power at the societal level (Burghardt, 1986; Longres, 1990). Marxian theory has helped social workers understand that, as part of the social welfare state, they have the potential to become agents of social control (Burghardt, 1986). On the other hand, social exchange theorists have suggested that people are rational and, although concerned with their self-interest, will interact fairly on a profit-and-loss basis. This utopian view of power relationships, particularly within the family, influenced the social systems approach to social work practice (Blau & Meyer, 1987; Longres, 1990).

Social workers also have been influenced by theorists who have examined power arrangements in the workplace. For example, Weber (1980) characterized power as a negative personal property, but argued that in industrialized societies, bureaucracy is intended to permit and regulate the legitimate use of power. His conceptualization led to an interest among social workers in organizational structure and how social workers can best function in bureaucracies (Blau & Meyer, 1987).

Furthermore, theorists have examined the personal effects on human developmental processes. For example, Goldenberg (1978) addressed the personal effects of acting as if "specific groups, types, or classes of people are both expendable and replaceable" (p. 9). He asserted that the experience of simultaneously being a member of society but being psychologically separated by oppression "continually undermines hope and subverts the desire to 'become'" (p. 3). He concluded that this process eventuates in aggrandizement for some individuals and marginalization for others. Radical social workers, who are concerned with power relationships in the therapeutic relationship, have long traced individual client difficulties to the power "organization of larger political, economic, or social structures" (Burghardt & Fabricant, 1987, p. 456).

Power also has been associated with preferential treatment, access to a disproportionate share of resources, and with the subordination of females, and racial and ethnic groups (Danziger, 1987). Wicker (1986) argued that "racism is more than prejudice. It is power plus prejudice" (p. 30). An outgrowth of these varying theoretical approaches has been the recognition that differential power is a marked feature in all complex societies (Anderson & Carter, 1984). In addition, power may be associated with the capacity to demean others and the ability to force an individual to do something against his or her will. Particularly in situations in which persons are forced to do something against their wills, power may be considered oppressive.

Although there are differences in power relations based on gender, ethnicity, and class, Davis, Leijenaar, and Oldersma (1991) have suggested seven common characteristics:

1. inequality in social resources, social position, political and cultural influences;
2. inequality in opportunities to make use of existing resources;
3. inequality in the division of rights and duties;
4. inequality in implicit or explicit standards of judgment, often leading to differential treatment (in laws, the labor market, educational practices, and so forth);
5. inequality in cultural representations: devaluation of the powerless group, stereotyping, references to the "nature" or (biological) "essence" of the less powerful;
6. inequality in psychological consequences: a "psychology of inferiority" (insecurity, "double-bind" experiences, and sometimes identification with the dominant group) versus a "psychology of superiority" (arrogance, inability to abandon the dominant perspective);
7. social and cultural tendency to minimize or deny power inequality: (potential) conflict often represented as consensus, power inequality as "normal." (p. 52)

Varying views on the nature of power have meant that the concept has been and remains multifaceted and highly contested (Lukes, 1974). The following sections present a discussion of key assumptions related to power from the general systems, ecological, and feminist perspectives.

POWER AND THE GENERAL SYSTEMS PERSPECTIVE:
BASIC ASSUMPTIONS

The concept of ethnosystems . . . emphasizes the interdependent, interrelatedness of ethnic collectivities . . . and makes it possible to study the variations in cultural patterns and social organization, language and communication, the degree of power over material resources, and political power. (Greene, 1991c, p. 249)

General systems thinkers are structural functionalist theorists who believe that social systems exist in relatively continuous harmony based on their maintenance of well-coordinated functions. The structuralists have examined power as an inherent, fixed property of persons and of structured systems (Parsons, 1951, 1964). In addition, hierarchies or status divisions in society reflect an institutionalized, but expected distribution of wealth, power, and prestige (Longres, 1990; Table 12.1). From this perspective, each system naturally develops a hierarchical system of power and control that underpins the social system's organizational capacity and is associated with how that social system achieves its organizational structure. In this manner, conflict and change leading to dysfunction are avoided, and the system remains well integrated. This view of power as being natural and necessary to group functioning has been applied in role theory, general systems theory, and many schools of family treatment (see Chapters 6 and 9 for a discussion of these theories).

One structuralist theorist who has had a strong influence on social work practice is Parsons. Parsons (1951, 1954) explained that power is a societal feature related to a community's or family's underlying structure and general capacity to meet collective obligations and goals. Parsons (1951, 1954) viewed each system as comprising a "natural" hierarchy of power and control based on consensus. He also suggested that hierarchical organization results in social stratification encompassing social class. He proposed that a social class status emerges when society ranks an individual on the basis of such indices as income, occupation, and education. That is, social stratification occurs and social class groups are formed. Social hierarchies center around socioeconomic statuses, race or skin color, ethnicity, religion, gender, health and physical abilities, age, and more recently in U.S. society, sexual orientation (Biddle & Thomas, 1966; Davis, 1991). The power hierarchies may be considered as institutionalized statuses and their associated inequities.

Table 12.1.   Power Issues in Social Work Practice

General systems theory

All social systems have an organizational structure and therefore have a status or
power hierarchy.

Personal and positional resource differentials are associated with differences in
power. Resources are an interpersonal factor influenced by gender,
ethnicity/race.

As a social system, the client–social worker relationship has inherent power issues,
which may mirror those found in the general society. Societal beliefs and practices tend to view professionals as authorities or experts over the lay public.

Ecological theory

Power is related to the reciprocal process of goodness-of-fit between person and
the environment.

A goodness-of-fit metaphor suggests that nutritive environments offer the necessary
resources, security, and support at the appropriate times and in the appropriate
ways. Such environments enhance the cognitive, social, and emotional development of community members.

When environments are not nutritive, the match tends to be poor. Hostile environments, in which there is a lack or a distortion of environment supports, inhibit
development and the ability to cope.

The client–social worker relationship goal is empowerment or a process of increasing personal, interpersonal, or political power to improve client's life situation,
knowledge, skills, or material resources.

Feminist theory

Power is unlimited and can be widely distributed through empowerment strategies.
Empowerment is a political act in which people take control over their own lives
and make their own decisions.

Power is a process in which people personally and collectively transform themselves. Power is derived from a person's internal energy and strength, and requires openness and a connection with others.

Whenever possible, the personal power between therapist and client approaches
equality.

Usually the notion of social class suggests that there is a group consciousness on the part of members, both of their own group and that of others. Status or power groupings in most communities also may vary by life-style and
access to services. Anderson and Carter (1984) suggested that when social
classes are clear and closed, there is little movement between and among
status groups. In addition, when status is assigned by some characteristic beyond a person's control, such as skin color, gender, national origin, or age, a
caste or castelike society exists (DuBois, 1969).

Testimony to this status phenomenon is the fact that the most powerful pre-
dictor of persistent poverty in the United States is race (Davis & Proctor,

1989). For example, there apparently is a permanent *underclass* in American society, which comprises those people who persist in poverty for several generations (Anderson & Carter, 1984; Longres, 1990). In the mid-1960s, urban analyst such as Kenneth Clark (1965) in *Dark Ghetto: Dilemmas of Social Power* argued that there was an urban crisis expressed in "a large subpopulation of low-income families and individuals whose behavior contrasted sharply with the behavior of the general population" (p. 88).

Questions have been raised and there is considerable debate by policy analysts, social science theorists, and social work activists about reasons for high rates of inner-city joblessness, teenage pregnancies, female-headed families, welfare dependency, serious crime, and civil rights demonstrations (Clark, 1965; Kerner Report, 1968; Moynihan, 1965; Thomas & Sillen, 1972; Wilson, 1985). Although the complex discussion is beyond the scope of this chapter, it is important to note that the origins of the underclass are still under debate and the implications for social work practice remain a serious concern (Lemann, 1986a,b; Williams, 1990)

The effects of socioeconomic forces on the lives of minority individuals have been conceptualized by several theorists using a systems perspective in cross-cultural social work. The systems perspective explains how power is distributed in U.S. society and brings attention to "how certain patterns of deployment of resources as well as certain legislative and administrative decisions place heavier burdens on minorities than on the general population" (Bush, Norton, Sanders, & Solomon, 1983, p. 111). For example, Chestang (1972) and Miller (1980) used a systems analysis to discuss the dual perspective, which portrays the impacts for clients who simultaneously live in relationship to two cultures representing unequal power: (1) the dominant or sustaining system, that is, the source of power and economic resources, and (2) the nurturing system, that is, the immediate social environment of the family and community. Miller (1980) suggested that the social worker's assessment of stress produced by institutional and dominant environment factors can lead to an understanding about "whether the target of change should become the client, the larger system, or both, or whether it is appropriate to intervene at all" (p. 60).

To view minority families, specifically African-American families, within the larger power context of other ethnosystems and societal institutions, Solomon (1976) developed the concept of an ethnosystem. An *ethnosystem* is defined as a "collective of interdependent ethnic groups with each group sharing unique historical and/or cultural ties and bound together by a single, political system" (p. 45). Competition between and among groups for scarce economic resources and labor accounts for differential power and, according to Wilson (1973), is a central factor of racial-group interaction in complex societies.

POWER AND THE ECOLOGICAL PERSPECTIVE: BASIC ASSUMPTIONS

Lack of power or powerlessness and helplessness are the root causes of poor social functioning and of the disorganization in people and in the systems that surround them. (Pinderhughes, 1978, p. 11)

The ecological perspective takes a transactional view of power relationships with goodness-of-fit between person and the environment as the underlying paradigm (Draper, 1979; Pinderhughes, 1983). A *goodness-of-fit* metaphor suggests that nutritive environments offer the necessary resources, security, and support at the appropriate times and in the appropriate ways. Such environments enhance the cognitive, social, and emotional development of community members. Goodness-of-fit is a reciprocal process: When an environment in which a person lives is nutritive, the person tends to flourish and the match tends to be good. When the environment is not nutritive, the match tends to be poor. Hostile environments, in which there is a lack or a distortion of environmental supports, inhibit development and the ability to cope (Greene, 1991c).

Pinderhughes (1978) has based her definitions of client power on assumptions from the ecological perspective. She suggested that "sound functioning in an individual or community requires, among other things, the ability to master the environment and to influence positively the forces affecting the ability to cope" (p. 10). Furthermore, human behavior must be understood from an ecological transactional framework encompassing the significance of culture and power. Viewing culture from a transactional perspective does not mean labeling group traits and other cultural symbols. Rather, it involves understanding how cultural symbols are maintained through interaction with the environment, other cultural groups, and the social structures that influence these groups (Pinderhughes, 1989).

Through this pattern of group interaction, diversity and status emerge: "[V]ia the mechanism of differentiation and stratification, society erects social structures that create further differences between these groups" (Pinderhughes, 1989, p. 153). How each group copes with its status position is key to the ecological perspective. This perspective requires that the necessary fit of the individual and family environment, encompassing food, shelter, money, education, recreation, and protection, is assured in an appropriate way (Germain, 1987). This definition of power, then, is "the capacity to influence for one's own benefit the forces that affect one's life space" (Pinderhughes, 1989, p. 154).

A family's sense of capacity or power to function effectively depends on its fit with the environment (Auerswald, 1971; Bronfenbrenner, 1986; Sotomayor, 1971; see Chapter 9 for a discussion of the family). However, many families face the burden of insurmountable environmental pressures and limited access to resources. They may be seen as ineligible for work, struggling with unresponsive educational systems, and blocked from entering the social and economic mainstream. Hence, a "cycle of poverty and exclusion is perpetuated" (Hartman & Laird, 1983, p. 189).

Minority individuals and families particularly face this ecological challenge (Harrison, Wilson, Pine, Chan, & Buriel, 1990). Ecological theorists believe that the ecological challenges facing ethnic minorities are not sudden, temporary economic calamities, but derive from a long history of oppression and discrimination. The process of discrimination often leading to poverty is seen as a

> cycle of powerlessness in which the failure of the larger social system to provide needed resources operates in a circular manner. . . . The more powerless a community the more the families within it are hindered from meeting the needs of their members and from organizing the community so that it can provide them with more support. (Pinderhughes, 1983, p. 332)

From the ecological perspective, then, power evolves through social structures when the majority or dominant group maintains control or power over subordinate groups. This process of social stratification also involves denying subordinates access to resources and controlling the expectations for lifestyles, life chances, and quality of life. In addition, a group's relative power affects how individuals and families perceive themselves and their life opportunities. Pinderhughes (1989) hypothesized that "these victim groups are maintained in relatively powerless positions where they serve as a mechanism for the system in which they exist" (p. 155).

POWER AND THE FEMINIST PERSPECTIVE: BASIC ASSUMPTIONS

Feminism is a transformational politics, a political perspective concerned with changing extant economic, social, and political structures. (Van Den Bergh & Cooper, 1986, p. 1)

Another group of modern theorists who have addressed the concept of power are the poststructuralists. Poststructuralists view the meaning of power as multiple, unfixed, and open to interpretation (Weedon, 1987; see Chapter 12). Poststructuralists tend to look at multiple meanings in relation to a particular social, political, and historical context (Sands & Nuccio, 1992). They argue that conceptions of power are needed to deal with *local power*— the microprocesses of everyday life (Foucault, 1983). This philosophy shifts the focus of power issues to "routine, habitual and practical features of human conduct in the constitution of social life" (Davis, Leijenaar, & Oldersma, 1991, p. 10; see Chapter 7 on social construction).

Because power "hovers everywhere and underlies everything," it is a primary concept in the analysis of social life (Giddens, 1984, p. 226). Giddens argued that the structural properties of social systems do not exist outside day-to-day, face-to-face interactions. Rather, power has the following five dimensions:

(1) Power is integral to social interaction, which includes but is not limited to, social institutions or political collectives.

(2) Power is intrinsic to human agency, which encompasses people's desires and intentions.

(3) Power is relational, involving relations of dependence and autonomy.

(4) Power is enabling as well as constraining, and includes restrictions and opportunities.

(5) Power is processual, which involves how people routinely construct, maintain, change, and transform their relations of power.

How power is conceptualized has been a central concern of feminist theorists. They reject the notion that power is limited and that people need to be placed into dichotomous conditions of haves and have-nots (Van Den Bergh & Cooper, 1986, p. 5). They do not accept that power needs to be viewed as limited, such as a limited supply of property or money, with the controllers of the supply dominating or censuring personal and societal behaviors (Hooyman, 1980). Instead, according to feminist theorists, power is unlimited and can be widely distributed through empowerment strategies rather than through domination. Empowerment, then, is viewed as a political act in which people take control over their own lives and make their own decisions. Hence, "the personal is political" is a major assumption of feminist theory (Van Den Bergh & Cooper, 1986, p. 612).

Feminist theorists also suggest that the traditional definition of power as expressed in the structuralist point of view involves an "imposition-from-without model" (Albrecht & Brewer, 1990, p. 4). This model, represented as Western and patriarchal, is defined in terms of who can maintain domination or control (Bricker-Jenkins & Hooyman, 1986). The contemporary feminist perspective on power differs in that power is not seen as a property or resource owned by those in control. Rather, power is expressed as a process in which people personally and collectively transform themselves. That is, power is derived from a person's internal energy and strength and requires openness and a connection with others (Albrecht & Brewer, 1990).

Although different branches of feminists share many ideas, they also speak in multiple voices on different philosophical and political ideas. Liberal feminists work to attain political rights and opportunities for all and to change the inequality that exists among men and women within the political system. Socialist feminists strive to eliminate oppression and the resulting sexism, racism, and classism stemming from patriarchal capitalism. Radical feminists believe in a society in which patriarchy no longer predominates, and women's caring and loving qualities will dominate society (Nes & Iadicola, 1989).

A theory of power relevant to women must define how women are valued as a social category, according to Davis, Leijenaar, and Oldersma (1991) in their book on the gender of power. However, Sands and Nuccio (1992) have questioned the social work profession's use of categories such as gender, as well as race, ethnicity, and class, when addressing its mission to overcome oppression. They suggested there is the danger that the "very categories promulgated to stem oppression are themselves oppressive in their superficiality" (Sands & Nuccio, 1992, p. 493). Indeed, they assert, the very construction of categories returns people, full circle, to oppressive hierarchical relationships. Instead, they proposed that practitioners need to be cognizant of clients' multiple voices.

For example, feminist theorists contend that it is not possible to describe the essential female or male. Such essentialism tends to treat historical and social constructions as fixed, natural, and absolute (Tice, 1990, p. 135). Feminist scholars have called for theories that "are nonuniversal, [but open to the] multiplicity and diversity of experiences" (Frazer & Nicholson, 1990, p. 21). Because feminist scholars are suspicious of any universal norms that fit all women and men, these scholars would "replace unitary notions of 'woman' with plural and complex descriptions of feminine gender identity" (Tice, 1990, p. 135).

Feminist theory also has addressed social work activities that are centered around social reform and the existing relationships of patriarchal power and authority (Hooyman, Summers, & Leighninger, 1988). For example, feminism posits that social roles should not be assigned solely on the basis of gender (Valentich, 1986). Although feminism places high value on women's experiences, it strives for equality of men and women. An androgynous sex role repertoire, or one that draws on both instrumental task roles and expressive nurturing roles, is encouraged. On the other hand, because social workers often want to advocate for a particular group as a category, such as the rights of women, using dichotomous categories often places the advocate in a dilemma about how to address a client's particular issues, needs, and vulnerabilities (Brown, 1990; Donadello, 1986; Sands & Nuccio, 1992). Therefore, the counterargument is made that the drive for equality and self-actualization should not deter the scholarly study and theory in women's development that is only in its infancy (Bricker-Jenkins, Hooyman, & Gottlieb, 1991).

POWER DIFFERENTIALS AND INTERVENTION STRATEGIES

If our institutional response and problem-solving endeavors are directed to the elimination of the powerlessness, then we are truly "starting where the client is." (Pinderhughes, 1978, p. 14)

Power is "an often unspoken but central dynamic in cross cultural encounters" and therefore needs to be addressed in the clinical social work relationship (Pinderhughes, 1989, p. 109). Political, economic, and social aspects of professional social work authority—the established right granted by society to make decisions on certain issues—also must be taken into consideration (Briar & Miller, 1971; Dworkin, 1990).

This section reviews and explores the power differential and control issues that may exist in the social worker–client relationship. Potential difficulties in providing a service that maximizes client competence and feelings of self-worth are noted.

General Systems Perspective

From a structuralist systems perspective, power that is viewed as legitimate, such as that associated with professional power, is called *authority*. The authority of the expert, such as a social worker, stems from education, knowledge, credentials, expertise, status, and agency position. Martin and O'Connor (1989) have asserted that the client–social worker relationship is an example of an authority relationship with the social worker in the advantaged position. From this perspective, the client–social worker relationship is "structured by the organization prior to the arrival of worker or client" (Martin & O'Connor, 1989, p. 104).

Furthermore, perceived differences in socioeconomic status are of importance to social workers because the proportion of people in poverty in the United States is increasing; poverty is a major factor in putting people at risk; and socioeconomic differences, among others, have profound influences on how individuals interact, communicate, and perceive the world. "Social work technology has developed from essentially middle-class conceptions of the universe" (Davis & Proctor, 1989, p. 260). Because cross-class helping relationships may be affected by the client-therapist status differential, practitioners working with economically different clients must ask, How does my economic status impact the extent to which I can be helpful?

From this perspective, the interviewer (social worker)–interviewee (client) interaction is one of reciprocal, mutual efforts of both participants to influence each other. However, because the interviewer has more power, the influence potential of that person is greater (Kadushin, 1972). The interviewer/social worker has reward power, or the power to control access to special services and to the therapy he or she dispenses. He or she also has expert power or specialized knowledge and skills and, in some cases, may have coercive power or the ability to control.

For these many reasons, social workers need to be aware of their own power biases as well as of techniques that will help them avoid power abuses. For example, Gutierrez (1990) has proposed that the goal of empowerment is to avoid replicating within the social worker–client relationship the relative powerlessness that a client experiences in the society. When applied cross-culturally with a particular cultural context in mind, empowerment may not lead inexorably to strategies for reducing hierarchy. For example, Hirayama and Cetingok (1988) have suggested that empowerment techniques with Asian immigrants would not be congruent with values that stress vertical relationships, interdependence, self-control, and acceptance. On the other hand, because hierarchical relationships may be found oppressive, great care should be taken by the practitioner to respect the client's culture and, at the same time, not engage in institutionalized power biases.

Ecological Perspective

According to one ecological theorist, the social worker, who is an expert who diagnoses, teaches, and treats, must be cautioned, particularly in cross-cultural social work, not to use the helping role to satisfy his or her own needs for power (Pinderhughes, 1983). Such oppression, the withholding of power by dominant groups, can only be addressed only through empowerment (Pinderhughes, 1983). To avoid this difficulty, interventions should be based on an understanding of power dynamics and the social worker should use strategies that enable clients to turn a sense of powerlessness into a sense of power. Such interventions focus on client strengths and reinforce coping mechanisms that exercise choice and self-assertion. They also may incorporate strategies that increase client information and knowledge of resource options.

In addition, an understanding of the interaction between oppressed people and an oppressing society also must involve an appreciation and respect for the special coping capacities and resources necessary to survive and function in a hostile environment. Draper (1979) contended that language used by African-Americans such as the adjective *bad* to mean *good* is an example of culturally based "behavior that is calculated to transform impotence into an active force" (p. 274). Draper furthered her argument by stating that phrases such as "Keep in your place" and "If you're black, stay back" function to diffuse hostility and gain power (p. 272).

Discrimination against minority groups and others serves a societal purpose of projecting "victim" status onto others, while the members of the dominant group are the beneficiaries—or are anxiety free (Bowen, 1978). According to Pinderhughes (1989), this process of societal projection makes it difficult for any practitioner to examine his or her own behaviors in the clinical encounter. She has suggested the following questions for monitoring practitioner behavior:

> If the societal projection process provides a sense of competence, stability, and lack of confusion for benefactors-beneficiaries but also reinforces anxiety and greater confusion for victims, and I, as the helper, am a member of the benefactor-beneficiary (or victim group), what does this mean for me in my work with clients who are also victims of this process? What does this mean if I, the clinician, am also a member of a victim group?
>
> Do I receive gratification in this possible double power role?
>
> Is this gratification a liability in the helping process?
>
> In my relationship with clients (victims), do I allow the goals pursued and the strategies used to be influenced by my professional role? (pp. 133–134)

Others have argued against the perspective of client as victim (Goldstein, 1983, 1990a, 1992; Weick, 1992). For example, Weick (1992) suggested that a strengths perspective toward human development assumes a form of individual power. In addition, Goldstein (1992) has argued that neither the concept of pathology nor the concept of strength is based on objective fact. Rather, each concept is socially constructed and reflects public and professional attitudes and beliefs (see Chapter 7 on social construction). The reflection of attitudes and beliefs is expressed in the situation of people who are positive for the human immunodeficiency virus (HIV), who prefer to be called "persons with AIDS" or "PWAs," rather than "AIDS victims."

Another example involves the various portrayals in the social work professional literature of how to view people who have faced domestic violence (Davis, 1987). Initially, wife abuse was seen as a problem affecting diverse women and was linked to societal forces outside the individual, such as norms permitting men to physically abuse women. Then, wife battering was viewed as one type of family violence; some theorists asserted that "victims" played a role in their own difficulty. The focus then shifted from providing services to women to focusing services on men who batter.

On the other hand, a systemic process of empowerment involves influencing the external social system to be less destructive and requires working with extrafamilial systems, such as churches, businesses, or schools. Making surrounding systems more responsive, addressing the power differential, and assisting clients to exert their personal, political, and economic power are the ultimate goals of empowerment. The need to make surrounding social systems more responsive is particularly keen for clients who experience "interacting oppressions" such as the multiple interacting effects of gender and race among women of color (Morris, 1993, p.99).

Empowerment then is "a process of increasing personal, interpersonal, or political power so that individuals can take action to improve their life situation" (Gutierrez, 1990, p. 149). Empowerment is gaining the capacity to manage emotions, knowledge, skills, or material resources in a way that makes more effective performance of valued social roles and receipt of individual satisfaction possible. The social worker who works using an empowerment model aims to reduce "institutionally derived powerlessness caused by social injustice and societal inconsistency" (Bush et al., 1983, p. 103). Persons who have belonged to stigmatized categories all their lives can be assisted by developing interpersonal skills and the performance of valued social roles (Solomon, 1976). Therefore, empowerment encompasses problem-solving strategies and the building of support networks.

To the extent that powerlessness may be an issue with every client who seeks help, empowerment may be viewed as a necessary component of all human services methods and techniques (Green, 1982). Empowerment as a goal of social work practice assumes that the knowledge and skills the practitioner uses in working with the client (system) will maximize the client's own effectiveness and opportunities. The client participates in a helping process that "redefines his [or her] self-worth, competence and ability to affect his [or her] social and physical worlds" (Solomon, 1978, p. 342). Although the goal of empowerment may erroneously seem relatively easy to attain, many theorists see it as difficult to achieve (Pinderhughes, 1976, 1989; Solomon, 1976). Unfortunately, many agencies designed to assist the poor and those less powerful hold power over their clients. As in any service provision, agency personnel and policies determine what services are available to whom and under what circumstances, for example, seemingly simple matters such as the times when services are available and how physical space is designed.

Problem solving through empowerment, however, may be impeded by several issues. Empirical studies have demonstrated that there often is little consensus between social workers and clients on such important matters as the definition of the problem, what interventions are needed, and the goals and outcome of treatment. These issues can remain areas of contention throughout the relationship or can bring about early termination of services. In addition, many current intervention approaches to problem solving tend to ignore the organizational or sociopolitical environment in which problem solving occurs (Greene, 1989). These forces often make clinical problem solving a "political act by which the participants seek to accomplish a more satisfactory redistribution of power and control" (Murdock, 1982, p. 418). By recognizing the omnipresence of conflict in social relationships (including the helping relationship), the practitioner can consciously adopt strategies to maintain mutual respect in the client–social worker relationship and to control the effects of power discrepancies (p. 420).

Advocacy, an approach closely aligned with empowerment, is another means of redressing power differentials between the client and social worker. Advocacy, which involves "acting as a partisan" in a social conflict and using one's professional expertise in the interest of the client (Harbert & Ginsberg, 1979, p. 234), can occur at three levels: (1) the individual level, focusing on the manner in which a certain client or group is assisted in a specific situation, such as the acceptance of a client for service; (2) the administrative level, centering on convincing decision-makers to alter agency regulations, such as the verification procedures used in public welfare; and (3) the policy level, influencing legislative or regulatory provisions, such as changes in health policy. Social workers operating as partisans attempt to influence another individual or group to make a decision that the person or group otherwise would not make, which concerns the welfare and interests of the client, who by definition is in a less powerful status than the decision-maker (Sosin & Caulum, 1983). Advocates, therefore, organize their social work activities around obtaining goods, services, other resources, and power for clients (Biegel, Shore, & Gordon, 1984).

Advocacy as an intervention strategy is concerned with the balance of power between the client as a member of a minority or other disenfranchised group and the larger society (Greene, 1988). The advocate generally takes action to rectify unfair or unjust practices and the inequitable distribution of resources (Green, 1982). From the advocate's point of view, the client's problems are not seen as personal or psychological deficits, but rather as stemming or arising from discrimination in social and economic opportunities (Dodson, 1981; Prunty, 1980). Techniques of intervention challenge those system's inequities that seem to contribute to or cause difficulties, rather than focus solely on the relief of the individual client.

"To negate advocacy on any level is to dismiss a basic tenet of social work practice" (Sosin & Caulum, 1983, p. 15). Advocacy on behalf of one or more clients implies that the condition facing the client has broader ramifications or exists at the macrosystems level. That is, rather than attempt to improve a difficulty on a case-by-case basis, the social worker takes measures such as testifying before boards of directors or legislative bodies about the overall need. Advocacy as an approach to intervention recognizes that many clients "have serious social systems problems and have spent a great deal of time, effort, energy and resources in trying to cope with them. . . . [Therefore, the social work advocate focuses on the] reality oriented problem" that the clients bring (Prunty, 1980, p. 183).

Feminist Perspective

Although there is not one definition of feminist therapy, many theorists view it as a collaborative process between client and practitioner that attempts to alleviate or remediate the social, cultural, and psychological barriers to women's optimal functioning. The goal of feminist counseling is remediation on both psychological and social levels. This view emphasizes a clarification of individual autonomy as well as an attempt to change structural properties in the family and in the economy (Russell, 1986; Valentich, 1986).

Through a number of therapeutic goals, practitioners may identify their own biases and better assist women to act on their own behalf. Seven general feminist helping principles, according to Van Den Bergh and Cooper (1987), are as follows:

1. A client's problems are interpreted within a sociopolitical framework. This underscores the notion of "the personal as political."
2. Automatic submission to traditional sex [gender] roles is questioned, yet supported for pursuing a free choice of life styles.
3. Treatment is focused on articulating and augmenting clients' strengths rather than centered on pathologies. Therapy seeks to be an empowering process, whereby clients increase their ability to control their environments to get what they need.
4. Encouragement is given to the development of an independent identity that is not defined by one's relationships with others.
5. Reassessment of women's relationships with other women is encouraged so that bonding between women is valued as highly as developing relationships with men.
6. Emphasis is placed on developing a balance between work and interpersonal relationships.
7. Whenever possible, the personal power between therapist and client approaches equality. (p. 613)

Feminist practitioners believe that it is important for the helping relationship to involve two equals. Theorists tend to see the social worker as expert as being detrimental to growth because of the dependency this view may generate (Bricker-Jenkins & Hooyman, 1984). As in all social work practice, the practitioner strives to treat the client with dignity and respect, but social worker expertise is shared. Skills tend to be externally and empowerment oriented, including problem solving, interpersonal, and life management skills, and participation in collective action, such as networking, and joining support and self-help groups (Bricker-Jenkins & Hooyman, 1984).

There is continuing concern with how sexist attitudes may effect practice and the profession. Renaming, or the right to describe and name one's own

Table 12.2. Guidelines for Power Parity in the Client–Social Worker Relationship

---

Recognize that the social worker has the potential to be an agent of social control and or social change. Bring awareness of sociohistorical issues of power, racism, and privilege of the general U.S. society to the client–social worker relationship.

Examine power issues related to practical features of everyday social life within the context of social, cultural, political, and historical contexts.

Recognize and deal with practitioner biases rooted in power statuses and offer strategies for bringing parity to the helping relationship.

Identify a client's psychologically issues related to oppression.

Identify social, structural, and institutional factors that produce client stress and inequalities.

Determine whether the target of change should become the client, the larger system, or both, or whether it is appropriate to intervene at all.

Employ empowerment and advocacy strategies that enhance client strengths.

---

experiences, has increasingly become the therapeutic and political goal shared by the civil rights and women's movement. It involves using new words for people, altering meanings through language, remembering old definitions, and expanding existing definitions (Van Den Bergh, 1982). The development of feminist therapies also has involved the reconceptualization of diagnostic categories (Brown, 1992). This reconceptualization was based on the idea that client assessment and treatment may reflect societal inequities and, therefore, may be racist, sexist, or heterosexist in nature. Hamilton and Jensvold (1992) have argued that an example of the misuse of diagnostic categories is the widespread, often misplaced diagnosis and treatment of women for depression, rather than addressing issues of status, poverty, employment, and family roles.

The skepticism about universal truths and concern for individualizing the client also is reflected in family treatment approaches (Hoffman, 1990; also see Chapter 7). For example, Hoffman (1990) contended that the family therapy literature was long dominated by a masculine vocabulary based on strategies that portrayed family members as either "one-up" or "one-down". She suggested that family therapists need to replace the notion of the feedback loop, which assumes a static communication and balance within families with the idea of "intersubjective loops of dialogue," which express multiple stories (p. 8). She went on to state that this intervention approach leads to empowerment of women and ethnic minorities within the treatment milieu.

Weick, Rapp, Sullivan, and Kisthardt (1989) also have proposed that "diagnostic categories establish classes of conditions with which clients are matched" (p. 351). They contend this problem deficit perspective sets up barriers for clients that can be overcome if social workers use an approach that is dedicated to enhancing client strengths. Increasingly, theorists and practitioners are examining the effects of scientific classification or categories of illness. For example, White (1988) has suggested that psychodiagnostic language has a political flavor that may be used to describe people as oppressed by problems. He has proposed interventions that aim to redefine problems through helping clients to separate themselves from the problem, describe themselves in new ways, and write an alternative story of family life.

Common features contained in the three power perspectives presented include respect for client strengths and an awareness of and attention to societal factors in problem definition (Table 12.2). Acknowledgement of power as a critical factor in shaping human behavior creates a therapeutic atmosphere in which clients can "achieve self-actualization without inhibiting that of others" (Bricker-Jenkins, 1991, p. 272).

Epilogue:
Power and the Social Work Profession ⎯⎯⎯⎯⎯⎯⎯

Carol T. Tully

The tumultuous social and political changes that occurred in the 1960s have had an impact on social work education that has lasted into the 1990s. The activist approach taken by minorities of color, women, lesbians and gays, as well as other disenfranchised groups in the 1960s led to a reexamination of curricula content related to cultural diversity that still is being implemented in schools of social work (Arnold, 1970; Council on Social Work Education, [CSWE], 1973, 1992; Dumpson, 1979; Glasgow, 1971). These ever-expanding parameters related to cultural diversity within a professional accreditation agency reflect the growing demands of the profession for better ways of providing services within an increasingly culturally diverse system. This section recounts how the Council on Social Work Education (CSWE) came to integrate lesbian and gay curriculum issues.

A STUDY OF ADVOCACY WITHIN THE SOCIAL WORK PROFESSION

Evolving from such accrediting bodies as the Association of Professional Schools of Social Work (1924) and the National Association of Schools of Social Administration (1942), CSWE, which emerged during the early 1950s, remains the primary accreditation agency for U.S. schools of social work (Kelly, 1980). Its organizational structure is typical of other bureaucratic models (Weber, 1946); consequently, CSWE reacts slowly to any organizational change (Thompson, 1967). Furthermore, when CSWE has viewed changes as negative, although necessary, it sometimes has erected organizational barriers to thwart or inhibit their implementation (Thompson, 1967).

The following historical overview traces the evolution of CSWE's Lesbian and Gay Commission, details the CSWE organizational "coming-out" process, and delineates CSWE's struggle by including unpopular policies in both its own organizational structure and its accreditation standards.

From Caucus to Commission: The Coming-Out Process

Theoretical models of the identification and integration of homosexual identities within individuals have tended to dichotomize by gender (see, for example, Grace, 1979; Lewis, 1984), but they also have shared certain characteristics. Because organizations are entities comprising individuals, they too may be perceived as having individualized philosophies and personalities (Strauss, 1972). Thus, when faced with organizational change, such as the emerging lesbian or gay man, organizations seem to move through four developmental phases: (1) identification, (2) investigation, (3) internal conflict, and (4) institutionalization.

Identification (1976–1977)

Moving away from the traditional definition of homosexuality as a mental illness, the American Psychological Association (APA) in 1973 removed homosexuality from its list of mental disorders and reclassified homosexuality as a sexual orientation (Tully, 1983). In 1975, the American Public Health Association and APA issued public policy statements deploring discrimination against lesbians and gay men (Tully, 1989), and in 1976 the CSWE Delegate Assembly passed the Gay Caucus's resolution to establish a gay task force within CSWE. Task force objectives centered on gathering information on homosexuality within social work curricula, rooting out discrimination against lesbian and gay social work faculty and students, and delineating further aims (CSWE, 1976).

Concurrently, in 1976, NASW developed a public policy statement on homosexuality, adopted in 1977 by the NASW delegate assembly (NASW, 1977). Partially because CSWE had never appointed a task force, and in response to NASW's public policy statement, a gay caucus of 14 members met on March 3, 1977, at the CSWE annual program meeting. From that caucus emerged the resolution mandating that CSWE create a "public policy statement on Gay Issues" (CSWE, 1977b); the resolution was passed by the house of delegates that year. The resolution also required that the CSWE board of directors appoint a task force to develop a curriculum on lesbian and gay issues related to social work and to develop guidelines that would assure the rights of both homosexual faculty and students.

Besides developing the first resolution CSWE would actually implement— the creation of a lesbian and gay task force within its organizational structure—the 1977 CSWE gay caucus formed as the Association of Social Work Educators Concerned with Lesbian/Gay Issues, supported by dues-paying members. The association would later become the source of political influence within CSWE.

As with all popular coming-out models (Lewis, 1984), the first stage is to identify differences or to reexamine issues based on new information. Following pressure from within CSWE and the lead of NASW, which had endorsed policies that protected lesbians and gay men from discrimination, CSWE was forced to examine its previously unwritten ideas about homosexuality. CSWE's association and the Ad Hoc Task Force on Lesbian/Gay Issues (appointed by the president of CSWE until late 1979) became the recognized organizational structures by which CSWE began to grapple with the complexities of sexual orientation issues.

Investigation (1977–1979)

The second phase of coming-out involves investigating the phenomenon (Lewis, 1984): During the end of the 1970s, CSWE began analyzing this newly identified issue. Because the Ad Hoc Task Force on Lesbian/Gay Issues was not to be officially appointed until 1979, the association was responsible for developing strategies that would become the major source of CSWE's eventual policies on lesbian/gay issues. The association met in April 1977 to develop organizational goals, identify common issues, create incentives for association members to join CSWE, and develop a plan to fill the 1978 annual program meeting with sexual orientation issues. However, the goal of supplying an abundance of lesbian/gay content at the 1978 annual program meeting was not realized because the CSWE program committee rejected most of the lesbian/gay proposals submitted (Tully, 1989).

Doubling in size from 1977, members of the association in 1978 vowed to continue submitting annual program meeting abstracts on lesbian/gay themes. They also promised to push the CSWE board of directors into appointing the gay task force created in 1976 by the house of delegates.

Internal Conflict (1980–1983)

During the early 1980s, CSWE began to grapple with the reality of its lesbian and gay members and the influence of the association. Thus it began the third phase of its own coming-out process: It experienced the internal conflict (Lewis, 1984) that any organizational change creates (Selznick, 1957). Announcing the appointment of the six-member Ad Hoc Task Force on Lesbian/Gay Issues at the 1980 annual program meeting created turmoil among association members because CSWE insisted on naming two heterosexuals to the task force, "for balance" (Tully, 1989, p. 9).

As a task force without organizational funding, the group spent significant time and energy devising fund-raising schemes ("Gay/Lesbian Task Force Meets," 1981, p. 11). Because CSWE did not provide funding for the task force, the association and task force became fiscally joined as a result of these financial constraints.

By 1981, the task force's two heterosexual members had resigned after failing to attend any meetings, and were replaced; a member of the task force acted as the liaison between the CSWE Ad Hoc Task Force on Lesbian/Gay Issues and the NASW Task Force on Lesbian and Gay Issues. The primary objectives of the CSWE task force were to continue to develop and examine social work curricula on lesbian/gay issues, to inquire about discrimination issues of lesbian/gay social work faculty and students, and to create CSWE accreditation standards that reflected lesbian/gay issues and needs. Tangentially, task force members played a continuing leadership role in the association and in developing and disseminating lesbian/gay social work curriculum content at the CSWE annual program meetings.

During the early 1980s, heated debates erupted within CSWE over proposed revised accreditation standards that stated, "Every aspect of the program's organization and implementation shall be conducted without discrimination on the basis of race, color, gender, age, creed, ethnic or national origin, handicap, or political or sexual orientation" (Evaluation Standards 11 and 12; CSWE, 1984, p. 102). Members also debated proposed revisions to the CSWE policy statement in terms of issues of sexual orientation that were included under "Special Populations" (7.3 Special Populations, CSWE, 1988a, p. 5). The debates pitted conservative religious schools and other conservative organizational members against more moderate and radical lesbian/gay advocates.

Some schools threatened withdrawal from CSWE, citing irreconcilable differences between their values and the values expressed by CSWE. All deplored CSWE's newly defined position on lesbian/gay issues (personal communication from T. D. Thompson of Asbury College, Wilmore, Kentucky, to Dorothy B. Daly, March 1981; personal communication from R. C. Bullock of Azusa Pacific College, Azusa, California, to Dorothy B. Daly, March 1981; personal communication from E. G. Kuhlmann of Eastern College, Saint Davids, Pennsylvania, to Dorothy B. Daly, February 1981; personal communication from E. B. Whipple of the National Association of Christians in Social Work, Los Angeles, to Dorothy B. Daly, March 1981). Virtually no CSWE constituency group was overlooked during this turmoil. Despite sometimes bitter confrontations, continuing advocacy and education efforts of the CSWE task force and its broad-based, grass roots support from the association, enabled both the current CSWE accreditation standards and curriculum policy statement to reflect a more tolerant view of homosexuality than previous CSWE policies.

Institutionalization (1984–1990)

Following the successes of the task force, association and task force members struggled to have equal status with other minority groups within CSWE's organizational structure. The task force made further progress, evident in CSWE's provision of a professional CSWE staff member to provide staff support for the task force. CSWE did not provide funds.

In 1984, with continuing pressure from CSWE members, CSWE's board of directors "elevated the Gay/Lesbian Task Force to the status of a Commission"—the Commission on Gay/Lesbian Issues in Social Work Education ("Gay/Lesbian Task Force Becomes a Commission," 1984, p. 8). Because the continuance of CSWE task forces must be evaluated annually, commissions are assured continual existence.

In addition to the goals established by the Gay/Lesbian Task Force, the Commission on Gay/Lesbian Issues in Social Work Education expanded its scope to include the development of a compendium of instructional readings on lesbian/gay issues to cover all the CSWE professional foundation areas outlined in the curriculum policy statement. In addition, the commission investigated funding sources for a volume dealing with social work education and practice in relation to AIDS ("Gay/Lesbian Task Force Becomes a Commission," 1984).

From 1985 to 1987, the commission settled into a regular routine of activities, but because of increasing organizational financial crises, no funds were ever provided to assist commission members in defraying their costs. The group expanded its mandate to include networking with other CSWE commissions and building an internal organizational infrastructure within CSWE.

Although the relationship between the commission and the association thrived, commission members realized that connecting with similar CSWE organizational entities would strengthen the position of each within the overall organization. Thus, commission and association members who also were members of other CSWE organizational entities (such as the Commission on Accreditation, Commission on Educational Policy, Commission on Minority Concerns, and Commission on the Role and Status of Women) began to build linkages between the Commission on Gay/Lesbian Issues in Social Work Education and other institutionalized CSWE organizational structures.

In addition to the bibliography, one of the tangible results of networking was the Commission on Accreditation's request to have the Commission on Gay/Lesbian Issues in Social Work Education develop a packet of materials related to the *Handbook of Accreditation Standards* (CSWE, 1984), which specifically delineated social work education standards on sexual orientation. The CSWE Division of Standards and Accreditation distributed this information to accredited programs of social work.

In 1987, some CSWE members moved to disband the Commission on Gay/Lesbian Issues in Social Work Education in the new organizational structure of CSWE. However, primarily because of the efforts of commission and association members and the connections that had been forged with other CSWE organizational structures, the commission survived the attack (CSWE, 1989b).

Although the commission continued to exist, the number of lesbian/gay-oriented presentations accepted for inclusion at the annual program meetings continued to decline from 1985 to 1989, whereas the content on AIDS-related materials increased. The identification of AIDS as only a homosexual issue was the outcome. For example, in 1989, the annual program meeting included eight lesbian/gay-oriented sessions, but five dealt with issues related to AIDS.

Aware of the continuing decline of extraneous lesbian/gay content, members of the commission and the association met in Chicago to discuss strategies for assuring lesbian/gay content in the 1990 annual program meeting in Reno, Nevada. They created a lesbian/gay symposium to be included in the meeting, which once accepted as a symposium for a single annual program meeting, "may request symposium status for the following year and have its specific theme (related to the overall Conference theme) appear in [CSWE's] 'Call for Papers'" (CSWE, 1989a, p. 72).

Having moved through the first three stages of coming out, CSWE currently is institutionalizing the issue through continuing presentations at annual program meetings; the continuation (through the 1988–1989 reorganization of the CSWE structure) of the Commission on Gay/Lesbian Issues in Social Work Education; and the continuing inclusion of gays and lesbians as a "special population" within the current curriculum policy statement (CSWE, 1988b, p. 125).

Curricular Implications

It is obvious that social work curricula need to reflect homosexually oriented content in courses and field instruction settings. Given the inclusion of lesbians and gays as a special population within the current curriculum policy statement (CSWE, 1988b), the fact that the Commission on Gay/Lesbian Issues in Social Work Education presented documentation to the CSWE Division of Standards and Accreditation in 1987, and that site visit teams do look for lesbian/gay-oriented material throughout the curriculum, considerably more attention is needed in curriculum development (Tully, 1989). The following sections describe areas in the social work curricula in which lesbian/gay issues are important, using the CSWE accreditation standards.

Evaluation Standard 11: Nondiscrimination

The nondiscrimination standard for both the undergraduate- and master's-level programs clearly states that "every aspect of the program's organization and implementation shall be conducted without discrimination on the basis of race, color, gender . . . or sexual orientation" (CSWE, 1988a, pp. 9, 18). Since this standard refers to nondiscrimination and not affirmative action, programs do not need to demonstrate affirmative action to the groups identified. They must, however, demonstrate that none of the minorities faces discrimination within the social work program (CSWE, 1988b). Thus, programs must provide evidence that every aspect of the program's organization and implementation is conducted without discrimination toward the identified groups; demonstrate that students are educated to work with and accept people with beliefs and practices different from those propagated by the program, field setting, or institution; and show that students are exposed to a variety of curricular materials that reflect the various viewpoints represented by the social work profession (CSWE, 1988b).

Evaluation Standard 12: Cultural Diversity

According to the undergraduate and master's standards on cultural diversity, "the program shall make specific, continuous efforts to assure the enrichment of the educational experience it offers by reflecting racial, ethnic and cultural diversity throughout the curriculum and in all categories of persons related to the program" (CSWE, 1988b). Because this standard is cross referenced to the special populations section of the curriculum policy statement, and ample empirical evidence exists that defines the lesbian/gay community as a unique subculture (Tully, 1983; Varnell, 1989), Evaluation Standard 12 provides further rationale for the inclusion of lesbian/gay-oriented content throughout the social work curriculum.

Evaluation Standard 4: Curriculum

Undergirded by the values and ethics embodied by the profession and the objectives of social work education (CSWE, 1988b, pp. 123, 125) and armed with explicit mandates in its accreditation standards on nondiscrimination and cultural diversity, attention has turned toward ways in which compliance could be documented through the curriculum. Because both the undergraduate- and graduate-level social work programs share the social work education goal that students shall integrate professional values, skills, and knowledge for competent social work practice (CSWE, 1988b), content on lesbian/gay issues (as well as on other oppressed minorities) ought to be infused across the curriculum from the entry-level courses, through the foundation content, and into the specialization segment of the curriculum. Thus, the first courses taken in any social work curriculum need to include appropriate content related to the reality that social workers, perhaps unknowingly, provide services to lesbians and gays.

Following the introductory classes, content related to lesbians/gays needs to be developed and implemented in the foundation content. The human behavior and social environment sequence provides an opportunity to examine lesbian and gay development across the life span and to discover their membership in families, groups, and organizations. Furthermore, students ought to have the chance to have knowledge of how lesbians and gays are affected by social, psychological, and cultural systems in which they are a minority.

The social welfare policy and services sequence provides an opportunity for students not only to begin to gain knowledge of the values and ethics surrounding the public policies and laws impacting lesbians and gay men but also to confront their own values about homosexuality. To accurately understand the history of social work and services delivery systems, social welfare policy and services courses must reflect and take pride in the lesbian leaders of the social work profession and the evolution of policies and services to all oppressed minorities—including homosexuals.

Social work practice courses need to sensitize students to look beyond the presumption of heterosexuality for all clients and provide appropriate interventive methods for dealing with lesbians and gays. Because social work practice occurs with individuals, groups, families, communities, and organizations, and because students are to gain competency with a variety of practice methods and models that represent the current state of the art in professional social work practice (CSWE, 1988b), practice courses present an opportunity for students to integrate knowledge, skills, and values related to social work practice with lesbians and gay men.

Courses designed for the research sequence not only enable students to learn how to do research with minorities but to read existing research on special populations. Thus, students become sensitized to the basis of scientific thinking, the acquisition of new knowledge, and how that knowledge is transformed into professional practice.

The foundation content dealing with field practicum engages students in a supervised experience in which they can safely apply social work skills, knowledge, values, and theory to actual practice. The field practicum also allows students to provide social work intervention with various special populations, including lesbians and gay men.

Finally, courses developed for the advanced curriculum, whether they are based on a conceptual framework of fields of practice, population groups, problem areas, or practice roles and interventive modes (CSWE, 1988b), must be developed to build on and reflect foundation content. Assuming the professional foundation content exhibits appropriate content related to all oppressed minorities, the advanced course curriculum and field practicum need to further refine and help students focus specifically on their own professional integration of the values, skills, and knowledge of social work. Based on the generalized goals of social work education, the mandates of the accreditation standards, the reports of visiting committees, and the needs of professional social work, content related to lesbians and gays (as well as all oppressed minorities) is appropriate at every level of the social work education continuum and in every social work course.

As the social work profession move into the 1990s, it is time again to revise the curriculum policy statement (Beless, 1989). To assure there is no erosion of previously accomplished goals, it is paramount that the existing CSWE policies on nondiscrimination, cultural diversity, and special populations be left intact and strengthened, if possible. To guarantee the continuing coming-out process for CSWE as well as the social work profession, all who care about oppression must advocate for the inclusion of appropriate language in the newly developing curriculum policy statement.

The early 1990s brought with it a revised curriculum policy statement that specifically identified gay and lesbian persons as a "population-at-risk" (Curriculum Policy Statement, CSWE, 1992, p. 112) on which social work programs must provide content. Created by the Commission on Educational Policy and Planning, this revised document, coupled with the developing accreditation standards, when implemented in 1995, will demonstrate a more complete institutionalization of policies related to lesbian and gay persons than at any other point in CSWE's history. Evolving as a specific requirement a specific requirement for social work curricula at a time when homosexuality as a life-style is being regularly attacked from the conservative right, puts CSWE and the schools it accredits on the cutting edge of the struggle for social justice.

References

Abramovitz, M. (1991). "Putting an end to double speak about race, gender, and poverty: An annotated glossary for social workers." *Social Work, 36*(5), 380–384.

Abramson, M. (1985). "The autonomy-paternalism dilemma in social work practice." *Social Casework, 66*(7), 387–393.

Abramson, P. R., Parker, T., & Weisberg, S. R. (1988). "Sexual expression of mentally retarded people: Educational and legal implications." *American Journal of Mental Retardation, 93,* 328–334.

Ackerman, N. (1954). *The psychodynamics of family life.* New York: Basic Books.

Ackerman, N. (1972). "Family psychotherapy—theory and practice." In G. D. Erikson and T. P. Hogan (Eds.), *Family therapy: An introduction to theory and technique.* Monterey, CA: Brooks/Cole.

Acosta, F. X., & Evans, L. A. (1982). "The Hispanic-American patient." In F. X. Acosta, J. Yamamoto, & L. A. Evans (Eds.), *Effective psychotherapy for low-income and minority patients* (pp. 51–82). New York: Plenum.

Adamek, R. J. (1982). "Testing the family role complementarity model." *Journal of Comparative Family Studies, 13,* 1–11.

Adams, K. A. (1980). "Who has the final word? Sex, race, and dominance behavior." *Journal of Personality and Social Psychology, 38*(1), 1–8.

Alba, R. D. (1985). *Italian-Americans: Into the twilight of ethnicity.* Englewood Cliffs, NJ: Prentice-Hall.

Albrecht, L., & Brewer, R. M. (1990). *Bridges of power: Women's multicultural alliances.* Philadelphia, PA: New Society.

Allen, J. A., & Burwell, Y. N. (1980). "Ageism and racism: Two issues in social work education and practice." *Journal of Education for Social Work, 16*(2), 71–77.

American Association of University Women. (1991). *Shortchanging girls, shortchanging America.* Washington, DC: Author.

American Psychiatric Association (1987). *Diagnostic and statistical manual of mental disorders.* Washington, DC: Author.

Amundson, J. (1991). "Diagnosis and treatment in another light." *Calgary Participator, 1*(3), 30.

Anderson, H., & Goolishian, H. (1992). "The client is the expert: A not-knowing approach to therapy." In S. McNamee and K. J. Gergen (Eds.), *Therapy as social construction* (pp. 25–39). Newbury Park, CA: Sage.

Anderson, R. E., & Carter, I. (1984). *Human behavior in the social environment: A social systems approach.* Hawthorne, NY: Aldine de Gruyter.

Anderson, T. (1991). *The reflecting team: Dialogues and dialogues about the dialogues.* New York: Norton.

Antonovsky, A., & Sagy, S. (1990). "Confronting developmental tasks in the retirement transition." *Gerontologist, 30*(3), 362–368.

Aponte, H. J. (1979). "Diagnosis in family therapy." In C. B. Germain (Ed.), *Social work practice: People and environments* (pp. 107–149). New York: Columbia University Press.

Aponte, H. J. (1985). "The negation of values in therapy." *Family Process, 24,* 323–338.

Aponte, H. J. (1987). "The treatment of society's poor: An ecological perspective on the underorganized family." *Family Therapy Today, 2,* 1–7.

Aponte, H. J. (1991). "Training on the person of the therapist for work with the poor and minorities." *Journal of Independent Social Work, 5*(3/4), 23–30.

Ardilla, R. (1982). "International developments in behavior therapy in Latin America." *Journal of Behavior Therapy & Experimental Psychiatry, 13,* 15–20.

Arnold, H. D. (1970). "American racism: Implications for social work." *Education for Social Work, 7–12.*

Aronson, H., & Overall, B. (1966). "Treatment expectation of patients in two social classes." *Social Work, 11*(1), 35–41.

Auerswald, E. H. (1971). "Families, change and the ecological perspective." *Family Process, 10,* 263–280.

Auerswald, E. H. (1986). "Thinking about thinking in family therapy." In H. C. Fishman and B. L. Rosman (Eds.), *Evolving models for family change* (pp. 13–27). New York: Guilford.

Auslander, G. K., & Litwin, H. (1988). "Social networks and the poor: Toward effective policy and practice." *Social Work, 33*(3), 234–238.

Bachelor, A. (1988). "How clients perceive therapist empathy. A content analysis of 'received' empathy." *Psychotherapy, 25*(2), 227–240.

Bachelor, A. (1991). "Comparison and relationship to outcome of diverse dimensions of the helping alliance as seen by client and therapist." *Psychotherapy, 28,* 534–549.

Baer, D. M. (1970). "An age-irrelevant concept of development." *Merrill-Palmer Quarterly, 16,* 238–245.

Baird, K. E. (1970). "Semantics and Afro-American liberation." *Social Casework, 51*(5), 265–269.

Baker, E. (1985). "Psychoanalyses and a psychoanalytic psychotherapy." In I. J. Lyn and J. P. Garske (Eds.), *Contemporary psychotherapies* (pp. 19–68). Columbus, OH: Charles E. Merrill.

Balgopal, P. R., Munson, C. E., & Vassil, T. V. (1979). "Developmental theory: A yardstick for ethnic minority content." *Journal of Education for Social Work 15*(3), 28–36.

Bartlett, H. M. (1970). *The common base of social work.* Washington, DC: National Association of Social Workers.

Bateson, G. (1972). *Steps to an ecology of mind.* New York: Ballantine.

Bateson, G. (1979). *Mind and nature: A necessary unity.* New York: Bantam.

Becker, H. S. (1958). "Problems of inference and proof in participant observation." *American Sociological Review, 23,* 652–660.

Becker, M. E. (1989). "The rights of unwed parents: Feminist approaches." *Social Service Review, 63*(2), 496–517.

Beless, D. W. (1989). "From the executive director." *Social Work Education Reporter, 37*(2), 1, 11.

Bem, S. L. (1974). "The measurement of psychological androgyny." *Journal of Consulting Clinical Psychology, 42,* 152–162.

Bem, S. L. (1981). *Bem sex role inventory professional manual.* Palo Alto, CA: Consulting Psychologist Press.

Bem, S. L. (1985). "Androgyny and gender schema theory: A conceptual and empirical integration." In T. B. Sonderegger (Ed.), *Nebraska symposium on motivation 1984: Psychology and gender.* Lincoln: University of Nebraska Press.

Bem, S. L. (1987). "Gender schema theory and the romantic tradition." In P. Shaver and C. Hendrick (Eds.), *Sex and gender* (pp. 251–271). Newbury Park, CA: Sage.

Berger, J., Fisek, M. H., Norman, R. Z., & Zelditch, M. Jr. (1977). *Status characteristics and social interaction: An expectation states approach.* New York: Elsevier.

Berger, J., & Zelditch, M. Jr. (Eds.). (1977). *Status, rewards, and influence: How expectations organize behavior.* San Francisco: Jossey-Bass.

Berger, R. M. (1983). "What is homosexual: A definitional model." *Social Work, 28*(5) 132–135.

Berger, R. M. (1984). "Realities of gay and lesbian aging." *Social Work, 29*(1), 57–62.

Berger, R. M. (1987). "Homosexuality: Gay men." In A. Minahan et al. (Eds.), *Encyclopedia of social work* (18th ed., pp. 795–805). Silver Spring, MD: National Association of Social Workers.

Berger, R. M., & Federico, R. (1982). *Human behavior: A social work perspective.* New York: Longman.

Berkman, L. F. (1983). "The assessment of social networks and social support in the elderly." *Journal of the American Geriatrics Society, 31*(12), 743–749.

Berkman, L. F., & Syme, S. L. (1979). "Social networks, host resistance, and mortality: A nine year follow-up study of Alameda County residents." *American Journal of Epidemiology, 109*(Feb.), 186–204.

Berkun, D. (1984). "Women and the field experience." *Journal of Social Work Education, 20*(3), 5–12.

Berlin, S. B. (1976a). "Better work with women clients." *Social Work, 21*(6), 492–497.

Berlin, S. B. (1976b). "Theory and practice in feminist theory." *Social Work, 26*(6), 447–454.

Berlin, S. B. (1980). "Cognitive-behavioral approaches." In A. Rosenblatt and D. Waldfogel (Eds.), *Handbook of clinical social work* (pp. 1095–1119). San Francisco: Jossey-Bass.

Bernal, G., & Ysern, E. (1986). "Family therapy and ideology." *Journal of Marital and Family Therapy, 12,* 129–135.

Bernardez, T. (1982, May). *Cultural countertransference in the psychotherapy of women.* Paper presented at the Annual Meeting of the American Academy of Psychoanalysis, Toronto.

Bernardez, T., & Stein, T. S. (1979). "Separating the sexes in group psychotherapy: An experiment with men's and women's groups." *International Journal of Group Psychotherapy, 29,* 493–502.

Berthold, S. M. (1989). "Spiritism as a form of psychotherapy: Implications for social work practice." *Social Casework, 70*(8), 502–509.

Berzoff, J. (1989). "From separation to connection: Shifts in understanding women's development." *Affilia, 4,* 45–58.

Beverly, C. (1989). "Treatment issues for Black alcoholic clients." *Social Casework, 70*(6), 370–374.

Biddle, B. J., & Thomas, E. (1966). *Race theory.* New York: Wiley.

Biegel, D. E., Shore, B. K., & Gordon, E. (1984). *Building supper and networks for the elderly.* Beverly Hills: Sage.

Biestek, F. P. (1951). "The principles of client-self-determination." *Social Casework, 32*(9), 369–375.

Bilides, D. G. (1990). "Race, color, ethnicity, and class: Issues of biculturalism in school-based adolescent counseling groups." *Social Work with Groups, 13*(4), 43–58.

Billings, A., & Moos, R. (1982). "Work stress and the stress-buffering roles of work and family measures." *Journal of Occupational Behavior, 3,* 215–232.

Billingsley, A. (1968). *Black families in White America.* Englewood Cliffs, NJ: Prentice-Hall.

Billingsley, A. (1969). "Black students in a graduate school of social welfare." *Social Work Education Reporter, 17*(2), 38–44.

Billingsley, A. (1971). *Black agenda for social work in the seventies.* Atlanta, GA: Atlanta University School of Social Work.

Billingsley, A. (1976). *The family and cultural pluralism.* Address at Baltimore Conference on Ethnicity and Social Welfare, Institute on Pluralism and Group Identity, New York.

Billingsley, A. (1987). "Family: Contemporary patterns." In A. Minahan et al. (Eds.), *Encyclopedia of social work* (18th ed., pp. 520–529). Silver Spring, MD: National Association of Social Workers.

Birren, J. E. (1969). "The concept of functional age, theoretical background." *Human Development, 12,* 214–215.

Black, R. B., & Weiss, J. O. (1991). "Chronic physical illness and disability." In A. Gitterman (Ed.), *Handbook of social work practice with vulnerable populations* (pp. 137–164). New York: Columbia University Press.

Blau, P., & Meyer, M. W. (1987). *Bureaucracy in modern society.* New York: Random House.

Blechman, E. A. (1984). *Behavior modification with women.* New York: Guilford.

Blechman, E. A. (1992). "Mentors for high-risk minority youth: From effective communication to bicultural competence." *Journal of Clinical Child Psychology, 21,* 160–169.

Block, J. (1968). "The white worker and the negro client in psychotherapy." *Social Work, 13*(2), 36–42.

Bloom, A. A. (1980). "Social work and the English language." *Social Casework, 61*(6), 332–338.

Bloom, M. (1984). *Configurations of human behavior.* New York: Macmillan.

Blue, T. (1986). *The teaching and learning process.* Washington, DC: National Education Association.

Blumer, H. (1969). *Symbolic interactionism.* Englewood Cliffs, NJ: Prentice-Hall.

Boehm, W. W. (1959a). *Curriculum study* (Vols. 1–12). New York: Council on Social Work Education.

Boehm, W. W. (1959b). "The social work curriculum study and its implications for family casework." *Social Casework, 40*(8), 428–434.

Boneparth, E., & Stoper, E. (1988). "Introduction: A framework for policy analysis." In E. Boneparth and E. Stoper (Eds.), *Women, power and policy* (pp. 1–19). New York: Pergamon.

Boss, P. G., & Thorne, B. (1989). "Family sociology and family therapy: A feminist linkage." In M. McGoldrick, C. Anderson, and F. Walsh (Eds.), *Women in families: A framework for family therapy* (pp. 78–96). New York: Norton.

Boss, P. G., & Weiner, J. P. (1988). "Rethinking assumptions about women's development and family therapy." In C. Falicov (Ed.), *Family transitions* (pp. 235–251). New York: Guilford.

Boulette, T. R. (1976). "Assertive training with low-income Mexican-American women." In M. R. Miranda (Ed.), *Psychotherapy with the Spanish-speaking.* Los Angeles: Spanish Speaking Mental Health Research Center, University of California.

Bowen, M. (1971). "Aging: A symposium." *Georgetown Medical Bulletin, 30*(3), 4–27.

Bowen, M. (1976). "Theory and practice of psychotherapy." In P. Guerin (Ed.), *Family therapy: Theory and practice* (pp. 42–90). New York: Garden.

Bowen, M. (1978). *Family therapy in clinical practice.* New York: Aronson.

Boxer, A. M., & Cohler, B. J. (1989). "The life course of gay and lesbian youth: An immodest proposal for the study of lives." *Journal of Homosexuality, 17*(3–4), 315–355.

Brainerd, C. J. (1978). "The stage question in cognitive-developmental theory." *Behavioral and Brain Sciences, 2,* 173–213.

Brayboy, T. (1971). "The Black patient in group therapy." *International Journal of Group Psychotherapy, 21,* 288–293.

Briar, S. (1961). "Use of theory in studying the effects of client social class on students' judgments." *Social Work, 6*(3), 91–97.

Briar, S. (1987). "Direct practice: Trends and issues." In A. Minahan et al. (Eds.), *Encyclopedia of social work* (18th ed., pp. 394–395). Silver Spring, MD: National Association of Social Workers.

Briar, S., & Miller, H. (1971). *Problems and issues in social casework.* New York: Columbia University Press.

Bricker-Jenkins, M. (1991). "The propositions and assumptions of feminist social work practice." In M. Bricker-Jenkins, N. R. Hooyman, and N. Gottlieb (Eds.), *Feminist social work practice in clinical settings* (pp. 271–303). Newbury Park, CA: Sage.

Bricker-Jenkins, M., & Hooyman, N. (1984). "Feminist ideology." Discussion paper presented at the annual program meeting of the Council on Social Work Education, Detroit, March 13. Silver Spring, MD: Feminist Practice Project, National Association of Social Workers.

Bricker-Jenkins, M., & Hooyman, N. (1986). *Not for women only: Social work practice for a feminist future.* Silver Spring, MD: National Association of Social Workers.

Bricker-Jenkins, M., Hooyman, N. R., & Gottlieb, N. (Eds.). (1991). *Feminist social work practice in clinical settings.* Newbury Park, CA: Sage.

Brodsky, A. (1973). The consciousness-raising group as a model for therapy with women. *Psychotherapy: Theory, Research, and Practice, 10*(1), 24–29.

Bromley, M. A. (1987). "New beginnings for Cambodian refugees or further disruptions." *Social Work, 32*(3), 236–239.

Bronfenbrenner, U. (1979). *The ecology of human development.* Cambridge, MA: Harvard University Press.

Bronfenbrenner, U. (1986). "Ecology of the family as a context for human development: Research perspectives." *Developmental Psychology, 32*(6), 723–742.

Brooks, C. M. (1974). "New mental health perspectives in the black community." *Social Casework, 55*(8), 489–496.

Brooks, W. K. (1986). "Human behavior/social environment: Past and present, future or folly." *Journal of Social Work Education, 22*(1), 18–23.

Broverman, I., Broverman, D., Clarkson, I., Rosekrantz, P., & Vogee, S. (1970). "Sex role stereotypes and clinical judgments of mental." *Journal of Consulting and Clinical Psychology, 34,* 1–7.

Brower, A., Garvin, C., Hobson, J., Reed, B., & Reed, H. (1987). "Exploring the effects of leader gender and race on group behavior." In J. Lassner, J. Powell, and E. Finnegan (Eds.), *Social groupwork: Competence and values in practice* (pp. 129–148). New York: Haworth.

Brown, J. E., & Slee, P. T. (1986). "Paradoxical strategies: The ethics of intervention." *Professional Psychology: Research and Practice, 17,* 487–491.

Brown, L. B. (1950). "Race as a factor in establishing a casework relationship." *Social Casework, 31*(3), 91–97.

Brown, L. S. (1990). "The meaning of a multicultural perspective for theory-building in feminist therapy." *Women and Therapy, 9*(1/2), 1–22.

Brown, L. S. (1992). "A feminist critique of the personality disorders." In L. S. Brown and M. Allow (Eds.), *Personality and psychopathology: Feminist reappraisals* (pp. 206–228). New York: Guilford.

Brown, P. A. (1976). "Racial social work." *Journal of Education for Social Work, 12*(1) 28–35.

Bruner, J. (1986). *Actual minds: Possible worlds.* Cambridge, MA: Harvard University Press.

Bruner, J. (1987). "Life as narrative." *Social Research, 54*(1), 11–22.

Bruner, J. (1990). *Acts of meaning.* Cambridge, MA: Harvard University Press.

Bryant, C. (1980). "Introducing students to the treatment of inner-city families." *Social Casework, 61*(10), 629–636.

Buckingham, S. L., & Rehm, S. J. (1987). "AIDS and women at risk." *Health and Social Work, 12*(1), 5–11.

Buckingham, S. L., & Van Gorp, W. G. (1988). "Essential knowledge about AIDS dementia." *Social Work, 32*(2), 112–115.

Burgest, D. R. (1973). "Racism in everyday speech and social work jargon." *Social Work, 18*(4), 20–25.

Burghardt, S. (1986). "Marxist theory and social work." In F. J. Turner (Ed.), *Social work treatment: Interlocking theoretical approaches* (pp. 590–617). New York: Free Press.

Burghardt, S., & Fabricant, M. (1987). "Radical social work." In A. Minahan et al. (Eds.), *Encyclopedia of social work* (18th ed., pp. 455–462). Silver Spring, MD: National Association of Social Workers.

Burke, J. L. (1982). "Suggestions for a sex-fair curriculum in family treatment." *Journal of Education for Social Work, 18*(2), 98–102.

Burrell, G., & Morgan, G. (1979). *Sociological paradigms and organizational analyses.* London: Heinemann.

Bush, J. A., Norton, D. G., Sanders, C. L., & Solomon, B. B. (1983). "An integrative approach for the inclusion of content on blacks in social work education." In J. C. Chunn, P. J. Dunston, and F. Ross-Sheriff (Eds.), *Mental health and people of color* (pp. 97–125). Washington DC: Howard University Press.

Butler, R. N. (1959). *An orientation to knowledge of human growth and behavior in social work education* (Vol. 6). New York: Council on Social Work Education.

Butler, R. N. (1969). "Directions in psychiatric treatment of the elderly: Role of perspectives of the life cycle." *Gerontologist, 9*(2), 134–138.

Butler, R. N., & Lewis, M. C. (1973). *Aging mental health: Positive psychological approaches.* St. Louis, MO: C. V. Mosby.

Butler, R. N., Lewis, M., & Sunderland, T. (1991). *Aging and mental health positive psychosocial and biomedical approaches.* New York: Macmillan.

Butler, S., & Wintram, C. (1991). *Feminist group work.* Newbury Park, CA: Sage.

Caceres, J. (1982). "Enuresis: Cortical control or social reinforcement?" *Behavior Therapist, 5*(2), 65–67.

Callnek, M. (1970). "Racial factors in countertransference: The black therapist and the black client." *American Journal of Orthopsychiatry, 40*(1), 39–46.

Camasso, M. J., & Camasso, A. E. (1986). "Social supports, undesirable life events, and psychological distress in a disadvantaged population." *Social Service Review, 60*(Sept.), 378–394.

Canda, E. R. (1989). "Religious content in social work education: A comparative approach." *Journal of Social Work Education, 25*(1), 36–45.

Caroff, P. (Ed.) (1982). *Treatment formulations and clinical social work.* Silver Spring, MD: National Association of Social Workers.

Carpenter, E. M. (1980). "Social services, policies, and issues." *Social Casework, 61*(8), 455–461.

Carter, E. A., and McGoldrick, M. (Eds.), *The family life cycle: A framework for family therapy.* New York: Gardner.

Castex, G. (1993, Feb.). *Using diversity in the classroom to understand diversity: Challenges and techniques.* Paper presented at Council of Social Work Education Annual Program Meeting, New York.

Cecchin, G. (1992). "Constructing therapeutic possibilities." In S. McNamee and K. J. Gergen (Eds.), *Therapy as social construction* (pp. 86–95). Newbury Park, CA: Sage.

Chafetz, J. S. (1972). "Women in social work." *Social Work, 17*(5), 12–18.

Chandler, S. M. (1980). "Self-perceived competency in cross-cultural counseling." *Social Casework, 61*(6), 347–353.

Chandler, S. M. (1986). "The hidden feminist agenda in social development." In N. Van Den Bergh and L. B. Cooper (Eds.), *Feminist vision for social work* (pp. 149–162). Silver Spring, MD: National Association of Social Workers.

Chapman, M. (Ed.) (1993). *Social and biological aspects of ethnicity.* New York: Oxford University Press.

Chau, K. L. (1989). "Sociocultural dissonance among ethnic minority populations." *Social Casework, 70*(4), 224–230.

Chau, K. L. (1990). "A model for teaching cross-cultural practice in social work." *Journal of Social Work Education, 26*(2), 124–133.

Chau, K. L. (Ed.). (1991). *Ethnicity and biculturalism: Emerging perspectives of social group work.* New York: Haworth.

Chess, W. A., & Norlin, J. M. (1988). *Human behavior and the social environment.* Boston: Allyn and Bacon.

Chestang, L. (1972). *Character development in a hostile environment* (Occasional Paper No. 3), School of Social Service Administration, University of Chicago.

Chestang, L. (1984). "Racial and personal identity in the black experience." In B. W. White (Ed.), *Color in a white society* (pp. 83–94). Silver Spring, MD: National Association of Social Workers.

Chilman, C., Nunnally, E. W., & Cox, F. M., Eds. (1988). *Variant family forms.* Newbury Park, CA: Sage.

Claiborn, C. D. (1982). "Interpretation and change in counseling for negative emotions." *Journal of Counseling Psychology, 30*(2), 164–171.

Clark, K. (1965). *Dark ghetto: Dilemmas of social power.* New York: Harper & Row.

Cochrane, G. (1979). *The cultural appraisal of development projects.* New York: Praeger.

Coleman, M., & Nelson, B. (1957). "Paradigmatic psychotherapy in borderline cases." *Psychoanalyses, 5*(3), 28–44.

Coleman, R. P., & Rainwater, L. (1978). *Social standing in America: New dimensions of class.* New York: Basic Books.

Collier, A. (1987). "The language of objectivity and the ethics of reframing." In S. Walrond-Skinner, and D. Watson (Eds.), *Ethical issues in family therapy* (pp. 118–126). New York: Routledge and Kegan Paul.

Collins, A. H., & Pancoast, D. L. (1976). *Natural helping networks: A strategy for prevention.* Washington, DC: National Association of Social Workers.

Collins, B. G. (1986). "Defining feminist social work." *Social Work, 31*(3), 214–219.

Compton, B., & Galaway, B. (1989). *Social work processes.* Chicago: Dorsey.

Conrad, R. D., Delk, J. L., & Williams, C. (1974). "Use of stimulus fading procedures in the treatment of situation specific mutism." *Journal of Behavior Therapy & Experimental Psychiatry, 5,* 99–100.

Cooley, C. H. (1902). *Human nature and the social order.* New York: Scribners.

Cooper, S. (1973). "A look at the effect of racism on clinical work." *Social Casework, 54*(2), 76–84.

Corey, G. (1986). *Theory and practice of counseling and psychotherapy.* Monterey, CA: Brooks/Cole.

Cornett, C., & Hudson, R. A. (1987). "Middle adulthood and the theories of Erikson, Gould, and Vaillant: Where does the gay man fit?" *Journal of Gerontological Social Work, 10*(3/4), 61–73.

Correa, V. I., Poulson, C. L., & Salzberg, C. L. (1984). "Training and generalization of reach-grasp behavior in blind, retarded young children." *Journal of Applied Behavior Analysis, 17,* 57–69.

Cottraux, J., Legeron, P. & Mollard, E. (Eds.). (1992). *Which psychotherapies in the year 2000?* Amsterdam: Swets & Zeitlinger.

Cottrell, L. S. (1969). "Interpersonal interaction and the development of the self." In D. A. Goslin (Ed.), *Handbook of socialization theory and research* (pp. 543–570). Chicago: Rand McNally.

Council on Social Work Education. (1970). *Manual of accrediting standards revisions.* New York: Author.

Council on Social Work Education. (1971). *Manual of accrediting standards revisions.* New York: Author.

Council on Social Work Education. (1973). *Guidelines for implementation of accreditation standard 1234A.* Mimeo, author, New York.

Council on Social Work Education. (1977). Gay caucus house of delegates resolution #3, annual program meeting.

Council on Social Work Education. (1976). House of delegates resolution, annual program meeting, Philadelphia, March.

Council on Social Work Education. (1981). *Commission on accreditation.* Proposed revised standards, actions and procedures (Document #81-200-3-R), author, New York.

Council on Social Work Education. (1982). *Curriculum policy statement.* New York: Author.

Council on Social Work Education. (1984). *Handbook of accreditation standards and procedures.* New York: Author.

Council on Social Work Education. (1988a). Curriculum policy statement. New York: Author.

Council on Social Work Education. (1988b). *Handbook of accreditation standards and procedures.* New York: Author.

Council on Social Work Education. (1989a). *Annual program meeting final program.* Washington, DC: Author.

Council on Social Work Education. (1989b). *Strategic plan.* Washington, DC: Author.

Council on Social Work Education. (1991–1992). *Handbook of accreditation standards and procedures.* Alexandria, VA: Author.

Council on Social Work Education. (1992). *Curriculum policy statement for master's degree programs in social work education.* Alexandria, VA: Author.

Crawford, S. (1987). "Lesbian families: Psychosocial stress and the family-building process." In *Boston lesbian psychologies collective edition* (pp. 195–214). Champaign-Urbana: University of Illinois Press.

Crawford, S. (1988). "Cultural context as a factor in the expansion of therapeutic conversation with lesbian families." *Journal of Strategic and Systemic Therapies, 7*(3), 2–10.

Crompton, D. W. (1974). "Minority content in social work education—Promise or pitfall?" *Journal of Education for Social Work, 10*(1), 9–18.

Cummerton, J. M. (1981). "Homophobia and social work practice with lesbians." In A. Weick and S. T. Vandiver (Eds.), *Women, power, and change* (pp. 104–113). Washington, DC: National Association of Social Workers.

Cutler, C. (1991). "Deconstructing the DSM III." *Social Work, 36,* 154–157.

Dahlheimer, D., & Feigal, J. (1991). "Gays and lesbians in therapy: Bridging the gap." *Networker* (Jan./Feb.), 44–49.

Dangel, R. F., & Polster, R. A. (1984). "Winning! A systematic, empirical approach to parent training." In R. F. Dangel, & R. A. Polster (Eds.), *Parent training* (pp. 162–201). New York: Guilford.

Danziger, S. (1987). "Poverty." In A. Minahan et al. (Eds.), *Encyclopedia of social work* (18th ed., pp. 294–302). Silver Spring, MD: National Association of Social Workers.

Das, S., Menon, M., Menon, G., Kamakshi, G., Krishnan, G. & Saraswathi, K. (1980). "Social workers in a psychotherapeutic setting: Workshop in behavior modification held at Government Hospital, Madras." *International Journal of Social Psychiatry, 26,* 109–117.

Davenport, J., & Reims, N. (1978). "Theoretical orientation and attitudes toward women." *Social Work, 23*(4), 306–309.

Davis, A., & Havighurst, R. J. (1958). "Social class and color differences in child rearing." In H. D. Stein and R. A. Cloward (Eds.), *Social perspectives on behavior* (pp. 419–431). New York: Free Press.

Davis, K. (1991). "Critical sociology and gender relations." In K. Davis, M. Leijenaar, and J. Oldersma (Eds.), *The gender of power* (pp. 65–86). Newbury Park, CA: Sage.

Davis, K., Leijenaar, M., & Oldersma, J. (Eds.). (1991). *The gender of power.* Newbury Park, CA: Sage.

Davis, L. (1979). "Racial composition of groups." *Social Work, 24,* 208–213.

Davis, L. (1981). Racial issues in the training of group workers. *Journal for Specialists in Group Work,* 155–160.

Davis, L. E. (1984). *Ethnicity in social group work practice.* New York: Haworth.

Davis, L. V. (1984). "Beliefs of service providers about abused women and abusing men." *Social Work, 29*(4), 243–250.

Davis, L. V. (1986). "Role theory." In F. J. Turner (Ed.), *Social work treatment* (pp. 541–563). New York: Free Press.

Davis, L. V. (1987). "Battered women: The transformation of a social problem." *Social Work, 32*(4), 306–311.

Davis, L. V., & Proctor, E. (1989). *Race, gender, and class: Guidelines for practice with individuals, families and groups.* Englewood Cliffs, NJ: Prentice-Hall.

Davis, M., Sharfstein, S., & Owens, M. (1974). "Separate and together: All black therapist group in the white hospital." *American Journal of Orthopsychiatry, 44,* 19–25.

de Amorin, A., & Cavalcante, G. F. (1992). "Narrations of the self: Video production in a marginalized subculture." In S. McNamee and K. J. Gergen (Eds.), *Therapy as social construction* (pp. 149–165). Newbury Park, CA: Sage.

de Anda, D. (1984). "Bicultural socialization: Factors affecting the minority experience." *Social Work, 29*(2), 101–107.

DeCasper, A. J. & Spence, M. J. (1986). "Prenatal maternal speech influences newborn's perception of speech sounds." *Infant Behavior and Development, 9,* 133–150.

DeHoyos, G. (1989). "Person-in-environment: A tri-level practice model." *Social Casework, 70*(3), 131–138.

DeHoyos, G., & Jensen, C. (1985). "The systems approach in American social work." *Social Casework, 66*(8), 490–497.

Delaney, A. J. (1979). *The black task force report.* New York: Family Service Association of America.

Delgado, M. (1977). "Puerto Rican spiritualism and the social work profession." *Social Casework, 58*(8), 451–458.

Deparle J. (1993, July 14). "Census reports a sharp increase among never-married mothers." *New York Times,* p. 1.

Derrida, J. (1976). *Of grammatology to G. C. Spivak.* Baltimore, MD: Johns Hopkins University Press.

Derrida, J. (1978). *Writing and difference.* Chicago: University of Chicago Press.

Deutsch, M., & Krauss, R. M. (1965). *Social Psychology.* New York: Basic Books.

Devore, W., & Schlesinger, E. G. (1981). *Ethnic-sensitive social work.* St. Louis, MO: C. V. Mosby.

Devore, W., & Schlesinger, E. G. (1987a). *Ethnic-sensitive social work practice* (2nd ed.). Columbus, OH: Merrill.

Devore, W., & Schlesinger, E. G. (1987b). "Ethnic sensitive practice." In A. Minahan et al. (Eds.), *Encyclopedia of social work* (18th ed., pp. 512–516). Silver Spring, MD: National Association of Social Workers.

DeWeaver, K. L., & Kropf, N. P. (1992). "Person with mental retardation: A forgotten minority in social work education." *Journal of Social Work Education, 28,* 36–46.

Diangson, P., Kravetz, D. F., & Lipton, J. (1975). "Sex-role stereotyping and social work education." *Journal of Education for Social Work, 11(3),* 44–49.

Dieppa, I. (1983). "A state of the art analysis." In G. Gipson (Ed.), *Our kingdom stands on brittle glass* (pp. 115–128). Silver Spring, MD: National Association of Social Workers.

Dion, K. (1985). Sex, gender, and groups: Selected issues. In V. E. O'Leary, R. K. Unger, & B. A. Wallston (Eds.), *Women, gender, and social psychology.* Hillsdale, NJ: Lawrence Erlbaum.

Dodson, J. (1981). "Conceptualizations of black families." In H. P. McAdoo (Ed.), *Black families* (pp. 23–36). Newbury Park, CA: Sage.

Dodson, J. (1988). "Conceptualizations of Black families." In H. P. McAdoo (Ed.), *Black families* (pp. 77–90). Beverly Hills, CA: Sage.

Doherty, W. J., & Boss, P. G. (1992). "Values and ethics in family therapy." In A. D. Gurman and D. P. Kniskern (Eds.), *Handbook of family therapy* (pp. 606–637). New York: Brunner-Mazel.

Dolnick, E. (1993, Sept.). "Deafness as culture." *Atlantic, 272*(3), 37–51.

Donadello, G. (1986). "Integrating the lesbian/gay male experience in feminist practice and education." In N. Van Den Bergh and L. B. Cooper (Eds.), *Feminist visions for social work* (pp. 283–298). Silver Spring, MD: National Association of Social Workers.

Dore, M., & Dumois, A. O. (1990). "Cultural differences in the meaning of adolescent pregnancy." *Families in Society: The Journal of Contemporary Human Services, 71*(2), 93–101.

Draper, B. (1979). "Black language as an adaptive response to a hostile environment." In C. B. Germain (Ed.), *Social work practice: People and environments* (pp. 267–281). New York: Columbia University Press.

Duberman, L. (1975). *The reconstituted family: A study of remarried couples and their children*. Chicago: Nelson Hall.

DuBois, W. E. B. (1969). *Darkwater voices from within the veil*. New York: AMS.

Dubray, W. H. (1985). "American Indian values: Critical factor in casework." *Social Casework, 61*(1), 30–37.

Duehn, W. D., & Mayadas, N. N. (1977). "The use of stimulus/modeling videotapes in assertive training for homosexuals." In J. Fischer, & H. Gochros (Eds.), *Handbook of behavior therapy with sexual problems* (Vol. II, pp. 431–438). Elmsford, NY: Pergamon.

Dumpson, J. B. (1979, March). *Education for practice with and for Black Americans: An historical perspective*. Paper presented at the Council on Social Work Education Annual Program Meeting, Boston.

Duncan, B. L., Solovey, A. D., & Rusk, G. S. (1992). *Changing the rules: A client directed approach to therapy*. New York: The Guilford.

Dunkel, J., & Hatfield, S. (1986). "Countertransference issues in working with persons with AIDS." *Social Work, 31*(2), 114–118.

Durrant, M., & Coles, D. (1991). "Michael White's cybernetic approach." In T. C. Todd and M. D. Selekman (Eds.), *Family therapy approaches with adolescent substance abusers* (pp. 137–174). Boston: Allyn and Bacon.

Dworkin, J. (1990). "Political economic and social aspects of professional authority." *Families in Society, 71*(9), 534–541.

Eagley, A. H. (1987). *Sex differences in social behavior: A social role interpretation*. Hillsdale, NJ: Lawrence Erlbaum.

Edelman, M. (1982). "The political language of the helping professions." In H. Rubenstein and M. H. Block (Eds.), *Things that matter: Influences on helping relationships* (pp. 63–76). New York: Macmillan.

Edgar, R., & Clement, P. (1980). "Teacher-controlled and self-controlled reinforcement with underachieving black children." *Child Behavior Therapy, 2*(4), 33–56.

Edwards, A. W. (1982). "The consequences of error in selecting treatment for blacks." *Social Casework, 63*(7), 429–433.

Edwards, E. D., & Edwards, M. E. (1980). "American Indians: Working with individuals and groups." *Social Casework, 25*(8), 498–506.

Edwards, E. D., Edwards, M. E., Daines, G., & Eddy, F. (1978). "Enhancing self-concept and identification with 'Indianness' of American Indian girls." *Social Work with Groups, 1*(3), 309–318.

Efran, J. S., Lukens, M. D., & Lukens, R. J. (1990). *Language structure and change: Frameworks of meaning in psychotherapy*. New York: Norton.

Else, J. F., & Sanford, M. J. (1987). "Nonsexist language in social work journals: Not a trivial pursuit." *Social Work, 32*(1), 52–58.

Ephross, P. H., & Greene, R. R. (1991). "Symbolic interactionism." In R. R. Greene and P. H. Ephross (Eds.), *Human Behavior Theory and Social Work Practice* (pp. 203–226). Hawthorne, NY: Aldine de Gruyter.

Ephross-Saltman, J., & Greene, R. R. (1993). "Social worker's perceived knowledge and use of human behavior theory." *Journal of Social Work Education, 2*(1), 88–98.

Erickson, A. G. (1987). "Family services." In A. Minahan et al. (Eds.), *Encyclopedia of social work* (18th ed., pp. 589–600). Silver Spring, MD: National Association of Social Workers.

Erikson, E. H. (1950). *Childhood and society.* New York: Norton.

Erikson, E. H. (1959). *Identity and the life cycle.* New York: Norton.

Erikson, E. H. (1963). *Childhood and society.* New York: Norton.

Erikson, E. H. (1964a). *Insight and responsibility.* Toronto: George J. McLeod.

Erikson, E. H. (1964b). "Inner and outer space: Reflections on womanhood." *Daedalus, 93.*

Erikson, E. H. (1968). *Identity, youth, and crisis.* New York: Norton.

Erikson, E. H. (1974). *Dimensions of a new identity.* New York: Norton.

Erikson, E. H. (1982). *The life cycle completed.* New York: Norton.

Eure, G. K., Griffin, J. E., & Atherton, C. R. (1987). Priorities for the professional foundation: Differences by program level. *Journal of Social Work Education, 23*(2), 19–29.

Ezell, M., & Gibson, J. W. (1989). The impact of informal social network on the elderly's need for services. *Journal of Gerontological Social Work, 14*(3/4), 3–18.

Falck, H. S. (1988). *Social work: The membership perspective.* New York: Springer.

Falicov, C. J., & Karrer, B. M. (1980). "Cultural variations in the family life cycle: The Mexican-American family." In E. A. Carter and M. McGoldrick (Eds.), *The family life cycle* (pp. 383–426). New York: Gardner.

Falk, H. S. (1988). *Social work: The membership perspective.* New York: Springer.

Farris, C. E., Neuhring, E. M., Terry, J. E., Bilecky, C., & Vickers, A. (1980). "Self-concept formation in Indian children." *Social Casework, 61*(8), 484–489.

Favor, C. (1986). "Religion, research, and social work." *Social Thought, 12,*20–29.

Federico, R. (1979). "Human behavior in the social environment within a human diversity framework." In B. Baer & R. Federico (Eds.), *Educating the baccalaureate social worker* (Vol. 2, pp. 181–208). Cambridge, MA: Balinger.

Feingold, E., & Werby, E. (1990). "Supporting the independence of elderly residents through control over their environment." *Journal of Housing for the Elderly, 6*(1/2), 25–32.

Ferster, C. B., & Skinner, B. F. (1957). *Schedules of reinforcement.* New York: Appleton-Century-Crofts.

Feagin, J. R. & Feagin, C. (1986). *Discrimination American style: Institutional racism and sexism* (2nd ed.). Malabar, FL: Robert Krieger.

Field, T. M., Woodson, R., Greenberg, R. & Cohen, D. (1982). "Discrimination and imitation of facial expressions by neonates." *Science, 218,* 179–181.

Findlay, P. C. (1978). "Critical theory and social work practice." *Catalyst, 1*(3), 53–68.

Fine, M., & Asch, A., Eds. (1988). *Women with disabilities: Essays in psychology, culture, and politics.* Philadelphia: Temple University Press.

Fiorito, G. & Scotto, P. (1992). "Observational learning in *Octopus vulgaris.*" *Science, 256,* 545–546.

Fischer, J. (1978). *Effective social work practice: An eclectic approach.* New York: McGraw-Hill.

Fischer, J., Dulaney, D. D., Fazio, R. T., Hudak, M. T., & Zivotofsky, E. (1976). "Are social workers sexists?" *Social Work, 21*(6), 428–433.

Fischer, J., & Gochros, H. L. (1975). *Planned behavior change: Behavior modification in social work.* New York: Free Press.

Fischer, J., & Miller, H. (1973). "The effect of client race and social class on clinical judgment." *Clinical Social Work Journal, 1*(2), 100–109.

Fischer, C. (1982). *To dwell among friends: Personal networks in town and city.* Chicago: University of Chicago Press.

Fischer, J., & Gochros, H. (1975). *Planned behavior change: behavior modification in social work.* New York: Free Press.

Fisher, D. D. V. (1991). *An introduction to constructivism for social workers.* New York: Praeger.

Fisher, R., & Ury, W. (1981). *Getting to yes: Negotiating agreement without giving in.* New York: Penguin.

Fitts, W. F. (1965). *Tennessee self-concept scale manual.* Nashville: Counselor Recordings and Texts.

Flynn, M. C., & Saleem, J. K. (1986). "Adults who are mentally handicapped and living with their parents: Satisfaction and perception of their lives and circumstances." *Journal of Mental Deficiency Research, 30,* 379–87.

Foa, E. B., Rothbaum, B. O., Riggs, D. S., & Murdock, T. B. (1991). "Treatment of posttraumatic stress disorder in rape victims: A comparison between cognitive-behavioral procedures and counseling." *Journal of Consulting and Clinical Psychology, 59,* 715–723.

Foster, M., & Perry, L. (1982). "Self-valuation among blacks." *Social Work 27*(1), 60–65.

Foucault, M. (1965). *Madness and civilization.* New York: Vintage.

Foucault, M. (1978). *The history of sexuality: Volume I. An introduction.* New York: Vintage Books.

Foucault, M. (1980). *Power/knowledge: Selected interviews and writings.* New York: Pantheon.

Foucault, M. (1983). "Afterword: The subject of power." In H. Dreyfees, and P. Rabenow (Eds.), *Michael Foucault: Beyond structuralism and hermeneutics* (pp. 208–226). Chicago: University of Chicago Press.

Fox, D. M. (1986). "AIDS and the American health policy: The history and prospects of a crisis of authority." *Milbank Quarterly, (Supplement 1), 64,* 7–33.

Fox, J. (1983). "Affective learning in racism courses with an experiential component." *Journal of Social Work Education, 19*(3), 69–76.

Francis, E. A., ed. (1973). *Black task force report.* New York: Council on Social Work Education.

Frank, J. (1963). *Natural helping persuasion and healing: A comparative study of psychotherapy.* Baltimore: Johns Hopkins University Press.

Franklin, D. L. (1986). "Does client social class affect clinical judgment?" *Social Casework, 67*(7), 424–432.

Franklin, P. L. (1985). "Differential clinical assessments: The influence of class and race!" *Social Service Review, 59*(1), 44–61.

Franklin, J. H. (1988). "A historical note on black families." In H. P. McAdoo (Ed.), *Black families* (pp. 23–26). Newbury Park, CA: Sage.

Fraser, M., Taylor, M. J., Jackson, R., & O'Jack (1991). "Social work and science: Many ways of knowing." *Social Work, 27*(4), 5–15.

Frazer, N., & Nicholson, L. J. (1990). "Social criticism without philosophy: An encounter between feminism and postmodernism." In L. J. Nicholson (Ed.), *Feminism/postmodernism* (pp. 19–38). New York: Routledge.

Frazier, E. ([1939] 1966). *The Negro family in the United States.* Chicago: University of Chicago Press.

Freedman, E. (1990a). "Fear of feminism? An interview with Estelle Freedman." *Women's Review of Books, 7*(5), February, 25–26.

Freedman, E. (1990b). "The black family's life cycle: Operationalizing a strengths perspective." In S. M. L. Logan and R. G. McRoy, *Social Work Practice with Black Families: A Culturally Specific Perspective* (pp. 55–72). New York: Longman.

Freeman, J. (Ed.). 1984. *Women: A feminist perspective.* Palo Alto, CA: Mayfield.

Freeman, M. L. (1990). "Beyond women's issues: Feminism and social work." *Affilia, 5*(2), 72–89.

Freire, P. (1973). *Education for critical consciousness.* New York: Seabury.

Freud, S. (1956). "On psychotherapy." In *Collected papers, Vol. I.* London: Hogarth, 256–268.

Freymann, J. G. (1974). *The American health care system: Its genesis and trajectory.* New York: MedCom.

Friedman, E. H. (1980). "Systems and ceremonies." In E. A. Carter and M. McGoldrick (Eds.), *The family life cycle: A framework for family therapy* (pp. 429–460). New York: Gardner.

Froland, C. (1982). "Community support systems: All things to all people?" In D. E. Biegel and A. J. Naparstek (Eds.), *Community support systems and mental health* (pp. 253–266). New York: Springer.

Fruggeri, L. (1992). "Therapeutic process as the social construction of change." In S. McNamee and K. J. Gergen (Eds.), *Therapy as social construction* (pp. 40–53). Newbury Park, CA: Sage.

Gallegos, J. S., & Harris, O. D. (1979). "Toward a model for inclusion of ethnic minority content in doctoral social work education." *Journal of Education for Social Work, 15*(1), 29–35.

Gallo, F. (1982). "The effects of social support networks on the health of the elderly." *Social Work in Health Care, 8*(2), 65–74.

Gambrill, E., & Richey, C. (1975). "An assertion inventory for use in assessment and research." *Behavior Therapy, 6*, 350–362.

Garbarino, J. (1983). Social support networks: RX for the helping professionals. In J. Whittaker, J. Garbarino, and Associates. *Social Support Networks: Informal Helping in the Human Services.* Hawthorne, NY: Aldine de Gruyter.

Garrison, V. (1977). "The Puerto Rican syndrome." In V. Crapanzano and V. Garrison (Eds.), *Case studies in spirit possession* (pp. 418–427). New York: Wiley.

Garvin, C. (1987). *Contemporary group work,* 2nd ed. Englewood Cliffs, NJ: Prentice-Hall.

Garvin, C. (1991). "Social learning and role theories." In R. R. Greene and P. H. Ephross, *Human Behavior Theory and Social Work Practice* (pp. 151–176). Hawthorne, NY: Aldine de Gruyter.

Garvin, C., & Ephross, P. (1991). Group theory. In R. R. Greene and P. H. Ephross, eds, *Human Behavior Theory and Social Work Practice* (pp. 177–202). Hawthorne, NY: Aldine de Gruyter.

Garvin, C., & Seabury, B. (1984). *Interpersonal practice in social work.* Englewood Cliffs, NJ: Prentice-Hall.

Gay/lesbian task force meets. (1981). *Social Work Education Reporter, 29*(1), 11.

Gay/lesbian task force becomes a commission. (1984). *Social Work Education Reporter, 52*(3), 8.

Geertz, C. (1973). *The interpretation of cultures.* New York: Basic Books.

Gelfand, D. E., & Fandetti, D. V. (1986). "The emergent nature of ethnicity: Dilemmas in assessment." *Social Casework, 67*(9), 542–550.

Genevay, B., & Katz, R. S., Eds. (1990). *Countertransference and older clients.* Newbury Park, CA: Sage.

Gergen, K. J. (1982). *Toward transformation in social knowledge.* New York: Springer.

Gergen, K. J. (1985). "The social constructionist movement in modern psychology." *American Psychologist, 40*(3), 266–275.

Gergen, K. J., & Gergen, M. J. (1983). "Narratives of the self." In T. R. Sabin and K. E. Scheibe (Eds.), *Studies in social identity.* New York: Praeger.

Gergen, K. J., & Morse, S. J. (1967). Self-consistency: Measurement and validation. *Proceedings of the 75th Annual Convention of the American Psychological Association, 2,* 207–208.

Germain, C. B. (1968). "Social study: Past and future." *Social Casework, 49*(7), 403–409.

Germain, C. B. (1970). "Casework and science: A historical encounter." In R. Roberts and R. Nee (Eds.), *Theories of social casework* (pp. 3–32). Chicago: The University of Chicago Press.

Germain, C. B. (Ed.). (1979). *Social work practice: People and environments.* New York: Columbia University Press.

Germain, C. B. (1981, June). "The ecological approach to people-environment transactions." *Social Casework, 62,* 323–331.

Germain, C. B. (1987). "Human development in contemporary environments." *Social Service Review, 61,* 565–578.

Germain, C. B. (1989). "Preface." In *Group work with the poor and oppressed* (pp. 1–2). New York: Haworth.

Germain, C. B. (1991). *Human behavior and the social environment: An ecological view.* New York: Columbia University Press.

Germain, C. B. (1992). "A conversation with Carel Germain on human development in the ecological context." In M. Bloom (Ed.), *Changing lives: Studies in human development and professional helping* (pp. 406–409). Columbia: University of South Carolina Press.

Germain, C. B., & Gitterman, A. (1980). *The life model of social work practice.* New York: Columbia University Press.

Germain, C. B., & Gitterman, A. (1987). "Ecological perspectives." In A. Minahan et al. (Eds.), *Encyclopedia of social work* (18th ed., pp. 488–499). Silver Spring, MD: National Association of Social Workers.

Gibbs, J. T. (1985). "Treatment relationships with black clients: Interpersonal U.S. instrumental strategies." In C. B. Germain (Ed.), *Advances in clinical social work practice* (pp. 179–190). Silver Spring, MD: National Association of Social Workers.

Gibbs, J. T., & Moskowitz-Sweet, G. (1991). "Clinical and cultural issues in the treatment of biracial and bicultural adolescents." *Families in Society,* 579–592.

Gibbs, P. (1986). "HBSE in the undergraduate curriculum: A survey." *Journal of Social Work Education, 22*(2), 46–52.

Gibson, R. C. (1987). "Reconceptualizing retirement for Black Americans." *Gerontologist, 27,* 691–698.

Giddens, A. (1984). *The constitution of society.* Cambridge: Polity.

Giesen, M., & McClaren, H. A. (1976). Discussion, distance, and sex: Changes in impressions and attraction during small group interaction. *Sociometry, 39*(1), 60–70.

Gilchrist, L. D., Schinke, S. P., Trimble, J. E., & Czetkovich, G. T. (1987). "Skills enhancement to prevent substance abuse among American Indian adolescents." *International Journal of the Addictions, 22,* 869–879.

Gilligan, C. (1982). *In a different voice.* Cambridge, MA: Harvard University Press.

Ginsberg, E. (1989). *School social work.* Springfield, IL: Charles C. Thomas.

Gitterman, A., & Shulman, L. (1986). *Mutual aid groups and the life cycle.* Itasca, IL: F. E. Peacock.

Glasgow, D. (1971). "The black thrust for vitality: The impact on social work education." *Journal of Education for Social Work, 7*(2), 9–18.

Glasgow, D. (1972). "Black power through community control." *Social Work, 17*(3), 59–64.

Gluck, N. R., Dannefer, E., & Milea, K. (1980). "Women in families." In E. A. Carter and M. McGoldrick (Eds.), *The family life cycle* (pp. 295–327). New York: Gardner.

Goffman, E. (1957). "Interpersonal persuasion." In B. Schaffner (Ed.), *Group processes: Transactions of the third conferences* (pp. 117–193). New York: Josiah Macy, Jr., Foundation.

Goffman, E. (1959). *The presentation of self in everyday life.* New York: Doubleday/Anchor.

Goffman, E. (1963). *Stigma: Notes on the management of spoiled identity.* Englewood Cliffs, NJ: Prentice-Hall.

Goffman, E. (1967). *Interaction rituals: Essays on face-to-face behavior.* Garden City, NY: Doubleday.

Goldberg, G. S., Kantrow, R., Kremen, E., & Lauter, L. (1986). "Spouseless, childless elderly women and their social supports." *Social Work, 31*(2), 104–112.

Goldenberg, I. I. (1978). *Oppression and social intervention.* Chicago, IL: Nelson Hall.

Goldenberg, I. I., & Goldenberg, A. (1991). *Family therapy: An overview.* Belmont, CA: Brooks/Cole.

Goldner, V. (1988). "Instrumentalism, feminism and the limits of family therapy." *Journal of Family Psychology* 1(1), 109–116.

Goldner, V. (1989). "Generation and gender: Normative and covert hierarchies." In M. McGoldrick, C. M. Anderson, and F. Walsh (Eds.), *Women in families: A framework for family therapy* (pp. 42–60). New York: Norton.

Goldstein, E. G. (1980). "Knowledge base of clinical social work." *Social Work, 25*(3), 173–178.

Goldstein, E. G. (1986). "Ego psychology." In F. J. Turner (Ed.), *Social work treatment* (pp. 375–406). New York: Free Press.

Goldstein, G. S. (1974). "Behavior modification: Some cultural factors." *Psychological Record, 24,* 89–91.

Goldstein, H. (1981). *Social learning and change: A cognitive approach to social services.* Columbia: University of South Carolina Press.

Goldstein, H. (1983). "Starting where the client is." *Social Casework, 64*(5), 267–275.

Goldstein, H. (1986a). "A cognitive humanistic approach to the hard-to-reach client." *Social Casework, 67*(1), 27–36.

Goldstein, H. (1986b). "Education for social work practice: A cognitive cross-cultural approach." *International Social Work, 29,* 149–164.

Goldstein, H. (1986c). "Toward the integration of theory and practice: A humanistic approach." *Social Work, 31*(5), 352–357.

Goldstein, H. (1990a). "Strength of pathology: Ethical and rhetorical contrasts in approaches to practice families in society." *Families in Society: The Journal of Contemporary Human Services, 71*(5), 267–275.

Goldstein, H. (1990b). "The knowledge base of social work practice: Theory, wisdom analogue of art." *Families in Society, 71*(1).

Goldstein, H. (1992). "Victors or victims: Contrasting views of clients in social work practice." In D. Saleeby (Ed.), *The strengths perspective in social work practice* (pp. 27–38). New York: Longman.

Gomez, M. R. (1990). "Biculturalism and subjective mental health among Cuban Americans." *Social Service Review, 64*(3), 374–389.

Good Tracks, J. G. (1973). "Native American noninterference." *Social Work, 18*(6), 30–34.

Goodban, N. (1985). "The psychological impact of living on welfare." *Social Service Review,* 403–421.

Goodenough, W. H. (1957). "Cultural anthropology and linguistics." In B. L. Garvin (Ed.), *Report of the seventh annual round table meeting on linguistics and language study* (pp. 104–127). Washington, DC: Georgetown University Press.

Gordon, W. (1964). "Notes on the nature of K." In H. Bartlett (Ed.), *Building social work. A report of a conference* (pp. 1–15). New York: National Association of Social Workers.

Gordon, W. (1983, May/June). "Social work revolution or evolution?" *Social Work 28*(3), 181–185.

Gottlieb, N. (1987). "Sex discrimination and inequality." In A. Minahan et al. (Eds.), *Encyclopedia of social work* (18th ed., pp. 561–569). Silver Spring, MD: National Association of Social Workers.

Gottschalk, S. S., & Witkin, S. L. (1991). "Rationality in social work: A critical examination." *Journal of Sociology and Social Welfare, 18*(4), 121–135.

Gould, K. H. (1984). "Original works of Freud on women: Social work references." *Social Casework, 65*(2), 94–101.

Gould, K. H. (1987). "Life model versus conflict model: A feminist perspective." *Social Work, 32*(4), 346–351.

Grace, J. (1979). *Coming out alive: A positive developmental model of homosexual competence.* Unpublished paper.

Granger, J. M., & Portner, D. L. (1985). "Ethnic- and gender-sensitive social work practice." *Journal of Social Work Education, 21*(1), 38–47.

Green, J. (1982). *Cultural awareness in the human services.* Englewood Cliffs, NJ: Prentice-Hall.

Green, S. L., & Hansen, J. C. (1989). "Ethical dilemmas faced by family therapists." *Journal of Marital and Family Therapy, 15,* 149–158.

Greene, R. R. (1984). "Ageism, death anxiety, and the caseworker." *Journal of Social Service Research, 7*(1) 55–69.

Greene, R. R. (1986). *Social work with the aged and their families.* Hawthorne, NY: Aldine de Gruyter.

Greene, R. R. (1988). *Continuing education for gerontological careers.* Washington, DC: Council on Social Work Education.

Greene, R. R. (1989). "The growing need for social work services for the aged in 2020." In B. S. Vourlekis and C. G. Leukefeld (Eds.), *Making our case: A resource book of selected materials for social workers in health care* (pp. 11–17). Silver Spring, MD: National Association of Social Workers.

Greene, R. R. (1991a). "Carl Rogers and the person-centered approach." In R. R. Greene and P. H. Ephross (Eds.), *Human behavior theory and social work practice* (pp. 105–122). Hawthorne, NY: Aldine de Gruyter.

Greene, R. R. (1991b). "Eriksonian theory: A developmental approach to ego mastery." In R. R. Greene and P. H. Ephross (Eds.), *Human behavior theory and social work practice* (pp. 39–78). Hawthorne, NY: Aldine de Gruyter.

Greene, R. R. (1991c). "The ecological perspective: An eclectic theoretical framework." In R. R. Greene and P. H. Ephross (Eds.), *Human behavior theory and social work practice* (pp. 261–296). Hawthorne, NY: Aldine de Gruyter.

Greene, R. R. (1991d). "General Systems Theory." In R. R. Greene and P. H. Ephross (Eds.), *Human behavior theory and social work practice* (pp. 2227–2260). Hawthorne, NY: Aldine de Gruyter.

Greene, R. R., & Ephross, P. H. (1991a). "Classical psychoanalytic thought, contemporary developments, and clinical social work." In R. R. Greene and P. H. Ephross (Eds.), *Human behavior theory and social work practice* (pp. 39–78). Hawthorne, NY: Aldine de Gruyter.

Greene, R. R., & Ephross, P. H. (Eds.). (1991b). *Human behavior theory and social work practice.* Hawthorne, NY: Aldine de Gruyter.

Greenson, R. (1955). "The borderline case." *Journal of American Psychoanalytic Association, 3*(2), 295–297.

Grief, G. (1987). "A longitudinal examination of single custodial fathers: Implications for treatment." *American Journal of Family Therapy, 15,* 253–260.

Griffin, J. E., & Eure, G. K. (1985). "Defining the professional foundation in social work education." *Journal of Social Work Education, 21*(3), 73–91.

Groves, B. M., Cassella, M., & Jacobs, J. (1981). "Dilemmas in role identification for low-income women." In A. Weick and S. T. Vandiver (Eds.), *Women, power, and change* (pp. 127–136). Washington, DC: National Association of Social Workers.

Groze, V., & Rosenthal, J. A. (1991). "A structural analysis of families adopting special-needs children." *Families in Society, 72*(2), 469–482.

Grunbaum, J. (1987). "Multi-directed partiality and the parental imperative." *Psychotherapy, 24,* 646–656.

Guidano, V. F. (1987). *Complexity of the self.* New York: Guilford.

Guidano, V. F. (1990). *The self in process: Towards a post-rationalist cognitive therapy.* New York: Guilford.

Guidano, V. F. (1991). *The self in process.* New York: Guilford.

Guidry, R. (1979). "A design for teaching human behavior in a generalists program." *Journal of Education for Social Work, 15*(2), 45–50.

Gutierrez, L. (1990). "Working with women of color: An empowerment perspective." *Social Work, 35*(2), 149–153.

Hagen, B. H. (1983). "Managing conflict in all-women groups." In Beth Glover Peed and Charles D. Garvin (Eds.), *Groupwork with women/groupwork with ˈen* (pp. 95–104). New York: Haworth.

Hagen, J. L., & Ivanoff, A. M. (1988). "Homeless women: A high risk population." *Affilia, 3*(1), 19–33.

Haley, J. (1963). *Strategies of psychotherapy.* New York: Grune and Stratton.

Haley, J. (1976). *Problem-solving therapy: New strategies for effective family therapy.* San Francisco: Jossey-Bass.

Hamilton, G. ([1940] 1951). *Theory and practice of social casework.* New York: Columbia University Press.

Hamilton, G. (1958a). "Foreword." In H. D. Stein, and R. A. Cloward (Eds.), *Social perspectives on behavior* (pp. xi–xiv). New York: Free Press.

Hamilton, G. (1958b). "A theory of personality: Freud's contribution to social work." In H. J. Parad (Ed.), *Ego psychology and casework theory* (pp. 11–37). New York: Family Service of America.

Hamilton, J. A., & Jensvold, M. (1992). "Personality, psychopathology, and depressions in women." In L. S. Brown and M. Ballou (Eds.), *Personality and psychopathology: Feminist reappraisals* (pp. 116–143). New York: Guilford.

Hanson, W. (1980). "The urban Indian woman and her family." *Social Casework,* 476–483.

Harbert, A., & Ginsberg, L. (1979). *Human services for older adults: Concepts and skills.* Belmont, CA: Wadsworth.

Hare-Mustin, R. T. (1978). "A feminist approach to family therapy." *Family Process, 17*(2), 181–194.

Hare-Mustin, R. T. (1980). "Family therapy may be dangerous for your health." *Professional Psychology, 11,* 935–938.

Hare-Mustin, R. T. (1986). "The problem of gender in family therapy." *Family Process, 26,* 15–27.

Hare-Mustin, R. T. (1989). "The problem of gender in family therapy theory." In M. McGoldrick, C. M. Anderson, and F. Walsh (Eds.), *Women in families: A framework for family therapy* (pp. 61–77). New York: Norton.

Hare-Mustin, R. T. (1990). "Sex, lies and headaches: The problem is power." In T. J. Goodrich (Ed.), *Women and power: Perspectives for family therapy* (pp. 61–83). New York: Norton.

Hare-Mustin, R. T., & Marecek, J. (1988). "The meaning of difference: Gender theory, past modernism and psychology." *American Psychologist, 43,* 445–464.

Harris, L. H., & Lucas, M. E. (1976). "Sex-role stereotyping." *Social Work, 21,* 390–395.

Harrison, A. O., Wilson, M. N., Pine, C. J., Chan, S. Q., & Buriel, R. (1990). "Family ecologies of ethnic minority children." *Child Development, 61,* 347–362.

Harrison, D. F., Wodarski, J. S., & Thyer, B. A. (Eds.). (1992). *Cultural diversity and social work practice.* Springfield, IL: Charles C. Thomas.

Harry, H. L. K. (1988). "Will your daughter marry one?" UCLA *Social Welfare, 1*(Spring), 5–6.

Hartman, A., & Laird, J. (1983). *Family-centered social work practice.* New York: Free Press.

Hartman, A., & Laird, J. (1984). *Working with adoptive families beyond placement.* New York: Child Welfare League of America.

Hartman, A., & Laird, J. (1987). "Family practice." In A. Minahan et al. (Eds.), *Encyclopedia of social work* (18th ed., pp. 575–589). Silver Spring, MD: National Association of Social Workers.

Hauserman, N., Walen, S. R., & Behling, M. (1973). "Reinforced racial integration in the first grade: A study in generalization." *Journal of Applied Behavior Analysis, 6,* 193–200.

Haussmann, M. J., & Halseth, J. H. (1983). "Re-examining women's roles: A feminist group approach to decreasing depression in women." In Beth Glover Reed and Charles D. Garvin (Eds.), *Groupwork with women/groupwork with men* (pp. 105–116). New York: Haworth.

Haviland, W. A. (1990). *Cultural anthropology.* Holt, Rinehart, and Winston.

Haworth, G. (1984). "Social work research, practice and paradigms." *Social Service Review* (Sept.), 343–357.

Hayek, F. A. (1978). *New studies in philosophy, politics, economics and the history of ideas.* Chicago: University of Chicago Press.

Hayes-Bautistista, B. (1978). "Chicago patients and medical practitioners: A sociology of knowing paradigm of lay-profession interaction." *Social Science and Medicine, 12,* 83–90.

Hearn, G. (1969). "Progress toward an holistic conception of social work." In G. Hearn (Ed.), *The general systems approach: Contributions toward an holistic conception of social work* (pp. 63–70). New York: Council on Social Work Education.

Heffer, R. W., & Kelley, M. L. (1987). "Mothers' acceptance of behavioral interventions for children: The influence of parent race and income." *Behavior Therapy, 18,* 153–163.

Hefferman, J., Shuttlesworth, J., and Ambroseno, R. (1988). *Social work and social welfare.* St. Paul, MN: West Publishing.

Heineman, M. B. (1981). "The obsolete scientific imperative in social work research." *Social Service Review, 58,* 371–397.

Heineman, M. B. (1982). "Author's reply." *Social Service Review, 56,* 312.

Hepworth, D. H., & Larsen, J. A. (1987). "Interviewing." In A. Minahan et al. (Eds.), *Encyclopedia of social work* (18th ed., pp. 996–1008). Silver Spring, MD: National Association of Social Workers.

Hepworth, D. H., & Larsen, J. A. (1990). *Direct social work practice.* Belmont, CA: Wadsworth.

Herdt, G. (1992). *Gay culture in America: Essays from the field.* Boston: Beacon.

Herr, J. J., & Weakland, J. H. (1979). *Counseling elders and their families.* New York: Springer.

Hersh, A. (1970). "Changes in family functioning following placement of a retarded child." *Social Work, 15*(1), 93–102.

Herskovits, M. J. ([1941] 1958). *The myth of the negro past.* New York: Random House.

Hipple, J. L., & Hipple, L. (1980). "Concepts of ideal woman and ideal man." *Social Work, 25*(2), 147–149.

Hirayama, H., & Cetingok, M. (1988). "Empowerment: A social work approach for Asian immigrants." *Social Casework, 69*(1), 41–47.

Hirsch, B. J. (1979). "Psychological dimensions of social networks: A multimethod analysis." *American Journal of Community Psychology, 7*(3), 263–277.

Ho, M. K. (1984). "Social group work with Asian/Pacific-Americans." In L. E. Davis (Ed.), *Ethnicity in social group work practice* (pp. 49–56). New York: Haworth.

Ho, M. K. (1987). *Family therapy with ethnic minorities.* Newbury Park, CA: Sage.

Ho, M. K. (1992). *Minority children and adolescents in therapy.* Newbury Park, CA: Sage.

Hoffman, L. (1985). "Beyond power and control: Toward a 'second order' family systems theory." *Family Systems Medicine 3*(4), 381–396.

Hoffman, L. (1990). "Constructing realities: An art of lenses." *Family Process, 29*(1), 1–12.

Hoffman, L. (1992). "A reflective stance for family therapy." In S. McNamee and K. J. Gergen (Eds.), *Therapy as social construction* (pp. 7–24). Newbury Park, CA: Sage.

Hogan, R. (1976). *Personality theory: The personological tradition.* Englewood Cliffs, NJ: Prentice-Hall.

Holland, T. (1989). "Values, faith, and professional practice." *Social Thought, 15,* 29–40.

Hollingshead, A. B., & Redlich, F. C. (1958a). "Social stratification and psychiatric disorders." In H. D. Stein and R. A. Cloward (Eds.), *Social perspectives on behavior* (pp. 449–455). New York: Free Press.

Hollingshead, A. B., & Redlich, F. C. (1958b). *Social class and mental illness: A community study.* New York: Wiley.

Hollis, F. (1964). *Casework: A psychosocial therapy.* New York: Random House.

Hollis, F. (1977). "Social casework: The psychosocial approach." In J. B. Turner (Ed.-in-chief), *Encyclopedia of social work* (17th ed., pp. 1300–1308). Washington, DC: National Association of Social Workers.

Holzberg, C. S. (1982). "Ethnicity and aging: Anthropological perspectives on more than just minority elderly." *Gerontologist, 22*(3), 240–257.

Hooks, B. (1984) *From margin to center.* Boston: South End.

Hooyman, N. R. (1980). "Toward a feminist administrative style." Paper presented at NASW First National Conference on Social Work Practice in a Sexist Society, Washington, DC, September,

Hooyman, N. R., & Cunningham, R. (1986). "An alternative administrative style." In N. Van Den Bergh and L. B. Cooper (Eds.), *Feminist visions for social work,* pp. 163–186. Silver Spring, MD: National Association of Social Workers.

Hooyman, N. R., & Kiyak, H. A. (1988). *Social gerontology.* Needham Heights, MA: Allyn and Bacon.

Hooyman, N. R., Summers, A., & Leighninger, L. Eds. (1988). *Women working together: A collection of course syllabi about women.* New York: Commission on the Role and Status of Women in Social Work Education, Council on Social Work Education.

Hopkins, T. J. (1973). "The role of the agency in supporting black manhood." *Social Work, 18*(1), 53–58.

Hopkins, T. J. (1980). "A conceptual framework for understanding the three 'isms'— Racism, ageism, sexism." *Journal of Education for Social Work, 16*(2), 63–70.

Hopps, J. G. (1987). "Minorities of color." In A. Minahan et al. (Eds.), *Encyclopedia of social work* (18th ed., pp. 161–171). Silver Spring, MD: National Association of Social Workers.

Howard, R., Lipsitz, G., Sheppard, F. & Steinitz, L. Y. (1991). "Sexual behavior in group residences: An ethics dilemma." *Journal of Contemporary Human Services, 72*, 360–365.

Hudson, W. W. (1978). "First axioms of treatment." *Social Work, 23*, 65–66.

Hudson, W. W. (1982). "Scientific imperatives in social work research and practice." *Social Service Review, 56*, 242–258.

Hunter, P., & Kelso, E. N. (1985). "Feminist behavior therapy." *Behavior Therapist, 8*(10), 201–204.

Hurtado, A. (1989). "Relating to privilege: Seduction and rejection in the subordination of white women and women of color." *Signs: Journal of Women in Culture and Society, 14*(4), 833–855.

Hyde, J. S. (1990). "How large are cognition gender differences: A meta-analysis." In J. M. Nielsen (Ed.), *Feminist research methods* (pp. 207–223). San Francisco: Westview.

Ifill, D. (1989). "Teaching minority practice for professional application." *Journal of Social Work Education, 25*(1), 29–35.

Imber-Black, E. (1991). "A family–larger system perspective." In A. S. Gurman and D. P. Kniskern (Eds.), *Handbook of family therapy* (pp. 583–600). New York: Brunner/Mazel.

Imre, R. W. (1971). "A theological view of social casework." *Social Casework, 52*(9), 578–583.

Imre, R. W. (1982). *Knowing and caring: Philosophical issues in social work.* Lanham, MD: University Press of America.

Jackson, D. D. (1965). "Family rules: Marital quid pro quo." *Archives of General Psychiatry, 12*, 589–594.

Jackson, D. D. (1977a). "Family rules: Marital quid pro quo." In P. Watzlawick and J. Weakland (Eds.), *The international view* (pp. 21–30). New York: Norton.

Jackson, D. D. (1977b). "The study on the family." In P. Watzlawick and J. Weakland (Eds.), *The interactional view* (pp. 2–20). New York: Norton.

Jackson, J. S., McCullough, W. R., & Gurin, G. (1988). "Family, socialization, environment, and identity development in Black Americans." In H. P. McAdoo, *Black families* (pp. 242–256). Newbury Park, CA: Sage.

Jacobson, N. S. (1983) "Beyond empiricism: The politics of marital therapy." *American Journal of Family Therapy, 11*, 11–24.

Janchill, M. P. (1969). "Systems concepts in casework theory and practice." *Social Casework, 15*(2), 74–82.

Jayaratne, S. (1980). "Characteristics and theoretical orientations of clinical social workers: A national survey." *Journal of Social Service Research, 4*(2), 17–30.

Jayaratne, S., & Ivey, K. V. (1981). "Gender differences in the perceptions of social workers." *Social Casework, 62*(7), 405–412.

Jenkins, J. H., & Karno, M. (1992, Jan.). "The meaning of expressed emotion: Theoretical issues raised by cross-cultural research." *American Journal of Psychiatry, 149*(1), 9–21.

Jenkins, J. O., Rahaim, S., Kelly, L. M., & Payne, D. (1982). "Substance abuse." In S. Turner, & R. T. Jones (Eds.), *Behavior modification with black populations: Psychosocial issues and empirical findings* (pp. 209–247). New York: Plenum.

Johnson, H. C. (1987). "Human development: Biological perspective." In A. Minahan et al. (Eds.), *Encyclopedia of social work* (18th ed., pp. 835–850). Silver Spring, MD: National Association of Social Workers.

Jones, I. (1979). "African-American clients: Clinical practice issues." *Social Work, 24*(2), 112–118.

Jones, R. T. (1982). "Academic improvement through behavioral intervention." In S. M. Turner, and R. T. Jones (Eds.), *Behavior modification with black populations: psychosocial issues and empirical findings* (pp. 121–149). New York: Plenum.

Joseph, M. V. (1987). "The religious and spiritual aspects of clinical practice: A neglected dimension of social work." *Social Thought,* 12–23.

Kadushin, A. (1972). "The racial factor in the interview." *Social Work, 17*(3), 88–98.

Kadushin, A. (1983). *The social work interview.* New York: Columbia University Press.

Kaplan, A. (1990). "Empathy and its vicissitudes." In J. Surrey, A. Kaplan, and J. Jordan (Eds.), *Work in progress: Empathy revisited* (pp. 6–12). Wesley, MA: Stone Center of Wesley College.

Kaufman, A. V. (1990). Social network assessment: A critical component in case management for functionally impaired older persons. *International Journal of Aging and Human Development, 30*(1), 63–75.

Keane, T. M., St. Lawrence, J. S., Himadi, W. G., Graves, K. A. & Kelly, J. A. (1983). Blacks' perceptions of assertive behavior: An empirical evaluation. *Behavior Modification, 7,* 97–111.

Kelley, M. L., McKay, S., & Nelson, C. H. (1985, Dec.). Indian agency development: An ecological practice approach. *Social Casework, 66,* 594–602.

Kelley, P., & Kelley, V. R. (1985, June). Supporting natural helpers: A cross-cultural study. *Social Casework, 66,* 358–366.

Kelly, G. A. (1955). *The psychology of personal constructs.* New York: Norton.

Kelly, J. A., St. Lawrence, J. S., Hood, H. V., & Brasfield, T. (1989). "Behavioral intervention to reduce AIDS risk activities." *Journal of Consulting and Clinical Psychology, 67,* 60–67.

Kelly, M. R. (1980). *A history of social work education.* Unpublished paper.

Kerner Report. (1968). *Report of the national advisory commission on civil disorders.* New York: Bantam.

Keesing, R. M. (1987). "Anthropology as interpretive quest." *Current Anthropology, 28,* 161–176.

Khanna, S., Desai, N. G., & Channabasavanna, S. M. (1987). A treatment package for transsexualism. *Behavior Therapy, 18,* 193–199.

Kim, B. (1973). "Asian-Americans: No model minority." *Social Work, 18*(3) 44–53.

Kim, N. S. (1979). "Multidimensional-behavioral treatment of interpersonal anxiety." *Behavior Therapist, 2*(5), 33–35.

Kimmel, D. C. (1990). *Adulthood and aging* (3rd ed.). New York: Wiley.

Kissman, K. (1991). "Feminist-based social work with single-parent families." *Families on Society, 72*(2), 23–28.

Kleinman, A. M. (1973). "Medicine's symbolic reality on a central problem in the philosophy of medicine." *Inquiry, 16,* 206–213.

Kleinman, A. M. (1978). "Rethinking the social and cultural context of psychopathology and psychiatric care." In T. C. Manschreck and A. M. Klunman (Eds.), *Renewal in psychiatry: A critical rationale perspective* (pp. 97–138). New York: Wiley.

Kluckhorn, C. (1951). "Values and value orientations." In T. Parsons and E. A. Shils (Eds.), *Toward a theory of action.* Cambridge, MA: Harvard University Press.

Kluckhohn, F. (1953). "Dominant and variant value orientations." In C. Kluckhohn and H. Murray (Eds.), *Personality in nature, society, and cultural* (2nd ed., pp. 342–357). New York: Alford A. Knopf.

Kluckhohn, F., & Stodbeck, F. L. (1961). *Variation in value orientations.* Westport, CT: Greenwood.

Knott, B. (1973). "Symbolic interaction and social work education." *Education for Social Work,* 24–30.

Kolberg, L. (1976). "Moral stages and moralization: The cognitive-developmental approach." In T. Lickona (Ed.), *Moral development and behavior* (pp. 31–53). New York: Holt, Rinehart and Winston.

Korittko, A. (1991). "Family therapy with one-parent families." *Contemporary Family Therapy, 12,* 625–639.

Kravetz, D. (1976). "Sexism in a woman's profession." *Social Work, 21*(6), 421–426.

Kravetz, D. (1982). "An overview of content on women for the social work curriculum." *Journal of Education for Social Work, 18*(2), 42–49.

Kropf, N. P., Schneider, R. L., & Stahlman, S. D. (1993). "The status of gerontology in baccalaureate social work education." *Educational Gerontology, 19*(7), 623–634.

Kuhn, D. R. (1990). "The normative crises of families confronting dementia." *Families in Society, 71*(8), 451–460.

Kuhn, T. S. ([1962] 1970). *The structure of scientific revolutions.* University of Chicago Press.

Kumabe, K. T., Nishida, C., & Hepworth, D. H. (1985). *Bridging ethnocultural diversities in social work and health.* Honolulu: University of Hawaii School of Social Work.

Ladner, J. (1971). *Tomorrow's tomorrow: The black woman.* Garden City, NY: Doubleday.

Laird, J. (1989). "Women and stories: Restoring women's self-constructions." In M. McGoldrick, C. M. Anderson, and F. Walsh (Eds.), *Women in families: A framework for family therapy* (pp. 427–450). New York: Norton.

Lakoff, G., & Johnson, M. (1980). *Metaphors we live by.* Chicago: University of Chicago Press.

Land, H., Nishimoto, R., & Chau, K. (1988). "Interventive and preventive services for Vietnamese Chinese refugees." *Social Service Review, 62*(Sept.), 468–483.

Latting, J. K. (1990). "Identifying the 'isms': Enabling social work students to confront their biases." *Journal of Social Work Education, 26*(1), 36–44.

Lax, W. D. (1992). "Postmodern thinking in a clinical practice." In S. McNamee and K. J. Gergen (Eds.), *Therapy as social construction* (pp. 69–85). Newbury Park, CA: Sage.

Lee, J. A. B. (1980). "The helping professional's use of language in describing the poor." *American Journal of Orthopsychiatry, 50,* 580–584.

Lee, J. A. B. (1989). *Group work with the poor and oppressed.* New York: Haworth.

Leighninger, R. D. (1977). "Systems theory and social work: A re-examination." *Journal of Education for Social Work, 13*(3), 44–49.

Lemann, N. (1986a). "The origins of the underclass," Part 1. *Atlantic Monthly, 257*(June), 31–35.

Lemann, N. (1986b). "The origins of the underclass," Part 2. *The Atlantic Monthly, 258*(July), 54–55.

Lever, J. (1976). "Sex differences in games children play." *Social Problems, 23*(4), 478–487.

Lewis, E. A. (1992). "Regaining promise: Feminist perspectives for social group work practice." *Social Work with Groups, 15*(2/3), 271–284.

Lewis, E. A., & Ford, B. (1990). "The network utilization project: Incorporating traditional strengths of African-American families into group work practice." *Social Work with Groups, 13*(4), 7–22.

Lewis, J. S. (1993). *Independent living among community based elderly: The impact of social support and sense of coherence.* Unpublished dissertation, University of Maryland, Baltimore.

Lewis, L. A. (1984). "The coming-out process for lesbians: Integrating a stable identity." *Social Work, 29*(5), 464–469.

Lewis, O. (1966). "The culture of poverty." *Scientific American* (Oct.), 19–25.

Lewis, R. G. (1980). "Cultural perspectives on treatment modalities with Native Americans." *Life Span Development,* 434–441.

Lewis, R. G., & Gingerich, W. (1980). "Leadership characteristics: Views of Indian and Non-Indian students." *Social Casework, 61*(Oct.), 494–497.

Lewis, R. G., & Ho, M. K. (1975). "Social work with Native Americans." *Social Work, 20*(2), 379–382.

Liebow, E. (1967). *Tally's corner.* Boston: Little Brown.

Lin, N., Simeone, R. S., Ensel, W. M., & Kuo, W. (1979). "Social support, stressful life events, and illness: A model and an empirical test." *Journal of Health and Social Behavior, 20,* 108–119.

Linton, R. (1936). *The study of man.* New York: Appleton Century Croft.

Linton, R. (1958). "Status and role." In H. D. Stein and R. A. Cloward (Eds.), *Social perspectives on behavior* (pp. 175–176). New York: Free Press. [Reprinted from *The study of man.* New York: Appleton Century Croft.]

Lipman-Blumen, J. (1976). "The implications for family structure of changing sex roles." *Social Casework, 57*(2), 67–79.

Lipsitt, L. P., & Kaye, H. (1964). Conditioning sucking in the human newborn. *Psychonomic Science, 1,* 29–30.

Lister, L. (1987). "Ethnocultural content in social work education." *Journal of Social Work Education, 20*(1), 31–39.

Lockheed, M. E., & Hall, K. P. (1976). "Conceptualizing sex as a status characteristic: Applications to leadership training strategies." *Journal of Social Issues, 32*(3), 111–124.

Logan, S. M. L. (1981). "Race, identity, and Black children: A developmental perspective." *Social Casework, 62*(1), 47–56.

Logan, S. M. L. (1990). "Black families: Race, ethnicity, culture, social class and gender issues." In S. M. L. Logan, E. M. Freeman, and R. G. McRoy (Eds.), *Social work practice with Black families: A culturally specific perspective* (pp. 18–37). New York: Longman.

Logan, S. M. L., Freeman, E. M., & McRoy, R. G. (Eds.). (1990). *Social work practice with Black families: A culturally specific perspective.* New York: Longman.

Longres, J. F. (1990). *Human behavior in the social environment.* Itasca, IL: F. E. Peacock.

Longres, J. F., & Bailey, R. H. (1979). "Men's issues and sexism: A journal review." *Social Work,* 26–32.

Lowe, R. (1991). "Postmodern themes and therapeutic practices: Notes towards the definition." *Dulwick Centre Newsletter, 3,* 41–53.

Lowenberg, F. M. (1988). *Religion and social work practice in contemporary American society.* New York: Columbia University Press.

Lowenstein, S. F. (1976). "Integrating content on feminism and racism into the social work curriculum." *Journal of Education for Social Work, 12*(1), 91–96.

Lowenstein, S. F. (1980). "Understanding lesbian women." *Social Casework, 61*(1), 29–38.

Lukes, C. A., & Land, H. (1990) "Biculturality and homosexuality." *Social Work, 35*(2), 155–161.

Lukes, S. (1974). *Power: A radical view.* London: MacMillan.

Lum, D. (1982). "Toward a framework for social work practice with minorities." *Social Work, 27*(3), 244–249.

Lum, D. (1986). *Social work practice and people of color: A process-stage approach.* Monterey, CA: Brooks/Cole.

MacDonald, G., Sheldon, B., & Gillespie, J. (1992). "Contemporary studies of the effectiveness of social work." *British Journal of Social Work, 22,* 615–643.

MacDonald, M. L. (1982). Assertion training for women. In J. P. Curran and P. M. Monti (Eds.), *Social skills training: A practical handbook for assessment and treatment* (pp. 253–279. New York: Guilford.

Mackey, J. E. (Ed.). (1973). *American Indian task force report.* New York: Council on Social Work Education.

Madanes, C. (1981). *Strategic family therapy.* San Francisco: Jossey-Bass.

Madanes, C. (1990). *Sex, love and violence: Strategies for transformation.* New York: Norton.

Madanes, C. (1991). *Strategic family therapy.* San Francisco: Jossey-Bass.

Mahoney, M. J. (1985). "Psychotherapy and human change process." In M. J. Mahoney and A. Freeman (Eds.), *Cognition and psychotherapy* (pp. 3–48). New York: Plenum.

Mahoney, M. J. (1988). "The cognitive sciences and psychotherapy: Patterns in a developing relationship." In K. S. Dobson (Ed.), *The handbook of cognitive-behavioral therapies* (pp. 357–386). New York: Guilford.

Mahoney, M. J. (1991). *Human change processes: The scientific Foundations of Psychotherapy*. New York: Basic Books.

Maier, H. W. (1987). "Human development: Psychological perspective." In A. Minahan et al. (Eds.), *Encyclopedia of social work* (18th ed., pp. 850–856). Silver Spring, MD: National Association of Social Workers.

Maki, M. (1990). "Countertransference with adolescent clients of the same ethnicity." *Child and Adolescent Social Work, 7*(2), 135–145.

Malinowski, B. (1954). *Magic science and religion*. New York: Doubleday.

Malone, D. M. (1990). "Aging persons with mental retardation: Identification of the needs of a special population." *Gerontology Review, 3*(1), 1–14.

Malott, R. W., Whaley, D. L., & Malott, M. E. (1991). *Elementary principles of behavior* (2nd ed.). Englewood Cliffs, NJ: Prentice-Hall.

Maluccio, A. (1979). Competence and life experience. In C. B. Germain (Ed.), *Social work practice: People and environments* (pp. 282–302). New York: Columbia University Press.

Margolin, G. (1982). "Ethical and legal considerations in marriage and family therapy." *American Psychologist, 7*, 789–801.

Markus, H. (1977). "Self-schemata and processing information about the self." *Journal of Personality and Social Psychology, 35*, 63–78.

Martin, J. M., & Martin, E. P. (1985). *The helping tradition in the black family and community*. Silver Spring, MD: National Association of Social Workers.

Martin, P. Y., & O'Connor, G. G. (1989). *The social environment: Open systems applications*. New York: Longman.

Martin, P., & Shanahan, K. A. (1983). "Transcending the effects of sex composition in small groups." *Social Work with Groups, 6*(3/4), 19–32.

Matsuoka, J. K. (1990). "Differential acculturation among Vietnamese refugees." *Social Work, 35*(4), 341–345.

Mattaini, M. A. (1990). "Contextual behavior analyses in the assessment process." *Families in Society, 71*, 236–245.

Mattaini, M. A. (1991). "Walden 1.9: Successive approximations." *Behavior and Social Issues, 1*(2), 53–60.

Maturana, H., & Varela, F. (1987). *The tree of knowledge*. Boston, MA: New Science Library.

Max, J. (1971). "Power theory and institutional change." *Social Service Review, 45*(3), 274–288.

Mayer, J., & Timms, N. (1969). "Clash in perspectives between worker and client." *Social Casework, 50*, 32–40.

McAdoo, H. P. (1978). The impact of upward mobility on kin-help patterns and reciprocal obligations in Black families. *Journal of Marriage and the Family, 40*, 761–778.

McAdoo, H. P. (1981). "Patterns of upward mobility in Black families." In H. P. Mcadoo (Ed.), *Black families* (pp. 155–170). Beverly Hills: Sage.

McDermott, C. J. (1989). "Empowering the elderly nursing home resident: The resident rights campaign." *Social Work, 34*(2), 155–157.

McDermott, F. E. (1982). "Against a persuasive definition of self-determination." In H. Rubenstein and M. H. Block (Eds.), *Things that matter influences on helping relationships* (pp. 77–88). New York: Macmillan.

McDonald-Wikler, L. (1987). "Developmental disabilities." In A. Minahan et al. (Eds.), *Encyclopedia of social work* (18th ed., pp. 422–434). Silver Spring, MD: National Association of Social Workers.

McGoldrick, M. (1982). "Ethnicity and family therapy: An overview." In M. McGoldrick, J. K. Pearce, and J. Giordano (Eds.), *Ethnicity and family therapy* (pp. 3–30). New York: Guilford.

McGoldrick, M. J. (1989). "Women through the family life cycle." In M. J. McGoldrick, C. M. Anderson, and F. Walsh (Eds.), *Women in families: A framework for family therapy* (pp. 200–226). New York: Norton.

McGoldrick, M. J. (1990). Presentation in the Georgia State University Professional Continuing Education Series, Atlanta, Georgia, October 26, 1990.

McGoldrick, M. J., Anderson, C. M., & Walsh, F. (1989). "Women in families and in family therapy." In M. J. McGoldrick, C. M. Anderson, and F. Walsh (Eds.), *Women in families: A framework for family therapy* (pp. 3–15). New York: Norton.

McGoldrick, M. J., Preto, N. G., Hines, P. M., & Lee, E. (1991). "Ethnicity and family therapy." In A. S. Gurman and D. P. Kniskern (Eds.), *Handbook of family therapy* (pp. 546–582). New York: Brunner/Mazel.

McIntosh, P. (1992). "White privilege and male privilege: A personal account of coming to see correspondences through work in Women's Studies." In M. L. Anderson and P. H. Collins (Eds.), *Race, class, and gender: an anthology* (pp. 70–81). Belmont, CA: Wadsworth.

McKamy, E. H. (1976). "Social work with the wealthy." *Social Casework, 57*(4), 254–258.

McLeod, M. (1986). "Systemic family therapy." *Individual Psychology Journal of Adlerian Theory, 42*, 493–505.

McNamee, S., & Gergen, K. J. (Eds.). (1992). *Therapy as social construction.* Newbury Park, CA: Sage.

McWhirter, D., & Mattison, A. (1984). *The male couple.* Englewood Cliffs, NJ: Prentice-Hall.

Mead, G. H. (1925). "The genesis of the self and social control." *International Journal of Ethics, 35*, 251–277.

Mead, G. H. (1934). *Mind, self, and society.* Chicago: University of Chicago Press.

Meisel, S. S., & Perkins, A. F. (1974). "The need for women's studies in education." *Journal of Social Work Education, 10*(3), 17–31.

Merton, R. K. (1957a). *Social theory and social structure.* Glencoe, IL: Free Press.

Merton, R. K. (1957b). "The role-set: Problems in sociological theory." *British Journal of Sociology, 8*, 110–120.

Merton, R. K. (1958). "Bureaucratic structure and personality." In H. D. Stein and R. A. Cloward (Eds.), *Social perspectives on behavior* (pp. 577–584). New York: Free Press.

Mest, G. M. (1988). "With a little help from their friends: Use of social support systems by persons with retardation." *Journal of Social Issues, 44*(1), 117–25.

Metress, S. P. (1985). "The history of Irish-American care of the aged." *Social Service Review, 59*(March), 18–31.

Meyer, C. (1973). "Direct services in new and old contexts." In A. Kahn (Ed.), *Shaping the new social work* (pp. 26–54). New York: Columbia University Press.

Meyer, C. (1982). "Issues in clinical social work: In search of a consensus." In P. Caroff (Ed.), *Treatment formulations and clinical social work* (pp. 19–26). Silver Spring, MD: National Association of Social Workers.

Meyer, C. (1987). "Direct practice in social work: Overview." In A. Minahan et al. (Eds.), *Encyclopedia of social work* (18th ed., pp. 409–422). Silver Spring, MD: National Association of Social Workers.

Meyer, C. (1993). *Assessment in social work practice.* New York: Columbia University Press.

Miller, D. (1987). *Helping the strong: An exploration of the needs of families headed by women.* Silver Spring, MD: National Association of Social Workers.

Miller, J. B. (1976). *Toward a new psychology of women.* Boston: Beacon.

Miller, J. B. (1984). *The development of women's sense of self.* Unpublished paper, Wellesley College, Wellesley, MA.

Miller, J. B., & Stiver, I. P. (1991). *A relational reframing of therapy work in progress.* No. 52, The Stone Center, Wellesley College, Wellesley, MA.

Miller, S. (1980). "Reflections on the dual perspective." In E. Mizio and J. Delany (Eds.), *Training for service delivery for minority clients* (pp. 53–61). New York: Family Service of America.

Minuchin, S. (1974). *Families and family therapy.* Cambridge, MA: Harvard University Press.

Minuchin, S., & Montalvo, B. (1971). "Techniques for working with disorganized low socio-economic families." In J. Halry (Ed.), *Changing families* (pp. 202–211). New York: Grune & Stratton.

Miranda, M. (Ed.). (1973). *Puerto Rican task force report.* New York: Council on Social Work Education.

Mirelowitz, S., & Grossman, L. (1975). "Ethnicity: An intervening variable in social work education." *Journal of Education for Social Work, 11*(3), 76–83.

Mizio, E. (1972). "White worker–minority client." *Social Work, 17*(3), 82–86.

Mizio, E. (1974). "Impact of external systems on the Puerto Rican family." *Social Casework, 55*, 76–83.

Mohan, B. (1980). "Human behavior, social environment, social reconstruction, and social policy: A system of linkages, goals, and priorities." *Journal of Education for Social Work, 16*(1), 26–32.

Mokuau, N. (1990). "A family-centered approach in native Hawaiian culture." *Families in Society, 71*(10), 607–613.

Montalvo, B. (1974). Home-school conflict and the Puerto Rican child. *Social Casework, 55*(Feb.), 100–110.

Montalvo, F. (1983). "The affective domain in cross-cultural social work education." *Journal of Social Work Education, 19*(2), 48–53.

Montiel, M., & Wong, P. (1983). "A theoretical critique of the minority perspective." *Social Work, 64*(2), 112–117.

Moon, M. S., Inge, K. J, Wehman, P., Brooke, V., & Barcus, J. M. (1990). *Helping persons with severe mental retardation get and keep employment: Supported employment strategies and outcomes.* Baltimore: Paul H. Brookes

Morales, J. (1992). "Community social work with Puerto Rican communities in the United States: One organizer's perspective." In F. G. Rivera and J. L. Erlich (Eds.),

Community organization in a diverse society (pp. 91–112). Boston: Allyn and Bacon.

Morawetz, A., & Walker, G. (1984). *Brief therapy with single-parent families.* New York: Brunner/Mazel.

Morell, C. (1987). "Cause is function: Toward a feminist model of integration for social work." *Social Service Review, 61*(1), 144–155.

Morin, S. F., & Garfinkle, E. M. (1978). "Male homophobia." *Journal of Social Issues, 54*, 29–47.

Morris, J. K. (1993). "Interacting oppressions: Teaching social work content on women in color." *Journal of Social Work Education, 29*(1), 99–111.

Mosteller, Susanne. (1963). "Value orientations of caseworkers and clients." *Smith College Studies in Social Work, 34*(1), 1–29.

Mount, B., & Zwernik, N. (1988). *It's never too early , it's never too late: A booklet about personal futures planning* (Publication #421-88-109). St. Paul, MN: Metropolitan Council.

Moynihan, D. P. (1965). *The negro family.* Washington, DC: Department of Labor.

Munson, C. E. (1981). "Symbolic interaction theory for small group treatment." *Social Casework, 62*(3), 167–174.

Murase, K., ed. (1973). *Asian American task force report: Problems and issues in social work education.* New York: Council on Social Work Education.

Murdock, A. (1982). "A political perspective on problem solving." *Social Work, 27*(5), 417–421.

Myerhoff, B. (1978). *Number our days.* New York: Dutton.

National Association of Social Workers. (1977). "Policy statement on homosexuality. Memo. Washington, DC.

National Association of Social Workers. (1978). *Code of ethics of the national association of social workers.* Silver Spring, MD: Author.

National Association of Social Workers. (1982). "Standards for social work in developmental disabilities." In *NASW Standards for Social Work in Health Care Settings* (pp. 15–21). Silver Spring, MD: Author.

National Commission on Neighborhoods. (1979). *People building neighborhoods. Final report to the President and Congress of the United States.* Washington, DC: U.S. Government Printing Office.

Needham, R. (1977). "Casework interventions with a homosexual adolescent." *Social Casework, 58*(7), 387–394.

Nelson, M., Nelson, B., Sherman, M., & Strean, H. (1968). *Roles and paradigms in psychotherapy.* New York: Grune & Stratton.

Nes, J. A., & Iadicola, P. (1989). "Toward a definition of feminist social work: A comparison of liberal, radical and socialist models. *Social Work, 34*(1), 12–21.

Newman, B. S. (1989). "Including curriculum content on lesbian and gay issues." *Journal of Social Work Education, 25*, 202–11.

Newman, B., & Newman, P. R. (1987). *Development through life: A psychosocial approach.* Homewood, IL: Dorsey.

Nichols, M. (1989). Sex therapy with lesbians, gay men, and bisexuals. In S. Leiblum & R. Rosen (Eds.), *Principles and practice of sex therapy* (pp. 269–296). New York: Guilford.

Nisbett, R., & Ross, L. (1980). *Human inference: Strategies and shortcomings of social judgment.* Englewood Cliffs, NJ: Prentice-Hall.

Noble, W. N. (1988). "African-American family life: An instrument of culture." In H. P. McAdoo (Ed.), *Black families* (2nd ed., pp. 44–53). Newbury Park, CA: Sage.

Northen, H. (1982). *Clinical social work.* New York: Columbia University Press.

Northen, H. (1987). "Assessment in direct practice." In A. Minahan et al. (Eds.), *Encyclopedia of social work* (18th ed., pp. 171–183). Silver Spring, MD: National Association of Social Workers.

Northen, H. (1988). *Social work with groups* (2nd ed.). New York: Haworth.

Norton, D. G. (1976). "Working with minority populations: The dual perspective." In B. Ross and S. K. Khinduka (Eds.), *Social work in practice.* New York: National Association of Social Workers.

Norton, D. G. (1978). *The dual perspective: Inclusion of ethnic minority content in the social work curriculum.* New York: Council on Social Work Education.

Nuckolls, K. B., Cassel, J., & Kaplan, B. H. (1972). "Psychosocial assets, life crisis and the prognosis of pregnancy." *American Journal of Epidemiology, 95*(May), 431–441.

O'Hanlon, W. H. (1993). "Possibility therapy: From iatrogenic injury to estrogenic healing." In S. Gilligan and R. Price (Eds.), *Therapeutic conversations* (pp. 3–17). New York: Norton.

Olson, C. S. (1988). Blue Ridge blues: The problems and strengths of rural women. *Affilia, 3*(1), 5–17.

Orlin, M. (1979–80). Beyond non-sexist practice to feminist social work. *Journal of Applied Social Sciences, 4*(1), 77–91.

Padilla, A., ed. (1980). *Acculturation theory, models, and some new findings.* Boulder, CO: Westview.

Palombo, J. (1985). "Self psychology and countertransference in the treatment of children." *Child and Adolescent Social Work Journal, 2*(1), 36–48.

Palombo, J. (1992). "Narratives, self-cohesion, and the patient's search for meaning." *Clinical Social Work Journal, 20,* 249–270.

Pancoast, D. L., & Collins, A. (1987). Natural helping networks. In A. Minahan et al. (Eds.), *Encyclopedia of social work* (18th ed., pp. 177–182). Silver Spring, MD: National Association of Social Workers.

Parsons, R. J. (1988). "Empowerment for role alternatives for low income minority girls: A group work approach." *Social Work with Groups, 11*(4), 27–46.

Parsons, R. J., Hernandez, S. H., & Jorgensen, J. D. (1988). "Integrated practice: A framework for problem solving." *Social Work, 33,* 417–421.

Parsons, T. (1942). "Age and sex in the social structure of the United States." *American Sociological Review 7,* 604–616.

Parsons, T. (1951). *The social system.* New York: Free Press.

Parsons, T. (1954). *Essays in sociological theory.* New York: Free Press.

Parsons, T. (1964). "Age and sex in the social structure." In R. L. Coser (Ed.), *The family: Its structure and functions* (251–266). New York: St. Martins.

Parsons, T., & Bales, R. F. (1955). *Family socialization and interaction process.* Glencoe, IL: Free Press.

Pavalko, R. (1986). *Social problems.* Itasca, IL: F. E. Peacock.

Paviour, R. (1988). "The influence of class and race on clinical assessments by MSW students." *Social Service Review, 62*(4), 684–693.

Peabody, S. A., & Gelso, C. J. (1982). "Countertransference and empathy: The complex relationship between two divergent concepts in counseling." *Journal of Counseling Psychology, 29*(3), 240–245.

Pedersen, P. (1976). "The field of intercultural counseling." In P. Pedersen, W. J. Lonner, and J. G. Draguns (Eds.), *Counseling across cultures* (pp. 17–41). Honolulu: University of Hawaii Press.

Pendagast, S., & Sherman, R. (1977). "Diagrammatic assessment of family relationships." *Social Casework, 59*, 465–476.

Pepitone, A. (1949). "Motivation effects in social perception." *Human Relations, 3*, 57–76.

Perlman, H. H. (1957). *Social casework: A problem solving process.* Chicago: University of Chicago Press.

Perlman, H. H. (1962a). "Intake and some role considerations." In C. Kassius (Ed.), *Social casework in the fifties* (pp. 163–174). New York: Family Service Association of America.

Perlman, H. H. (1962b). "The role concept and social casework: Some explanations." *Social Service Review, 36*, 17–31.

Perlman, H. H. (1965). "Self-determination: Reality or illusion?" *Social Service Review, 39*(4), 410–421.

Perlman, H. H. (1968). *Persona: Social role and responsibility.* Chicago: University of Chicago Press.

Perry, D. G., & Bussey, K. (1979). "The social learning theory of sex differences: Imitation is alive and well." *Journal of Personality and Social Psychology, 37*, 1699–1712.

Petr, C. G. (1988). "The worker-client relationship: A general systems perspective." *Social Casework, 60*(10), 586–596.

Petro, O., & French, B. (1972) "The Black client's view of himself." *Social Casework, 53*(8), 466–474.

Pierce, C. H., & Risley, T. R. (1974). "Improving job performance of neighborhood youth corps aides in an urban recreation program." *Journal of Applied Behavior Analysis, 7*, 207–215.

Pilisuk, M., & Minkler, M. (1980). "Supportive networks: Life ties for the elderly." *Journal of Social Issues, 36*(2), 95–115.

Pinderhughes, E. B. (1978). "Power, powerlessness, and empowerment in community mental health." *Black Caucus Journal*, 10–15.

Pinderhughes, E. B. (1979). "Teaching empathy in cross-cultural social work." *Social Work, 24*(4), 312–316.

Pinderhughes, E. B. (1982). "Family functioning of Afro-Americans." *Social Work, 27*(1), 91–96.

Pinderhughes, E. B. (1983). "Empowerment for our clients and for ourselves." *Social Casework, 64*, 331–338.

Pinderhughes, E. B. (1989). *Understanding race, ethnicity, and power: The key to efficacy in clinical practice.* New York: Free Press.

Pinkston, E. M. & Linsk, N. L. (1984). *Care of the elderly: A family approach.* Elmsford, NY: Pergamon.

Pins, A. M. (1970, March). "Entering the seventies: Changing priorities for social work education." *Social Work Education Reporter, 18*(1), p. 30.

Piven, F. F., & Cloward, R. (1971). *Regulating the Poor.* New York: Pantheon Books.

Podair, S. (1967). "How bigotry builds through language." *Negro Digest, 16*, 35–41.

Polanyi, M. (1958). *Personal knowledge.* Chicago: University of Chicago Press.

Polkinghorne, D. E. (1988). *Narrative knowing and the human sciences.* Albany, NY: State University of New York Press.

Polsky, H. (1969). "System as patient: Client needs and system function." In G. Hearn (Ed.), *The general systems approach: Contributions toward a holistic conception of social work* (pp. 5–11). New York: Council on Social Work Education.

Popper, K. R. (1959). *The logic of scientific discovery.* London: Hutchinson.

Posner, W. (1961). "Basic issues in casework with older people." *Social Casework, 42*(5–6), 234–239.

Poster, M. (1989). *Critical theory and poststructuralism: In search of a context.* Ithaca, NY: Cornell University Press.

Poverny, L. M., & Finch, W. A. (1988). "Gay and lesbian domestic partnerships: Expanding the definition of family." *Social Casework, 69*(2), 116–121.

Prager, E. (1980). "Evaluation in mental health: Enter the consumer." *Social Work Research and Abstracts, 16*, 5–10.

President's Commission on Mental Health. (1978). *Report to the President.* Washington, DC: U.S. Government Printing Office.

Pridgen, N. H. (1991). "At the agency community-based counseling services for deaf and hard-of-hearing individuals." *Families in Society, 72*(3), 174–176.

Priest, S. (1990). *The British empiricists.* New York: Penguin.

Proctor, E. K., & Davis, L. E. (1983). "Minority content in social work education: A question of objectives." *Journal of Education for Social Work, 19*(2), 85–93.

Prunty, H. (1980). "The 'how-tos' of advocacy for the caseworker." In E. Mizio and J. Delaney (Eds.), *Training for service delivery to minority clients* (pp. 181–188). New York: Family Service of America.

Queralt, M. (1984). "Understanding Cuban immigrants: A cultural perspective." *Social Work, 29*(2), 115–121.

Queiro-Tajalli, I. (1989). "Hispanic women's perceptions and use of prenatal health care services." *Affilia, 4*(2), 60–72.

Raskin, N. (1985). "Client-centered therapy." In S. J. Lynn and J. P. Garske (Eds.), *Contemporary psychotherapies models and methods* (pp. 155–190). Columbus, OH: Charles E. Merrill.

Reamer, F. G. (1988). "Aids and ethics: The agenda for social workers." *Social Work, 33*(5), 460–464.

Rebecca, M., Hefner, R., & Olishanshy, B. (1976). "A model of sex-role transcendence." In A. G. Kaplan and J. P. Beau (Eds.), *Beyond sex role stereotypes* (pp. 90–97). Boston: Little Brown.

Red Horse, J. G. (1980a). "American Indian elders: Unifiers of Indian families." *Social Casework, 25*(8), 490–492.

Red Horse, J. G. (1980b). "Family structure and value orientation in American Indians." *Social Casework, 25*(8), 462–467.

Reed, B. G. (1979). Differential reactions by male and female group members in the presence of male or female authority figures. *Dissertation Abstracts International, 40, 7.*

Reed, B. G., & Garvin, C. D. (Eds.) (1983). *Groupwork with women/groupwork with men: An overview of gender issues in social group work practice.* New York: Haworth.

Reed, B. G., & Garvin, C. D. (in press). "Feminist thought and group psychotherapy: Feminist principles as praxis." In B. de Chant (Ed.), *Women and group psychotherapy: gender, theory and practice.* New York: Guilford.

Reid, W. J., & Hanrahan, P. (1982). "Recent evaluations of social work: Grounds for optimism." *Social Work, 27,* 328–340.

Reiss, D. (1981). *The family construction of reality.* Cambridge, MA: Harvard University Press.

Reissman, L. (1958). "A study of role conceptions in bureaucracy." In H. D. Stein and R. A. Cloward (Eds.), *Social perspectives on behavior* (pp. 221–227). New York: Free Press.

Renfrey, G. S. (1992). "Cognitive-behavior therapy and the Native American client." *Behavior Therapy, 23,* 321–340.

Reynolds, B. C. (1951). *Social work and social living.* New York: Citadel.

Reynolds, V., Falger, V. S. E., & Vine, I. (Eds.). (1986). *The sociobiology of ethnocentrism: Evolutionary dimensions of xenophobia, discrimination, racism and nationalism.* Athens, GA: University of Georgia Press.

Rhodes, S. L. (1977). "Contract negotiation in the initial stage of casework." *Social Service Review, 51,* 125–140.

Rhodes, S. L. (1980). "A developmental approach to the life cycle of the family." In M. Bloom (Ed.), *Life span development* (pp. 30–40). New York: Macmillan.

Ribes, E. (1985). "Human behaviour as operant behavior: An empirical or conceptual issue?" In C. F. Lowe, M. Richelle, D. E. Blackman, & C. M. Bradshaw (Eds.), *Behaviour analysis and contemporary psychology* (pp. 117–133). Hillsdale, NJ: Lawrence Erlbaum.

Rice, L. N., & Greenberg, L. S. (1984a). "The new research paradigm." In L. N. Rice and L. S. Greenberg (Eds.), *Patterns of change: An intensive analysis of psychotherapy process.* New York: Guilford.

Rice, L. N., & Greenberg, L. S. (Eds.) (1984b). *Patterns of change: An intensive analysis of psychotherapy process.* New York: Guilford.

Richards, S. A., & Jaffee, C. L. (1972). "Blacks supervising whites: A study of interracial difficulties in working together in a simulated organization." *Journal of Applied Psychology, 56,* 234–240.

Richmond, M. (1917). *Social diagnosis.* New York: Russell Sage Foundation.

Richmond, M. (1922). *What is social casework?* New York: Russell Sage Foundation.

Ridley, C. (1984). "Clinical treatment of the nondisclosing black client—A therapeutic paradox." *American Psychologist, 39*(11), 1234–1244.

Ridgeway, C. L. (1982). "Status in groups: The importance of motivation." *American Sociological Review, 47,* 76–88.

Ridgeway, C. L. (Ed.) (1992). *Gender, interaction, and inequality.* New York: Springer-Verlag.

Rivera, F. G., & Erlich, J. L. (1992). "Introduction: Prospects and challenges." In F. G. Rivera and J. L. Erlich (Eds.), *Community organization in a diverse society* (pp. 1–26). Boston: Allyn and Bacon.

Roberts, D. (1993a). "Nubia: The unfolding story of a storied land." *Smithsonian, 24*(3), 90–103.

Roberts, D. (1993b). "Out of Africa: The superb artwork of ancient Nubia." *Smithsonian, 24*(3), 90–100.

Robertson, M. E. (1970). "Inclusion of content on ethnic and racial minorities in social work curriculum." *Social Work Education Reporter, 18*(1), 47.

Rodwell, M. K. (1987). "Naturalistic inquiry: An alternative model for social work assessment." *Social Service Review,* 231–246.

Rogers, C. R. (1957). "The necessary and sufficient conditions of therapeutic personality change." *Journal of Consulting Psychology, 21,* 95–103.

Rogers, C. R. (1961). *On becoming a person.* Boston: Houghton Mifflin.

Rogers, C. R., & Dymond, R. F. Eds., (1957). *Psychotherapy and personality change.* Chicago: University of Chicago Press.

Romero, D. P. (1977). "Biases in gender-role research." *Social Work, 22*(3), 214–218.

Romero, J. T. (1983). "The therapist as social change agent." In G. Gibson (Ed.), *Our kingdom stands on brittle glass* (pp. 86–95). Silver Spring, MD: National Association of Social Workers.

Rosenhan, D. L. (1984). "On being sane in insane places." *The Invented Reality.* New York: Norton.

Rosenzweig, S. (1936). "Some implicit common factors in diverse methods of psychotherapy." *American Journal of Orthopsychiatry, 6,* 412–415.

Roth, S. (1989). "Psychotherapy with lesbian couples: Individual issues, female socialization and the social context." In M. McGoldreck, C. Anderson, and F. Walsh (Eds.), *Women in families: A framework for family therapy* (pp. 286–307). New York: Norton.

Roth, S., & Murphy, B. C. (1986). "Therapeutic work with Lesbian clients: A systemic therapy view." In J. C. Jansen and M. Ault-Riche (Eds.), *Women and family therapy* (pp. 78–88). Rockville, MD: Aspen.

Rothman, J., Gant, L. M., & Hnat, S. A. (1985). "Mexican-American family culture." *Social Service Review, 59*(2), 197–215.

Rubin, A. (1985). "Practice effectiveness: More grounds for optimism." *Social Work, 30,* 469–476.

Ruckdeschel, R. A. (1985). "Qualitative research as a perspective." *Social Work Research and Abstracts, 21,* 17–21.

Ruiz, J. (Ed.), (1973). *Chicano task force report.* New York: Council on Social Work Education.

Russell, B. (1956). *Logic and knowledge.* London: Allen & Unwin.

Russell, M. (1986). "Teaching feminist counseling skills: An evaluation." *Counselor Education and Supervision, 25*(4), 320–331.

Russo, N. F. (1991). "Reconstructing the psychology of women: An overview." In M. T. Notman, and C. C. Nadelson (Eds.), *Women and men: New perspectives on gender differences* (pp. 43–61). Washington, DC: American Psychiatric Press.

Ryan, A. S. (1985). "Cultural factors in casework with Chinese-Americans." *Social Casework, 66*(6), 333–340.

Ryan, C. C., & Rowe, M. J. (1988). "Aids: Legal and ethical issues." *Social Casework, 69*(6), 324–333.

Ryan, W. (1971). *Blaming the victim.* New York: Pantheon.

Ryders, R. G. (1987). *The realistic therapist: Modesty and relativism in therapy and research.* Newbury Park, CA: Sage.

Saafir, R. K. (1982). "Implementing community programs: The Black perspective in behavioral community psychology." In S. M. Turner, & R. T. Jones (Eds.), *Behavior modification in black populations: Psychosocial issues and empirical findings* (pp. 301–325). New York: Plenum.

Saari, C. (1986a). "The created relationship: Countertransferences and the therapeutic culture." *Clinical Social Work Journal, 14*(1), 39–51.

Saari, C. (1986b). *Clinical social work treatment: How does it work?* New York: Gardner.

Saari, C. (1991). *The creation of meaning in clinical social work.* New York: Guilford.

Saigh, P. A., & Umar, A. M. (1983). "The effects of a good behavior game on the disruptive behavior of Sudanese elementary school children." *Journal of Applied Behavior Analysis, 16,* 339–344.

Saleebey, D. (1988). *Theory and the generation and subversion of knowledge.* Unpublished paper, School of Social Work, University of Kansas, Lawrence.

Saleebey, D. (1989). "The estrangement of knowing from doing: Profession in crisis." *Social Work, 70,* 556–563.

Saleebey, D. (1992). "Introduction: Power to the people." In D. Saleebey (Ed.), *The strengths perspective in social work Practice* (pp. 3–17). New York: Longman.

Sanders, D. S. (1974). "Educating social workers for the role of effective change agents in a multicultural, pluralistic society." *Journal of Education for Social Work, 10*(2) 86–91.

Sanders, D. S. (1975). "Dynamics of ethnic and cultural pluralism: Implications for social work education and curriculum innovation." *Journal of Education for Social Work, 11*(3), 95–100.

Sands, R. G. (1988). "Sociolinguistic analysis of a mental health interview." *Social Work, 33*(2), 149–154.

Sands, R. G., & Nuccio, K. (1992). "Past-modernization feminist theory and social work." *Social Work, 37*(6), 489–502.

Sands, R. G., & Richardson, V. (1986). "Clinical practice with women in their middle years." *Social Work, 31,* 36–43.

Sanville, J. (1987). "Creativity and constructing of the self." *Psychoanalytic Review, 74,* 263–279.

Sanzenbach, P. (1989). "Religion and social work." *Social Casework, 70,* 571–572.

Sanzenbach, P., Canda, E. E., & Joseph, M. (1989). "Religion and social work: It's not that simple." *Social Casework, 70*(9), 571–575.

Sarbin, T. R. (1986). *Narrative psychology.* New York: Praeger.

Satir, V. (1967). *Conjoint family therapy.* Palo Alto, CA: Science and Behavior Books.

Schacter, S. (1964). "The interaction of cognitive and physiological determinants of emotional state." In L. Berkowitz (Ed.), *Advances in experimental social psychology* (Vol. 1). New York: Academic.

Schank, R. C., & Abelson, R. P. (Eds.) (1990). *Scripts, plans, goals and understanding.* Hillsdale, NJ: Lawrence Erlbaum.

Schilit, R., Clark, W. M., & Shallenberger, E. A. (1988). "Social supports and lesbian alcoholics." *Affilia, 3*(2), 27–40.

Schilling, R. F., Schinke, S. P., Blythe, B. J., & Barth, R. P. (1982). "Child maltreatment and mentally retarded parents: Is there a relationship?" *Mental Retardation, 20,* 201–209.

Schinke, S. P., Botvin, G., Trimble, G., Orlandi, M., Gilchrist, L., & Locklear, B. (1988). "Preventing substance abuse among Native American adolescents." *Journal of Counseling Psychology, 35,* 87–90.

Schinke, S. P., & Gilchrist, L. D. (1978). "Adolescent pregnancy: An interpersonal skill-training approach to prevention." *Social Work in Health Care, 3,* 159–167.

Schlesinger, E. G., & Devore, W. (1979). "Social workers view ethnic minority teaching." *Journal of Education for Social Work, 15*(3), 20–27.

Schneider, S. W. (1989). *Intermarriage: The challenge of living with differences between Christians and Jews.* New York: Free Press.

Schnelle, J. F. (1991). *Managing urinary incontinence in the elderly.* New York: Springer.

Schon, D. (1983). *The reflective practitioner: How professionals think in action.* New York: Basic books.

Schultz, R. (1976). "Effects of control and predictability on the physical and psychological well-being of the institutionalized aged." *Journal of Personality and Social Psychology, 33,* 563–573.

Schwartz, A. (1984). "The contribution of cognate disciplines to micro practice." In M. Dinerman and L. L. Geisman (Eds.), *A quarter-century of social work education* (pp. 93–114). Silver Spring, MD: National Association of Social Workers & Council on Social Work Education.

Schwartz, M. C. (1973). "Sexism in the social work curriculum." *Journal of Social Work Education, 9*(3), 65–70.

Schwartz, M. C. (1974). "Importance of the sex of worker and client." *Social Work, 19*(2), 177–185.

Scott, C. A. (1971). "Ethnic minorities in social work education." In A. M. Pins et al. (Eds.), *The current scene in social work education* (pp. 24–25). New York: Council on Social Work Education.

Scott, D. (1989). "Meaning construction and social work practice." *Social Service Review,* March, 39–51.

Seltzer, M. M., Ivry, J., & Litchfield, L. C. (1987). "Family members as case managers: Partnership between the formal and informal support networks." *Gerontologist, 26*(6), 722–728.

Seltzer, M. M., Litchfield, L. C., Lowy, L.,& Levin, R. J. (1989). "Families as case managers: A longitudinal study." *Family Relations, 38*(3), 332–336.

Seltzer, M. M., Seltzer, G. B., & Litchfield, L. C. (1982, June). *Community opposition to community residence: A study of factors related to community response.* Paper presented at the meeting of the American Association on Mental Deficiency, Boston.

Selznick, P. (1957). *Leadership in administration.* New York: Harper and Row.

Shafer, R. (1983). *The analytic attitude.* New York: Basic Books.

Shapiro, T., & Hertzig, M. E., Eds. (1988). "Normal growth and development." In *American Psychiatric Press Textbook of Psychiatry* (pp. 91–121). Washington, DC: American Psychiatric Press.

Shaw, M. E. (1976). *Group dynamics: The psychology of small group behavior.* New York: McGraw-Hill.

Shaw, M. E. (1983). *Group dynamics: The psychology of small group behavior.* New York: McGraw-Hill.

Sheridan, N. J., Bullis, R. K., Adcock, C. R., Berlin, S. D., & Miller, P. C. (1992). "Practitioners' personal and professional attitudes and behaviors toward religion and spirituality: Issues for education and practice." *Journal of Social Work Education, 28*(2), 190–203.

Sherman, S. N. (1976). "The therapist and changing sex roles." *Social Casework, 57*(2), 93–96.

Shernoff, M. J. (1984). "Family therapy for lesbian and gay clients." *Social Work, 29,* 393–396.

Shibutani, T. (1961). *Society and personality.* Englewood Cliffs, NJ: Prentice-Hall.

Shields, S. A. (1987). "Women, men and the dilemma of emotion." In P. Shaver and C. Hendrick (Eds.), *Sex and gender* (pp. 229–250). Newbury Park, CA: Sage.

Shon, S., & Ja, D. (1982). "Asian families." In M. McGoldrick, et al. (Eds.), *Ethnicity and Family Therapy* (pp. 208–228). New York: Guilford.

Shulman, L. (1981). *Identifying, measuring, and teaching helpful skills.* New York: Council on Social Work Education.

Shulman, L. (1984). *The skills of helping individuals and groups.* Itasca, IL: F. E. Peacock.

Shulman, L. (1991). *Interactional social work practice.* Itasca, IL: F. E. Peacock.

Sider, R. C., & Clements, C. (1982). "Family or individual therapy: The ethics of modality choice." *American Journal of Psychiatry, 139,* 1455–1459.

Siegel, D. I. (1985, June). "Homogeneous versus heterogeneous areas for the elderly." *Social Service Review, 59,* 216–238.

Simon, B. K. (1960). *Relation between theory and practice in social casework.* New York: National Association of Social Workers.

Simon, B. (1970). "Social casework theory: An overview." In R. Roberts and R. Nee (Eds.), *Theories of social casework* (pp. 353–394). Chicago: University of Chicago Press.

Siporin, M. (1975). *Introduction to social work practice.* New York: Macmillan.

Siporin, M. (1980). "Ecological systems theory in social work." *Journal of Sociology and Social Welfare, 7,* 507–532.

Siporin, M. (1986). "Contribution of religious values to social work and the law." *Social Thought, 12*(4), 35–50.

Siqueland, E. R. & Lipsitt, L. P. (1966). "Conditioned head-turning in human newborns." *Journal of Experimental Child Psychology, 3,* 356–376.

Skinner, B. F. (1953). *Science and human behavior.* New York: Free Press.

Skinner, B. F. (1966). "The phylogeny and ontogeny of behavior." *Science, 153,* 1205–1213.

Skinner, B. F. (1971). "A behavioral analysis of value judgements." In E. Tobach, L. R. Aronson, & E. Shaw (Eds.). *The biopsychology of development* (pp. 543–551). New York: Academic.

Skinner, B. F. (1975). "The shaping of phytogenic behavior." *Journal of the Experimental Analysis of Behavior, 24,* 117–120.

Skinner, B. F. (1985). "Cognitive science and behaviorism." *British Journal of Psychology, 76,* 291–301.

Skynner, A. C. R. (1981). "An open-systems, group analytic approach to family therapy." In A. S. Gurman and D. P. Kniskern (Eds.), *Handbook of family therapy* (pp. 39–84). New York: Brunner, Mazel.

Sluzki, C. E. (1990). "Negative explanations drawing distinctions, raising dilemmas, collapsing time externalisation of problems: A note on some powerful conceptual tools." *Residential Treatment for Children and Youth, 7*(3), 33–37.

Smith, F. E., & Stuart, P. (1982). "Integrating ethnic and minority group history into social welfare policy and history courses." *Journal of Education for Social Work, 18*(3), 101–108.

Sokolovsky, J., & Vesperi, M. D. (1990). "The cultural context of well-being in old age." *Generations, 15*(1), 21–24.

Solomon, B. B. (1976). *Black empowerment: Social work in oppressed communities.* New York: Columbia University Press.

Solomon, B. B. (1982, July). *Power, the troublesome factor in cross-cultural supervision.* Paper presented at Smith College School of Social Work, Amherst, MA.

Solomon, B. B. (1987). "Human development: Sociocultural perspective." In A. Minahan et al. (Eds.), *Encyclopedia of social work* (18th ed., pp. 865–866). Silver Spring, MD: National Association of Social Workers.

Solomon, B. B. (1991). "Social work values and skills to empower women." In A. Weick and S. T. Vandiver (Eds.), *Women, power and change* (pp. 206–214). Washington, DC: National Association of Social Workers.

Sophie, J. (1986). "A critical examination of stage theories of lesbian identity development." *Journal of Homosexuality, 12*(2), 39–51.

Sosin, M., & Caulum, S. (1983). "Advocacy: A conceptualization for social work practice." *Social Work, 28*(1), 12–18.

Sotomayor, M. (1971). "Mexican-American interaction with social systems." *Social Casework, 51*(5), 316–322.

Sotomayor, M. (1977). "Language culture and ethnicity in developing self-concept." *Social Casework, 58*(4), 195–203.

Soyer, D. (1960). "Reverie on working with the aged." *Social Casework, 50*(5), 291–294.

Specht, R., & Craig, G. J. (1982). *Human development: A social work perspective.* Englewood Cliffs, NJ: Prentice-Hall.

Speck, R., & Attneave, C. L. (1971). "Social network intervention." In J. Haley (Ed.), *Changing families* (pp. 312–332). New York: Grune & Stratton.

Speck, R., & Attneave, C. L. (1973). *Family network.* New York: Vintage.

Spencer, M. B., & Horowitz, F. D. (1973). "Effects of systematic social and token reinforcement on the modification of racial and color concepts attitudes in black and preschool children." *Developmental Psychology, 9*, 246–254.

Spiegel, J. P. (1968). "The resolution of role conflict within the family." In N. W. Bell and Ezra F. Vogel (Eds.), *The family* (pp. 361–380). Glencoe, IL: Free Press.

Spiegelman, A. (1991). *Maus.* New York: Pantheon.

Spradley, J. P. (1979). *The ethnographic interview.* New York: Harcourt, Brace, Jovanovich.

Sprung, G. M. (1989). "Transferential issues in working with older adults." *Social Caseworker, 70*(10), 597–602.

Staats, A. W., & Butterfield, W. H. (1965). "Treatment of nonreading in a culturally-deprived juvenile delinquent: An application of reinforcement principles." *Child Development, 36*, 925–942.

Stack, C. (1974). *All our kin.* New York: Harper & Row.

Stack, C. (1975). *All our kin—Strategies for survival in a Black community.* New York: Harper and Row.

Starrett, R. A., Mindel, C. H., & Wright, Jr., R. (1983). "Influence of support systems on the use of social services by the Hispanic elderly." *Social Work Research and Abstracts, 19*(4), 35–40.

Stein, H. D., & Cloward, R. A. (Eds.). (1958). *Social perspectives on behavior.* New York: Free Press.

Stewart, A. J., Franz, C., & Layton, L. (1988). "The changing self: Using personal documents to study lives." *Journal of Personality, 56*(1), 41–73.

Stewart, B., & Nodrick, B. (1990). "The learning disabled lifestyle: From reification to liberation." *Family Therapy Case Studies, 5*(1), 60–73.

Stiles, W. B. (1988). "Psychotherapy process-outcome correlations may be misleading." *Psychotherapy, 25,* 27–35.

Stockard, J., & Johnson, M. M. (1992). *Sex and gender in society.* Englewood Cliffs, NJ: Prentice-Hall.

Strauss, G. (1972). "The personality v. organization hypothesis." In W. Nord (Ed.), *Concepts and controversy in organizational behavior* (pp. 332–434). Pacific Palisades, CA: Goodyear.

Strean, H. S. (1974). "Role theory." In F. J. Turner (Ed.), *Social work treatment,* pp. 314-342. New York: Free Press.

Strean, H. S. (1978). *Clinical social work theory and practice.* New York: Free Press.

Sudarkasa, N. (1988). "Interpreting the African-American family organization." In H. P. McAdoo (Ed.), *Black families* (2nd ed. pp. 27–43). Newbury, CA: Sage.

Sue, D. W., & Sue, D. (1990). *Counseling the culturally different: Theory and practice* (2nd ed.). New York: Wiley.

Sue, S., & Zane, N. (1987). "The role of culture and cultural techniques in psychotherapy: A critique and reformulation." *American Psychologist, 42*(1), 37–45.

Sutherland, R., & Woodward, J. L. (1940). *Introduction to sociology.* New York: Lippincott.

Swenson, C. (1979). "Social networks, mutual aid and the life model of practice." In C. B. Germain (Ed.), *Social work practice: People and environments* (pp. 215–266). New York: Columbia University Press.

Taggart, M. (1985). "The feminist critique in epistemological perspective: Questions of context in family therapy." *Journal of Marital and Family Therapy, 11,* 113–126.

Taggart, M. (1989). "Epistemological equality as the fulfillment of family therapy." In M. McGoldrick, C. M. Anderson, and F. Walsh (Eds.), *Women in families: A framework for family therapy* (pp. 97–106). New York: Norton.

Task Force on Lesbian and Gay Issues. (1977). *National Association of Social Workers Policy Statement.* Washington, DC: National Association of Social Workers.

Taylor, R. J., & Chatters, L. M. (1986). "Patterns of informal support to elderly Black adults: Family, friends, and church members." *Social Work, 31*(6), 432–438.

Thomas, A., & Sillen, S. (1972). "The mark of oppression." In A. Thomas & S. Sillen, *Racism and Psychiatry* (pp. 45–56). New York: Brunner/Mazel.

Thomas, E. J. (Ed.). (1967). *The socio-behavioral approach and applications to social work.* New York: Council on Social Work Education.

Thomas, S. A. (1977). "Theory and practice in feminist therapy." *Social Work, 22*(6), 447–454.

Thomlison, R. J. (1984). "Something works: Evidence from practice effectiveness studies." *Social Work, 29*, 51–56.

Thomlison, R. J. (1986). "Behavior therapy in social work practice". In F. J. Turner (Ed.), *Social work treatment* (3rd ed., pp. 131–154). New York: Free Press.

Thompson, J. D. (1967). *Organizations in action.* New York: McGraw-Hill.

Thorne, B., & Yalom, M. (1982). *Rethinking the family: Some feminine questions.* New York: Longman.

Thyer, B. A. (1981). "Behavioral social work: A bibliography." *International Journal of Behavioural Social Work and Abstracts, 1*, 229–251.

Thyer, B. A. (1985). "Textbooks in behavioral social work: A bibliography." *Behavior Therapist, 8*, 161–162.

Thyer, B. A. (1987a). "Contingency analysis: Toward a unified theory for social work practice." *Social Work, 32*, 150–157.

Thyer, B. A. (1987b). *Treating anxiety disorders.* Newbury Park, CA: Sage.

Thyer, B. A. (1988). Radical behaviorism and clinical social work. In R. Dorfman (Ed.). *Paradigms of clinical social work* (pp. 123–148). New York: Guilford.

Thyer, B. A. (1991). "Behavioral social work: It is not what you think." *Arete, 16*(2), 1–9.

Thyer, B. A. (1992a). "A behavioral perspective on human development." In M. Bloom (Ed.), *Changing lives: Studies in human development and professional helping* (pp. 410–418). Columbia: University of South Carolina Press.

Thyer, B. A. (1992b). "The term 'cognitive-behavior therapy' is redundant (letter)." *Behavior Therapist, 15*, 112, 128.

Thyer, B. A. (1992c). "Single system research designs." In R. M. Grinnell (Ed.), *Social work research and evaluation* (4th ed., pp. 94–117). Itasca, IL: F. E. Peacock.

Thyer, B. A., & Hudson, W. W. (1987). "Progress in behavioral social work: An introduction." *Journal of Social Service Research, 10*(2–4), 1–5.

Thyer, B. A., & Maddox, M. K. (1988). "Behavioral social work: Results of a national survey on graduate curricula." *Psychological Reports, 63*, 239–242.

Thyer, B. A., Thyer, K. B., & Massa, S. (1991). "Behavior analysis and therapy in the field of gerontology." In P. K. H. Kim (Ed.), *Serving the elderly: Skills for practice,* (pp. 117–135). Hawthorne, NY: Aldine de Gruyter.

Thyer, B. A., & Wodarski, J. S. (1990). "Social learning theory: Towards a comprehensive conceptual framework for social work education." *Social Service Review, 64*, 144–152.

Tice, K. (1990). "Gender and social work education: Directions for the 1990's." *Journal of Social Work Education, 26*(2), 134–144.

Tidwell, B. J. (1971). "The black community's challenge to social work students to confront their biases." *Journal of Social Work Education for Social Work, 7*(3), 59–65.

Tiefer, L. (1987). "Social constructionism and the study of human sexuality." In P. Shaver and C. Hendrick (Eds.), *Sex and gender* (pp. 70–93). Newbury Park, CA: Sage.

Timberlake, E. M., & Cook, K. O. (1984). "Social work and the Vietnamese refugee." *Social Work, 29*(2), 108–112.

Tobin, J. (1986). "Counter transference and failure in intercultural therapy." *Ethos, 14*(2), 120–143.

Tomm, K. (1990). "A critique of the DSM." *Dulwich Centre Newsletter,* Volume 3 (pp. 5–8). Adelaide: Dulwich Centre Publications.

Towle, C. (1960). "A social work approach to courses in growth and behavior." *Social Service Review, 34,* 402–414.

Trader, H. P. (1977). "Survival strategies for oppressed minorities." *Social Work, 22*(1), 10–13.

Traitner, W. I. (1984). *From poor law to welfare state: A history of social welfare in America* (3rd ed.). New York: Free Press.

Trepper, T. (1987). "Senior editor's comments." In W. S. Tseng and J. Hsu (Eds.), *Culture and family problems and therapy,* xi–xii. New York: Haworth.

Truax, C. B. (1966). "Therapist empathy, warmth, genuineness and patient personality change in group psychotherapy: A comparison between interaction unit measures, time sample measures, and patient perception measures." *Journal of Clinical Psychology, 71,* 1–9.

Truax, C. B., & Carkhuff, R. R. (1966). "Therapist empathy genuineness and warmth and patient therapeutic outcome." *Journal of Consulting Psychology, 30,* 395–401.

Tseng, W. S., & Hsu, J. (1991). *Culture and family problems and therapy.* New York: Haworth.

Tsui, P., & Schultz, G. L. (1985). "Failure of rapport: Why psychotherapeutic engagement fails in treatment of Asian clients." *American Journal of Orthopsychiatry, 55,* 561–569.

Tully, C. T. (1983). *Social support systems of a selected group of older women.* Doctoral dissertation, School of Social Work, Virginia Commonwealth University, Richmond.

Tully, C. T. (1989, March). *Minority contributions to social work: A lesbian and gay chronology.* Paper presented at Annual Program Meeting, Council on Social Work Education, Chicago.

Tully, C. T., & Greene, R. R. (In press). *Cultural diversity comes of age: A study of coverage, 1970–1991.*

Turner, F. J. (1974). *Social work treatment.* New York: Free Press.

Turner, S. M., & Jones, R. T. (Eds.). (1982). *Behavior modification in Black populations: Psychosocial issues and empirical findings.* New York: Plenum.

Tylim, I. (1982). Group psychotherapy with Hispanic patients: The psychodynamics of idealization. *International Journal of Group Psychotherapy, 32*(3), 339–350.

U.S. Bureau of the Census. (1987). *Statistical abstract of the United States.* Washington, DC: USGPO.

Valentich, M. (1986). "Feminism and social work practice." In F. J. Turner (Ed.), *Social work treatment* (pp. 564–580). New York: Free Press.

Valentich, M., & Gripton, J. (1984). "Ideological perspectives on the sexual assault of women." *Social Service Review, 58*(3), 448–461.

Valentine, C. A. (1971). "Deficit, difference, and bicultural models of Afro-American behavior." *Harvard Educational Review, 41,* 135–141.

Van Den Bergh, N. (1982). "Renaming: Vehicle for empowerment." In J. Penfield (Ed.), *Women and language in transition* (130–136). Albany, NY: State University of New York Press.

Van Den Bergh, N., & Cooper, L. B. (1985). *Feminist visions for social work.* Silver Spring, MD: National Association of Social Workers.

Van Den Bergh, N., & Cooper, L. B. (Eds.). (1986). *Feminist visions for social work.* Silver Spring, MD: National Association of Social Work.

Van Den Bergh, N., & Cooper, L. B. (1987). "Feminist social work." In A. Minahan et al. (Eds.), *Encyclopedia of social work* (18th ed., pp. 610–618). Silver Spring, MD: National Association of Social Workers.

Van Hasselt, V. B. (1987). "Behavior therapy for visually handicapped persons." In M. Hersen, R. Eisler, & P. M. Miller (Eds.), *Progress in behavior modification, 21,* 13–44.

Varnell, P. (1989). "The future of gay ethnicity." *Southern Voice, 7*(Dec.), 24.

Visher, E., & Visher, J. S. (1987). "Treating families with problems associated with re-marriage and step relationships." In C. Chilman, E. Nunnally and F. Cox (Eds.), *Variant family forms—Families in trouble* (Vol. 5, pp. 222–224). Beverly Hills, CA: Sage.

Visher, E., & Visher, J. S. (1988). *Old loyalties, new ties.* New York: Brunner/Mazel.

von Glaserfeld, E. (1984). "An introduction to radical constructivism." In P. Watzlawick (Ed.), *The invented reality: Contributions to constructivism* (pp. 18–40). New York: Norton.

Wahler, R. G., & Erickson, M. (1969). "Child behavior therapy: A community program in Appalachia." *Behaviour Research and Therapy, 7,* 71–78.

Walsh, F., & Scheinkman, M. (1989). "Fe(male): The hidden gender dimension in models of family therapy." In M. McGoldrick, C. M. Anderson, and F. Walsh (Eds.), *Women in families: A framework for family therapy* (pp. 16–41). New York: Norton.

Walters, E. T. & Bryne, J. H. (1983). "Associative conditioning of single sensory neu-rons suggests a cellular mechanism of learning." *Science, 219,* 405–408.

Wanderer, Z. & Ingram, B. L. (1991). "The therapeutic use of tape-recorded repeti-tions of flooding stimuli." *Journal of Behavior Therapy and Experimental Psy-chiatry, 22,* 31–35.

Wasser, E. (1964). "The sense of commitment in serving older persons." *Social Case-work, 45*(8), 443–449.

Watson, B. (1993, August). "Navajo code talkers: A few good men." *Smithsonian, 24*(5), 34–35.

Watzlawick, P. (1984). *The invented reality: How do we know what we believe we know?* New York: Norton.

Weber, M. (1946). "Bureaucracy." In J. M. Shafritz, and P. H. Whitbeck, Eds. (1978), *Classics of Organization Theory* (pp. 37–42). Oak Park, IL: Moore.

Weber, M. (1958a). "Class states, party." In H. D. Stein and R. A. Cloward (Eds.), *So-cial perspectives on behavior* (pp. 351–362). New York: Free Press.

Weber, M. (1958b). "The essentials of bureaucratic organization." In H. D. Stein and R. A. Cloward (Eds.), *Social perspectives on behavior* (pp. 564–571). New York: Free Press.

Weber, M. (1980). "Class status party." In V. Jeffries and H. E. Ransford (Eds.), *Social stratification: A multiple hierarchy approach* (pp. 89–98). Boston: Allyn & Bacon.

Weick, A. (1981). "Reframing the person-in-environment perspective." *Social Work, 26*, 140–143.

Weick, A. (1983). "Issues in overturning a medical model of social work practice." *Social Work, 28*(Nov./Dec.), 467–471.

Weick, A. (1986). "The philosophical contest of a health model of social work." *Social Casework, 67*, 551–559.

Weick, A. (1987). "Reconceptualizing the philosophical perspective of social work." *Social Service Review, 61*, 218–230.

Weick, A. (1992). "Building a strengths perspective for social work." In D. Saleeby (Ed.), *The strengths perspective in social work practice* (pp. 18–26). New York: Longman.

Weick, A., Rapp, C., Sullivan, P. W., & Kisthardt, W. (1989). "A strengths perspective for social work practice." *Social Work, 34*(4), 350–354.

Weimer, W. B. (1977). "A conceptual framework for cognitive psychology: Motor theories of the mind." In R. Shaw and J. Bransford (Eds.), *Perceiving, acting, and knowing* (pp. 267–311). Hillsdale, NJ: Lawrence Erlbaum.

Weiner, J. P., & Boss, P. G. (1985). "Exploring gender bias against women: Ethics for marriage and family therapy." *Counseling and Values, 30*, 9–23.

Weiss, B. S., & Parish, B. (1989). "Culturally appropriate crisis counseling: Adapting an American method for use with IndoChinese refugees." *Social Work, 34*(3), 252–254.

Wellman, B. (1981). "Applying network analysis to the study of support." In B. H. Gottlieb (Ed.), *Social networks and social support* (pp.171–200). Beverly Hills: Sage.

Wesley, C. (1975). "The women's movement and psychotherapy." *Social Work, 20*(2), 120–124.

Westcot, M., & Dries, R. (1990). "Has family therapy adapted to the single-parent family?" *American Journal of Family Therapy, 18*, 363–371.

Wetzel, J. W. (1976). "Interaction of feminism and social work in America." *Social Casework, 57*(4), 227–236.

Wetzel, J. W. (1986). "A feminist world view conceptual framework." *Social Casework, 67*(3), 166–173.

Whitaker, J. K., & Gabauno, J. (1983). *Social support networks.* Hawthorne, NY: Aldine de Gruyter.

White, M. (1986). "Negative explanation restraint and double description: A template for family therapy." *Family Process, 25*(2), 169–183.

White, M. (1988, Summer). "The externalizing of the problem and the reauthoring of lives and relationships." *Dulwich Centre Newsletter,* pp. 3–20. Adelaide: Dulwich Centre Publications.

White, M. (1993). "Deconstruction and therapy." In S. Gilligan and R. Price (Eds.), *Therapeutic conversation* (pp. 22–61). New York: Norton.

White, M., & Epston, D. (1990). *Narrative means to therapeutic ends.* New York: Norton.

White, R. W., & Watt, N. F. (1981). *The abnormal personality.* New York: Wiley.

Whitehurst, G. J., & Valdez-Menchaca, M. C. (1988). "What is the role of reinforcement in early language acquisition?" *Child Development, 34*, 430–440.

Whiten, A. & Ham, R. (1992). "On the nature and evolution of imitation in the animal kingdom." In P. J. B. Slater, J. S. Rosenblatt, C. Beer, & M. Milinski (Eds.), Advances in the study of behavior (Vol. 21, pp. 239–282). New York: Academic.

Whitman, B. Y., Graves, B., & Accardo, P. J. (1989). "The mentally retarded parent in the community: Identification and method and needs assessment survey." American Journal of Mental Deficiency, 91, 636–638.

Whittaker, J. K. (1983). "Mutual helping in human service practice." In J. K. Whittaker, and J. Garbarino, Social Support Networks: Informal Helping in the Human Services (pp. 29–70). Hawthorne, NY: Aldine de Gruyter.

Whittaker, J. K., Garbarino, J., & Associates (Eds.). (1983). Social support networks: Informal helping in the human services. Hawthorne, NY: Aldine de Gruyter.

Whorf, B. L. (1956). Language thought and reality. New York: Wiley.

Wicker, D. G. (1986). "Combating racism in practice and in the classroom." In N. Van Den Bergh and L. B. Cooper (Eds.), Feminist visions for social work (pp. 29–44). Silver Spring, MD: National Association of Social Work.

Williams, L. F. (1990). "Working with the black poor: Implications for effective theoretical and practice approaches." In S. M. L. Logan, E. M. Freeman, R. G. McRay (Eds.), Social work practice in the black families (pp. 169–192). New York: Longman.

Wilson, M. D., & McReynolds, L. V. (1973). "A procedure for increasing oral reading rate in hard-of-hearing children." Journal of Applied Behavior Analysis, 6, 231–240.

Wilson, W. J. (1973). Power, racism, and privilege. New York: Free Press.

Wilson, W. J. (1985). "Cycles of deprivation and the underclass debate." Social Service Review, 59(4), 541–559.

Wilson, W., & Calhoun, J. (1974). "Behavior therapy and the minority client." Psychotherapy: Theory, Research and Practice, 11, 317–325.

Wingspread Report. (1978). Strengthening families through informal support systems. Racine, WI: Johnson Foundation.

Winter, S. K. (1971). "Black man's bluff." Psychology Today, 5, 39–43, 78–81.

Wodarski, J. S., & Bagarozzi, D. A. (1979). Behavioral social work. New York: Human Sciences.

Wolf, J. H. (1985). "'Professionalizing' volunteer work in a Black neighborhood." Social Service Review, 59(Sept.), 423–434.

Wolfe, D. A., St. Lawrence, J., Graves, K., Brehony, K., & Kelly, J. A. (1982). "Intensive behavioral parent training for a child abusive mother." Behavior Therapy, 13, 438–451.

Wood, G. G., & Middleman, R. R. (1992). "Groups to empower battered women." Affilia, 7(4), 82–95.

Woodman, N. J. (1981). "Social work with lesbian couples." In A. Weick and S. T. Vandiver (Eds.), Women, power, and change (pp. 114–126). Washington, DC: National Association of Social Workers.

Woodman, N. J. (1987). "Homosexuality: Lesbian women." In A. Minahan et al. (Eds.), Encyclopedia of social work (18th ed., pp. 805–812). Silver Spring, MD: National Association of Social Workers.

Wright, R., Kail, B. L., Creecy, R. F. (1990). "Culturally sensitive social work practice with black alcoholics and their families." In J. M. L. Logan, E. M. Freeman and

R. G. McRoy (Eds.), *Social work practice with black families: A culturally specific perspective* (pp. 203–222). New York: Longman.

Wyatt, G. E., Strayer, R. G., &. Lobitz, W. C. (1976). "Issues in the treatment of sexually dysfunctioning couples of Afro-American descent." *Psychotherapy: Theory, Research and Practice, 13,* 44–50.

Wyche, K. F. (1993). "Psychology and African-American women: Findings from applied research." *Applied and Preventive Psychology, 2,* 115–121.

Zammuner, V. L. (1987). "Children's sex-role stereotypes." In P. Shaver and C. Hendrick (Eds.), *Sex and gender* (pp. 272–293). Newbury Park, CA: Sage.

Zarit, S. (1980). "Group and family intervention." In S. Zarit (Ed.), *Aging and mental disorders* (pp. 322–349). New York: Free Press.

Ziter, M. L. P. (1987). "Culturally sensitive treatment of black alcoholic families." *Social Work, 32*(2), 130–135.

Zuckerman, M. (1990). "Some dubious premises in research and theory on racial differences." *American Psychologist, 45,* 1297–1303.

Biographical Sketches
of the Contributors ―――――――――――――――――――

Robert G. Blundo is Assistant Professor at the School of Social Work, Louisiana State University.

Karen Frankel is an MSW graduate of the University of Georgia School of Social Work.

Paul Gallant is an assistant professor of social work at the University of Georgia.

Charles Garvin is professor of social work and director of the joint doctoral program in social work and social science at the University of Michigan. He is author of such widely used text books as *Contemporary Group Work: Interpersonal Practice in Social Work,* and co-author of Generalist Practice: A Task Centered Approach. He has written extensively in the theory and practice of social work in groups.

Beth Glover Reed is an associate professor at the University of Michigan. She has written extensively on such topics as feminist practice, substance abuse among women, and implications of cultural diversity. She has provided leadership for many years to the race and gender committee of her school of social work.

Roberta R. Greene, MSW, Ph.D. is currently professor and associate dean at the School of Social Work University of Georgia. She is the author and or co-author of three other texts in the Aldine series. Her many articles reflect her interest in the integration of theory and practice in clinical social work. Her perspective on the profession is derived from a career in agency clinical practice, social work organization and educational experience, and the belief that social work issues should be addressed in public policy.

Nancy P. Kropf, Ph.D. is the assistant director of the Gerontology Center and assistant professor of social work at the University of Georgia. She authored several articles and chapters on gerontology, developmental disabilities social work education. Additionally, she has co-edited a book, *Gerontological Social Work* with Robert L. Schneider.

Judith S. Lewis, MSW, Ph.D. is an assistant professor at Tulane University School of Social Work, New Orleans, Louisiana. She has taught and been Director of Field Instruction of the social work program, Auburn University, Alabama.

Joan Ephross Saltman is a temporary assistant professor at Millersville University, Millersville, PA. She has recently completed her Ph.D. dissertation at the University of Maryland at Baltimore. Using a symbolic interaction theoretical framework, her dissertation research focused on the intervention preferences of social workers with Jewish-Christian intermarried couples.

Kathryn H. Thompson is an Assistant Professor and Director of the Atlanta Office of the University of Georgia School of Social Work. Dr. Thompson received her B.A. from Birmingham-Souther College in 1958, B.D. from Yale University in 1961, MSW from Smith College School for Social Work in 1963, and Ph.D. in Career Development from the College of Education at Georgia State University in 1986. Her research is focused on adult and career development of women. She chairs the Faculty Committee on Gender Issues, and was the 1993 recipient of the National NASW Lifetime Achievement Award. For many years, Dr. Thompson has utilized role theory in teaching generalist practice and adult development courses and in applications to evaluations of service systems (P.A.S.S) focused on deviancy and stigmatized roles.

Bruce A. Thyer, MSW, Ph.D. is Professor of Social Work and Adjunct Professor of Psychology at the University of Georgia, and Associate Clinical Professor of Psychiatry and Health Behavior at the Medical College of Georgia. Dr. Thyer is the co-editor, with Dianne Harrison and Walter Hudson, of *Cultural Diversity and Social Work Practice* (Springfield, IL: Charles C. Thomas), published in 1992. His most recent article is titled "Assessing students' attitudes relative to cultural diversity: A review of selected measures". This work was co-authored with Dorothy Carrillo and Carol Holzhalb, and will appear in the *Journal of Social Work Education*.

Carol T. Tully, BA, University of Arizona, MSW, Ph.D., Virginia Commonwealth University. She is currently an Associate Professor of Social Work at Tulane University in New Orleans where she is also Director of Field Instruction. Dr. Tully's primary areas of research are in the areas of gerontology, gay and lesbian issues, and higher education curriculum development and implementation. Past work has been related to social support systems of

older women, elder abuse, aging and homelessness, social work faculty qualifications, issues associated with the social supports of hearing impaired lesbians and gay men, lesbian functioning in a heterosexist culture, curriculum
development, accreditation issues, and social work practice. She is currently involved in an examination of feminist theory as it relates to systems theory. Dr. Tully teaches courses in the areas of clinical practice and research.

Index

Acculturation, 31
Advocacy for diverse curriculum
  evaluation standards of, 241–243
  historical overview of, 2–3, 235–236
  identification phase of, 236–237
  implications for, 240
  institutionalization phase of, 239–240
  internal conflict phase of, 237–238
  investigation phase of, 237
African Americans
  case illustration with, 143
  civil rights movement and, 22
  diversity content in human behavior
    theory and, 21–22
  family life cycle of, 159–160,
    166–167
  identity and, 85
  personal meaning and, 69
  role prescription for "manhood" and,
    102
  single mothers and, 143–144
Aged, 7
American Indians
  case illustration with, 141, 143
  ecological approach and, 214
  family forms and, 161
  noninterference and, 30
  role expectations of female, 102
  social work practice and, 14
  term of, 4
Asian Americans, 85, 112, 214
Assertiveness, 197
Assessment, 57–59 (See also Social
  work assessment)
Assimilation, 31
Attitudes, of social worker, 12–15
Authority, professional, 52–54
Autonomy, 82–83, 90

Behavior Code, 136–137
Beliefs, group, 195
Biculturalism, 31, 157
Blacks (See African Americans)
Blaming the victim theory, 29

Change, 29, 125–127
Chinese Americans, 50–51, 67, 214
Clarification, 48–49
Class variances, 7–8
Client-social worker relationships
  countertransference and, 49–50
  Freud and, 49–50
  language and, 72–73
  Rogers and, 40–47
  role theory and, 110–114
  transference and, 49, 114
Clinical diagnosis, 57
Codependency, 90
Collective behavior, 60
Communications, 194
Conditioned response, 137
Conditioned stimulus (CS), 137
Consciousness, 196–197
Consciousness-raising, 22, 29, 174, 197
Constructionist theory
  biological propensities and, 122
  change and, 125–127
  defining, 115–116
  intervention and, 127–128
  knowledge and, 124, 129–130
  language and, 123–124
  meaning and, 123
  mind and, 124
  myths and, 125
  narrative and, 123–124
  personal experiences and, 122–123
  power and, 129–130